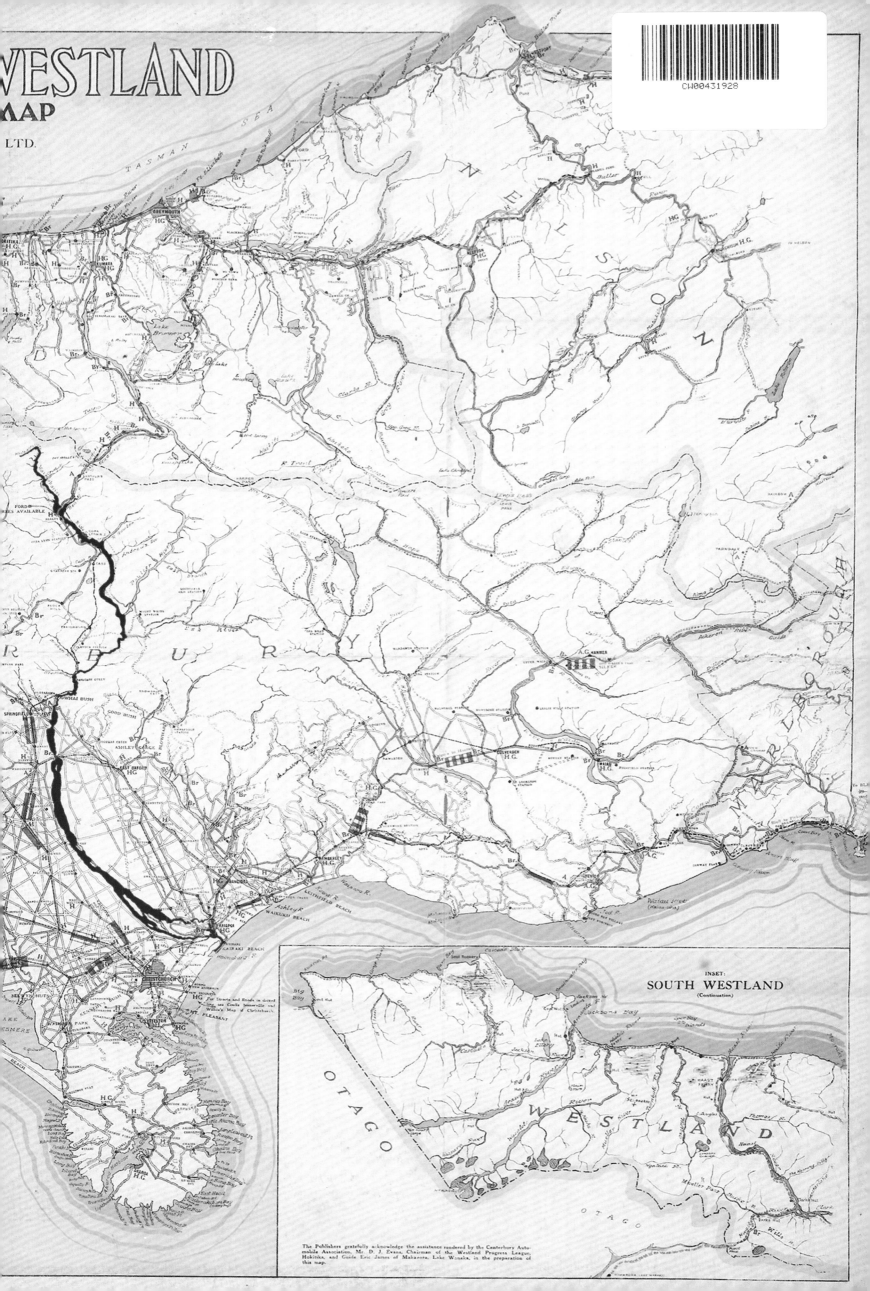

WESTLAND
MAP

LTD.

INSET:
SOUTH WESTLAND
(Continuation)

The Publishers gratefully acknowledge the assistance rendered by the Canterbury Automobile Association, Mr. D. J. Evans, Chairman of the Westland Progress League, Hokitika, and Guide Eric James of Makarora, Lake Wanaka, in the preparation of this map.

WAIMAKARIRI

What others have said about
Waimakariri

"...This story has been told superbly...the 400 photographs that complement the 200,000 words of the text are sometimes breathtakingly beautiful, often dramatic and always relevant...the whole large-format book is remarkably good value. A true Cantabrian can scarcely do without it."

...A comprehensive story of the river, its exploration and the development of communications, farms, ferries and bridges, the National Park, recreation, mountaineering, and the lives of those who live along its banks..."

...A river to be respected by everyone. This book will certainly enhance that respect. It is the Compleat Waimakariri."

– Christchurch *Press*

"...Canterbury has been well written about in personal, regional or sectional histories, but this tale is quite different in its use of the dominating influence of a great river on a whole population. The coldness of the river itself is swept aside by the warmth of this outstanding addition to our works of historical importance."

– *Observer*

"...The Waimakariri is the biggest of the Canterbury rivers which for millennia have been draining the alpine catchment to build up the plains."

...The river has a wide compass and so has the book. With an eagerness matching that of the river Logan sweeps through the terrain of farming and exploration; ferries and bridges; gold on the West Canterbury coast and the triumphs of engineering to build roads and a rail tunnel to get to it; mountaineers past and present; the pioneers who canoed and their grandchildren who jet-boat on the provocative waters."

...This is a prestige publication and must become a standard reference work for the region."

– *Sunday Star Times*

"...This is the most comprehensive book ever written about a New Zealand river, its land and its people and it is one of the best, if not the best."

Everything connected with this book is on a grand scale and it sets a new standard in regional histories."

...The book is the result of six years research and writing. In a word it is superb."

– Christchurch *Star*

WAIMAKARIRI

AN ILLUSTRATED HISTORY

ROBERT LOGAN

Phillips&King
PUBLISHERS

Published by Phillips and King Publishers
Private Bag 4748
Christchurch
New Zealand

First published by the author for Logan Publishing Company 1987
Reprinted October 2008 in a facsimile edition with a Publishers'
Note and new cover.

The author has asserted his moral rights in the work.

ISBN 978-0-9583315-5-5

Cover design by Quentin Wilson
Printed in Hong Kong

Contents

Publishers' Note

A journalist, mountaineer and 'part-time non-university historian', Robert Logan began work on *Waimakariri: An Illustrated History* as a retirement project; it dominated six years of his life. He presented the concept to the main New Zealand publishers of the day, Whitcoulls and A.H. & A.W. Reed. Both were sceptical about the potential market for a 'lavishly illustrated, colour-splashed, coffee-table, history book'. They felt colour was unnecessary in a history book, that the readership would be too small and that the proposed volume would be too large and too expensive. Logan, however, was undeterred.

His son John's Gisborne company, Logan Print, printed the book, which was designed by the Logans themselves. Binding was completed in Christchurch. Robert and his wife Alice handled the sales and distribution in Canterbury. Such was his faith in the project that he printed 3000 copies, banking on the fact that sales would ensure his recovery of the $100,000 production cost. The retail price in 1987 was an enormous $55, for a large hardback of an unusual size. There was no allowance in his pricing for an author's royalty. His satisfaction came solely from the enthusiastic response his book received from the media and the support he got from the book-buying public.

Such success is rare for a self-published work, but Robert Logan not only had the writing talent to tell the story of Canterbury's greatest river, but also the requisite design and layout skills (in the days before computer typesetting and page design) to produce the book. He also managed the marketing, distribution and publicity. His achievement was the more impressive in a depressed retail market still stunned by the share market crash of October 1987. On top of this there was a truck drivers' strike that threatened the delivery of stock for the vital Christmas market.

Newspaper reviews were lavish with their praise. 'Superb,' said the *Christchurch Star*. *The Press* described it as 'The Compleat Waimakariri'. The *Sunday Star -Times* said 'it must become a standard reference work for the region'. The pre-Christmas weeks were busy for the Logans as booksellers realised they had a local bestseller on their hands and began sending courier vans to their home in Soleares Avenue on Mount Pleasant for urgent supplies. On Christmas Eve Robert and Alice found themselves inching their way through crowds of shoppers in Cashel Mall to deliver copies directly to the book counter at Whitcoulls.

The book has been out of print for many years but still sits on the Christchurch City Libraries list of the 10 most borrowed New Zealand books. Second-hand copies are hard to find and fetch premium prices.

The Logan family is delighted to see the book back in print some 20 years after its initial publication. The original printer's plates have long since disappeared so each page had to be individually scanned; this edition, printed in Hong Kong, is therefore a facsimile of the original. We have designed a new dust jacket and have added attractive endpapers.

As independent publishers we greatly admire the tenacity and perseverance Robert Logan showed in seeing the original publication to fruition. We thank the Logan family for their support in reprinting this important contribution to the story of Canterbury.

Brian Phillips
Philip King
Christchurch
October 2008

Introduction

The Waimakariri could be the most historically interesting of all our rivers, not just because it has threatened—and continues to threaten—more people and property than any other in the country, but also because it provides the route for both road and railway across the Southern Alps. The coach drive through the gorges and over the pass was the most exciting in New Zealand; the railway journey still is.

The Canterbury settlement's earliest days were disturbed by the sight of Waimakariri flood water flowing down the Avon, even into Cathedral Square; of engineers in despair of this mischief-maker in their midst; and of husky gold diggers off to make their fortunes on the West Coast—they left in their wake such a ferment of greed and envy that a thousand men had to hack, dig and blast a road up the river and over the mountains to bring the gold to Christchurch.

The pilgrims, exhausted by their climb over the Port Hills from Lyttelton in 1850, were glad to drop their burdens at the first fresh-water stream, already named Avon. There they put up simple huts where Christchurch was to stand. How were they to know the Avon was an old course of the Waimakariri and that, had they arrived a little sooner, an enormous flood would have swept them out to sea, huts and all? Some years passed before they became properly aware that *sundry indications show/that here a river used to flow.*

Much of the tale of those early days had to do with keeping the Waimakariri on course—and out of the city. The gold rush came in the middle of a decade of great floods, and while engineers struggled on the lower plains to keep the banks intact, the upper valley came alive with the urgent search for a pass to the Coast.

Explorers found a way for the road, men built it with pick, shovel and wheelbarrow through the worst of winters, sheepfarmers pushed up the valley and established their stations, seafarers sailed their little ships across the bar into Port Kaiapoi, engineers came to the conclusion nothing could be done with their rogue river (not even a bridge), and adventurers crossed the passes and climbed the mountains. These and many others—hoteliers, coach drivers, gold seekers, canoeists in the gorge, railway tunnellers and track-layers—all help tell the story of *Waimakariri.*

Many outstanding men contribute to that story. Of these none played a greater part than Edward Dobson, Canterbury's first provincial engineer, who grappled with the problems of bridges, floods, exploration and road building. Supporting roles were played by his sons George and Arthur. Charles Torlesse surveyed much of the plains near the river, climbed one of its mountains and explored in the headwaters. Joseph Pearson pushed through the gorges to open up the tussock country for sheepfarmers. There were many others, all true pioneers and part of Canterbury's history.

The world of these notable and adventurous men and the river they had so much to do with could be portrayed better if more of that history had been recorded at the time. So much was never written, or if it was is lost or undiscovered, yet the author's years of research have proved rewarding. And they have been sustained by his affection for the river. He swam and fished in it as a boy, coxed rowing crews on its lower reaches, and waded Kaiapoi streets awash with its flood waters. Later he tramped its riverbeds, climbed its mountains, and endured its storms. This book, he supposes, is some kind of personal memorial to that affection, and a sharing of the past.

In the upper Waimakariri the scenery is varied. In written descriptions words like grand and beautiful predominate. Of course beauty is forever in the eye of the beholder, and here there is much to behold, especially when snow covers the tops and the clouds are ornamental. Yet when Torlesse first saw the land beyond Castle Hill in 1858 he so disliked it that he wrote of "crossing the wretched Broken River country which gave me positive pain to look at from its barren and misshapen appearance". On the other hand when David McLeod, who in time was to own both Cora Lynn and Grasmere stations, paused there on his first visit in 1926 he found it "all so peaceful and beautiful that I lingered there longer than I should".

Although there was a long time between them the scene had not changed much except that the highway to the Coast had been added. As many years before as since McLeod's visit the peace he found at Broken River might have been shattered by the oaths and whipcracks of wagoners splashing their teams through the river or the tramp of diggers marching past to the goldfields. But that would be about all. Even the coaches stopped in 1906, and for 30 more years until the Waimakariri was bridged at Klondyke only a few travellers passed that way.

Now up to 2000 people a day motor over Porter's Pass into the valley, mostly on their way to the skifields or en route to and from the West Coast. A growing proportion, including the skiers, make the valley their destination, perchance to "linger there longer than they should". If they are in danger of getting "hooked" on the history behind the scenery, this book should be strong bait.

For those who might wonder, it should be explained that *Waimakariri* climbs fences at times, going across the Alps when it must to complete Canterbury projects which reached their conclusions in Westland. The most difficult and dramatic part of building the road, for example, took place there.

The author has made some assumptions and judgements, the better to serve history's ends, but only sparingly and after close study. As to factual errors, their complete removal is a process which seldom reaches finality; hopefully there are none of consequence in these pages.

The River—Facts and Figures

Making 19th century New Zealanders speak of distances in kilometres may be as incongruous as reading that an 1864 workman on two pounds a week was paid four dollars, but now and the future must belong to the metrics. Accordingly most measurements in these pages have been metricised except in direct quotations. For those who still find miles come easier than metres, these equations should help:

1 mile = 1.609km : 1km = 0.621 mi.
1 foot = 0.305m : 1m = 3.28ft.
1 acre = 0.404 hectares : 1ha = 2.471 acres.
1 sq.mile = 2.589 sq.km : 1 sq.km = 0.386 sq.mi.

The Waimakariri River is 151km (94mi) long and flows in a south-easterly direction from its source in the Southern Alps to where it enters the Pacific Ocean on Pegasus Bay about 15km north of Christchurch's Cathedral Square. Its lower reaches flow within 5km of the city's nearest suburbs and even less from the north runway of Christchurch International Airport.

The river has a catchment area of 3562 sq.km, the largest of the four principal North Canterbury rivers (the others: Waiau, 3310; Rakaia, 2910; Hurunui, 2670). Of this area 2500 sq.km is in the mountains and the balance on the Canterbury Plains. For half its length the river is bounded by ranges nearly 2000m high. For about 23km it flows through the snowy ramparts and beech-forested heights of its alpine birthplace; for another 67km through tussock, scree and forested uplands (including the top sheep runs and the gorge); and then for 61km across the gently-sloping plains to the sea. The gorge is 24km long.

About 46km of the main divide are drained by the Waimakariri and its tributaries, which have their primary sources in glaciers on Mounts Rolleston and Armstrong on the divide and Mounts Murchison and Wakeman on the Shaler Range, and in the sprawling headwaters of its largest tributary, the Poulter River. The principal catchment areas are:

Main river above Mt White Bridge, 478 sq.km.
Poulter River, 481 sq.km.
Esk River, 388 sq.km.
Broken River, 396 sq.km.

The mean annual flows of these four main sources, measured in cubic metres per second (cumecs) are 52, 36, 11 and 12 respectively. The estimated annual rainfall varies from 5950mm (234in) near the main divide, to 2000mm (78in) at Klondyke Corner (Bealey confluence), to about 900mm (35in) at the Gorge Bridge, to 600mm (23in) near the mouth. The whole river has an average discharge of 116 cumecs measured at the old main highway bridge north of Christchurch. Since reliable records began in 1930 the highest flood, in 1957, measured 3990 cumecs. The banks along the lower river are designed to contain a flood of 4730 cumecs.

Tributaries in the upper river, from the divide to the Gorge Bridge, are the White, Crow, Anti-Crow, Bealey, Cass, Hawdon, Poulter, Esk, Broken and Kowai rivers. The Eyre River in its diversion channel enters about 15km from the sea, and the Kaiapoi River close to the mouth. This latter, the channel of which once carried the main Waimakariri, drains a large plains area lying to the north by way of the Cust River, the Cam River, and various smaller contributors including some which originate in Rangiora.

The 356,400 hectares of Waimakariri catchment is predominantly in high production pasture (97,600ha), forest (74,600ha) and semi-natural valley and mid-altitude tussock (60,950ha). There are 58,000ha of snow tussock country, a majority of which has less than 40% coverage. Low production pasture accounts for 20,500ha and riverbeds for 16,000ha.

The upper catchment measures 249,000ha and includes much of Arthur's Pass National Park and Craigieburn Forest Park. The greater part (53%) is occupied land mostly leased to runholders through pastoral leases and pastoral occupation licences issued by the Crown and the University of Canterbury. Over 72,000ha of this is of little or no productive value, but the remaining 60,400ha is on lower slopes with better soils and is generally suitable for pastoral farming.

Much of the overall responsibility for this country rests with the North Canterbury Catchment Board and one of its principal management issues concerns erosion and soil conservation. Original research work by its first soil conservation officer, R.D. Dick, established that grasslands above 1000m were unable to sustain sheep-grazing without damage to the environment. With this in mind the board has since 1964 followed a policy of retiring high ground, and in the last 20 years some 25,000ha has been withdrawn from stock use, requiring the erection of nearly 60km of fencing.

Areas of the top runs, with retirement figures bracketed, are as follows: Castle Hill, 11,443ha (4600ha); Flock Hill, 13,973ha (2400ha); Craigieburn, 6678ha (nil); Mount White, 49,804ha (nil); Grasmere-Cora Lynn, 9698ha (6500ha). Nearer Porter's Pass 5300ha of Brooksdale, 3400ha of Mt Torlesse, 1300ha of Benmore and 1800ha of Woodstock have also been retired.

In the Waimakariri's 67,500ha of indigenous forest, mountain beech is the dominant species, with some small stands of red beech and silver beech, mainly in the upper Poulter. The forests increase in richness and diversity as rainfall increases towards the main divide, at the same time

as the timberline lowers to about 1250m. Above this altitude there is still a wealth of flowering shrubs, mosses and lichens, while in the area's extensive screes are to be found many other beautiful specimens. The principal plants with alpine associations are buttercups, mountain daisies, bluebells, mountain foxgloves, mountain eyebrights, spaniards and gentians.

Twelve species growing within the Waimakariri basin are on the rare and endangered list. There are four within the Castle Hill Nature Reserve, including the Castle Hill buttercup which is unique in the world to that location. There are now over 300 specimens of this flower which before protection was doomed to destruction.

Bird watchers (and shooters) are all too familiar with the species most frequently found on the Waimakariri. It is the black-backed gull, which on the plains section of the river is numbered in tens of thousands, and even in the upper reaches is twice as numerous as the banded dotterel. Other species seen in reasonable numbers are the pied oystercatcher, the paradise shelduck and the Canada goose. According to a recent survey there are still wrybill plovers on the river, a species now considered to be endangered in New Zealand and the only bird in the world with a beak bent laterally to the right, apparently to help it forage for food under riverbed stones.

How does the Waimakariri rate scenic-wise? Remembering the beholder's eye, the basin tussock country has a special charm for many, and with the highway passing through is of course the most familiar. The beauty of the remote headwaters is reserved for the keen tramper, and the hidden gorge for the jetboater and canoeist. In its resource survey the Catchment Board lists two separate assessments made by screening slides of New Zealand scenery to representative audiences asked to grade their reactions. In the first, on a scale of 0-16 +, the gorge section of the Waimakariri and that part above the Crow River in the headwaters were both rated 17, or "exceptional". In the second, on a 0-9 scale, these same sections rated 6.78 and 7.02.

The Waimakariri is assuredly the most "public" river in the South Island, perhaps in New Zealand, in that it is used by more people more frequently in more ways than any other. The Catchment Board in the course of a recreational survey has assembled figures which show the estimated annual adult "visits" to the river and its catchment area. Among these are the following: salmon angling, 78,000; trout angling, 64,000; estuarine fishing, 35,000; jetboating, 30,000; whitebaiting, 13,500; power boating and water skiing, 3000; yachting, 3000; and canoeing and rafting, 1200.

In addition about 25,000 people are estimated to use the river and lake banks for picnicking, 20,000 for walking and tramping, and 14,000 for swimming, and to these can be added an assortment of horse and trailbike riders, rowers, hunters, game shooters, mountaineers and skiers. The latter now go in their thousands to the Craigieburns and Arthur's Pass each season to enjoy the snow on the river's five skifields; in 1986 35,000 went to the Porter Heights field alone.

Unsung Heroes. *Construction of the two great upper Waimakariri projects, the road and railway, were largely accomplished by men working with picks and shovels. These two, posed outside their Midland railway home with their cat, would be in many respects typical of their road-building forebears 35 years earlier.* N.Z. Railways

Sloven's Stream country *up which the railway heads towards Cass. It is invisible in the slight gorge of the stream away to the left. At right foreground is the Rosa Hut track down which Brassington stumbled after the fatal rafting disaster in the Waimakariri Gorge. (See Chapter 15,* Adventure in the Gorge).

Acknowledgements

The author's thanks are extended to the many people who have helped in greater or lesser degree with *Waimakariri,* especially the following: The North Canterbury Catchment Board for permission to use material from its surveys, in particular the 1986 Resource Survey; the board's chairman, Richard Johnson, and staff members Bob Reid, Brian Dwyer and Alan Norton; David McLeod for encouragement and material; Sister Angela Hill for details and photographs of the Dobson family; *The Press* for permission to reprint pictures; the Canterbury Museum's Josie Lang (library), David Harrowfield (archives) and Joan Woodward (photographs); the Canterbury Public Library's Sue Sutherland and Richard Greenaway; the Alexander Turnbull Library, Wellington; the Hocken Library, Dunedin; sheep station owners or managers, Marmaduke Spencer-Bower (Claxby and Woodstock), Ray and Rhonda Marshall (Mount White), Hamish and Philippa Innes (Flock Hill), Fenton and Louise Westenra (Craigieburn) and Max Smith (Castle Hill); M.J.O. ("Duke") Dixon for a memorable day jetboating in the gorge, and Guy Mannering and Bob Radley for additional jetboat material; N.Z. Railways Publicity Branch for photographs and information; Bob Meyer of the N.Z. Railway & Locomotive Society; Graham Rhind for reading over some chapters for their improvement; and to the following for additional help: Grace Adams, Tom Ayers (Kaiapoi Museum), Gordon Buchanan, Tom Beckett, Jack Cochrane, Doug Dick, Ken Dobson, Robin Drake, Jack Ede, Chris Fenwick, Tom Ferguson, Bob Gormack, Doug Harris, Felix Harvey, Don Hawkins, John Hendon (M.E.D.), Sir Charles Hilgendorf, Kay Holder (A.P.N.P.), Jan Kitson, Diana Lancaster, Sir John McAlpine, Jane Mears, Deryck Morse, Doreen Murie, Gerald Nanson, Leith Newell, Tom Newth, Dorothy Pascoe, John Patterson (Lands & Survey), Alison Powell, Nui Robins, John Sampson, Roy Sinclair, Rob Sutherland, Bert Thompson, Ivan Tucker, and George Urry.

In addition a special debt is owed to the Lovell-Smith coaching reminiscences in Canterbury Museum, to L.G.D.Acland's *Early Canterbury Runs,* and to my friend Don Hawkins' *Beyond the Waimakariri* for essential material in Chapters 7, 8 and 9 respectively.

It was an advantage to have such a useful family to thank: my wife, Lal, not only for her interest and encouragement, but for her meticulous copy and proof reading; daughter Sally Dunford and son Geoffrey Logan, who also read the manuscript and suggested improvements; and especially my elder son John, who generously threw the resources of Logan Print Limited behind the project to produce the finished book.

The Photographs. Sources and photographers are acknowledged where known. Many pictures are copied from old publications, where poor quality had to be balanced against usefulness. Most of the remainder, in colour and monochrome, are from the author's 35mm Pentax.

CHAPTER ONE

Early Days

When the first Europeans came to Canterbury there would be local Maoris still around in whose time a great flood in the Waimakariri River had swept down the Avon, one of its ancient courses to the sea. Such a disaster is strongly implied by the discovery 25 years ago of a kanuka log buried under two metres of river shingle in a pit on Avonhead Road, adjacent to Christchurch Airport, which when carbon dated was found to be less than 200 years old. No minor fresh overflowing into the Avon, such as happened frequently in the 1860s, could have been responsible for such a depth of shingle, but possibly the whole river in high flood, temporarily following one of its several overflow channels to the Pacific Ocean.

Some years passed before the Canterbury pilgrims comprehended the seriousness of this threat to the very core of their colonising venture, but by 1860, when Samuel Butler arrived, the first efforts had been made to keep the river away from the city. Butler, a man who seemed to know the way of most things, and was later the author of *Erewhon* and many other books, had this to say after one of his journeys across the plains.

They (the bullock team) are now going down into an old riverbed formerly tenanted by the Waimakariri, which then flowed into Lake Ellesmere, ten or twelve miles south of Christchurch, and which now enters the sea at Kaiapoi, twelve miles to the north of it. Besides this old channel it has others which it has discarded with fickle caprice for the one in which it happens to be flowing at present, and which there appears some reason for thinking it is soon going to tire of. If it eats about a hundred yards more of its gravelly bank in one place the river will find an old bed several feet lower than its present. This bed will conduct it into Christchurch. Government had put up a wooden defence, at a cost of something like two thousand pounds, but there was no getting any firm standing ground, and a few freshes carried embankment, piles and all, away, and ate a large slice off the bank into the bargain; there is nothing for it but to let the river have its own way.

The pilgrim fathers were not disposed to give in as easily as that, though the river so sorely tried them that *The Press* was moved to describe it as "this incomprehensible torrent". Protecting the city became a major preoccupation in the 1860s, when floods kept breaking out and muddying the Avon to the alarm of all. It became a kind of white-man's-burden on top of the already heavy load of colonising a new land, and one which, although carried with less anxiety today, has never quite gone away.

The Maoris who lived on the banks of the Waimakariri at Kaiapoi, on the other hand, had come to terms with the river long before Europeans arrived, and lived there because the fishing was good and the waterfowl plentiful. Their canoes ferried travellers across the river bound for Kaiapohia, the fortress pa in the swamps near Woodend, six or seven kilometres north of Kaiapoi. Among these were the first white men,

Samuel Butler, *who was 25 years old in 1860 when he arrived in Canterbury, was described by contemporaries as "a small dark man with penetrating eyes", who passed the solitary hours in his station hut far up the Rangitata River playing Bach fugues on the piano he had carted there on a bullock dray. E.R. Chudleigh spoke of him as "nearly as dark as a Maori" and "very nearly if not quite an infidel". John Hardcastle said when he was a boy going to the smithy one day he saw a man leading a horse away. The blacksmith watched the stranger well along the road in silent wonder, then said, "See 'im? 'E don't believe in Gawd!" The man was Butler.*

shadowy figures from the past who were probably shipwrecked sailors or runaway whalers (one said to be heavily tattooed), who left no record of their adventures. Only one of their number left even a name, and that was Smith — a trader's agent killed at Kaiapohia in 1829 during the first attack on the pa.

Joseph Price *(1810-1901), who came to Australia in 1829 in a ship which carried 140 women convicts. Visited New Zealand in 1831 and later settled at Price's Valley on Banks Peninsula where he farmed until his death. He had two wives, the first a Maori of the Ngai-tahu tribe named Kiri Kararina, and the second Jane Scott, whom he married in Sydney in 1848.*

Joseph Price was the first man to leave a written record of his association with the Waimakariri. He was a member of the crew of the barque *Vittoria,* trading out of Sydney for flax, which anchored at Rhodes Bay (Purau) in Port Cooper (Lyttelton Harbour) in June or July of 1831. Years later Price recalled all too briefly (and none too clearly) the events of that visit:

The trading master ... went overland from Port Cooper to Kaiapoi, and under the pilotage of a Maori we took the barque around to the same place. In this journey we lost our way and had difficulty to find the entrance to the river. We remained two nights in Kaiapoi and were treated by the natives most hospitably ... We got from the Maoris some pigs and flax in exchange for powder and muskets, blankets and tobacco. The pigs and flax were sent to Raupaki and were taken to the bay now known as Rhodes Bay where we lay.

The trading master was a man named Williams. He knew that if he wanted to do business he had to go to Kaiapohia but Price's words fail to make clear whether the *Vittoria* actually sailed into the Waimakariri. If it did, the flax would hardly have been sent to Rapaki. The inference is strong that the ship failed in its mission and returned to anchorage at Purau and that Price then followed Williams on foot to the pa.

Long trek. *This view from the Port Hills (excepting civilisation's changes) is similar to that which confronted Williams and Price before embarking on their 30 kilometre walk to Kaiapohia (1). The mouth of the Waimakariri River is marked (2).*

Williams would have Maori guides for his march over the Port Hills by the Rapaki track and through the swamps to the Waimakariri. His view from the hills included the plains where Kaiapohia lay 30km due north, on the far side of the river. At that time the Waimakariri flowed in two separate channels a considerable distance apart, enclosing a large island. There were canoes at the mouth of Kaikanui Creek for crossing one branch, and again further north for the other. The latter was most likely where Alexander Baxter later established his ferry, about where the bridge stands today in the heart of Kaiapoi.

By then Williams would be over the main obstacles in his path and facing the walk along the sandhills to Kaiapohia.* When Price followed he would doubtless be accompanied by several members of the crew to help with the packing. He spent two nights at the pa. The hospitality of the Maoris "extended itself as far as to accommodate us not only with fish and potatoes, but also with a female bed companion for each of us, but unfortunately my inamorata happened to be about 80 years of age, and consequently not the most desirable of companions".

When trading was finished and the flax and pigs carried to the boats at Rapaki and loaded into the *Vittoria,* the ship sailed through the heads and round to Akaroa for more trading; there young Joe Price was compensated to some extent with a much younger and more attractive bedmate.

Williams and Price and their helpers were among the first Europeans to stand on the banks of the Waimakariri, cross it in canoes, and no doubt enjoy for their supper some of its prized roast duck — whatever interpretation is put on Price's somewhat ambiguous recollections. They were also possibly the last white men to live, however briefly, within the palisades of Kaiapohia, already in the final dramatic year of its total destruction by Te Rauparaha. One can but mourn that in his recollection of things past Joseph Price did not record more fully the details of life within the great pa by day as well as by night.†

Left: *The Kaiapohia monument, marking the pa site, is located down a side road north of Woodend township.*
Below: *An early artist's conception of the famous Ngai-tahu stronghold sacked by Te Rauparaha in 1831.*
Kaiapoi Museum.

One estimate of the Maori population in Canterbury at the turn of the century puts the figure at about 5000, possibly halved before 1830 by civil wars and a peculiar "eat relation" feud. Te Rauparaha's bloody massacre at Kaiapohia in the autumn of 1832, plus the forced captivity of many more who were taken off to the North Island, left only a few hundred survivors in the area. Of these, a few lived on the lower Waimakariri and the remainder elsewhere in the province at choice localities such as Port Levy. To some extent the population increased later, a change which had its genesis in the North Island when Tamihana, a son of Te Rauparaha, became an ardent Christian. His Ngati-toa tribe, warmed by the new teachings, celebrated conversion by returning their Ngai-tahu slaves to Canterbury.

Tamihana himself came south and lived for a time among these repatriates and the remnant of Ngai-tahu which had escaped his ferocious father. His Christian influence must have been powerful, for he moved among them in safety. Other changes, the direct consequence of contact with traders, whalers

and missionaries, saw the Maori equipped with iron cooking pots, clay pipes and tobacco, and a smattering of the English language.

This was the way they were in 1840 when the first European settlers arrived to till the soil at Riccarton, seven kilometres south of the Waimakariri River. Malcolm McKinnon and his wife, a man named Shaw and his wife, and another named Ellis struggled hard to establish themselves but after 18 months had to admit defeat. Soon after their departure William and John Deans arrived and took up where they left off. These resourceful Scots succeeded with the first farming venture on the Canterbury plains and were able to give a helping hand to other settlers as they arrived.

The Deanses, taking a break from their exertions, one day walked up the Waimakariri almost to the foothills, when the river prompted John to observe that he had never seen one which ran so fast. By contrast he noted that below their place it was "deep and still as a lake". In these two observations he exposed the essence of "the Waimakariri trouble" — the fact that the river had not yet established a uniform gradient to the sea.

The pioneers who were to have more intimate contact with the Waimakariri over the next few years topped the Port Hills on December 15, 1848. They were the advance guard of the Canterbury Association sent to prepare the way for the pilgrims: Captain Joseph Thomas, chief surveyor, William Fox, the Association's agent, and two assistant surveyors, Thomas Cass

Thomas Cass, *one of the original surveyors of Canterbury, arrived in New Zealand in 1841 and surveyed in Northland until 1844. He was chief surveyor for Canterbury from 1851 to 1857 and his name is enshrined in a Kaiapoi street, a hill and bay near Lyttelton, and the river between Grasmere and Cora Lynn stations. He built himself a cottage in Oxford Terrace which with additions became the Royal Hotel (later the Grenadier and now demolished).*

and Charles Torlesse. It was Torlesse's second trip to New Zealand, and of these four he was to have the closest and most eventful association with early Canterbury.

Charles Obins Torlesse *was 23 years old when he arrived in Canterbury. He was the first man to climb a Waimakariri mountain, which Captain Thomas named after him, and the first to explore the river's headwaters. He built the first house at Rangiora, acquired the big Fernside run, and increased his holdings until for a time they embraced nearly 30,000 hectares, including much of Lees Valley.*

---

* For Kaiapoi residents and collectors of historical quirks it is interesting to note that as Williams began the last stage of his journey he was probably walking, nearly enough, along the track which has since become Williams Street, by which the old Main North Road passes through the town. It was of course not named for him, but for *four* other gentlemen of the same name who at various times served as mayor of the borough. Coincidence certainly has more than one long arm.

† Price returned to Canterbury later and took up land on Banks Peninsula at what is still known as Price's Valley, opposite Lake Ellesmere, where he raised a large family and lived to age 91.

Almost as soon as the survey party had made contact at Riccarton they set forth to explore the North Canterbury plains. A howling nor'wester fought them on the walk north to the Waimakariri, where the waves on the river, whipped up by the wind, were sufficient to delay their crossing and force a camp on the south bank. At five o'clock next morning they were ferried across by the Maoris, then walked on to the pa at Kaiapoi where there was a collection of whares and pataka.

After breakfast they continued to the Ashley River. The journey, extending over several days, took them to Oxford and then round the base of the wooded hills to the Waimakariri again, near Woodstock. They found the river unfordable, no doubt because the nor'wester had brought heavy rain to the mountains, and had to fight their way through thick manuka scrub along the north bank to get back to Kaiapoi. The weather was oppressively hot, too hot for their dog Sailor. Already gored by a wild pig, he expired on the way from thirst.

On December 29 Torlesse took four of his men, including a large Maori named George Tuwhia, and moved up the south bank of the river to Coldstream Pass (Gorge Bridge). Again the weather was nor'west, hot and dusty to the point that Torlesse was induced to cool off in the river more than once. Holidays were rare in the 19th century, but perhaps New Year's Day was on the calendar by then. At any rate on that fine summer morning of January 1, 1849, Torlesse took George, "the big fellow", and left camp for a day free of survey duties.

The pair moved further up the south bank and tackled one of the 1850 metre peaks of the mountain range confronting them. They climbed steadily over interminable scree to the summit, which they reached at 4 p.m. A strong, cold wind greeted them on top, but it was warm on the east side, where Torlesse recorded that he drank "deliciously cold snow water".

Sheltering there he sketched the plains and hills and noted that he could see the Ashley and Waipara rivers far to the north. They descended by a shorter route and reached John Hay's hut at Makarika at 9 p.m. Torlesse paid Tuwhia two shillings and six pence for his day on the mountain. Maoris had never previously shown interest in climbing peaks and he may have been the first of his race to do so.

John Hay's Hut *at Makarika, on the Kowai River, in which Torlesse sought shelter after his climb. Apart from the Deans's establishment at Riccarton, this was the only other building on the Canterbury Plains at that time. Hay was one of a family of early Banks Peninsula settlers.*
J.E. FitzGerald/Canterbury Museum.

The main survey of the Mandeville plain (between the Waimakariri and Ashley rivers and extending about 24 kilometres in from the coast) was not started until the spring of 1849. Meanwhile the surveyors explored South Canterbury, laid out Lyttelton town, the Lyttelton-Sumner road, and the Bridle track. While Torlesse was down south in March the survey ship *Acheron* anchored in Lyttelton. Keen to see something of the country he was plotting on his charts the master, Captain John Lort Stokes, organised a trip to Mount Grey. A short, fat fellow (once described by Thomas Cass as "a most mysterious man"), he must have found the 80km return journey over scrubby, swampy plains rather more trying than pacing the *Acheron's* deck.

Rubicon Peak *(or Mount Torlesse as it is now called) was probably the one climbed on New Year's Day, 1849, by Charles Torlesse. He would have ascended by the right-hand skyline ridge, with rather less snow about than in this springtime picture.*

The number of Maoris living at Kaiapoi at this time was possibly between 30 and 50. Most of them would be on hand when the Stokes entourage arrived at the Waimakariri looking for the ferry canoes. The journal of the *Acheron,* supposedly written by an expedition member named Hansard, describes the crossing and how Dr Forbes, one of their number, shot a paradise duck, "a fine bird, nearly as large as a goose". The lagoons near the mouth of the river were at the time alive with the birds.

Hansard wasn't happy with his canoe, which leaked, and he asked to be landed. The point where he came ashore was occupied by a dozen or more Maori women ready to welcome him with cries of "Airemai! Airemai!" The rather prim Mr Hansard later wrote:

This hubbub was accompanied by a complimentary waving of mats and blankets. As the wearers had no other covering, there was an unusually liberal display of charms usually left to the imagination, and on which in one or two instances even the shepherd Paris might have thought no scorn to sit in judgement—but the majority! faugh! Reeking with putrid shark's oil cap a pie—their faces bedaubed in alternate lines of red and blue, these venerable harpies presented an appearance truly diabolical. All smoked short pipes. The vagaries of one ancient dame particularly interested me. Holding "the clay" to her lips and inhaling with all her might, she repeatedly poked a lighted stick into the bowl. But all in vain—nothing remained but a residuum of dust and ashes, which joined to the woodsmoke nearly choked her. Desirous to terminate this embarrassment, I offered a supply of the weed. She was most clamorously grateful, chattered a great deal, which I *did not* comprehend, and made overtures for a vestal embrace, which I *did*. Flight saved me like Joseph of old; only more discreet than he, I left not my coat in her grip...

The Stokes party canoed up the North Branch, probably to the site of present-day Kaiapoi, where they pitched their tents and cooked a good meal of duck, with potatoes generously provided by the Maoris. Next morning Hansard and his friends rose with the dawn, stripped, ran down the dewy grass on the bank and plunged into the chilly river, much to the astonishment of the natives. This, he said bravely, brought on a pleasant reaction, by which time a good fire had been kindled and breakfast was on the way.

Later they strolled through the three detached groups of huts forming the village and were amused by a lad with a large red and brown parrot swinging about on the end of a long pole. Two other young Maoris were trying to start a fire by the traditional method of rotating a pointed stick on a flat board. Their efforts ended in but a wisp of smoke.

Further along the riverbank they came to the fenced court of the second village section. There a breakfast party was enjoying a meal of dried eel and fern root, the latter pounded on a great stone by two elderly crones. Hansard was distressed by the sight of a girl "with remarkably soft, dove-like eyes" who was beating

Ruataniwha *was the name of a Maori kainga, or unfortified Maori village, situated on the Cam River at Kaiapoi. It would be typical of a number of small native settlements in the vicinity, each with its own choice eeling spot on the river, as encountered by the* Acheron *party. This 1850 painting was probably by William Fox.*

out grain on a mat with a small club. She claimed her back was broken. Dr Forbes examined her and found she had a spine injury.

On her had devolved every domestic drudgery, and a large proportion of field labour. Her attempt to lift from the fire a large iron pot in which the Maoris universally cook their meals reduced her to the distressing condition of a helpless cripple. It is more than probable that her brutal husband was smoking before that same fire, an unconcerned spectator of the whole.

By March 29 Stokes and his party had completed their trip to Mount Grey and returned to the river, where they were again welcomed by the natives, this time with a huge stew of potatoes and wild duck. They were entertained by more of these early Waimakariri riverbank residents—a good-looking young woman cradling the head of her handsome lover, picking the lice from his head and transferring them quickly to her own ruby lips; an old hag at the same occupation but from a tatty blanket; a tall chief who strode about with his infant son on his shoulders, wrapped in a scarlet blanket; a man who had been to Sydney, and who talked incessantly about Te Rauparaha; and two pretty girls of perhaps 10 and 12 years of age who followed a great black-bearded middle-aged ruffian wherever he went—on enquiry they turned out to be his wives. Hansard wrote:

An old crone sits scorching her knees close to our blazing logs, who has been converted by the Catholic Mission. She is puffing away from a short dingy pipe, the bowl of which holds thrice an ordinary allowance, and devoutly crosses herself each time she applies it to her lips. Poor soul!—all she knows of Christianity is probably comprised in that one expressive symbol of our Common Faith. The Kiapoa men disown her, professing to be protestants—"No do that, no do that, all same as Bishop!"

The day was bright and warm when Stokes gave the signal for the journey to continue, and everyone enjoyed the experience of paddling down the North Branch to the main river. There were so many ducks flying overhead that every gun was in use. Hansard's canoe brought up the rear of the convoy; the gun of one of its passengers exploded and the charge "rattled amongst the advance guard, not sparing the Captain's broadcloth. He however shook himself, and finding no hurt that required surgery, administered a sharp and not undeserved rebuke to the thoughtless offender". With that near thing safely survived, and a good haul of duck in hand, the party disembarked, said goodbye to the Maoris and the Waimakariri, and began the walk back to Riccarton.

Torlesse continued his survey work through the long summer of 1849-50. Occasionally he suffered from rheumatism, a complaint worsened by the conditions under which he lived and worked. In October he built a house of sorts at Kaiapoi to serve

as a more secure base for his operations, the first building of any kind between the Waimakariri and Waipara rivers—a plain house with four rooms (kitchen, sitting-room, office and bedroom). His affairs were cheered in October by the arrival of an old friend, John Cowell Boys, who had been with him during his first visit to New Zealand. Now, a fully fledged surveyor, he had come to help with the work.

November and December of 1850 were exciting months which saw the arrival of John Robert Godley, the Canterbury Association's chief agent and one of its principal promoters, and a few weeks later the First Four Ships and their complement of settlers. Godley wanted to do a quick tour of North Canterbury to see the country before the pilgrims arrived. Torlesse and Boys were no doubt delighted to learn that they were to act as guides for the party, and more so that Godley's charming wife, Charlotte, was coming along. Their pleasurable anticipation was heightened when they met the lady herself who was, Torlesse said, his very *beau-ideal* of a woman.

John Robert Godley, *chief agent of the Canterbury Association and generally referred to as the Founder of Canterbury, whose statue stands in Cathedral Square, guided the fortunes of the settlement through its first critical years. The months of delay in communicating with the Association in England at a time when crucial decisions had to be taken, led Godley to consider himself "a Nero on the spot" with "a Board of Angels in London".*

Charlotte Godley, *who with her husband John made one of the first expeditions into North Canterbury, before the First Four Ships arrived. She made a profound impression on all who met her (see Torlesse's admiring remarks in this chapter) and in Edward Ward's opinion was "an exceedingly nice person, very pretty and a good specimen and example to lady colonists".*
Canterbury Museum.

The party, including the Godleys' little boy Arthur, aged three, assembled at the Deans house at Riccarton on the morning of December 5, when Torlesse and Boys found they were to share the expedition with several others. A character named Hunter Brown, who owned a station on the Waipara and who happened to be at Deans's looking for runaway bullocks, joined in. He was, said Mrs Godley, "a sort of cross between a whaler, the roughest of seamen, and a German student". Still another was Frederick Weld (later Sir Frederick, Premier of New Zealand), of Flaxbourne station on the Marlborough coast, who would go with them as far as Rangiora on the long journey to his home. A man named Bill Holland, who had something to do with the Deans farm, came along to lead Mrs Godley's horse. He was, she said, "a very knowing man, a sort of horse breaker and cattle driver, who ... told us all what to do".

Charlotte Godley, in her *Letters from Early New Zealand,* described the first night's camp on the banks of the Waimakariri in graphic terms:

I assure you *camping* is the best fun possible ... the evening, after the fire was lighted, was very pleasant. The flax bushes and grass grew all about, higher than our tent, so that we seemed almost in a shrubbery; about ten yards behind our tent, along a little native path by the river, the fire was lighted, with drift wood from the river, and round it we all established ourselves most comfortably, waiting for tea, which was soon ready. It was great fun all sitting round the blaze, which the evening was just cold enough to make us appreciate, Arthur and I quite wrapped in Mr Weld's opposum-skin cloak ... which is as good as a house to live in.

As it got dark, a party of natives, who had been assembling at some huts across the river, came over in a canoe to pay us a visit, and sit down by our fire. The chief was funnily dressed out for the evening in white cotton stockings without shoes, white trowsers, a black waistcoat and jacket, and a most wonderful beaver hat.

The gentlemen had a sort of shed, built of long sticks, and sailcloth laid over it, with one side open to the fire; but till we were all asleep in the tent we heard them singing and laughing.

Next morning we were up early, and found the fire lighted, and tea but no milk; broiled eels, which the natives had caught for us in the river ... and as soon as breakfast was over, we had to pack all our goods and tents, and then cross the river in a canoe, the horses having to be swum over. After a very short walk, we went the rest of our morning's journey in a canoe up the river [the Cam], the banks of which were very pretty, as we got to the bush. My husband shot some wild ducks, and we lay in the boat, very pleasantly, and were paddled to the spot where we were to get on our horses again.

At Rangiora, where the party camped at the edge of the bush, Weld presented Mrs Godley with a bouquet featuring the flower of a cabbage tree. She expressed much sorrow at his departure next morning and admiration for his intention to walk the 150 miles or so to his station at Flaxbourne. Little Arthur lost his trousers at Rangiora. In the evening gloom they were, as his mother recorded, thrown on the fire by his father along with the branch on which they had been hung to dry.

After another camp at Oxford, including a rest day (it being Sunday), the Godley expedition headed for Riccarton. The principal feature on this part of the journey was the crossing of the Waimakariri at Courtenay. Mrs Godley found this "very disagreeable":

The bed is of shingle and about three-quarters of a mile broad, over which run eight or nine streams ... these are always shifting their bed, besides that an extra warm day sends down more or less flood from the snow mountains; and so, though safe one day, you may find the same place impassable the next, and the water runs so clear that it is difficult to guess at the depth. None of our party had crossed where we did before, and though I was quite safe, myself, with Holland leading my horse, who understands these rivers well, it was not quite so with my husband, who *of course* would go first, though he had taken Arthur before him for the crossing, and in one stream, just at the edge, I had the pleasure of seeing his horse, and Mr Boys', sink in over their tails as they tried to rise at the bank; the place was too deep, and the bottom not firm. Arthur was tossed off on the ground, and they all scrambled out, very little wet, but it was very unpleasant to *see* from the other side, where I was. One very disagreeable part is that, when the water runs so fast, it makes everyone who is not used to it as giddy as possible. I fancied the horse was standing still, pawing the ground, and the stream getting more and more rapid, and so I hear others say.

With the crossing safely accomplished by all hands Charlotte Godley left her husband to bathe in the river while she pressed on across the plains with the hot wind at her back and a threatening sky above, to the welcome shelter of the Deans farm at Riccarton. A few days later the main body of Canterbury Association pilgrims began arriving at Lyttelton on the *Charlotte Jane, Randolph, Sir George Seymour* and *Cressy*.

CHAPTER TWO

The Great Floods

The land on the banks of the lower Waimakariri was green and pleasant, except when the wind blew from the north-west. Then great clouds of dust from the wide shingle beds upstream made life unpleasant, and worse, often heralded the arrival of floods within the week. For people from gentler climates the nor'wester was a trying experience. All too soon they discovered it could gust like the hot breath of some mountain giant with big lungs and a bigger bucket. This unpleasant fellow, if he couldn't blow them down, scuttled them with great spates of water sloshed down the river. They found it difficult to reconcile rising floodwaters with a dry wind, blue skies and summer heat. In spring, of course, they suspected melting snow, but the Waimakariri soon showed it could produce floods any time of the year except midwinter, when hopefully the giant was asleep.

However the earliest settlers on Kaiapoi Island, between the north and south branches of the river, were not too much troubled by nature's extremes because for most of the first decade the river was reasonably well-behaved. The maps showed that it rose in the foothills like the Ashley and the Selwyn, and its potential for serious mischief was so little understood that Christchurch grew up alongside its own quiet little stream without suspecting that "Avon" was just another name for a rampaging Waimakariri of the distant past, which some day might return.

It was not until the late 1850s, when Joseph Pearson and Charles Torlesse reported on their separate expeditions beyond the gorges, that people learned the Waimakariri they knew on the plains was only half the river. Because much of its length runs in country hidden behind front ranges the settlers had no way of knowing that the weather gods blew quite different bugles in the mountains to what they sounded on the plains, so that floods would always be difficult to predict. The first big one, incredibly there on a fine summer day, with not a drop of rain to explain the phenomenon, was not only a surprise but a portent for the future.

The Waimakariri was such an ill-disciplined affair as it flowed across the plains that in places it occupied a bed almost three kilometres wide, and then split into two separate rivers between which lay Kaiapoi Island, a desirable block of land about 11 kilometres long and five or six kilometres across, containing some of the most fertile soil in Canterbury. This, combined with its proximity to ready markets, attracted a host of arable land farmers—up to 40 in the first decade. They counted themselves fortunate to have such rich soil to till.

But they also found they had two unruly rivers to contend with, and two names for both because the Waimakariri's official title was Courtenay. If that was not too much of a difficulty, pronouncing the native name was. They heard the Maoris' musical cascade of syllables, easy on the ear but not the articulation, and they came up with their own variations, like Waimakaridie, Waimacarry, Wye McReedy and Waimukruddi; even Whimicindi and Why Mack. Some took years to get it right and even longer to learn that one of its several meanings was *River of Cold Rushing Water*.

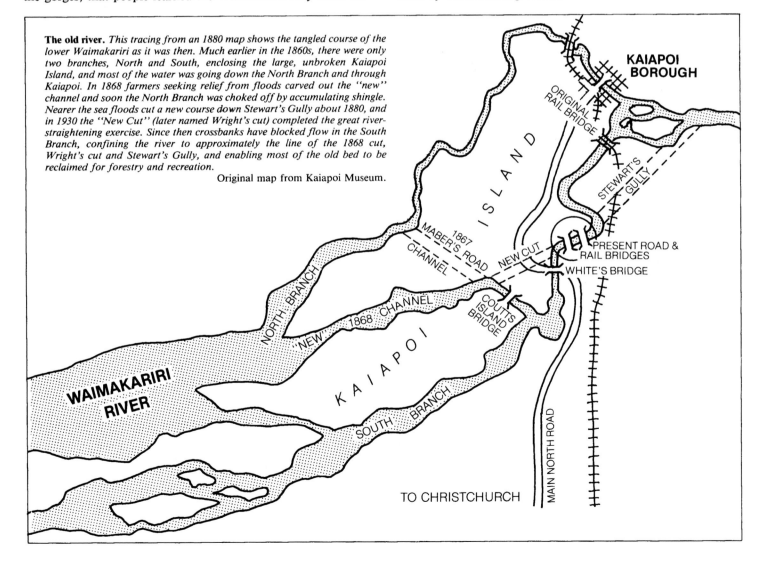

The old river. *This tracing from an 1880 map shows the tangled course of the lower Waimakariri as it was then. Much earlier in the 1860s, there were only two branches, North and South, enclosing the large, unbroken Kaiapoi Island, and most of the water was going down the North Branch and through Kaiapoi. In 1868 farmers seeking relief from floods carved out the "new" channel and soon the North Branch was choked off by accumulating shingle. Nearer the sea floods cut a new course down Stewart's Gully about 1880, and in 1930 the "New Cut" (later named Wright's cut) completed the great river-straightening exercise. Since then crossbanks have blocked flow in the South Branch, confining the river to approximately the line of the 1868 cut, Wright's cut and Stewart's Gully, and enabling most of the old bed to be reclaimed for forestry and recreation.*

Original map from Kaiapoi Museum.

In 1858 a couple of worrying "freshes" came down and overflowed on to farm land. One carried Dudding's ferry out to sea, causing some alarm; there was concern in the city too. Flood water escaped into the old channels along the south bank and the Avon rose high enough to sweep away and overturn the wash-house of William and Mary Tod in Wood Lane. Christchurch was well served at the time by witty versifiers, one of whom seized the opportunity to pen these lines about a local civil engineer, W.B. Bray, who worried about the river:

> At Avonhead lives Mr Bray,
> Who every morning used to say,
> "I should not be much surprised today
> If Christchurch city were swept away
> By the rushing, crushing, flushing, gushing Waimakariri
> River."
>
> He told his tale and he showed his plan,
> How the levels lay and the river ran;
> The neighbours thought him a learned man,
> But wished him further than Ispahan,
> With his wearing, tearing, flaring, scaring Waimakariri River.

The main trouble with the Waimakariri was its gradient. This averaged 1 in 200, which is about par for the course of Canterbury's snow-fed rivers, but whereas the Rakaia and Rangitata continued this grade to the sea, the Waimakariri flattened out for the last 15km. From there on the easier pace allowed its load of flood-borne detritus to be dumped on what could be called the terminal face of its "fan" or "cone", leading in turn to the instability of course described by Butler. At some unspecified time in the distant future the river, left to itself, would have completed its plains-building exercise right to the sea, and would then have resembled more closely its more orderly brothers further south.

But meantime, settling comfortably into a larger and more leisurely bed, it formed islands with names like McLean's, Templar's and Bailes's, immediately above where it split in two to enclose Kaiapoi Island. The town of Mandeville which was supposed to be sited hereabouts grew up instead much further east where Kaiapoi developed, half on the island and half on the "mainland". As the North Branch began to carry most of the water, continual flooding beset Kaiapoi to the extent that in the first three years of its existence the town suffered 16 disastrous floods and spent nearly all its revenue trying to keep the river at bay.

At "The Groynes" *children paddle and splash in what was once the South Branch of the Waimakariri. The massive concrete blocks were poured as part of works to protect Belfast, Chaneys and the Main North Road.*

The slowly-rising level of the riverbed spawned a number of troubles. On the northern side both the Eyre and Cust tributaries were long since choked off and, with nowhere to go, created the great Ohoka-Rangiora swamp. On the south bank, in the Courtenay-Halkett region, the river repeatedly tried to escape into old channels which headed directly for Christchurch, while lower down it would break out and flood the Belfast-Chaneys flats and threaten the Main North Road. The most southerly channel flowed through the present Groynes picnic spot, continued along behind the Belfast Hotel, swung north to the old White's Bridge and beyond to near the present motorway bridges, and from there north-east to join the North Branch near where the freezing works now stand.

The year 1859 brought the most serious flood scare of the decade. On February 2 water poured over Kaiapoi Island farms and through the streets of Kaiapoi itself, while a considerable overflow escaped into the Avon and renewed alarm in Christchurch. *The Lyttelton Times* was moved to comment that since it was obvious the Waimakariri was not in the habit of keeping to one bed for long, if the country was to be colonised the river would have to be civilised. Crosbie Ward, one of the several Ward brothers who emigrated from Ireland and settled in Canterbury, was a handy man with a pen. Among his topical verses of the time were these:

> Christchurch lies a little low,
> Hey, hey, the level o't;
> Above the tide a foot or so,
> Hey, hey, the level o't.
>
> And when about the town you go,
> Sundry indications show
> That here a river used to flow.
> Hey, and that's the — o't!

Another rhyme recorded the misfortune of a man named Rowley, who built his house by the Waimakariri at Halkett, not realising how recklessly it could change course when in flood:

> As young Mr Rowley one morning was going
> With a barrel on wheels to the river for drink,
> Instead of a mile off he found it was flowing
> Five yards from the house and a foot from the brink.
> The river was tumbling, the banks they were crumbling,
> Poor Rowley had scarcely got time to jump round,
> When very soon after, from basement to rafter,
> The whole of his house disappeared from the ground.

Rowley noted with alarm that a broad stream was heading in the general direction of the city, and hurried there to warn the townsfolk and describe the fate of his house. At the time the whole body of the river was pressing against the south bank near his place and there were no protective works to prevent overflows into old channels* leading towards the Halswell, Avon and Styx rivers. The occurrence focussed attention on the danger and led to construction of the first recorded protective works designed to keep Waimakariri water out of the Avon. There was much speculation about the reality of the threat to the city. *The Press* did nothing to comfort its readers by reminding them that the river could well sweep the whole town away:

There can hardly be a less pleasant matter for contemplation than the fact that a huge torrent is bowling down to the sea at the rate of knots at a distance of some 20 to 30 miles from the capital, and at an elevation of from three to four hundred feet above the tops of the houses, and that it has a tendency to break out of bounds and come rushing over the plains, to the certain destruction of everything in its path.

The thought of the Waimakariri in full cry, an impressive sight at any time, coursing down the Avon and through the city, perhaps converting Cathedral Square into a shingled waste, made many townspeople tremble whenever they saw a nor'west arch and felt the warm wind blow. The curving path of the river across the plains, with the convex side to the south, suggested it had only to straighten course to head directly for the city. And loose talk about "huge torrents" and "certain destruction" intensified the apprehension of people living on the outside of the curve.

But all these urban anxieties were based only on possibilities. In Kaiapoi and on the Island destructive floods were already grim realities. Even keeping the North Road open to traffic where it ran near the river was a problem with no easy solution. Provincial Engineer Edward Dobson designed and built a breakwater to protect the road, but the river was doing its best (or worst) to remove it (and coincidentally to water down his professional reputation). He could hardly be blamed—he was an expert on railway construction, not obstreperous colonial rivers.

*These are plain to any observant motorist on the Old West Coast Road between Yaldhurst and Courtenay.

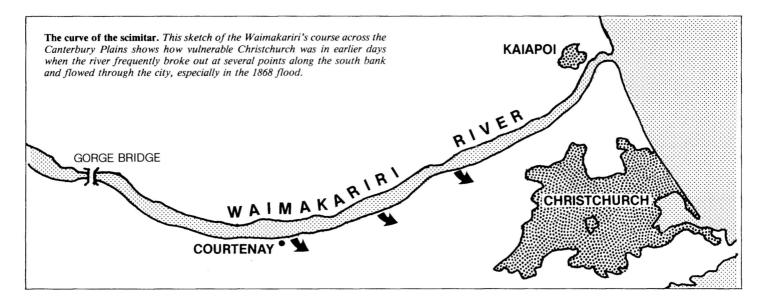

KAIAPOI

GORGE BRIDGE

RIVER

WAIMAKARIRI

COURTENAY

CHRISTCHURCH

The subject was discussed by the Provincial Council on August 11, 1863. Dobson said he thought the breakwater was working well, but others were not convinced and suggested they should get an engineer from Nelson or Melbourne, where it was understood good men were available who knew something about rivers (but not, as was remarked, as many as in Canterbury where happily everyone was an engineer when it came to knowing what was best to be done). *The Press* again:

A Committee has been sitting on the subject of the celebrated Waimakariri breakwater, and upon the subject generally of educating that tricksy and mischievous river. There is something related to water which renders all enquiries in which it is concerned painfully unsatisfactory. One gentleman says none of the breakwater has ever been carried away; another says thirty feet of it were gone when he saw it. One says it is doing its work capitally, sending the stream to the opposite side of the river; another says that it can be of no possible use at all; and a third says the bank has been falling away much more rapidly since the breakwater was built. The Committee recommend that the breakwater shall go on again to a limited extent. It is resolved to give the old river as large a dose of breakwater as can be administered for 500 pounds.

The Waimakariri remained unimpressed by frustrated engineers and droll editorial writers. It just kept rolling along, as rivers do, making sure at irregular intervals that nobody who lived within a far call of its banks slept too peacefully. This applied especially to farmers on the island. On September 28, 1863, they sent a delegation to wait on the Provincial Superintendent to draw attention to their individual and collective perils. *The Press* had more to say:

No sooner have we got rid of the obnoxious question of the breakwater below the bridge than a new feat of this incomprehensible torrent attracts our attention. All our readers who study the maps will know that about 10 miles from the sea the river divides itself into two branches which reunite just below the town of Kaiapoi; the two branches enclose a tract of country which is called Kaiapoi Island. The great body of water has hitherto run down the southern branch, but for some reason not accounted for, the water has broken through the shingle bed which lies at the upper mouth of the northern branch of the river, and is gradually but very rapidly taking possession of that course as its principal channel to the sea. The result is that a very large tract of country which has been brought into cultivation is in danger of being totally destroyed.

This threat to the island's existence carried with it an even greater danger to Kaiapoi now that the main Waimakariri was flowing through town. Soon there was scouring on the north bank where the river entered the Charles Street straight; the rebound carried it across to Raven Street; and in between a shingle bank formed. The river's quiet reaches began to assume the unruly characteristics of the South Branch. Town councillors watched these developments with apprehension, as well they might.

But Kaiapoi's predicament left the Provincial Council largely unmoved. Their attitude was that if people chose to build a municipality in such a highly vulnerable place, they had no legitimate claim on provincial money chests. Apart from that the council was convinced, mainly on the advice of its consulting engineer, W.T. Doyne, that there was no way Kaiapoi or the island could be saved except by an expenditure many times their worth. There were some councillors who had the safety of Christchurch so firmly in mind that the further the river strayed north the better.

All this was not enough to stop James Heyward, one of the island's leading farmers, from firing his own shot in the battle for survival with this letter addressed to the Provincial Secretary. He may not have known how to spell the Waimakariri's name, or when to take a breath between sentences, but he did know he and his neighbours were in deep trouble unless they could get help. He wrote:

Sir, — I beg to call your attention to the state of the river Whimacindi and the damage through the overflowing of all lands laying on the north branch and the centre of the Island Kaipoi that you may lay it before the Government that something may be done in time as the river is daily getting worse it is at present overflowing its banks for miles and flooding the surrounding cultivated land although there is no fresh but the main part of the water is coming into the north branch which used to be a small stream easily fordable even in a fresh but is now dangerous to cross at any time on horseback. I have myself eight acres ploughed part sown which is mostly perished with the water flooding it from the river and most of the other it will be useless to sow for fear of it being the same and all of my neighbours are in the same predicament not only our fences washed away but some are in danger of their houses and farm buildings going the same way and unless something be done soon nearly the whole of my farm above three hundred acres will be useless and the state of our roads through the overflowing of the river are almost impassable and you will find on examination that there is no exaggeration in what I have above stated and that I have not complained before urgent necessity compels me to do so.

I remain, yours respectfully,
JAMES HEYWARD*

The Kaiapoi River. *All that remains of the once rampant North Branch which in 1864-5-6 was damaging nearby farm lands and undermining Edward Dobson's unfortunate Girder Bridge (from the site of which this photograph was taken).*

*Heyward ran a large and important farm on Kaiapoi Island which supplied the market with 300 pigs a year and cropped 200 acres. He came to New Zealand in 1855 via Australia as a passenger on the famous voyage of the brig *Graphic*, then owned by William Sefton Moorhouse, who filled the ship with horses and 27 passengers. They were 58 days crossing the Tasman and the passengers ate the horses which were not thrown overboard. Heyward was supposed to be the man who got lost in the flax bushes in Cathedral Square and asked the way to Christchurch. —*Note from Macdonald Biographies (Canterbury Museum).*

In the face of that what could the Government do? It sent George Thornton, an assistant engineer, to cut a channel 400ft long, 50ft wide and several feet deep to divert some of the North Branch water back where it belonged. In a month it was 300ft wide and much of the river had returned to the South Branch. The cost was included in the 3642 pounds spent that year on the Waimakariri.

A further response was to commission Consulting Engineer Doyne to make a comprehensive report on the whole question. This gentleman plainly had a deep respect for Canterbury's big rivers. When in flood, he said, "they are gigantic torrents spreading over shingle beds from one to two miles in width, and moving forward with a force and noise which convey a sense of awe and grandeur".

Doyne presented his first report in July, 1864. Referring to the Waimakariri and especially to that part below the division into the North and South branches above Kaiapoi Island, he said:

From this point, for nearly four miles to the east, the river has spread out to a width of from 1½ to 2 miles, and consequently so diminished the force of the current that, during the freshes, all the materials brought down have accumulated in this space, and formed a barrier higher than the level of the banks on each side, rendering a change in the course of the river inevitable.

Doyne said the cost of adequate control works would be prohibitive and quite beyond the resources of the province. He thought Christchurch could take assurance from the river tending towards a more northerly course, but if something beyond natural ends was required, then "a set of levels should be taken to decide whether any works should be entered upon for the protection of Christchurch against an impending calamity".

This was cold comfort for Kaiapoi and the islanders, abandoned now to their own devices, and nature's. Mr Beswick, who represented Mandeville district on the Provincial Council, was smartly on his feet at the next meeting to criticise Doyne for his "do-nothing" report. He was in no mood to "lie down under that, it would be like a ship springing a leak and the carpenter crying out, 'It's no use working the pumps or trying to save the ship; we must all go down'." But the Secretary for Works replied that Mr Doyne had not said that nothing could be done but that it would cost more than the worth of all the property it would save. And, said the Secretary, five of the six other engineers in the province agreed. (The exception was James Wylde, who lived in Kaiapoi.) Provincial Superintendent Samuel Bealey supported this view but took on himself the responsibility of a modest expenditure for temporary protection works. Thomas Cass, the Chief Surveyor, agreed with Doyne, while the newspapers, conscious that the bed of the river was slowly rising, fell to wondering what would happen next. It was the turn of *The Lyttelton Times* to be facetious. Commenting on Doyne's proposal to let nature take its course, it said:

Kaiapoi Island it seems has before it the prospect of being destroyed but the destruction is to be conducted by strict rule and in accordance with sound theory, so grief for the loss when it occurs must be subdued by admiration for the method. Science requires that no bungling interference shall thwart her laws and if an ignorant multitude will only have patience they shall in time see the island swept into the Pacific, bearing a surveyor and theodolite in full work, a dumpy level on its legs and a qualified engineer tracing the last words of his report and recording the fulfilment of his theory, and shall people give praise to science, for the island shall be lost according to law.

The real problem of course was that no engineer in 1864 could match his resources against the requirements of the job. The solution, as *The Press* said many times, was to confine the river to a single, narrow, straight channel from Courtenay to the coast, to maintain a sufficient velocity when in flood to carry the shingle out to sea. This would have required enormous excavations and stopbanks, for the construction of which the finance, engineering skills and machinery simply didn't exist. This work was not done until 30 years into the next century although Edward Dobson, far ahead of his time, envisaged a canal across the island to straighten the river's course. Meantime Kaiapoi and the island had no alternative but to live with

periodic flooding, while Christchurch held its breath every time the "Waimak" splashed a little water in its direction.

The islanders and townsfolk threw up banks as high as they could afford to keep the newly-vigorous North Branch at bay, and hoped for the best. They had learned that the really big floods came in spring and early summer, but in 1865 they were reminded abruptly that this was not always so. In March the river sent down "a very heavy fresh" which submerged most of the island, taking with it some late crops and the house of Charlie Brown, a small farmer. In a fit of compassionate generosity the Provincial Council gave him 120 pounds to build a new one but they were not disposed to do more.

The same flood caused a disturbance to the dead as well as the living by threatening Kaiapoi's Sneydstown cemetery. When the burial ground was laid out the North Branch was a lazy little stream flowing some distance away. Since it now comprised almost the entire flow of the Waimakariri, in flood it swirled past the cemetery within a few feet of the graves.

Citizens called a public meeting to consider what should be done. They heard that for 150 pounds the river might be put in its place, but caution and respect for the dead demanded an immediate removal of the cemetery's occupants to a safer haven.

A new site was secured in a better place and the Provincial Council offered 20 pounds towards the cost of transferring the bodies. The men hired for this task were blamed later for not doing their work properly, because the next big flood stranded a coffin containing a woman's body on Edward Wilson's farm downstream. The police were called and the woman was re-buried in the new cemetery. No one knew whether this was an isolated case or whether a whole fleet of coffins had gone sailing down the North Branch. With all that water it was thought they would have no trouble Crossing the Bar.

The March flood was only the precursor of what was to be a long year of affliction. In May "the heaviest fresh for years" flooded over the banks so hopefully erected, swept across the island and poured into Kaiapoi streets. People grew tired of cleaning up after being so frequently muddied. They were looking forward to the winter as being the only time free from worry, when perhaps for a while they could sit around and talk of other things (of politics or the news from America that President Lincoln had been assassinated). Recovery from the last flood always seemed to be only the getting-ready for the next one. Relaxation and its pleasures were tempered with fears of what spring might bring.

Canterbury's nor'west arch, *a familiar sight as the fohn wind prepares to blow, has always meant rain in the mountains and possible floods in the Waimakariri. This shot from Christchurch's estuary shows sail-boarders enjoying their sport before the big breeze arrives.*

The river had a lively programme arranged. For openers "a considerable flood" arrived on October 4, but in terms of what was to come it was no more than a warning. Still, it ate a chunk out of the approach to White's old bridge in Kaiapoi and chewed away at the north bank along Charles Street until there were four gaps, including one rather too close for comfort to the new Swing Bridge on the main street.

Exactly one month later the fourth of November was a trying day with scorching heat and a strong, dusty nor'wester. People spent an uncomfortable night wooing sleep. Some families in

Edward Dobson *(1816-1908) — a photograph probably taken about 1860 when he was 44. As Provincial and Railways Engineer he was grappling with the immense and complex public works programme demanded by the new colony. His immediate worries would be how to bore the Lyttelton railway tunnel through the hard volcanic rock of the Port Hills, and how to keep the unruly Waimakariri in its place. And soon he and his sons would be exploring in the river's headwaters for a pass to the West Coast.*

Sneydstown (immediately north-west of Kaiapoi) who finally dozed off were awakened in the small hours by the cackling of fowls. Arising to investigate they found themselves up to their knees in water in their own bedrooms. Daylight showed the whole countryside to be one sheet of water as far as the eye could see, with just the tops of the fences still visible.

The weather continuing hot, children went swimming along Ohoka Road that day. Some stout fellows with a punt rescued a number of women and children from places where the water was getting too deep. None of the banks had held against the onslaught.

The old cemetery was now largely gone. So were the approaches to Edward Dobson's Girder Bridge over the North Branch, on the road to Rangiora. In response to entreaties Dobson and Secretary of Works John Hall hurried out with local dignitaries Beswick, Birch, Dudley and Rickman to inspect the damage. Extra protective works were authorised. There were mutterings from upstream where some of the larger landowners proposed to take matters into their own hands and put the river back in the South Branch where it belonged.

Floods and what to do about them were now dominant in most minds. On November 7, two hundred people crammed into the Kaikanui Hotel at Kaiapoi for a public meeting to argue the merits of alternative control schemes. Some were for banks generally, some for banks in specified places, others for cutting Dobson's canal across the island, and still others for a barrier at the entrance to the North Branch. Eventually the standard Canterbury solution was reached — a committee was appointed.

But the committee was too slow off the mark. Their deliberations, hardly begun, were overtaken by another flood and another public meeting. They had to scramble to get something ready in time, and came up with a bank "15ft wide at base, faced with sods, extending from Hassall's to Sneyd's properties, to cost 150 pounds". This, they considered, would prevent all flooding for at least 10 years.

It is not recorded whether the second public meeting thought the prospect of complete flood protection at 15 pounds a year to be blatant extravagance or absolute lunacy, but it was rejected on the spot. Instead, the meeting thrashed out its own specification for a bank "a quarter mile long, 16ft wide at base, 8ft wide at top, and 4ft high", cost unknown, guarantee unmentioned. In view of what was coming, it made no difference.

Workmen started building the new bank on the following Monday morning, but had made little progress by Wednesday when the river rose again. Workers leaned on their shovels and watched the yellow tide flow past them into Sneydstown.

A third public meeting was held in the Kaikanui Hotel. The owner, William White, the builder of bridges, offered to fix the whole vexing business for 10,000 pounds on a "no cure, no pay" basis. The nature of his scheme was not reported, but the meeting rejected it, which was probably lucky for William White.

James Wylde *was assistant provincial engineer under Edward Dobson until the White's Bridge controversy. He lived at Kaiapoi during the period the Waimakariri flowed through that town and was thus more personally involved with the flood threat than his contemporaries, but his efforts to control the river were no more effective for that.*

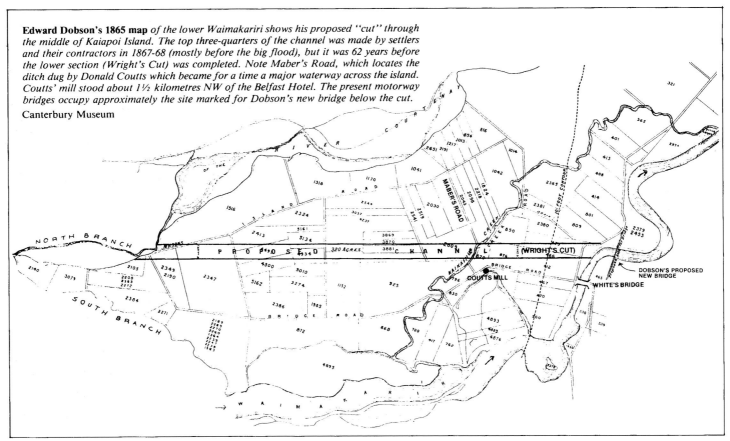

Edward Dobson's 1865 map *of the lower Waimakariri shows his proposed "cut" through the middle of Kaiapoi Island. The top three-quarters of the channel was made by settlers and their contractors in 1867-68 (mostly before the big flood), but it was 62 years before the lower section (Wright's Cut) was completed. Note Maber's Road, which locates the ditch dug by Donald Coutts which became for a time a major waterway across the island. Coutts' mill stood about 1½ kilometres NW of the Belfast Hotel. The present motorway bridges occupy approximately the site marked for Dobson's new bridge below the cut.*

Canterbury Museum

With that out of the way, the meeting fell to criticising the Provincial Council for its "do-nothing" attitude and the engineers for their failure to produce a workable solution. Hours of discussion saw midnight come and go, and with it most of those present. Finally, almost in desperation, it was decided to accept whatever the engineers might have to offer—and thus ended a decidedly useless evening made worse, one of those present maintained, because "public meetings should never be held in public-houses".

The wild Waimakariri *in full spate during one of its seasonal floods, whipping up high pressure waves. The original banks thrown up by early settlers and engineers were no match for the river in one of these moods.*
The Press

The north-west wind blew incessantly through spring and summer of 1865. On November 24 the dust flew and the gale uprooted trees and carried away house roofs. In the city the Provincial Council was meeting in its brand-new chambers in Durham Street, which were the admiration of all, but councillors had difficulty hearing speeches above the roar of the wind. About this time Doyne's "Second Report on Canterbury Rivers" was being considered. While this recommended that nothing be done to save Kaiapoi Island, the news for Christchurch was all good. Armed with the levels he had previously suggested, Doyne told the meeting that while the contour lines and general lie of the land appeared to put Christchurch in a most critical position, the danger was actually non-existent. A protracted study of the terrain had revealed that beneath the Courtenay-to-Fendalltown channel there ran an underground river which gathered in almost all the overflow water and diverted it back into the main Waimakariri so that only a small part of any flood would ever reach the Avon.

This was tremendous news for the city. If not everyone found it easy to believe, most were willing to make the effort. Meanwhile, farmers on Kaiapoi Island and residents of the town, lacking any such morsel of faith or hope, put up the hard cash to raise the banks before the next flood.

On December 11 Edward Dobson produced *his* report on "Waimakariri Encroachment", which recommended embankments on the upper side of the island but warned that these might push the river further to the north, "to the utter ruin of settlers in that part of the Mandeville district". How then to save all three local disaster areas—Kaiapoi Island, Kaiapoi town, and Ohoka swamp-dwellers?

There was only one way, said Dobson, and that was to excavate his canal across the island from Mason's Corner to a point below White's Bridge on the South Branch. Initially this would be 100 metres wide and one metre deep. The fall of 2.8m per kilometre would ensure that the river did most of the work itself by scouring out an ample waterway—a new "middle branch" which would replace both the old branches.

Instead of bridging the canal to take the North Road, Dobson proposed that the road be taken further down to a new bridge below the junction. He estimated the cost of the whole scheme at 24,000 pounds including 5000 pounds for the bridge. No mention was made of compensation for landowners in the firing line or for possible damage claims if the river developed an appetite for adjacent farmland.

The canal idea was agreeable but hazardous. Most neighbouring farmers, no matter how simple their arithmetic,

could figure that three streams were better than two when it came to getting flood waters safely past their properties, assuming the old branches would act as overflow channels. And while Edward Dobson must have felt some unease about letting loose a river like the Waimakariri in an artificial course, at least the scheme would get rid of that obstinate contraption, White's Bridge, which refused to wash away and pained him every time he saw it.

But this was really no time for consideration of such matters. The spring floods were over, the 15th anniversary of the province was a subject for celebration, and Christmas was just around the corner. The hot weather wasn't the best for roast beef and plum pudding, but it was good for kids on holiday and picnickers on willowed banks. On December 22 the *Times* reminded all its readers that now was the season for rejoicing and relaxation.

Unhappily next day it had to print this message sent down on the new telegraph line from Bealey: THUNDERSTORMS ACCOMPANIED BY HEAVY RAIN ALL DAY. RIVERS ABOVE THIS IMPASSABLE. WAIMAKARIRI AND BEALEY UP SEVERAL FEET IN LAST FEW HOURS AND RISING RAPIDLY. NOW RAINING IN TORRENTS.

The great Christmas Day flood of 1865 was on its way. It came charging down the gorge like a wild animal in a granite cage and swept out on to the plains, a mile wide and looking for trouble. There it prowled to and fro until it reached Courtenay, where enough escaped to give Christchurch a fright. The remainder, by far the greater part, rushed on towards the sea, fought to cram itself into the twin channels at Kaiapoi Island and spilled out over the surrounding countryside until it drowned the more lowly dwellings to the eaves.

Canterbury had never seen so much water before. It was by far the worst flood ever experienced, the most destructive, the most heart-breaking for settlers already reeling from a succession of lesser blows. Wylde estimated the damage at a colossal 70,000 pounds. Up in the mountains it swept away miles of the new West Coast highway, only just completed in the Bealey and Otira gorges. Kaiapoi municipality, already groggy from the earlier bouts with the river, almost sank beneath the mud. As farmers began to talk of quitting, an air of hopelessness spread over the land, no less tangible than the sea of floodwater which met the eye in every direction.

Communications being what they were in 1865, first reports published in the newspapers on December 26 were devoted mainly to what happened in the city. The *Times* reported:

Something like the casualty so long dreaded for Christchurch has at length occurred. Yesterday (Monday) morning Mr Templar of Coringa station found his place surrounded by water which had issued from the Waimakariri some 12 to 15 miles from Christchurch. A strong though shallow stream was passing over the nearby level plain and found its way at last into that part of the old riverbed which leads into the Avon. Mr Templar lost no time in announcing the matter to the proper authorities, and by an early hour of the morning, Mr Hall, Mr Stevens, Mr Jollie, Mr Dobson, and his Honor the Superintendent were informed. His Honor, with Messrs Hall and Dobson, set off as soon as

Looking upriver *today from Kaiapoi's main highway bridge, showing the "Swing" footbridge. The riverbed has been narrowed to half what it was in the mid-1860s when almost all the Waimakariri flowed down this North Branch course.*

practicable to examine the origin of the danger and the extent of the mischief done; and at the same time Mr Thornton, the assistant engineer, was despatched to see that the bridges and other means of communication were preserved from injury.

Christchurch residents, noting the swollen and discoloured Avon, felt greatly concerned, but when it failed to rise further their worries disappeared. One bridge on Fendalltown Road was removed to avoid trouble lower down and the approaches of another were washed away. But the city escaped lightly and Mr Doyne and his underground theory were loudly acclaimed.

The only news from the country that morning was that Kaiapoi Island was believed to be badly flooded and several cases of danger to life had been reported. Two men, Messrs Monk and Ashcroft, had rescued some women and children by swimming their horses across the river; the women had been up to their waists in water.

Next morning the *Times* was able to print the news from the north. It is a delightful example of leisured and informative 19th century newspaper reporting from the Kaiapoi correspondent's pen, here somewhat abridged for reasons of space:

For the second time in two months it is our painful task to have to record the disastrous effects of a flood in the Waimakariri. It will be remembered that, early in November last, the whole of Sneydstown and that portion of the town Kaiapoi situated on the island were more or less inundated, in consequence of the breaking away of a portion of the river bank near Hassall's farm. To prevent a recurrence of this evil, subscriptions were made, and an embankment of such size, thickness and stability was erected as to be calculated to be perfectly capable of resisting a heavier fresh than had been known for many years. By this means confidence was re-established, and a general sense of security from flood obtained amongst the inhabitants of the island. As the holidays were near at hand, preparations were made by one and all to celebrate the advent of Christmas-day in the true old English style. Invitations to join in the Christmas fare were freely given and accepted, picnics were arranged; and up to Friday night everything might be said to be going as merry as a marriage bell. Alas, however, for the mutability of human affairs, all were doomed by a great calamity, which will cause the Christmas of 1865 to be long remembered.

On Saturday morning the joyous countenances of the inhabitants were made to assume a most anxious look by the appearance in the public papers of a telegram from the Bealey, announcing the rapid rise of the Waimakariri. The river in Kaiapoi was keenly watched, when it soon became perceptible that the stream was rapidly rising; and, in fact, so quickly did it augment in volume, that notwithstanding the tide was running out from 9 a.m., yet the river rose about two feet between the hours of 12 noon and 2 p.m. The scorching nor'westers of the previous two days were more than remembered; and as it was also rumoured that it had been raining heavily in the hills for two days, preparations were made for the worst. At three o'clock the river was in many places level with the top of its banks, and shortly after, it began to overflow at the end of Fuller Street west. Great anxiety was felt in the town and fears were expressed during the morning as to the stability of the embankment at Hassall's, when about half past three in the afternoon, the news arrived in town that the bank had given way, and the river was pouring upon Sneydstown. The volume of water making its way through the gap was something terrible to look at. The current had swept everything before it; post and rail fences, mud banks, haystacks, and gorse hedges had all disappeared.

In town, the stream was found to be coming down the river with increased velocity, and some anxiety was felt for White's old bridge, which was known to be in a very shaky condition, and furthermore that if it gave way, it would probably severely damage the new bridge. Precautionary measures were promptly taken, by removing the unsafe part, which was done without accident. About 12 midnight, the whole of the streets on the south side of the river, except the North Road, were impassable. As a proof of the rapidity with which the water rose at this time, we may mention that in the course of two hours on Saturday night, it rose a full 20 inches in the houses in Peraki Street. Shortly after 12 o'clock on Saturday night the water began to retreat, and continued doing so all Sunday, when the crowns of the road were again passable. Beyond this, however, it did not subside, as the footpaths, houses and gardens were knee-deep all day. At about 11 o'clock on Sunday night the water began to rise once more, and by four o'clock on Monday morning it had again covered the streets. It continued rising, until many of the streets were more like rivers than anything else, the current in some places being a perfect rapid. At 8 o'clock the whole of the houses and properties lying to the west of the

North Road, and north of and including both sides of Ohoka Road, were without an exception from three to five feet under water. On the north side of the river affairs were not quite so bad, although a great number of houses and gardens were flooded to a depth of three to four feet. The worst sufferer on this side was undoubtedly the Rev. W.W. Willock, whose property, unfortunately, lies some feet lower than his neighbours.

As soon as day broke on Monday morning, the most strenuous efforts were made by those unaffected by the flood to relieve their neighbours in distress. The streets presented a most busy and at the same time distressing aspect, men on foot, on horseback, and in boats, to the number of 29 or 30, being engaged in rescuing the persons and property of the inundated from danger. The streets were pretty well strewed with firewood, post and rails, tubs, boxes, tin dishes, and in some instances might be seen a number of fowls taking a compulsory voyage of discovery on a floating log of wood.

During Tuesday afternoon Mr Rickman's malt-house, which was built on a sod foundation, fell in with a loud crash, the sods having become softened by the water. The new bridge also had a narrow escape from being seriously damaged by a portion of an old jetty which was washed against it with great violence. The bridge was very severely shaken. All the empty houses on dry ground were at once taken possession of, by those who had no friends and who could not obtain accommodation at the hotels. To estimate the extent of the damage done would be impossible, but this is certain, it is the most disastrous occurrence that has ever been known in Canterbury.

Kaiapoi scenes *during the 1923 flood, which from all accounts was not to be compared with those of the 1860s. The lower pictures were taken in the Sidey Quay area and show the local brewery under siege.* Weekly Press

Mr Wylde had always strongly opposed the Doyne argument that nothing could be done to save the Island. Now the *Times* came out vigorously on his side: "It is indeed monstrous that a credulous acceptance of a theory which can be successfully disputed should cause the Government to stand idly by while property is being destroyed wholesale, and life itself endangered by the flooding of the Waimakariri."

This said, the newspaper hastened to open a relief fund for sufferers from the flood. A few days later posters appeared on fences in Cathedral Square announcing a concert to help raise money. Although virtually penniless, the Kaiapoi municipal council scraped together 100 pounds and the Government sent a man to list individual cases of hardship.

One of the most notable characteristics of the Christmas Day flood was its duration. It was in reality two separate floods with peaks only a day apart. As late as December 28 most of Kaiapoi was still under water, to a depth of a metre in Sneydstown. The Government's Swing Bridge in Kaiapoi and the Girder Bridge upstream from Sneydstown were both damaged, but White's Bridge over the South Branch stood unharmed against the torrent. White's old bridge in Kaiapoi on the North Branch was dismantled shortly after the flood; a decision for this had been taken some time previously.

"Please God, no more!" could well have been the supplication of Kaiapoi people when the river rose again on January 3. Nothing having been done to the breached banks,

A plain warning. *Civil Engineers like Edward Dobson and William Bray were well aware of the Waimakariri threat to Christchurch, as this 1866 letter from Dobson shows:*

Provincial Engineers' office
Chch Oct. 17. 1866

Sir.

I have the honour to report that during the recent fresh in the Waimakariri an opening has been formed in the bank of shingle immediately below the timber breakwater, seventeen miles from Christchurch . . . . . . there is very probability that considerable flooding will take place both in the Fendalltown river & in the river itself during the freshes which may be expected during the months of November & December.

I do not apprehend any immediate danger of the main body of the stream coming down the Fendalltown river, but as the Waimakariri is now setting strongly against the South bank, it is probable that in a few years by the scouring of the shingle a very considerable portion of the river will return to its old channel & flow through Christchurch.

V. obedient servant

E. Dobson
Provincial Engineer

To the Secretary of Public Works

Canterbury Museum

water overflowed into the streets again. But it was only a small flood and no great harm was done.

"I am of the opinion that Kaiapoi may be protected for a time by earthen embankments, but I do not consider that it is possible to execute any engineering works which will save either the town or the island from being ultimately destroyed by the encroachments of the river," said Edward Dobson a week later, remembering the remarkable spectacle of the Christmas flood at its height. This was hardly a Happy New Year message for the beleaguered farmers and townsfolk, but Christchurch didn't fare much better. He was concerned, said the Provincial Engineer, whether the river might not flow permanently down Templar's dry bed. He had found that the shingle bank preventing this formed a very inefficient protection and might well be scoured away in a single fresh. If the river did escape into Templar's channel and from there into the Avon "it would be impossible to calculate the extent of the destruction of property which would ensue." He proposed to begin a detailed survey so that some action could be recommended.

A month later the news was no better. Since the Christmas flood, Dobson said, a great body of water was flowing down old channels which had been dry for years and finding its way into the Avon. It was quite possible that succeeding freshes might throw the main Waimakariri in that direction. He suggested raising and straightening the south bank at Courtenay and sowing it with broom and wattle. "I think this construction would remove all present danger to Christchurch," he added hopefully.

Meanwhile at Kaiapoi repairs were made to the banks between Hassall's and Sneyd's properties. When the next flood came on January 23 some parts of the island were again submerged, but the bank held.

The islanders were a hardy lot. The great majority considered the excellence of the land sufficient justification for risking another crop, but Henry Engelbrecht, who almost drowned on Christmas Day, decided he could do better elsewhere and left for Oxford. Another two or three followed, but the remainder stayed on and gave thought to how their properties might be better protected. Among those whose farms were substantially flooded (more or less in order of severity) were: John Taylor, John Humphrey, Joseph Clark, Thomas Hughes, John Maindonald, Henry Maindonald, James King, John Maber, John Wilson, James Heyward, Frank Lawry, James Whitmore, George Lainey, William Shaw and Richard Mason.

The whole question of the Waimakariri was an unexpected, unwanted and continuing vexation for the Canterbury Provincial Council. Since 1863 the sum of 7000 pounds had been spent on three embankments along the river—one near Watson's Halfway House in the Courtenay area, another downstream at Sandy Knolls, and a third 11km further on near McLean's, in each case to block an old overflow channel. The council agreed that it must do what it could to contain the river and maintain lines of communication but in the wider context it had to accept that floods were acts of God and somewhat beyond their jurisdiction. If Kaiapoi people chose to live in Kaiapoi, and island farmers to farm on the island, that was, alas, their problem. The Government repeated that it was not prepared to build large and expensive works to protect them or their property. After much haggling and endless correspondence, Kaiapoi got 500 pounds to spend on river banks.

Of course if the river failed to take the great curve and shot into the Avon, that would be a different matter altogether. On Dobson's recommendation the sum of 2000 pounds was found for work at Courtenay to protect the city. With this he built two large shingle banks, "each half a mile long, three feet high, and 10 feet wide at the top, placed at an upward angle to the stream where the main overflow took place". Men with shovels and wheelbarrows laboured for weeks to build them. It was expected that in this way a kind of eddy or backwater would turn the overflow back to the river.

Faint hope. The Waimakariri flooded again on October 12, 1866. Christchurch eyebrows rose at the sight of dead sheep floating down the discoloured Avon, noted to be very much

Refugees. *A Kaiapoi family with babe in arms, forced to leave their home by floodwaters, seeks shelter on higher ground in Kaiapoi's domain. Scenes like this would be common in 1865 and 1868; this one was during the 1923 disaster.* Weekly Press

above normal. When the water in the main river receded, one of Dobson's massive 1000 pound "dam banks" was nowhere to be seen.

That gentleman was naturally disturbed. The river had taken a set towards the south bank, he warned, and if allowed its way could well return to the old channels and head towards the city. With likely November and December floods in mind he advised people living near the Avon to be ready for the worst. Meanwhile he promised to keep a sharp eye on the situation.

"Every attempt which has been made to deal with this river has proved a failure," intoned *The Press,* "and yet it is important that something be done before it is too late." But what?

James Balfour, a marine engineer, was brought in to give an opinion. The complexities of the Waimakariri were simple compared with the rhetoric of his 22-page document, but the conclusions were no different, and nothing resulted from his expensive survey.

Virtually abandoned by the Government, the people of Kaiapoi formed a voluntary organisation in 1867 to raise the banks behind Sneydstown, an improvement which kept the borough dry through several small floods that year. The island farmers agreed that Dobson's canal was the solution for them, and set in train its excavation from Mason's Corner down the island to divert the North Branch into the South below Donald Coutts' flourmill. Coutts had already dug a canal along Maber's Road across the island to serve his flourmill, and this was now taking considerable North Branch water. In both cases the river did most of the work once it was given a start, but much good land had to be surrendered to satisfy its appetite along the new courses. The increased flow of water in the South Branch caused problems lower down, where the North Road was frequently endangered, but no matter how big the floods, William White's amateur-designed bridge across the river on the Main North Road stood its ground.

The fateful year of 1868 dawned beneath an angry sky of foreboding. A correspondent of the *Times* marvelled at the comparative indifference of the public. Engineers, he wrote, were riding up to Courtenay and contemplating the waters there with no more influence than King Canute. If the river came down the Avon in force, Christchurch would very soon be a wild waste of shingle. "I think, Sir," he added, "it behoves us all to look out in time."

There was not much time left. The periodic discolouration in the Avon kept the subject alive in the city, while on Kaiapoi Island the settlers organised contractors to dig their canal. When they had time they pitched in themselves. The risky work made exciting progress when freshes in the river helped things along. The January 17 flood found them ploughing guide lines for the water to follow and working vigorously with spades and shovels, directing overflows into new channels. It was almost as though they knew the greatest flood of all was coming.

George Lainey left his farm to join his brother-in-law, John Maber, for an afternoon on the job. When it was time to go home he took a short cut by crossing the Maber's Road stream, by then a considerable torrent. Waving farewell to his brother-in-law he plunged into the river, "but seemed to lose all command of himself as soon as he was in the water, was washed off his legs immediately, and disappeared". The tragedy cast a gloom over the island and intensified the seeming futility of the struggle.

By this time even the City Council was alarmed; they sent a deputation on January 23 to exhort the Superintendent to do something, anything, towards the protection of the city. The thousands of pounds already spent had produced nothing of value, they said, and the future was looking grim. But the Superintendent (W.S. Moorhouse) was not impressed. He reminded them that all of the engineers had recognised long ago that any scheme to adequately discipline the river was beyond the present resources of the province. The deputation left with the usual assurance that the Government had the matter firmly in hand.

As January turned to February, the Waimakariri was getting ready to show who was boss in this battle. And for the first time, unlike 1865, it would have a number of allies to help produce the deluge which history has nominated the greatest of them all.

The flood which swamped Canterbury along with most of the South Island east coast on Tuesday, February 4, 1868, was a surprise to local people. The couple of inches of rain which fell in Christchurch occasioned no particular concern, and if a telegram came from Bealey it would be only to report a similar fall there.

Summer had been kind that year. Grain crops were among the best yet and prices promised well. The fruit trees were laden. Feed was plentiful and stock was in good shape. January's end brought a week of beautiful, fine, sunny weather, and farmers everywhere looked forward to a bumper harvest.

Then the rain came in from the north-east. From that quarter it usually began gently, but the showers which fell shortly after dark on the Sunday evening of February 2 were heavier than normal. The downpour continued all night and towards Monday morning the wind increased to a violent gale, knocking the crops about and covering the ground beneath the fruit trees with much of the expected harvest.

Still there was no hint of what was to come. In the 18 years since the pilgrims had stepped ashore at Lyttelton, possibly they had not experienced a wet easterly gale sweeping across the plains. To such a wind the Canterbury foothills present much the same obstacle as the alps to the nor'wester—a barrier against which rainclouds drop their burden. For what happened back in the hills one must turn to Lady Barker's *Station Life in New Zealand*. Her husband, Frederick Broome, owned Broomielaw station near Whitecliffs. She was there on that Sunday evening, and this is what she wrote:

About 11 o'clock we were all sauntering about out of doors, finding it too hot to remain in the verandah; it was useless to think about going to bed; and it was agreed that some great change in the weather was due. There was a strange stillness and oppression in the air. We noticed immense banks and masses of clouds but they were not in the quarter from which our usual heavy rains come ... about midnight, after a very few premonitory drops, the rain came down liberally in sheets. The noise on the wooden roof was so great that we had to shout to each other to make ourselves heard. This heavy rain continued without a break for 24 hours, when it changed to heavy, broken showers and drizzle.

Within hours every creek and river along the foothills was a raging torrent as the yellow flood swept towards the plains. From about Craigieburn down, the Waimakariri also rose in considerable flood, but the real mischief came from the smaller rivers, the Ashley, Okuku, Makerikeri, Cust, Eyre, Kowai, Hawkins and Selwyn. By Monday morning all were running bank to bank, and shortly without banks at all as the enormous volume of water swept them away and poured out across the plains, converting the landscape into one vast lake. In North Canterbury, where the Ashley flowed unchecked through Southbrook and parts of Rangiora, the lie of the land saw this water, and that from the Eyre and Cust, directed towards the North Branch of the Waimakariri, where it flowed out to sea through a half-drowned Kaiapoi.

Here is what the local correspondent of *The Press* had to say:

When on Tuesday morning the people of Kaiapoi perceived the north-east gale which lasted since Sunday, and had done any amount of damage to corn crops, as well as most thoroughly threshing the fruit trees, none of them dreamt that the whole of that luxuriant agricultural district between the Waimakariri and the Ashley would be flooded to such an alarming extent. But such has been the case. We hear from authentic information that the whole Mandeville district, between these two rivers, is one great sheet of water. The view, as far as the eye can see from any high eminence, is of a magnificent lake studded with islands here and there, on which the owners of the submerged habitations have fled for refuge, only too well pleased they are beyond the flood, with no recourse but to await the abatement of the waters, shut out from all assistance on whatever patches of ground they had been lucky enough to reach—nor how slowly the day dragged on as with hearts filled with anxiety they watched the onward spread of the continually rising waters.

It was six o'clock that morning before early risers in Kaiapoi realised what was happening. As the river swelled before their eyes they took alarm and hastened to warn people on low-lying ground to remove possessions to upstairs floors or to the houses of neighbours who were better placed.

The Kaiapoi river came up so quickly that by 7.30 a.m. the 1865 high-water mark on the Swing Bridge was already submerged. Downstream from the bridge gangs of men worked to save stores of wool and grain, fighting the clock as the tide rose about them. Great stacks of sawn timber awaiting shipment at the wharves had their departure date forcibly advanced as stick by stick they floated off to sea.

The timber was joined on the river by a fascinating procession of flood debris from hundreds of farms upcountry — sheds, outhouses, farm animals dead and alive, gates, fowlhouses, wheelbarrows, posts and rails, hay bales, trees, even the odd beehive—all observed with interest by a miserable, rain-soaked crowd gathered at the Swing Bridge to preside over its fate. Some were busy with long poles trying to keep the piles free of debris. It was an unequal battle.

By midday the creaking structure was almost submerged beneath a surging bow wave, and it seemed only a matter of time before it yielded to the pressure. A stray boat came floating downstream, further impeding the flow of water; there was a loud crack—probably a bolt snapping—and the northern part of the bridge between the approach and the swing section broke loose and sailed away, narrowly missing the schooner Spray at anchor off Revell's wharf. Kaiapoi was now effectively divided in two.

The "tiger" escapes. *Events like this have not been seen on the Waimakariri for many years, but once were all too frequent as inadequate banks collapsed and flood waters spread far and wide over the countryside. From a photograph taken by the author in 1950 immediately above the north end of the old Main Highway Bridge.*

"Throw the Engineers Overboard"!

There was growing opposition to civil engineers in Canterbury in the mid-1860s. The new colony required immense development works, and men who were competent to take charge of such projects were highly thought of—and well paid. But as the years passed, and all the engineering know-how of the province failed to find a satisfactory answer to the Waimakariri question, a degree of disillusion found its voice.

Strangely the first move came from within the engineers' own ranks. James Wylde, C.E., suggested at a Provincial Council meeting that the river might be better handled by "practical men without engineering credentials". Wylde, who lived by the river at Kaiapoi, had always opposed the opinion of his fellows that nothing could be done about the lower reaches, but his own track record was poor. He once spent 1500 pounds on works at the top end of Kaiapoi Island and saw them all disappear with the next flood. In 1866 he proposed that the Superintendent should consider the appointment of a Board of Conservators. There was no doubt in his mind, he said, that the whole of the country surrounding the Waimakariri was liable to be destroyed, and in his view enough had been heard from experts on that subject.

Edward Jollie agreed. He also thought the danger was imminent and that the river might go into the Islington channel (leading to Lake Ellesmere) as well as into the Avon. If allowed to go on for even six months it might be in Christchurch by that time, when it would be too late.

Joseph Beswick from Kaiapoi, never one to mince words, thought they should "throw the engineers overboard altogether". The only work which had stood against the river was one built without benefit of engineering advice. (He would be referring to White's Bridge.)

Council rejected Wylde's motion by 27 votes to 10, but not before representative Murray-Aynsley had taken a verbal swipe at W.T. Doyne, the engineer who made the first two comprehensive reports on Canterbury rivers. He had heard that Doyne had been paid the enormous sum of 16,000 pounds for his services to Canterbury, and he would like to see details "laid on the table".

Murray-Aynsley exaggerated, but not by too much. When the figures were produced they showed that between 1854 and 1865 Doyne was paid 11,696 pounds for his work on provincial projects, mainly in connection with the Great South Railway (about a million dollars in 1986 currency).

Wylde had his way in the end. Three years later the Council gave the amateurs their chance by appointing a Board of Conservators, with Richard Harman as chairman. Christchurch has not been flooded since.

Nearly every street in town was under water. In many horsemen riding on errands of mercy found their mounts swimming beneath them. Men with boats worked tirelessly to rescue families marooned in trees or on house tops. In south Kaiapoi the water was generally about two metres deep, but in some places cottages which were awash to the eaves in 1865 were now completely out of sight. The house of Dr Dudley, chairman of the town council and one of the leaders in the campaign for better river control, was submerged to within inches of the ceiling. The Magistrate's Court, due to sit that day, could not do so for the best of reasons — the courthouse was full of water. By three o'clock in the afternoon it appeared that only five houses in all Kaiapoi remained untouched. Many who had moved to the homes of friends were forced to move again along with their hosts.

Unlike the 1865 flood, which maintained a high level for days, the water receded quickly this time. As communications were restored, news trickled through to reveal the full devastation in the countryside. The Ashley Bridge had gone and most others had suffered the same fate or were badly damaged. Two children were drowned near Southbrook. Even Maoris on their high ground at Tuahiwi were flooded; their memories could not recall this happening before. Two men at Cust who went to rescue horses were trapped; one survived a dreadful night by tying himself to a flax bush with the rope he had brought for the horses. One family spent the night on the roof of a stable; another escaped only minutes before their house collapsed. Farmers everywhere stared ruin in the face, their crops, livestock, newly-harvested wheat, fences, even haystacks and sheds, all gone with the flood. Thousands of dead cattle, sheep, pigs and poultry drifted away to lodge against fences — until they in turn gave way under the pressure. Debris of all kinds covered the mud-clotted fields and, as the clouds finally dispersed and the hot sun came out, an all-pervasive stench filled the air. It was difficult for anyone surveying this desolate scene to recall the green fields as they had been, and the soft weather and rosy prospects of only the week before.

As no river level recordings were kept in those days, comparisons between the great floods are largely guesswork. The facts suggest that in 1865 the Waimakariri ran higher than in 1868, if only because for the latter the heavy rainfall was confined to the front ranges. Kaiapoi Island farmers escaped relatively lightly in 1868 perhaps because of the Maber's Road channel across the island and the partly-excavated "Dobson" canal. There could be other reasons why more water escaped into Christchurch in 1868, such as the river having developed a pronounced set to the south. After the flood it was discovered that the bank near Courtenay had been scoured out by an overflow.

Christchurch, while it certainly suffered the worst flood in its history, escaped without serious damage. The *Times* reported that ...

Monday morning was unattended by the slightest alarm, and although the Avon was observed to be slightly discoloured, this was attributed to storm water from the nearby roads and streets. Shortly after 10 a.m. a perceptible rise was noted. Towards noon the alarm caused by this was further increased by gentlemen arriving from Fendalltown who reported that the Waimakariri had broken all bounds, and was making its way towards the Avon in greater volume than ever before known. By one o'clock the banks below the Madras Street bridge had been topped and the road on either side speedily became flooded. Shortly after 3 p.m. the overflow began at Gloucester Street, the river being level with the buttresses of the Government footbridge, Lane's mill, and the Montreal Street bridge, and flowing over the flooring of the Worcester Street bridge.

By 7 p.m. the whole of the block containing the post office and market place (Victoria Square) was knee-deep in water, while both Victoria Street and Colombo Street bridges were cut off from pedestrians. Hansom cabs and four-wheelers were busy ferrying passengers. At midnight the overflow appeared to have reached full depth, with the water level waist deep in the post office. The flood extended along Worcester Street into Cathedral Square to the Godley statue, and it was said that during the evening T.S. Mannering, the sheepfarmer, who happened to be in town, rowed a boat into the Clarendon Hotel. A large gap appeared in the approach to the Colombo Street bridge, and some time in the night the Worcester Street bridge sailed downstream and had to be secured by ropes to avoid further damage.

The main destruction appeared to be in Fendalltown, where some buildings collapsed, many sheep were lost, and fences and culverts destroyed. "The roar of the water passing through Mr Johnstone's property was more like a mountain torrent than an ordinary stream," wrote a reporter. A horseman riding into the city found the water up to his saddle-flaps, while in Mr Grigg's house in Merivale it was a metre deep. For the first time there seemed also to be serious overflows near McLean's and Templar's islands which sent substantial streams down Harewood Road into Papanui, and further north into the Styx River. Much of Fendalltown, Merivale, Papanui and the north of the central city were again under water, and there was severe flooding along the Avon in the business area.

Dr A.C. Barker lived on the north side of Worcester Street between Cathedral Square and Oxford Terrace. Here are extracts from a letter he wrote to a friend:

The flood so long predicted by Mr Bray has come at last, and my pretty garden amongst others is now several feet under water. All yesterday there was violent rain and this morning the river began to rise. Before communication was broken off we heard that Kaiapoi was under water. Then that all the bridges had been swept away. And now at half past ten at night the flood is closing round my house, having long ago filled the kitchen and put out the fire. It is now creeping at the rate of about 4 or 5 inches an hour up the steps. I am most unwilling to abandon the house, as the flood though very deep is from the flatness of the country not violent and I don't like unnecessarily to round up my friends in the middle of the night. Should it rise much higher I shall I think send for a cab or something of the sort and ship off the children to some friend's house on drier land. It is strange that this should have occurred just as Lord Lyttelton had come out to visit us — we are, or were, to give him a breakfast the day after tomorrow! I can't help thinking where we may be by that time.

Lord Lyttelton, after whom Lyttelton town and harbour are named, was a member of the management committee and a financial backer of the Canterbury Association. The function in his honour was the social event of the season, but the attendance was much reduced — invited country gentry were all marooned on their sheep stations.

The work of cleaning up after the flood kept North Canterbury occupied for weeks, and for longer than that sea breezes wafted inland the smell of rotting carcases strewn for miles along Pegasus Bay beaches. Most of the timber washed away from the wharves at Kaiapoi came back on the sands, where it was quickly gathered by scavengers with sharp eyes and insensitive noses. It was said that a man at Woodend built himself a four-roomed cottage from his booty, while another named Jones was found to have 6000ft of flotsam timber stacked in his shed. He and others were taken to court by the real owners but most of the cases were dismissed.

The flood in the Avon was the talk of the town while it lasted but was quickly overshadowed and almost forgotten as news of the disasters elsewhere began to filter through, especially from North Canterbury. Each day brought fresh news of enormous damage and loss throughout the land, and it was a long time before Canterbury recovered from what was termed "the saddest and most universal catastrophe the province has yet known".

The Waimakariri in Christchurch. *On several occasions in the 1860s the Avon swelled and sometimes overflowed with flood water from the big river. This 1868 photograph shows the scene at the Gloucester Street bridge with the Provincial Government buildings on the far bank, taken the day after the flood's midnight peak.*
Canterbury Museum

CHAPTER THREE

The Explorers

The year 1865 was one to remember in Canterbury. That was the year of the great gold rush to Westland and the men who hurried over the mountain passes to try their fortunes on the diggings. It was the year the Canterbury Provincial Government, needled by public clamour, ordered explorers into the Waimakariri headwaters and pushed the highway over Arthur's Pass. And it was the year the Waimakariri sent down its greatest flood, unsettling all who lived near its lower reaches. The year also brought big changes in other ways. As it ended, Cobb's coaches were being readied to run between Christchurch and Hokitika and the electric telegraph was about to link the two towns with the magic of instant communication.

There was much to do before the road could be built. No obvious route presented itself across the Southern Alps between East and West Canterbury. These were the days before "separation", when there were only three provinces in the South Island—Nelson, Canterbury and Otago—and each extended from the Pacific Ocean in the east to the Tasman Sea in the west.

For nearly everyone who lived in Canterbury the Southern Alps held all the terrors of the unknown. Their knowledge of the back country, and of Westland beyond the Alps, was virtually nil.

The Maoris, having been around much longer, knew that the established greenstone route from the West Coast lay to the north over Hurunui Saddle. This long, circuitous and dangerous journey involved many crossings of two large rivers, Hurunui and Taramakau. Edward Dobson was familiar with that country—he was the first European to cross the saddle, in 1857. But the gold rush was centred on Hokitika, much further south, and a shorter route had to be found, possibly from the headwaters of the Waimakariri River.

It was natural that the Waimakariri should come to mind first since it lay in what was perceived to be the right general direction. Yet for 100 kilometres the north-west horizon was dominated by ranges of almost continuous mountains, seldom less than 2000m high. Closer inspection revealed the only gap—where the Waimakariri flowed out on to the plains.

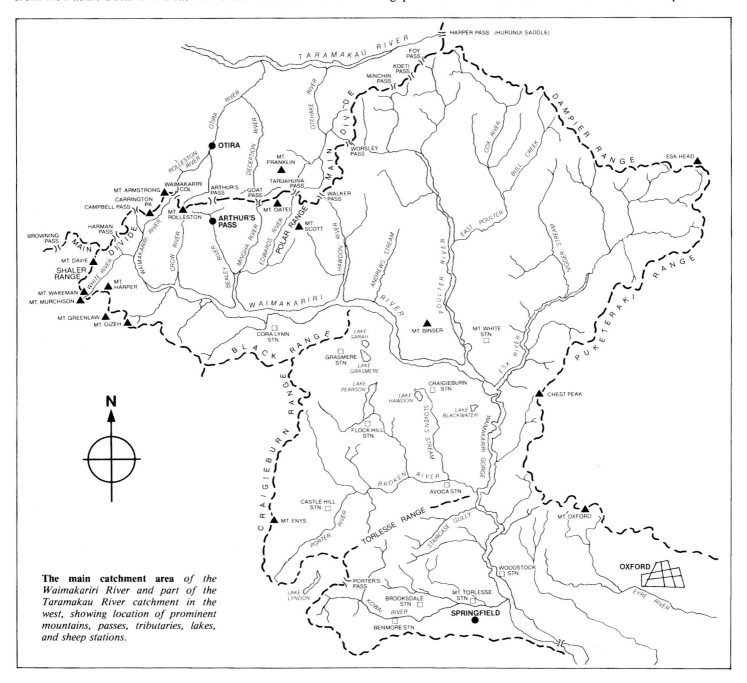

The main catchment area *of the Waimakariri River and part of the Taramakau River catchment in the west, showing location of prominent mountains, passes, tributaries, lakes, and sheep stations.*

Here surely was the way to the West Coast, except for one thing: travel up the river was made almost impossible by a 24km gorge of ferocious proportions. The search had to be extended further south to where, on the descending shoulder of the Torlesse Range, Porter's Pass gave access to comparatively easy country in the open Waimakariri basin, and from there a practical way to the main divide.

Surveyor Thomas Cass, interested in the subject, frequently asked local Maoris whether they used the Waimakariri on their journeys to and from the West Coast, but their answers were always in the negative. On the other hand explorers Leonard Harper and Arthur Dobson (second son of the Provincial Engineer) were both assured by the Coast Maoris that there was a pass to the Waimakariri from the headwaters of the Otira River, a tributary of the Taramakau River. But, they always added, it hadn't been used in their time.* This was tenuous evidence, yet within a few years this pass would be carrying the main highway across the Southern Alps, with coaches rattling through the Waimakariri valley bearing men travelling west, not for greenstone like the Maori, but for gold.

Part 1: From Pearson to Butler

It was gold of a different kind which lured the first explorers into the upper Waimakariri. They were Joseph Pearson and his companion Sidebottom seeking the golden tussock hills and basins so desired by sheep farmers. When they pushed through the lower Waimakariri Gorge in February, 1857, they were richly rewarded. There, spread before them as they broke through the encircling hills, lay 100,000 hectares or more of ideal sheep country — the great rolling expanses which were to become the Craigieburn, Grasmere and Mount White runs.

Joe Pearson, a Cumberland man who spoke with a broad Cumberland accent all his life, arrived in Lyttelton in early 1851 with a shipload of sheep belonging to his employer Joseph Hawdon, a successful Australian cattle and sheep man. His mission was to find suitable pastoral land in Canterbury for Hawdon and his friends, who had struck a bad patch in Victoria with drought and fire. In the course of his work for Hawdon, Pearson was twice credited with saving the life of a fellow cattle drover, Robert Heaton Rhodes, who also became a prominent figure in Canterbury.

Why it took Pearson more than five years to apply himself to his original assignment for Hawdon has never been explained, unless he was kept too busy with his own affairs. These included taking up stations near Oxford: Burnt Hill for himself and View Hill for John Christie Aitken, an associate of Hawdon's. For several years he lived at View Hill and managed both stations from there. Among his activities it was said he made the second overland journey between Canterbury and the Wairau, in 1852, and some time later he crossed the Waimakariri and climbed on to the Torlesse Range to get a view into the upper reaches of the river beyond the gorge. What he saw from there were glimpses of an untrodden region which begged closer inspection.

To a man standing high on an eastern buttress of the Torlesse Range the way to this country was plainly up the river's gorge, winding away to the north along the base of the Puketeraki Range. The likeliest eminence Pearson climbed for his view would be Peak 1114m between Otarama and Staircase, and from this he would have been able to assess most of the possibilities and difficulties. Returning to View Hill he and Sidebottom, a station hand, loaded three packhorses with supplies and set out on their adventure.

They found reasonable travelling to begin with but as they progressed the difficulties increased. The Staircase locality, where the river is locked between precipitous gorge walls, must have been a sore trial to both men and horses, but they got through somehow. Once past Staircase easier terraces high above the river gave access to a reasonable crossing of Broken River, and beyond that to the tussocked flats and hill slopes of the basin itself.

Here was a sheep man's paradise, a land of wide open spaces watered by lakes and streams draining south and east into the Waimakariri. Moving north over this country Pearson continually met with vistas to both left and right of new pastoral reaches, of soaring hills and well-grassed valleys. Soon the Waimakariri appeared free of its gorge, opening out into still further expanses of promising sheep country extending back north and north-east and drained by several large tributaries coming from the general direction of the Southern Alps main divide.

Pearson spent some weeks in the basin, exploring and firing the primeval tussock growth which everywhere had to be removed before sheep could graze. The glare and smoke from their awesome fires was clearly visible across the ranges from Christchurch, where it was a talking-point among concerned citizens. Then, with their food supplies almost gone they retreated the way they had come, back to the comparative luxury of the station at View Hill. †

At Burnt Hill homestead. *Joseph Pearson, by this time an old man, poses before his home with his wife and various descendants. Explorer, sheepfarmer and "father of Oxford", he was devoted to his Sarah (seated), who predeceased him by only four months.*

Joseph Pearson's map showing proposed run boundaries was submitted to the Waste Lands Board and signed in October, 1857, by W.G. Brittan, the Chief Commissioner, approving selections for Joseph Hawdon, Thomas Woollaston White, John C. Aitken, and Pearson himself.

The map includes many of the names by which prominent features are known today, which must have been given by Pearson. These include:

Broken River	Lake Blackwater
Esk River	Lake Pearson
Poulter River	Lake Grasmere
Mount Binser	Lake Charlotte
Sloven's Creek	Paketirake
Windy Creek	Lake Letitia

Some time later Lake Charlotte became Lake Sarah, named for Pearson's wife, and Windy Creek (pronounced with a long "i") became Winding Creek. Lake Letitia was named after White's wife, or possibly Charles Bowen's wife. Lake Hawdon is shown on the map without a title. Pearson named Grasmere after the lake in Westmoreland, and the Esk for any one of the numerous Esk Rivers in the British Isles. Sloven's Creek would be so-named because of its sluggish ways, but no explanation comes easily for Poulter, Binser or Charlotte (unless the last-named was for Godley's wife).

Pearson gave his own name to the largest lake but must have stopped short in contemplation of his companion Sidebottom, even though his name bore an obvious affinity with lakes. Paketirake would be Pearson's version of Puketeraki, the range

---

*The Maori was no stranger in the Waimakariri. Many artefacts have been found at or near Castle Hill, including recently a woven back-pack, and there are cave drawings there. The remains of Maori ovens were discovered at the Bealey River mouth, and it is said that an adze was found in the Otira Gorge.

†Previously published accounts of Pearson's journey described his route as being over Porter's Pass, but David McLeod is convinced Pearson went by way of the gorge, and the writer concurs. Had he come over the pass he would have needed to walk through the attractive Castle Hill country with his eyes shut; he makes no mention of it. On the contrary there is a section of Waimakariri below Staircase marked on his map as "Gorge above View Hill station", which is some evidence of his route.

Promised land. *This was some of the upper Waimakariri sheep country Joseph Pearson discovered in 1857 when at last he broke free of the gorges. The view from Bold Hill looks across Broken River, with Sloven's Creek coming in beneath its Midland line viaduct. The railway winds up Sloven's valley towards St. Bernard's Saddle before descending to Cass. The view embraces land occupied by five runs — Avoca with its station buildings in the pine trees, Flock Hill across the river, Craigieburn (on which stands Mount St. Bernard at left), and Grasmere in the distance. Beyond Bullock Hill and across the Waimakariri, part of Mount White run shows on the slopes of Mount Binser.*

forming the eastern boundary of the region, which musterers later shortened to Pakety.

Charles Torlesse followed Pearson into the upper Waimakariri in 1858. His association with the river was a lengthy and varied one, beginning when he climbed the mountain which bears his name, lying south-west of the lower gorge, from where he could see into the upper valley. He had much to do with the lower reaches of the river in the course of his survey work on the Mandeville Plains for the Canterbury Association. After that he took up farming at Rangiora, and at Snowdale and other sheep stations in Ashley River country. From Lees Valley he climbed to the top of the Puketeraki Range early in 1858 and could see still further into the upper Waimakariri. Resolved to visit it, he entered into an arrangement with John Ollivier, Provincial Secretary, "that I should go and sketch the upper Courtenay country for 10 shillings per 1000 acres that should be taken up".

He and his mate Fred Revell left Rangiora with their horse Rosi in early February with provisions for an extended journey in the mountains. They called on Joseph Pearson for advice and directions but found him surprisingly uncooperative. Worse, Rosi broke free and bolted for home. Poorly started, the explorers had to trudge 40km back to Rangiora and begin again.

By the night of February 9 they were camped a short distance above Porter's hut on the west branch of the Kowai River. Next morning they crossed Lyndon Saddle (Porter's Pass) and, skirting the lake, made their way down Porter River to Broken River, where they camped. Torlesse had no liking for this place — he christened it "The Howling Ravine".

Apparently Rosi didn't like Broken River country either. She bolted again and Revell had to go back five kilometres for her. But by day's end they had reached Iona Pass* and the following day went down the river to Lake Pearson and then east to a grove of trees with a pond, where they camped and bathed and caught some young paradise ducks. This may have been at the tiny lake called Vagabond's Inn.

*Torlesse's Iona Pass would be the summit of Craigieburn Cutting, separating the Broken River country from the Lake Pearson district. Like the famous Scottish island it tends to be gradual on one side and steeply rocky on the other. He also named the river Iona, but some time later this became the Craigie (or Cragy) Burn, a suitable name for a small stream in rough country. Later again the words were joined in popular usage and adopted for the nearby mountain range and sheep station, but the title on the bridge, "Craigieburn Stream", must strike Scots motorists as passing strange.

They were now in the heart of Hawdon country but saw nobody at Craigieburn (Flock Hill) or Grasmere. Torlesse spent the day roaming the tussocked expanses of Sloven's Creek, probably wondering where the Waimakariri had gone (it is six kilometres away to the east, quite invisible in its deep gorge), while Revell stayed in camp to nurse a sore foot, make some damper, and prepare the ducks for supper. Torlesse was unlikely to have found any new grazing country north of Broken River, but back at camp roast duck would be some compensation.

Charles Torlesse *was a nephew of Edward Gibbon Wakefield, on whose colonising ideas the Canterbury Association was based. When Wakefield discovered that Torlesse had been sent to New Zealand with Captain Thomas he objected strongly, declaring his nephew to be entirely unsuitable, being "conceited, intractable, of unamiable temper and requiring a tight hand". Nevertheless Torlesse served Canterbury well as surveyor, sheepfarmer and explorer, and after 18 years in the province returned to England where he died in 1866.*

Next day they moved around Mount St. Bernard and camped in the Waimakariri near Mount Binser. In fine weather they continued their journey upriver, camping one night at a place where there was "very fine soil", with plenty of feed for Rosi. This could have been near the Bealey River, or the Crow.

The weather remained fine on February 18 for their excursion into the headwaters. They walked up broad shingle and tussock expanses in the upper river, a slight nor'west breeze in their faces, heading towards the great bulk of the Shaler Range and Camp Spur. From here on Torlesse's diary entries are largely bereft of description which would detail their progress, so that it is not possible to do more than guess how far up the river they went.

Ollivier's brief required Torlesse to "fix the position of the principal hills ... numbering, lettering, or naming them ... and sketch in the woods, swamps, and base of mountains and the snowline", but the explorer appears to have ignored these directions. His only relevant diary entry is as follows:

Left the loads and Rosi to feed and walked up to nearly the head of the Courtenay or where it spills from the main range of mountains and where its tributaries enter with such a rush as to block up their channels leaving the water to ooze underneath. Pretty, wooded, cheerful-looking country particularly compared with what we had passed but very limited, very excellent soil on the flats, the wasting from steep wooded hills and volcanic rocks.

Retreating from the upper Waimakariri, Torlesse turned his attention to the Poulter River, the largest of the tributaries, which joins the Waimakariri about 40km downstream from Bealey. It extends tentacles for another 40km into a great fan-shaped piece of country, much of it heavily forested, between Worsley Pass and the Dampier Range. In the Poulter gorge Torlesse and Revell had to wade through deep water and make camp before reaching more open country. After a day's rest they pushed on through another gorge, but both felt so poorly that they camped again without bothering to pitch the tent. Torlesse spent a wretched night with pains, aches and diarrhoea for which "Fred made me two pots of arrowroot". Much improved after a further day's rest, they pushed on towards a watershed Torlesse thought might be with the Hurunui but "could not pass on account of the rock, wood and water and turned down again".

Having changed direction from north to west, Torlesse would be heading for Worsley Pass and not watershedding with the Hurunui but with the Otehake. He used some of Pearson's names on his map and added a number of his own: Green Hill, Castle Hill, Snow Cup, Steven Hill, Forest Peak, Gray Hill, Peveril Peak, Quail Hill, etc. He was also responsible for naming White Hill (Mount White), possibly because he was aware that on Pearson's map Thomas Woolaston White's name was pencilled in for that block of country between the Poulter and Esk rivers. White himself did not appear on the scene until 1860.

Retreating from the Poulter, Torlesse and Revell made their way back to civilisation. The arrangement with the Government resulted in Torlesse being paid 250 pounds, a handsome sum for which more might have been expected; Revell got 20 pounds, about eight weeks pay at worker rates. *The Lyttelton Times* had this to say of the exploit:

Mr Torlesse has returned from an expedition to survey the district round the head of the Waimakariri, and reports unfavourably of the country. He had travelled up the river to its source, which is in the Snowy Range, about 30 miles from the West Coast; also to the source of the northerly branch or the Waitawiri, from which point, with a very short interval, water appears to flow into the Hurunui. Mr Torlesse reports that except the country which has already been taken up for pastoral purposes, there does not appear to be any available land in more than very limited patches. The country generally consists of forest or mountain, intersected by ravines, and wide shingle beds. There was nothing of interest to be noted in the course of the survey.

Whether or not he gave thought to such an honour, reports such as this created for Charles Torlesse a further niche in Canterbury history, the distinction of having been the first explorer to reach the source of the Waimakariri. His position is properly that in 1858 he explored further up the river than any man before him. His own diary entry uses the suitably loose term — *nearly* to the head of the Courtenay.

The entry is vague; Ollivier's brief to name prominent features is ignored; his map is off course in the upper reaches. How far he went is not known, but it might be indicated by his non-

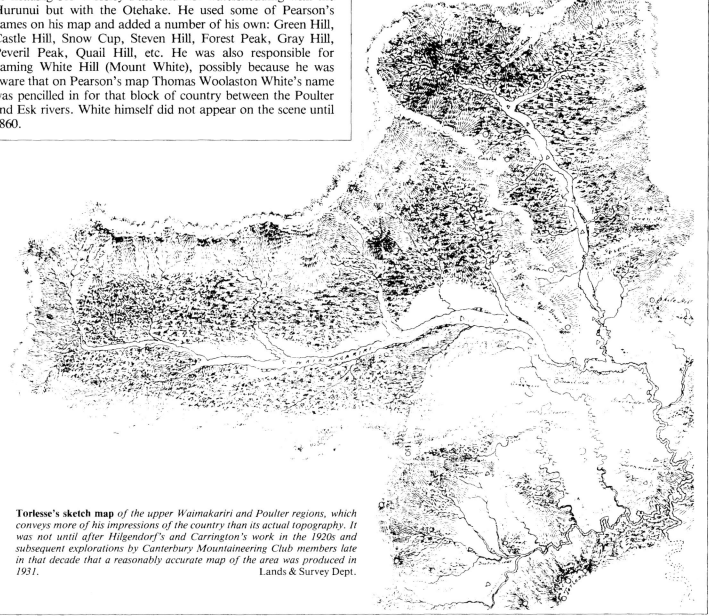

Torlesse's sketch map *of the upper Waimakariri and Poulter regions, which conveys more of his impressions of the country than its actual topography. It was not until after Hilgendorf's and Carrington's work in the 1920s and subsequent explorations by Canterbury Mountaineering Club members late in that decade that a reasonably accurate map of the area was produced in 1931.* Lands & Survey Dept.

mention of such an eminence as Carrington Peak, which smites the eye a good dozen kilometres short of the actual source. The first man to this lofty fountain-head was Jack Smith, builder of the road over Arthur's Pass, when he climbed to the glaciated Waimakariri Col (1753m) in 1865.

At the time, when the search for a road pass to the West Coast was much in the public mind, Torlesse wrote that he was

... under the distinct impression that the land between the head of the Waimakariri and the West Coast was of no great elevation and that there is a possibility of an available road being formed on a ridge from about the source of the Waimakariri in the direction of the river Okitiki.

No conjecture explains what possessed him to join the fray with this strange observation. The Hokitika River lies 32km from the Waimakariri across a jumble of high peaks and deep valleys, of which he could have no knowledge from any point he reached in 1858. A defective memory? An over-active imagination? The most likely explanation is the affliction from which he was soon to die.*

Samuel Butler *at a later stage of his young manhood. After nearly discovering Arthur's Pass in 1860 he promised to return for a second look, but never went back. Had he done so, Arthur's Pass could well have been Butler's Pass. There is a Butler Saddle at the head of the Lawrence River, a Rangitata tributary, from where he saw Whitcombe Pass leading into Westland and the shadowy outline of his mythical Erewhon. Had he been first to Arthur's Pass, who knows?—the Otira Gorge might have been the way to Nowhere.*

Samuel Butler, the young sheepfarmer and explorer who was later to achieve international literary fame, was next after Torlesse in the list of Waimakariri explorers. He went alone with his horse Doctor in 1860. His impressions of the river make interesting reading:

The Waimakariri flows from the back country out onto the plains through a very beautiful narrow gorge. Above the lower cliffs, which descend perpendicularly into the river, rise lofty mountains to an elevation of several thousand feet; so that the scenery here is truly fine.

The back country of the Waimakariri is inaccessible by dray, so that all the stores and all the wool have to be packed in and packed out on horseback. This is a very great drawback, and one which is not likely to be soon removed. In winter time, also, the pass which leads into it is sometimes entirely obstructed by snow, so that the squatters in that part of the country must have a harder time of it than those on the plains. They have the bush, however, and that is an important thing. ...There is a magnificent mountain chain of truly Alpine character at the head of the river, and ... in parts the scenery is quite equal in grandeur to that of Switzerland, but far inferior in beauty. How one does long to see some signs of human care in the midst of the loneliness!

I saw one saddle low enough to be covered by bush, ending a valley some miles in length, through which flowed a small stream with dense bush on either side. I firmly believe that this saddle will lead to the West Coast, but as the valley was impassable for a horse, and as, being alone, I was afraid to tackle the carrying of food and blankets, and to leave Doctor, who might very probably walk off whilst I was on the wrong side of the Waimakariri, I shirked the investigation. I certainly ought to have gone up that valley.

Butler was not the only man to feel regret at not having taken a closer look at Arthur's Pass. Three years before him another explorer, Leonard Harper, intended to investigate it from the west. Describing his crossing of Hurunui Saddle (later named Harper Pass in his honour), he says:

About 12 miles below the Saddle we crossed a deep rapid river running into the Taramakau. This river, the Otira, the natives told me, rises in the same place as that of the same name running east ... and that out of that Eastern Otira the Waimakariri takes its rise, and not from a lake as had been supposed. They also told me there was a pass up the gorge of the Otira into comparatively open country on the east side, but that it was very much more inaccessible than the Taramakau Pass, and therefore had not been used in their memory. I intended, however, to attempt it on my return journey, but was prevented by bad weather, lack of food, and by the fact that I had no boots, from trying it.

Leonard Harper's memorable West Coast journey, extending south to Big Bay beyond the Haast River, demolished not only his boots but also his trousers. At Lake Sumner on the way home, before he could make a decent appearance at the homestead he had to shelter in the scrub while a companion went in search of a fresh pair.

Part 2: Arthur Dudley Dobson

Among Waimakariri explorers' names that of Sir Arthur Dudley Dobson must be best known in the National Park today. His memory is kept alive by the fact that both road and rail use his pass to reach the West Coast, and by the impressive monument erected in his honour on the summit. It reminds every traveller that he, as a young man of 22, discovered the pass in 1864, and commemorates an important date in Canterbury history.

Arthur Dobson was not seeking such fame when he went up the Bealey River in March of that year; he was looking for an easy way to get his horses to the West Coast. Chief Surveyor Thomas Cass was pleased with the young man's contract survey work on the Coast, and agreed with Dobson's suggestion that a couple of horses would help things along if they could be got there. He wondered if there was a better route across the Alps than Hurunui Saddle—perhaps a pass out of the Waimakariri. He agreed to pay Dobson extra for a modest investigation before the young man returned to his contract.

Taking with him his younger brother Edward Henry, then aged 16, Arthur Dobson established a base at Cora Lynn sheep station on the Cass River, from where the brothers rode their horses through the Waimakariri and up the Bealey valley. Reaching the gorge they continued on foot, climbing through thick bush to the summit until they could look down into the Otira Gorge. Arthur could see immediately that this was no

place for horses, and with that turned back for home. No doubt he was anxious to get on with his work before winter set in.

A proper search for routes out of the Waimakariri would have entailed a stronger party, a thorough exploration of all the "available" passes (there are nine of them), and a crossing of the most suitable one to connect with the established track in the Taramakau valley. From north to south the passes (as they were named later) are: Foy, Koeti, Minchin, Worsley, Walker, Taruahuna, Goat, Arthur's and Harman, any one of which could have been best. When all were inspected next year not one proved suitable for a road or even a bridle track, and eventually "Arthur's" was reluctantly chosen by his father, Edward Dobson, as the best of a bad lot.

Before returning to Christchurch the brothers, spending a last night at Cora Lynn, were persuaded by Francis Goldney to make another visit to the pass, ostensibly to look for sheep country.*

This time, with two high-country men added to the party, it was crossed successfully as far as the mouth of the Otira Gorge. A reason why they did not continue a few miles further to the Taramakau Valley was that Arthur Dobson thought he was in the Arahura, not the Otira.

His formal report, lodged with the Chief Surveyor on his return to Christchurch, condenses both expeditions into the one

*In *Beyond the Waimakariri* D.N. Hawkins says that Torlesse died during a trip to England of a brain fever from which he had suffered for some years.

*Although they had been farming opposite the Bealey River for some years before the Dobsons came up the valley, and must have viewed the way to Arthur's Pass many times from the high ground of their run, the Goldneys (or their shepherds) seem never to have had their curiosity aroused sufficiently to make an expedition of their own into the Bealey valley.

and pays rather small tribute to what must have been valuable contributions from his companions, especially in surmounting the difficulties of the gorges:

After leaving the horses I followed the creek bed up for about 1½ miles, when the creek became so full of boulders and cascades that I was obliged to climb up the cliffs which formed the banks of the creek, to a terrace on the west side.

I found this terrace covered with black and white birch, but open and very good travelling. After pushing through the bush for about 60 chains, I came on to the saddle, which is an open valley about a mile long, covered with grass and low scrub, and full of small waterholes.

Crossing the saddle I descended a bank about 100 feet high (thickly covered with scrub) into the Arahura (?), which is of considerable size, even at this point, and is formed chiefly by a stream which flows in from the SW, conveying the drainage from the glaciers on the west face of Mount Rolleston

For half a mile from the foot of the saddle the river bed is 5 and 6 chains wide and offers very good travelling, when it suddenly contracts and flows through narrow gorges for 2½ miles, the river bed being full of enormous boulders.

At present it is very bad travelling from the saddle to the open river bed on the west side. The scrub is so thick that one must of necessity keep the river bed, and during our journey we were frequently obliged to lower ourselves down the cliffs with our swag slings, and wade through water holes up to our shoulders, with our swags on our heads.

All this would be avoided by a line cut through the bush on the east side of the river, and very easy gradients would be obtained by a little side cutting here and there.

I was accompanied on the trip by Mr F.B. Goldney, John Marshall, and one of my brothers. Mr Goldney entertained me most hospitably during my stay in the Waimakariri country, and found all the stores for the expedition.

As can be seen, this was hardly a factual account of proceedings. There is much of interest in a letter written some years later by the young brother, Edward Henry, who recalled the occasion thus:

We got to the Bealey in the afternoon and it was just lovely — the sun was shining brightly and lots of blue ducks were swimming about in the pools and back waters. No one had been known ever to have gone up the valley before and everything was in its natural state, no burnt bush or other abominations. We went well up the valley past an island of bush that used to be there, to a pleasant flat for the horses, tons of good feed. We tethered the horses and camped there, and next morning taking some provisions but no tent we started up the river.

Arthur Dobson, Explorer *(1841-1934) discovered the pass named after him in 1864. He enjoyed a long and distinguished career as surveyor and civil engineer in Westland, Nelson, Canterbury and Australia. He was for some years in partnership with his father in Christchurch, later becoming city engineer, and in 1931 was knighted for his services to the province.* **Right:** *His memorial column on the pass.*

We followed this until the cliffs and water combined stopped us, and then climbed up to the tops of the cliffs. It was very bad going then, for the rough blocks of stone were covered with deep moss and there was always a danger of falling between them. However, we got through without anything more serious than scraped legs and got to the top of the pass before dark, then we made a shelter to camp in and dried out our clothes, as we were wet to the waist. Next day Arthur took bearings of the most notable features and we essayed to climb up the mountain, but when we got a few hundred feet up, Arthur could recognise some of the mountains on the West Coast, also the moving shingle stopped us. We stayed in our shelter that night and came back to camp early and rode back to Cora Lynn.

Then another trip was decided on and Mr Goldney and a man named Marshall and Arthur and I went back. We camped at the same place, and leaving me to look after the camp, the others went over the pass in the vain hope of finding some open country. They were away two nights and the morning after their return the weather was bad, so we had to stay in camp that day. The day after, the weather cleared and we all returned to Cora Lynn.

The subsequent importance of the discovery invites a closer look at the events of that week in March, 1864. Of interest is the recollection by Sir Arthur in his *Reminiscences*, written when he was an old man, that "Mr Goldney was very anxious to know if there would be any chance of finding sheep country, and said he would be pleased if I would go over the saddle again". Arthur Dobson must have said at the time that he saw no sheep country from the pass. Could there have been other reasons, then, why the Goldneys wanted to see the pass more fully explored?

There were, of course. A bridle track across the divide, or better still a road, would be of inestimable value to Cora Lynn. As the nearest sheep station to a possible West Coast meat market, it would be ideally placed for that trade. As well, a good road to Christchurch would be welcome if only to remove one of the curses of Cora Lynn. The station was on the Cass River at the extreme southern end of the run, cut off from most of its country by the precipitous butt end of the Black Range, falling steeply to the river and requiring two fords of the Waimakariri and much riverbed travel, all of which would be eliminated by a road around the bluffs.

If these were not sufficient good reasons for taking a further look at the pass there was another: second thoughts often assail failed or incomplete explorations. Back at Cora Lynn that night there would be much talk around the fire in the primitive homestead. From this, growing more aware of the possible future importance of his discovery, Arthur Dobson may have

Arthur's Pass. *The long open space on the pass itself shows clearly in this photograph looking north from Mount Bealey (1823m). Beyond is the Otira valley with Mount Alexander (1958m) in the background across the Taramakau River.*　　　　　　　　　　　John Sampson.

begun to doubt that he should be returning to Christchurch to report a mission so obviously only half completed. For whatever reason a decision was made to give the pass another try, this time with a bit more push behind it. Frank Goldney rustled up some provisions, added his head shepherd, Jack Marshall, to the party (and one of the station dogs), and away they went.

This time, according to Edward Henry, he was left at Camping Flat with the horses. The others swagged over the pass and tackled the gorge. The trip was a rough one in which the skills and energies of all would be fully employed, wading deep pools and climbing over huge boulders. At one place they had to make a sapling ladder to descend a bluff; the dog was lowered in a sling. They reached the open valley at the mouth of the gorge and that was about as far as they went. No grazing land was found, of course, because none existed, but at least they had proved that the passage was negotiable, if with great difficulty. All then returned to Canterbury and to Edward and the horses at Camping Flat.

Thomas Cass, the Chief Surveyor, filed away Arthur Dobson's report for future reference; for the present there was no public demand for a new route across the Alps.

Arthur Dobson did not name the pass he had crossed—that came later when brother George made the second crossing a year later and casually referred to it as "Arthur's" pass. But he did name a nearby peak Mount Rolleston after the Provincial Secretary of the time. The Bealey River he named after the Provincial Superintendent, and the Devil's Punchbowl for Old Nick himself. Francis Goldney is remembered in the Goldney Ridge rising west from the pass, and the Goldney Glacier on Mount Rolleston. John Marshall missed out in the futurity stakes, but somewhere in the gorge there is, or was, a Sling Dog Gully.

Concerned that after all he might have been in the Otira valley and not the Arahura as he had imagined (the Arahura is seven or eight miles away to the west as the kokako might fly, over wild and broken country), Arthur Dobson made a point of leaving the Taramakau on his next trip to the Coast to investigate the Otira. He must have remembered that the Mawhera chief, Tarapuhi, had told him the pass lay up that river, and soon proved the point when he recognised the mouth of the gorge. As always, familiarity smoothes the most difficult paths, and he would feel some annoyance at not having completed the job properly in the first place. The easy journey up the Otira was for him almost a final act of association with the pass of his discovering. Others, including his father, would take hold of this labyrinthine passage and forge it into a highway fit for Cobb's coaches.

There was no urgency—the gold rush was still nearly a year away. He had much to do on the Coast and he was soon back in the Taramakau Valley and on his way. The upper Waimakariri was left to the sheep. It came to life again only when the gold fever struck. In the interval, exploration was limited to a few excursions by sheepmen and their friends, about which little is known. Walker and Pearson took a mule to the top of Walker Pass at the head of Hawdon River. Henry Worsley, Percival, Leech, and Thomas went up the Poulter and discovered Worsley Pass. Joseph Hawdon sent his head shepherd McRae and a party into the Hawdon valley. They crossed Walker Pass, skirted along the divide and returned to the Poulter via Worsley Pass. *The Lyttelton Times* announced that a member of this group was none other than the great man of golden fable, Albert Hunt himself—could there be gold in them thar hills? But no, a correction appeared a few issues later. It wasn't Albert at all; merely another, ordinary, Hunt.

Part 3: Eyes West — the Background

All eyes seemed to be looking west in that year of 1865, up the valley of the Waimakariri in hopes of prosperity or in fear of what the river might do next. In the event the hopes turned mainly to disappointment and the fears were dissolved with time and effort. But while it lasted, the year had more than its share of great events and issues, bravery and foolishness, hardship and adventure. The climax came with Christmas when the Waimakariri ran amok and destroyed whole sections of the new highway across the mountains, flooded much of the northern plains, and changed the Avon from a sleepy little river into a raging torrent. For many it turned the festive season into a time of alarm and despair.

When the year began, European contact with the upper Waimakariri had been limited to the expeditions of half-a-dozen adventurers. When it ended, a new wave of explorers had investigated almost every pass across the divide and chosen the least difficult. They were followed by surveyors, engineers, contractors and the hundreds of labourers who came to build the road over "Arthur's" pass to the coast.

The Canterbury population, at the time about 32,000, carried heavy burdens establishing itself in the new land, making the roads, railways, bridges and other public works needed for orderly colonial development. In addition the province had recently embarked on a major project, the Lyttelton tunnel. There was sense in this because it would provide a short and practical link between the settlement and its port.

But a 150 mile road through unknown mountains, impenetrable forests and unbridgeable rivers, leading God knew where—that was another thing altogether. What then persuaded this provincial community to consider such a costly and possibly useless enterprise, a highway up the Waimakariri and over the Alps, when their well-being so obviously needed all their resources on the plains, and the expensive hole in the hill was only part dug?

The answer lay in a simple four-letter word: *Gold.*

Plainly Canterbury was seduced by the prospect of quick riches. Somewhere over there beyond the hills on the western horizon was a prize to quicken the blood. They might not have heard of Arthur Clough but his verse was appropriate:

And not by eastern windows only,
When daylight comes, comes in the light,
In front the sun climbs slow, how slowly,
But westward, look, the land is bright!

Wistful eyes staring at the morning's sunlit ranges could be turned green with envy when they looked south to where Dunedin was waxing fat on the affluence of its successful goldfields. People were upset to read items like this published every week in the morning newspapers:

LATEST FROM OTAGO: The usual weekly escort arrived in Dunedin yesterday afternoon bringing 18,452 ounces of gold.

Why, it was asked, should Otago enjoy all the good fortune? Where was Canterbury's goldfield? Where indeed? Julius Haast, the new Provincial Geologist, appeared to have no answer. The only gold he had discovered was away on the far side of the mountains, and a thorough search of likely places nearer home had been without success. Some people, like Paddy, thought if Haast was a real geologist he should be able to find gold anywhere. And if he couldn't, then why was he paid so much?

The Provincial Council had no answer to such conundrums; instead it put up a thousand pounds for the discovery of a payable goldfield anywhere within reasonable distance of Christchurch. But not *too* close! Conservatives among the population were upset at the thought of bearded rowdies digging up their carefully-planned settlement. (When the gold rush arrived, one newspaper consoled its readers that at least the discovery was in the most remote corner of the province.)

A thousand pounds represented about 10 years' work for a labouring man, so the reward soon worked miracles. Gold was found everywhere—in the Waimakariri, the Rakaia, the Hurunui, on Banks Peninsula, in the Malvern Hills, even in the gizzards of ducks! One Jack Bowman, a well-sinker and practical joker, grabbed a handful of brass filings from Anderson's foundry and threw them down a well he was digging in Colombo Street, creating a sensation for a few hours among gullible passers-by. Companies were started on all sides. Harold Henry de Bourbel's doorpost was covered with plates listing the companies of which he was legal manager: the Moonlight, the Lamplight, the Candlelight, and so on. There was even a Canterbury Gold Prospecting Association which met in Cobb's offices with John Ollivier in the chair. But the gold found in Canterbury was never in payable quantities, or it was "fool's gold", or the kind that drove Mary's man home to the mountains of Mourne. The real stuff, largely undiscovered, lay across the divide in West Canterbury awaiting the digger's spade.

A gold rush, it was said, comes when its time has come. That time had come in California, in Victoria, and in Otago, but not yet in West Canterbury. Scattered finds in 1862 were not enough to trigger the avalanche. Several expeditions organised in Christchurch set sail from Heathcote or straggled over the Hurunui Saddle and down the Taramakau to the coast, but they met with mixed fortune and excited nobody.

There was a flurry of interest in March, 1863, when *The Press,* suddenly alert to the prospects, predicted an imminent discovery. Although the West Coast was a part of the province, to the average Cantabrian of that time it might as well have been on the dark side of the moon. There was little to persuade adventurers to try the skimpy track leading from North Canterbury over the Hurunui Saddle. When Hokitika became the centre of goldfield activity the most suitable pass geographically was Browning's Pass, between the Wilberforce (a Rakaia tributary) and Arahura rivers. At 1412m it was too high and would be snowbound for much of the year, and in any case it was too rugged for road builders.

The one remaining communication alternative was by sea. That way Hokitika was much closer to Nelson than to Lyttelton, and even Melbourne was in the running for the goldfields trade. It was natural, therefore, that a demand should arise for more direct access. Should a gold rush eventuate, thundered. *The Press,* an escort would be needed immediately to bring the gold to Christchurch. It continued:

The Government of Canterbury can have but one duty and that is to get a road to that district with the least possible delay. If there be a paying goldfield it is a matter of life and death to us. It is not yet too late in the season to send expeditions up both the Rakaia and the Waimakariri in search of the requisite route.

Life or death it might be for the editor of *The Press,* but the Provincial Government was unmoved. Thomas Cass, the Chief Surveyor, who plainly read his morning newspaper, was not so sure. He summoned one of his staff, Henry Whitcombe, and sent him off on what was to be a fatal errand. "Start in the north and work south," advised Cass, but Whitcombe had his own ideas.

Ignoring the Waimakariri, he went up the Rakaia in April, 1863, ill-equipped and ignorant of the hazards awaiting him. He crossed the pass out of the Rakaia since named for him, almost starved to death struggling down the gorges on the other side, reached the sea and then, weakened by hunger and fatigue, drowned in the breakers at the mouth of the Taramakau.

A spate of other drownings followed on the Coast, of men engaged in exploration and survey work. Interest in the region waned. The golden seduction of Canterbury lost its impetus and fluttered listlessly through the spring, summer and autumn of 63-64. West Canterbury was left to its rainy isolation, except that the Government established a survey station at Mawhera (Greymouth) and the survey itself was started in the spring of 1863. The northern block was entrusted to Arthur Dobson, then 21 years of age.

Left:
John Hall *served throughout the life of the Canterbury Provincial Council (1853-76) and was then a Member of Parliament, serving as Colonial Secretary in the Fox ministry, as Postmaster-General, and later as Prime Minister. He was a small, lightly-built man, with a face described as "boyish" as a young man. He owned Rakaia Terrace station at Hororata and at one time the site of Christchurch railway station, which he sold for 6000 pounds. Described by* The Lyttelton Times *as "standing without reproach in all relations of life—as a friend, employer, landlord, neighbour and patriarch—and beloved and respected by those who knew him best". Was knighted for his services.*

Right:
Samuel Bealey, *the third Superintendent of Canterbury, succeeded to that office when Moorhouse resigned in 1863. He had headed a movement to get Robert Wilkin to stand, but he refused and Bealey was elected instead. He was better at managing his own affairs than the other superintendents but the job of running Canterbury was considered somewhat beyond him. He was well liked, and with the aid of bouyant land sales plus the administrative talents of John Hall and William Rolleston he presided adequately over a lively development period. He went back to England in 1867. His properties, sold in 1882, fetched 36,862 pounds, a not inconsiderable fortune.*

About this time there was a slight resurgence of interest and parties of newly-arrived immigrants were hustled into the Waitohi Gorge to improve the Hurunui track. A sum of 4000 pounds was voted for a road of sorts into the Waimakariri valley, and by December it was completed as far as Lake Pearson. Runholders in the valley had to subsidise the work by freeholding land equivalent in value to half the road expenditure.

But none of this activity could stem the feeling that West Canterbury was more of an embarrassment than an asset. *The Lyttelton Times* declared flatly that no more money should be spent there or on roads to get there, but thought it might make a good penal colony. In January, 1864, the work parties on the Hurunui were withdrawn. In May the Government decided to abandon the Mawhera depot, effective from August.

Enter Albert Hunt, New Zealand's most famous (or infamous) gold digger. One day in July, 1864, he came marching out of the Hohonu, near the lower Taramakau, with enough gold in his swag to persuade resident agent William Revell to back his claim for the Government's thousand-pound reward. A modest rush started and interest in the district revived. The Government back-pedalled and decided not to close the Mawhera depot after all. Instead it gave Revell a couple of policemen in case he needed them.

On August 11 Superintendent Samuel Bealey rose in Council and said:

From the information which has recently been made public, it appears probable that an important goldfield will shortly be established on the West Coast. I propose to cause a survey to be made, in order to determine the best line of road for rendering the district easily accessible from the settled portions of the province.

Was this the spieler coming with the bags of gold, to woo Miss Canterbury Eighteen-Sixty-Four? If so he was a great disappointment because nothing happened for at least another six months. Meanwhile the precious summer days drifted past unused. Soon shivering roadbuilders, fighting winter's rain and snow in the gorges, would desperately wish them back.

Promising finds and small rushes continued throughout the second half of 1864, but the opinion grew that the West Coast would never provide more than "tucker diggings". Then some better news came from the Totara River and Donnelly's Creek, south of Hokitika, and quite unexpectedly the fuse was lit. Three hundred men rushed there and others followed until by Christmas there were upwards of 1000 men on West Canterbury goldfields. Most exciting was the news that 1400 ounces of gold had been won.

But still the cautious Cantabrians hesitated, unable or unwilling to accept the rumours filtering through from the Coast. Even in late January of 1865 Secretary of Public Works John Hall was heard saying there was no reason to believe a goldfield existed, and even less to believe that it would be permanent. The official proclamation was put to one side.

The rush went on regardless. Westland's time had come. For thousands of men on goldfields in Otago, Nelson and Marlborough a change was in the air. They raised their heads from spent workings, bent an ear to some kind of 19th century ESP, and heard the call of a new eldorado: *Okitiki!* Suddenly, irresistibly, Westland was the place to be. The great rush of '65 was "on".

The news broke in Christchurch on the morning of Saturday, February 25. "Broke" is possibly too strong a word. In the featureless typography of early newspapers the short item was given no more prominence than a dozen others on the same page, but it was enough to cause a flurry of activity in Provincial Council executive circles. Crucial and urgent decisions had to be taken in matters such as a goldfield proclamation and possibly a gold escort.

Weekend executive meetings agreed that Revell should be appointed West Canterbury Resident Magistrate, and that Provincial Secretary William Rolleston should go to the Coast via Wellington to set up an administration. That done he was to negotiate with the banks to see what could be arranged to get the gold flowing to Christchurch.

By Tuesday morning the news had stirred up the populace in the city and no wonder, for here at last was the opportunity for Canterbury to match Otago's golden prosperity. Cries arose for a shorter land route across the Alps and an armed escort to bring home the booty.

Gold! The magic of the word, the dream of affluence it generated, was reinforced by the sight of a steady stream of rough-looking fellows marching through the city, heading along Papanui Road towards Kaiapoi and Hurunui. More than anything else this brought home to Christchurch the reality of events and the imminent prospect of untold wealth. In the 14 years of the city's life nothing like it had been seen before.

Merchants enjoyed a run on blankets, miners' picks and shovels, miscellaneous hardware, clothing, tents and boots. Many of the miners, hardy fellows, walked all the way from Otago. Others came by boat to Lyttelton, breasted the Bridle Track, shaded their eyes to the north, and hurried on through town. Caught up in the excitement of the moment, local men from all walks of life hastily equipped themselves and joined the throng. Families were deserted, their farewell tears sweetened by promises of certain wealth and quick return. Cobb & Co. put on extra coaches for the run to Waitohi and crammed them full. In 10 days more than a thousand men marched through Kaiapoi, providing townsfolk there with something new in the way of entertainment—there was "much excitement and nothing else is talked of". Twenty-five hundred men crossed White's new bridge over the Waimakariri River in three weeks. Some objected to the threepenny toll and threatened to throw the tollkeeper in the river. He fled to town demanding police protection.

The merchants and citizens of Christchurch quickly realised that they were, in the main, only sideline spectators to all this activity. The real game for the high stakes was being played out in some far corner of their own province, yet the prizes, lamentably, were going to others. "Summer's passing," mourned *The Press,* "and the gold is slipping from our grasp." The merchants put their heads and purses together and counted out a careful 200 pounds for the discovery of a route to the Coast suitable for a dray road. The question of what the

Provincial Council was doing had a short answer: it was in recess. Isaac Luck, chairman of the town council, stepped into the breach and called a public meeting for Thursday night.

This was short notice, but when the time came the new town hall was packed to the doors—a noisy demonstration of how completely the gold fever had gripped the city. The agenda found universal favour: "To urge the Government to establish a gold escort, make a road, and undertake other necessary works for developing the West Coast goldfields".

Among those on stage was William Wilson, a member of the Provincial Council. He assured the meeting that the approaches of the Otira Pass were open and easy, and perfectly free from obstruction. He had heard, he said, of a man who had "planted" 40 pounds weight of gold until he could send it over to Christchurch by the escort. (This statement was greeted with loud applause.)

The Canterbury Provincial Government buildings *on the corner of Armagh and Durham streets in Chistchurch were the powerhouse of executive administration during the gold rush days. They survive as the only remaining provincial government buildings in New Zealand, and (except for the cyclist and traffic lights) appear much the same as they were in 1865. Currently they house various functions of the Department of Justice. The impressive stone council chamber stands out of the picture to the right.*

Secretary for Works John Hall, representing the Government, told the meeting how Arthur Dobson had discovered a pass the previous year, and promised that if investigations presently being made by his brother George were favourable, a road would be built over it without delay. (Cheers.)

Also on stage was William Sefton Moorhouse, the great tunnel protagonist, who was both a past and future Superintendent. To the man who launched the Lyttelton tunnel, a road over the mountains would be child's play. He agreed wholeheartedly that the dray road should be built immediately. He had no fear of the prosperity of the West Coast goldfields, but there was one thing wrong — the gold should be coming to Christchurch! (Prolonged applause.)

Moorhouse, whose personal finances were often in a state of chaos, failed to explain exactly how the gold would benefit Christchurch. This was always something of a mystery but in the public mind the precious metal automatically equated with prosperity and that was all they needed.

Postmaster Bishop had something to say but the noisy meeting never discovered what it was. He advanced to the front of the platform, "but being unable to make himself heard, he sat down again amidst laughter and cheers".

And so in high good humour the meeting broke up and everyone went home to bed, convinced that the soon-to-be-realised Great Dray Road would see sacks of yellow metal coming across the alps every week. Perhaps some of them dreamt that night of a rainbow arching across the mountains to the proverbial pot of gold. They were not to know that the anticipated riches would prove just as elusive as was the promise at rainbow's end. *The Lyttelton Times* did its best to dispel the fantasies. Next morning it warned that the road would be far more difficult to build than was imagined, and that the gold escort "was not a wise proceeding".

But the tide of public enthusiasm was too insistent for talk like that. Whatever reservations Bealey, Rolleston, Hall and

A Colour Camera's
WAIMAKARIRI

The river *from above the Gorge Bridge, looking towards the snow-capped Torlesse Range.*

The fascinations of history combine with scenery to enhance the Waimakariri's image, with so much to admire along the West Coast Road where once the coaches rattled past on iron-shod wheels and passengers anticipated Mrs Cloudesley's hot scones at Castle Hill. Here the changing seasons bring warm browns and yellows in summer and autumn, the candid white of fresh snow in winter, and the delicate greens of new growth in spring. The alpine regions have a different, more dramatic beauty, and while some of this may be viewed from road and rail, much is reserved for the skier, the tramper, and the mountaineer.

Right: *The splendid barrier of the Torlesse Range separates Canterbury's plains from the inland sheep runs— a 2000m snowy rampart in winter photographed here from Sheffield. The summits, left to right are Castle Hill (or Tawera, the highest), Torlesse (or Rubicon), Back Peak and Otarama. To get round the range the road goes left over Porter's Pass and the rail to the right up the Waimakariri River.*

Below: *Once across the Torlesse Range yet another 2000m mountain chain, the Craigieburns, presents itself. Fortunately the required pass (Iona or Craigieburn Cutting, extreme right) is easy. Here the sun's first rays on a crisp winter morning light frosty tussocks as the road sweeps over Porter River Bridge on its way to Castle Hill (centre).*

Below right: *Autumn's brilliance enhances this view of the Craigie Burn Bridge and Purple Hill beyond.*

Above: *Sheep graze among the soft pastoral contours and bluff limestone outcrops on Castle Hill station, against a background of misted Craigieburns.*

Below left: *Oxford-based horse-riding safaris into Waimakariri country are becoming more popular.* Innes collection.

Below: *One of the modern developments along the West Coast Road surely never imagined by old-time coach passengers is this 1980s alpine resort village taking shape on the sunny flats opposite the old Castle Hill Hotel site. Since this photograph was taken the number of houses completed has risen to 38.*

company might have had they were bound to press on with something, anything. As Hall recalled later, no government not pledged to action in those circumstances would have stood for a day.

The stream of diggers marching along Victoria Street was more than enough to keep the pot boiling in the city. At the Government offices in Armagh Street important decisions were being made. George Thornton, the assistant engineer, was made Inspector of Roads, with authority over construction in the Taramakau valley.

At the same time John Hall pondered the problem of top control in his department. Four years previously, Provincial Engineer Dobson had resigned from that position to devote himself to constructing the Lyttelton tunnel, with the title of

Edward Dobson
M.Inst.C.E.

When his employment as Canterbury's first Provincial Engineer ended abruptly in 1869, Edward Dobson left Christchurch to live and work in Australia. Some amazement was expressed at the time "that this splendid man was allowed to leave Canterbury without a word of thanks or an expression of regret, without a gesture from the Provincial Council or a function from its citizens. How many dinners were given and toasts drunk to pompous nobodies; and yet he departed unhonoured and unsung." Perhaps the answer lay in this additional comment: "He was brusque, abrupt, and given to plain speaking. His uncompromising honesty and independence of character have of themselves raised against him a host of critics."

Edward Dobson, *a formal portrait taken during his early Canterbury days. He was described by Julius Haast as "a strong man who knew his own mind and spoke it". He lived to age 92, as did his wife Mary and their son Arthur.* Turnbull Library per Ken Dobson

Edward Dobson arrived at Lyttelton on the *Cressy,* one of the First Four Ships, on December 27, 1850, with his two eldest sons, George and Arthur, leaving behind him in England his wife Mary and four younger children, and a substantial career as an engineer, surveyor and architect. He was then 34 years old. He bought land at Sumner and built a clay-floored, cob-walled house on the site of the present Marine Hotel. Mary and the other children joined him exactly a year later, on December 27, 1851.

Until he was appointed Provincial Engineer in 1854 at a salary of 300 pounds a year, the family's finances were somewhat strained. In his reminiscences Arthur could remember helping George milk the cows and pack butter and cheese up the Richmond spur to Mount Pleasant and down to Lyttelton for sale. On the way back they dragged down logs from Jollie's bush for firewood and threw them over the cliffs behind the house.

Edward Dobson's 14-year term of office saw him design, build, or oversee such projects as the Sumner road to Lyttelton, the Lyttelton railway tunnel and much of the early railway system on the plains, the first roads to connect the scattered settlement, development of the Port of Lyttelton, the road to Akaroa, draining the great Rangiora swamp, and the highway over Arthur's Pass to Hokitika, regarded at the time as "a brilliant achievement".

No man had more to do with the Waimakariri River in those troubled days. It was his task — a hopeless one at the time — to stop it breaking out and flooding the plains. In this work, as in others, he did not shrink from exceptional measures. When the river took to the North Branch and threatened Kaiapoi he laid out a bold plan to make a 6km cut across Kaiapoi Island to give the river a new course which would be safer for both Christchurch and Kaiapoi. The plan was rejected, but island farmers saw it started, and that is where the river runs today.

But his greatest Waimakariri work was exploring the headwaters in association with son George. Most of the six weeks he spent up the river were swept by storms, when he worked in the wet or sheltered in a tent writing up his journals, listening to the rain and the keas calling from the misty hillsides. His comprehensive report on the region was a model of its kind. Canterbury was fortunate to have as its chief engineer a man who, while cultured and highly-educated, could still don old clothes, hoist a swag on his back, and tackle the hard and sweaty toil of genuine exploration, rugged gorges, flooded rivers, tent camps and all. It was a far cry from his home environment and his wife and family (there were 10 children: George, Arthur, Mary, Caroline, Edward, Maria, Robert, Emily, Herbert and Collet).

The problems he faced in a new and undeveloped country were numerous and complex, and inevitably he had his failures — a bridge or two gone with the floods, a slump in the sea wall at the port, river controls predestined not to succeed, and iron-hard volcanic rock in the Lyttelton tunnel which so wore down everyone who worked there that the finished job earned more criticism than praise.

Edward Dobson returned to Christchurch in 1878 and set up in private practice with his son Arthur (later Sir Arthur). Both lived to become grand old men of Canterbury's pioneering days. Obituary tributes to the father were warmly appreciative — "His name and services are indissolubly connected with the early history of the Province of Canterbury" — but the most generous was accorded him much earlier in his career when in 1861, after he was unhorsed while crossing a flooded Rakaia River, *The Press* said: "There is no single man in this country whose life is more valuable, whose loss would be more felt, and whom it would be more difficult to replace."

He was a great walker, even in very old age, remembered by one of his grandchildren on her way to school, "striding along with his shiny top hat, frock coat, elastic-sided boots, and a gold-topped walking stick". Johannes C. Andersen, a Canterbury historian, remembered him well:

Mr Dobson was a familiar figure in the streets of Christchurch till well on in my years and days. I often met him coming along Chancery Lane or Gloucester Street. He wore a roomy grey top hat, and usually held a key at the end of a piece of red tape in his right hand, and this key he twirled as he walked like a revolving planet at right angles to his line of march. He smiled affably to acquaintances as they passed, between whiles blowing out his cheeks as he emitted his breath. Sometimes, perhaps on colder days, the key was safely stowed and as he walked leisurely along (I never saw him hurried) he kept his hands, one above the other, Maori carving fashion, flat on his waistcoat in the region of his greatest periphery.

Edward Dobson's name is perpetuated in a mountain, glacier and river in the province's remote south-west corner, but there are permanent reminders of his work nearer at hand almost everywhere in Canterbury, most strikingly in the railway tunnel through the Port Hills and State Highway 73 across the Southern Alps — and in the Waimakariri River, for it was he who began the long and frustrating task of making it run safely to sea.

Railways Engineer. His salary remained the same at a thousand pounds a year, and it would appear that he made himself available when required as a kind of Acting or Honorary Provincial Engineer. Now Hall hurried to ask whether he would consider becoming Consulting Provincial Engineer. Yes, said Dobson, he'd be agreeable to that, no doubt reflecting that the more his title changed the more his job was the same.* Plainly the machinery of executive organisation was being prepared for something exceptional.

To satisfy the public that the Government was being suitably active, a more visible decision was taken. On the morning of Tuesday, March 7, a hurriedly-assembled armed escort of mounted policemen, led by Commissioner Shearman, was sent up the North Road bound for Hurunui and the coast, hopefully to return soon with bulging saddle bags. Mouths gaped in

Kaiapoi as the escort rode through. Here was proof indeed that the way to the goldfields, the route by which to secure the bounty, was not in the west but by the Great North Road. Local dignitaries immediately called a public meeting to promote the northern route.

Among the speakers was one Robert Day, who had packed provisions over the Hurunui Saddle recently, and he voted it a very good route. Not only that, but while he was in the Taramakau he had gone up the Otira out of curiosity and from what he had seen he thought it would be difficult to make a track there, where the boulders were four and five feet high. His opinions were cheered to the rafters. Up with the Hurunui, down with the Otira!

And it was nearly so, because none of the passes out of the Waimakariri proved to be what was wanted.

Part 4: The Dobsons and the Picnic Party

When news of the gold rush reached Christchurch on February 25 John Hall correctly anticipated that there would be an immediate public demand for a shorter route to the Coast. He called for Arthur Dobson's report of the previous year detailing his discovery of the pass which was soon to be named after him, and noted that while the Canterbury approach was relatively easy and the undulating summit provided good travelling, some difficulty was likely to be experienced in the Otira Gorge on the western side.†

Hall's apprehensions were quieted somewhat when he read the paragraph which Arthur Dobson had added to the effect that any difficulties in the gorge could be avoided by a line cut through the bush on the east side of the river, and that very easy gradients would be obtained by a little side cutting here and there.

Hall was not to know that these words seriously underplayed the obstacles in the gorge. He summoned George Dobson, eldest son of the Consulting Engineer, and instructed him to organise a

George Dobson, Explorer (1840-1866) looks here as if reluctant to have his portrait taken. Popular with family and friends, and bluntly honest like his father, he was an energetic and promising young surveyor-engineer when his career was cut short by his untimely death on a West Coast forest track. He was the Waimakariri's most wide-ranging pioneer explorer, and his tragic death generated anger and sorrow on both sides of the Alps. Even his murderer was said to express regret at having to kill "such a nice young fellow".

small party to inspect the route and cut a bridle track over it with the least possible delay. If the job proved more difficult than anticipated he was to hire workmen from wherever he could. The secretary was confident the track would be in place within a few weeks.

The youthful party of George Dobson (then 24), Matt Russell, and one Anderson left Christchurch on February 27, 1865. They took two days to reach Cora Lynn and another to Camping Flat, where a man named O'Brien took charge of the horses. Another day brought them to the summit of the pass where they camped in heavy rain.

Next morning, March 3, George had his first look down the steep western slopes of the pass into the canyon of the Otira Gorge. He regarded it with some concern. His journal reads:

Followed down the Otira to the commencement of the gorge, having reconnoitered which I was determined on taking the swags down half at a time, so left the flour, and started down with the remainder of the stores. Found it very rough travelling down the gorge, so climbed the cliffs on the east side, hauling up our swags after us by the slings,

and pushed them through the bush till we came to a shingle creek falling in from the east, where we camped, and commenced cutting a track through the bush to avoid this part of the gorge.

March 4th: Finished cutting the track by which this part of the gorge is avoided, marked both ends by breaking down the branches of the trees outside, brought down the flour, and leaving it at the

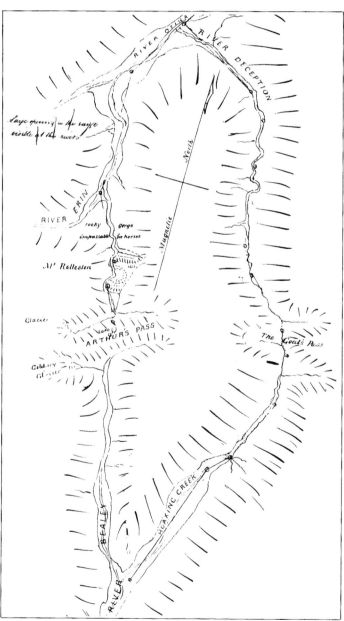

George Dobson's map drawn in 1865 by the explorer shows the proximity of his brother Arthur's Pass (920m) to the one he discovered, "The Goat's Pass" (1076m) between Deception River and "Hoaxing Creek" (Mingha River).
Canterbury Museum.

*Later in 1865 he was reappointed to his old position as Provincial Engineer.

†Arthur's Pass in fact runs north and south, due to the layout of the main divide in that part of the Southern Alps. North equates with west.

Goat Pass. *This winter photograph from Mount B'limit shows the shady side of Goat Pass (1076m) descending to Mingha River headwaters. Above the pass is Westland's Mount Franklin (2088m), another of the national park's higher peaks, standing between the Deception and Otehake rivers. This is now the pass for Coast-to-Coast runners.*

bottom of the track, shifted camp down through the rest of the gorge and three miles down the open riverbed where we could see a large double-peaked hill on the north side of the Taramakau.

With this the second crossing of Arthur's Pass was accomplished, but George felt he couldn't recommend it as a route. Any path or road through there would have to go in the bed of the river and every flood would require it to be built anew. Looking for alternatives he decided that the river which joined the Otira lower down warranted closer inspection. It headed in the right direction and looked promising.

Anderson's heart wasn't in exploration. He wanted to try his luck on the goldfields and asked to be released. George gave him a share of the provisions and let him go, "knowing the uselessness of arguing with a man touched with the yellow fever". With a brief farewell he and Russell turned up the new river with high expectations.

The valley promised well. The river had no gorge of any consequence and the two young men made good time along the relatively easy banks and among the boulders in the bed. But mountain travel in unknown regions often disappoints, and when they rounded a spur and caught their first sight of the pass it looked exceptionally high and steep. The slopes leading to the summit were very loose, requiring them to climb at one stage on hands and knees. George reluctantly accepted that any road built there would be constantly out of repair and because of the height could be rendered useless by snow for the greater part of the year.

His frustration is reflected in the names he entered on his sketch map — Deception for the river which had led them to the pass, The Goat's Pass for the saddle itself, and Hoaxing Creek* for the river on the east side which is now known as the Mingha, down which they then went to join the Bealey and return to Cora Lynn.

*These names appearing on Dobson's map cannot be put in doubt by later writings which attribute the name Deception to railway surveyors. They would also appear to dispose of the story that the pass was so named because somebody drove goats over it bound for the West Coast. About 1890 Hoaxing Creek was renamed Mingha after Mrs Mingha Wilson, wife of the chief engineer and manager of the Midland Railway Company. She was, she said, reluctant about this and agreed only because she thought her name had a Maori ring to it.

Back in Christchurch the whole town was waiting impatiently to hear that the track to the golden coast was cut and ready for immediate use. There was much grumbling when George announced that not only was this not so but in his view the route was not worth persisting with:

I am of the opinion that it will be impractical to construct a line of road for horse traffic in the Otira Gorge, due to the precipitous nature of the hillsides. Such a road would have to be made in the bed of the river, which in places is almost a cascade, falling with great violence over immense boulders in a very narrow valley, between two perpendicular walls of rock. The cost of constructing even a horse track would be immense, and the road would require repairing, or very probably entire reconstruction every time a fresh occurred in the river.

When these brave words were published in the newspapers next morning there was a howl of anguish. *The Press* was especially critical, refusing to believe that because of the problems of a mere mile or so, no matter how difficult, the route could not be forced. Surely some way could be found to build a path over, round, or through the obstructions of such a short section when the remainder, as George Dobson admitted in his report, presented no great obstacle. It was conceded that the young man was a worthy explorer, but was his engineering judgement sufficiently mature? A more seasoned experience must be brought to bear on the subject, and who better for this than Dobson senior?

Some critics — and he had plenty — might say that Edward Dobson was currently sheltering in his tunnel, away from the slings and arrows of provincial engineering strife. The fact that many of his public works were not going well — the Girder Bridge, Lyttelton Harbour works, Waimakariri protection — could have been a factor. He would not be looking for a challenge like a road over the Alps, the difficulties of which (if his sons had properly informed him) could exceed those of all the others.

But who else was there to send?

With the cries of road-blocked empire-builders and frustrated gold-seekers ringing in his ears. Secretary Hall seized his pen and wrote:

> Public Works Office, Christchurch,
> Canterbury, New Zealand.
> 14th March, 1865.

Edward Dobson, Esq., C.E.,
Christchurch.

Sir, — I am directed by his Honor the Superintendent to acquaint you that the Government is desirous of obtaining as speedily as possible the report of an Engineer upon the practicability and cost of forming a bridle track either through or above the gorge of the Otira, a tributary of the Taramakau, recently explored by Mr George Dobson. If the present condition of the works of the Lyttelton and Christchurch [railway] will enable you to absent yourself for a week or 10 days, his Honor will feel obliged if you will undertake this task, and he will authorise any expenditure which you may find it necessary to incur for this purpose.

> I have the honor to be, Sir,
> Your obedient servant,
> JOHN HALL, Secretary for Works.

In those days everyone was someone else's obedient (and sometimes even humble obedient) servant, but Edward Dobson knew who was what. Besides, he had a strong family involvement. He packed his bags and readied his horse. It was something at least that all they wanted was a bridle track.

"An urgent necessity" was how the newspapers were now describing the project as they pressed the Government to "get on with it". Hurrying to comply, Hall began arrangements which would have Jack Smith, the road contractor working in the Waimakariri basin, concentrate his efforts near Lake Pearson so that his gang would be on hand should they be needed.

As for young George, he was told to get on his horse and find a better pass, if there was one to be found. For the second time in a month he found himself riding the lonely trail to the west. And, added Hall, if he did stumble over something better, he was to be sure to contact his father for a second and more experienced opinion.

White's Accommodation House *still stands only a few metres from the Old West Coast Road at Courtenay, screened from sight by thick shrubbery. Now 122 years old and derelict, it hosted the Dobson and FitzGerald exploration parties on their way up the Waimakariri in 1865.*

When Edward Dobson rode out of Christchurch on the afternoon of Wednesday, March 15, following his son on the track to the west, the Waimakariri River kept him company for several miles. Part of his route lay through the sandy knolls and old channels where the river threatened to overflow when in flood, the scene of many of his none-too-successful efforts to keep it at bay. Rivers, roads, bridges, railways, tunnels—and now an alpine crossing—such was the life of a civil engineer. All had their worries, and likely he viewed the present prospect with no great enthusiasm. He stopped for the night at White's accommodation house at Courtenay.

Next morning the faint track led him across the plains towards the hills. Directly ahead lay the great bulk of the Torlesse Range. Soon the track and the river would part company, one to climb over the southern buttress of the range, the other to skirt the northern slopes in its deep gorge. Near Kowai Pass (Springfield) he met with son George, Matt Russell, and two others, John Browning and Edward Cahill. Browning was a member of the provincial survey staff, a small, lively, impulsive fellow spending his holidays exploring for the fun of it. Cahill was a road engineer lately arrived from Otago. He was interested in communication with the West Coast and only that week had offered to build the road in return for toll fee rights, a proposition the Government was quick to reject.

Together the five rode up the Kowai River to the foot of Porter's Pass, where they spent the night at Thomas's homestead. Next morning they continued up the steep, southern-slope track on the spur leading to the summit.* Gaining a high pass is often a rewarding experience for the traveller, opening up with the last few steps vast panoramas of new country. Not so Porter's. Although higher than Arthur's Pass it reveals only a shallow, swampy valley aptly named Starvation Gully, which carries the eye abruptly and at no great interval to the scarred face of Mount Lyndon. Apologists for the view (or lack of it) may excuse it on the ground that this is Rakaia country, or advise the viewer to return when winter snows have worked their enchantment.

More picturesque, as the five horsemen soon found, was the little Rakaia lake called Lyndon, nestling at the base of its mountain namesake, providing their pilgrimage with a welcome splash of colour. After that it was back into Waimakariri country again (the watershed saddle is so low it is often unnoticed) to watch the scenic delights of tussocked slopes and purpled hills unfold as they rode north towards Castle Hill and Lake Pearson.

And certainly this is intriguing country, once covered by a huge glacier, above which some of the higher peaks stood as islands. The great ice-plough carved the smaller mountains into their distinctive shapes and when it retreated aeons ago a considerable lake formed about them. Gradually the lake filled with shingle deposits from the main rivers, forming a vast plateau which in many respects is a continuation of the Canterbury Plains, but on a much higher level.

The area is bounded on the east by the Torlesse and Puketeraki ranges and on the west by the Craigieburn and Black ranges, all rising to between 1900m and 2200m. It is alive with names to stir the imagination. There are Red, White, Blue, Brown, Green, Purple, Cloudy, Foggy, Baldy, Bullock, Whale,

*The road up the northern side of the spur, where it is today, was not built until 1871.

Table, Long, Flock, and Castle hills; a Hog's Back, a Puffer, assorted Mounds of Misery, a couple of Sugar Loaves, some Candlesticks, a Broken river, and creeks called Ghost, Pig, and Bull; a No Man's Land, a Romulus and Remus, a Gog, a Magog, and even an Og, a Hallelujah Flat, and two mountains called Misery and Horrible, both on the Black Range.

No place, it might be thought, for the faint of heart. Torlesse, the first white man to see it, from his own distant peak in 1849, thought it "a romantic and chaotic mass of mountains". But on his second and closer look from the Puketeraki Range he was not so sure. "The scene," he wrote, "did not strike me as promising a smiling or cheerful home. It chilled me to look at it."

Everything has its imperfections, of course, but many another traveller has since been warmed by the predominant grandeur, colour and shapely variety of this country with its hills and valleys, terraces, slopes, flats, limestone outcrops, and clearwater lakes and rivers, through which the road weaves an almost tentative path among the tussocks and shingled heights, finding level going or easy grades nearly all the way.

Explorers crossing Waimakariri. *This copy of a water-colour by Sir William Fox shows an early exploration party fording the river below the gorge under the telescopic eye of a gentleman posed atop the bank.*

Along this path rode the Dobsons and their companions. The afternoon sun, slanting across the ridges, shadowed them to Pearson, the lake with the hourglass figure, and just beyond they topped the Ribbonwood Fan and for the first time saw that breath-taking view of the Grasmere country backgrounded by the Alps. Soon they were at Hawdon's station, where they stayed the night.

Next day the explorers parted company. Browning and Cahill, who were free agents, left to examine the headwaters of the Waimakariri, while the Dobsons and Russell crossed the valley and went up the Hawdon tributary bound for Walker Pass. Hawdon's head shepherd McRae had just returned from his round trip over Walker and Worsley passes, and the engineer thought he should look at these with a roadbuilder's eye.

The approach to Walker Pass was easy but on the other side the descent to the Taramakau River via the Otehake was a nightmare. The Dobsons and Russell were soon involved in a frustrating physical argument with the Otehake's notorious gorges. On March 21 they "climbed all day among precipices" and camped for the night "on the cliffs in a crow's nest built up of logs and brushwood".

Plainly this was no country for roads. Trying to extricate themselves they toiled all one day to gain two miles. Finally on March 24, cold and wet, they struggled back to Grasmere. It had taken nine days to learn one of the region's primary lessons—keep out of the Otehake.

This was about the length of time—"a week or 10 days"—that Edward Dobson was expected to be away from Christchurch.

While he was trudging down the Hawdon in the rain and searching out a ford across the flooding Waimakariri, *The Press* was recording the public's great anxiety for news of his mission. However Dobson had no plans for an early return. Browning was back from the headwaters to tell of a pass he had discovered ("Browning's" pass, later renamed Campbell Pass), while nearby Jack Smith (the road contractor) and his men were camped awaiting instructions. There were pressing decisions to be made and a wet Sunday enjoying Hawdon's hospitality was just the time and place for Dobson to make them. The three plans evolved were:

1. Jack Smith and his men were to move up the Bealey and establish themselves at Camping Flat, below Arthur's Pass.
2. Edward Dobson would follow next day and set the men to work on a track before leaving for the upper Waimakariri to inspect "Browning's" pass.
3. George Dobson (and Matt Russell) would leave immediately to investigate passes from the Poulter River. He was to cross the divide to the Taramakau valley, then go up the Otira and Rolleston rivers and cross "Browning's" pass to rendezvous with his father in the upper Waimakariri.

None of these plans worked but they all had a common destination far up the main river, where Smith found himself because he missed the turnoff at Bealey, Edward Dobson because he had no alternative but to follow, and George Dobson because that was where he was told to go — not that he reached it by the route intended.

As anyone who owns a map can see at a glance, the Rolleston River doesn't lead to Campbell Pass but to the very high Waimakariri Col on the shoulder of Mount Rolleston. To make his father's plan work George would have needed to go further down the Taramakau and turn up the Taipo River to Tumbledown Creek.

Edward Dobson had spent Monday, March 27, at Hawdon's, working on maps and sketches and no doubt recovering from the rigours of his Otehake adventures. Next day he went over to Cora Lynn station across the Cass, "from where Mr Goldney kindly accompanied me for some miles to point out the fords", and proceeded up the Bealey. Arrived at Camping Flat to find nobody there he retraced his steps until he found Smith's tracks. These led him up the Waimakariri, but darkness closed in at the Crow River junction, where he camped. It had been a long and unsatisfactory day in which he had covered about 38 kilometres and still was unsure of the road party's whereabouts. That night there was a sharp frost. The middle-aged engineer from Sumner, alone in the mountains, was certainly roughing it, but he was camped in a beautiful place. In those days the flats in the Crow valley were grassed and dotted with occasional trees, enhancing the impressive mountain views. It was like some ornamental park landscaped to seduce the passer-by from his intended destination.*

Wednesday's dawn revealed enough of a daybreak glimpse up the Crow River to show Edward Dobson that there was no pass there — "the glacier descends to the bush", he noted. But Mount Rolleston made the view worth looking at. Then it was on up the Waimakariri for another eight or nine kilometres to the small grassy flats below "Browning's" pass. There, unable to reconcile where they were with where they should be, stood Jack Smith and his men.

History does not record what the engineer said to the contractor but now that the parties were joined Dobson wasted no time. He and Smith set out immediately to explore the further reaches of the river. Soon they came to the Waimakariri Falls where the river is converted into a spectacular cascade almost completely hidden in a labyrinth of gloomy precipices. Dobson was not impressed with the valley by which they had come — "little more than a mass of loose boulders and shingle between vertical walls of rock, with glaciers at their summits" — and at the falls he turned back, thinking it "not worth while to risk life and limb by climbing to the watershed".

But Jack Smith, adventurous fellow, pressed on alone. It is strange country. The great red-rock walls which abound on all

sides are magnificently primitive — good base stock for a Stonehenge — and the steep way through them towards the open upper valley is complicated by river crossings and bluffs.

In the valley Smith found himself confronted by a glacier and hemmed in between Mount Rolleston on one side and Mount Armstrong on the other. But he kept on, finding a way up one of the lateral moraines beside the ice, "aided by a light fall of snow", until he had climbed steeply to the Waimakariri Col (1753m) and could look down into the rock-bound Rolleston River.

A waterfall, *sprayed by an autumn wind, makes its small contribution to the infant Waimakariri River. Up this barren cirque in 1865 Jack Smith struggled alone to Waimakariri Col, birthplace of the river; but in those days a glacier flowed down this high-level valley.*

This exploit gave Jack Smith the honour of being the first man to reach the true source of the Waimakariri River and the first to climb to glacial heights in what is now Arthur's Pass National Park. It is about all we know of him. Of his greater achievement as the man who built the road over Arthur's Pass, nothing is known except for passing references and criticisms in the reports of engineers and supervisors. He has long since been lost in the frequence of his name.

While Smith was mountaineering, Dobson was setting the men to work on a track through the bush on the west side of the river "to enable me to ascertain the practicability of making a road in side cutting up to Browning's Pass". The summit of this pass lies well back, out of sight from the river. It is likely that Edward Dobson had no idea how high it was — 1266m above sea level and therefore snowed in for much of the year. Had he known, he would hardly have wasted four or five days on it. The men worked on the track all day Thursday and Friday, March 30 and 31, and were sleeping the sleep of honest toilers on the Friday night when a storm came over the pass and blew down all their tents.

Storms of a different kind were brewing in Christchurch, where impatience was growing to know what was going on in the mountains and when the much-publicised bridle track would be ready. A Chamber of Commerce deputation, irked with the Government's failure to inform, waited on Superintendent Bealey that same Friday to ask about progress with the road to Westland. Mr Bealey assured his visitors that right then Mr Dobson was at work cutting the track over Arthur's Pass. In fact, of course, the only sign of life at Arthur's Pass that day was George Dobson coming through from Otira.

As it happened more exciting things than Chamber of Commerce deputations were developing in the city. John Edward FitzGerald, first man ashore from the first of the first four ships, original Superintendent of Canterbury, and founder of *The Press,* was apparently not entirely convinced that the Dobsons were to be trusted in the back country. Impulsive as ever, he was organising an exploration party of impressive standing to journey into the upper Waimakariri. On March 29 he wrote to the Superintendent:

Dear Bealey, — It is clear that the right pass has not been found. If the Government would assist with expenses I am prepared to start with a party of which Mr Harman, Mr White, and Mr Browning will form

*A onetime climbing companion of the author's, George Doig, on passing this spot always swore that when he was an old man he would return and pitch his tent in these idyllic surroundings, there to sit in idleness savouring them to the full. Unfortunately George didn't live long enough, and in any case nature has swept away his Elysium and replaced it with barren shingle.

part. We shall be six in all. And we will explore the Middle or head branch of the Waimakariri—the old Maori pass to the Arahura.

FitzGerald thought about 70 pounds would be a sufficient contribution from the Government but Bealey, in a generous mood or from a fondness for round figures, made it 100 pounds provided they started immediately. FitzGerald replied on March 31 that he proposed to take two wagons to the farthest point possible on the Waimakariri, then to make survey expeditions into the passes at the head of the river and if any suitable pass was found, to push on to the West Coast or at least as far as the diggings in the Arahura.* His note to Bealey concluded: "P.S. We start at 9 o'clock tomorrow morning. As the expenses will considerably exceed the grant we take no servants."

Before detailing the adventures of the Picnic Party, as FitzGerald's group was promptly nicknamed, it would be as well to get Edward Dobson out of the upper Waimakariri. On the morning FitzGerald's coaches were leaving Christchurch the men camped below "Browning's" pass were setting up their

Left:
Richard James Strachan Harman *(1826-1902), the discoverer of Harman Pass when he was a member of FitzGerald's "Picnic Party". A civil engineer, he started his life in Canterbury in 1851 as a land and estate agent, and shortly as a runholder. He was a member of the Provincial Council, and at one time its treasurer, a keen sportsman, chairman of the first Board of Conservators set up to protect the city from the Waimakariri, and was responsible for much of the planting and beautifying of Christchurch.*

Right:
James Edward FitzGerald, *first Superintendent of Canterbury, was an impulsive Irishman, variously described as "handsome, volatile, gifted, and unstable as water". A contemporary praised him thus: "His fine instincts, generosity and manly frankness aided to raise the whole tone of public life in which he moved." He retired from the superintendency in 1857 for health reasons and then represented the province in London as Emigration Officer. Returning to New Zealand he founded* The Press *in Christchurch in 1861, and in 1867 became Comptroller and Auditor-General to Central Government in Wellington.*

Carrington Peak, *"towering sheer, huge and close", dominates this late-summer view from the White-Waimakariri junction, where George Dobson and Matt Russell, and later Harman, Browning and Johnstone camped during their 1865 explorations. Edward Dobson, Jack Smith and their work party pitched tents further up the Waimakariri beyond the bush-covered spur, and started a track to the left towards Campbell Pass. One of the favoured railway routes was by a tunnel under Carrington Peak.*

tents again after the storm and drying out their blankets. In the afternoon they went back to track cutting. But Dobson had by now reached a cross gully which could not be passed without great difficulty and expense. To reach the top of the waterfall which is such a feature of the Waimakariri approach to the pass would require 2.5km of side cutting on a hillside too loose to afford a secure foundation for a road. This, he declared, was a fatal objection, and with that he abandoned the attempt.

A tradition of wet Sundays was setting in and this gave the men a day off on April 2. The great cliffs of Carrington Peak came alive with small waterfalls as the heights disappeared into the clouds. The only men stirring in the Waimakariri valley were the unfailingly peripatetic George Dobson and his running mate who, rain or no rain, were making their way upriver. At the forks George turned up the White River and pitched a tent on the edge of the bush (ever since a favourite camping spot and now the site of Carrington Hut). From this point the Waimakariri valley continues to the north while shortly the

*FitzGerald's intentions were good but his geography was astray. There is no single pass between the Waimakariri and the Arahura.

White turns almost due south, so that the two main branches oppose each other on the map.

Harman's is the only pass out of the White valley which crosses the main divide. The way to the saddle is by a steep, narrow, rock-walled canyon, filled for much of the year with avalanche snow. Down it tumbles the Taipo-iti ("Little Devil") River. There is no room in this formidable place to orchestrate the grade-saving manoeuvres needed for a road. What possessed the Picnic Party explorers a week later to persist with the crossing, which in turn leads to greater difficulties in the Taipo River over the pass, can only be explained by their unhindered enthusiasm. George Dobson required but a perfunctory inspection of the ravine to dismiss it out of hand, and he correctly presumed that any other pass out of the White could lead only to the Wilberforce.

But where, oh where was Father? Only one place remained—somewhere further up the main river. So there George directed his steps and at last found what he was looking for—the whole party by then packing up for the long walk back to Bealey. It is not known what Edward Dobson thought when he saw his son approaching from downriver instead of over "Browning's" pass as he had been directed, and he would be disappointed to learn that the Poulter exploration had failed to discover a suitable pass.

On the way back a surprise was in store. In the distance men could be seen approaching over the shingled wastes. Surely not the Picnic Party already! The newcomers turned out to be a score of rather rougher fellows heading, as they fondly imagined, for the Arahura diggings. They had come from the south by way of Lake Lyndon and followed the explorers' tracks. They were promptly turned about and marched back to Bealey.

With the diggers the party was now about 35 strong. They camped that night in the lower valley of the Bealey, and as they sat around their fires Edward Dobson could be satisfied that a thoroughly professional investigation had been made of all available passes, and that there were no hidden alternatives. The danger was past that FitzGerald's shining knights of amateur exploration might still find some golden road for their pumpkin coaches. Reality was more prosaic: the road would have to go over Arthur's rough and rocky pass, a proceeding that promised to be no fairy-tale affair. Life for all who worked there would be hard and unyielding. The preliminaries were over, the engineer-explorer decided, and it was time to get Jack Smith and his pick-and-shovel men to work.

Back in Christchurch the papers and the public, stimulated by anticipation of the Picnic Party's adventures in the mountains, were growing still more impatient (and more than a little scornful) in all matters connected with the Dobson expedition. It was by then three weeks since they had left town. Edward Dobson hastened to write a note to John Hall, knowing that it would reach the newspapers almost immediately. In it he gave the news that Arthur's Pass had been chosen for the bridle track, and added:

I am afraid that the Government will share the impatience of the public at the time this survey has taken, but the country is so rough, and the difficulty of getting through the bush is so great, that it has only been through great exertion on the part of all concerned that I have been able so soon to arrive at a definite result.

There must have been jubilation in the city that at last the decision was made, and more than a little conjecture about the outcome should Mr FitzGerald's enterprise discover a better pass than Arthur's. This they could well do (in the public mind), being six men of high standing, led by a former Superintendent, including in their ranks an Engineer and an Explorer, and with their initial thrust into the wilderness powered by Cobb's coaches. It was all very romantic and exciting.

But mountain gods not only have no hearts, they seem to enjoy deflating cherished hopes. FitzGerald's men were about to learn some of the facts of life in the Snowy Ranges.

The Picnic Party left Christchurch on a day which impressed some sceptical onlookers — April 1. They made a shaky start. Twenty-seven kilometres out they discovered one of the vehicles, a light wagon, was unlikely to survive the journey. A halt was called at White's accommodation house and Captain Anderson, the head driver, rode back to Christchurch to get a trusty Concord coach as a replacement. None was available there and he had to ride on to Kaiapoi for one.

The leather-sprung American-built coaches were so named because they came from Concord, U.S.A. Riding through the night on his urgent errand the Captain may well have thought of himself as a latter-day Paul Revere, whose own midnight ride (but lately publicised by Longfellow's famous poem) actually passed through a town called Concord. Be that as it may, by seven o'clock in the morning Anderson had secured the wanted vehicle and delivered it safely to Courtenay, after which he had to face the long and difficult drive to the west where no coach had been before.

The party comprised J.E. FitzGerald, leader; R.J.S. Harman, a civil engineer and land agent; R.R. Armstrong, an immigration officer; J.S. Browning, surveyor (returned only recently from the upper Waimakariri); and R.R. Johnstone. Captain Anderson was a superb driver and horseman who came to New Zealand with Cole and Hoyt when they brought coaches and horses over from Australia at the time of the Otago gold rush and set up the Cobb & Co. operation here.

While all were waiting at White's for Anderson's return coincidence produced Edward Cahill, Browning's recent companion in exploration, who was riding past on his way to Christchurch. He was persuaded to join the expedition and return to the mountains.

According to *The Lyttelton Times,* which may have taken some satisfaction from the incident, "a messenger had to be sent back to town from a considerable distance for some forgotten articles, and after all, when it was too late to be remedied, it was found that though dog, gun, powder and shot had been provided, the caps had been forgotten".

On the steep climb up Porter's Pass Anderson had to use both teams of horses to bring up the coaches one at a time, and it took two hours to get all to the top. They reached Castle Hill station on the evening of April 2 and drove to Grasmere next day — three days for what is now much less than half that in hours. Trackless from there on, they jolted down the Cass riverbed to the Waimakariri and pushed on over the shingle,

The "road" to Harman's Pass *up the Taipoiti Gorge. No place for even a bridle track, said George Dobson, the first man to view it during his search for a suitable pass out of the Waimakariri. This is a late November photograph in a snowy year.*

through the river and along the scrubby flats to the Bealey for their fourth camp. They were much impressed with the mountains, "which reared themselves aloft with the most picturesque variety of abrupt outline".

In the morning George Dobson hove in sight on his way from Arthur's Pass to the Poulter to tidy up the last exploration chores there. His journal entry is laconic: "Met Messrs FitzGerald and Harman at the mouth of the Bealey, with two of Cobb's coaches." A diarist with the Picnic Party was wordier:

Wednesday, 5th: The morning broke misty and thick, and colder. Met George Dobson and two men on the Bealey flat. They seemed much astonished to see Cobb's coaches so far in the interior. Mr Dobson had been exploring in the same country to which we were now bound, and he stated it to be totally impracticable for a road. However, it was considered there was enough doubt whether the most probable pass had been looked for to keep the party from entire disappointment.

Prospects for dramatic discoveries were now greatly reduced but having come so far the expedition decided to bounce the coaches another four or five miles over the riverbed to the Crow River junction and for a little beyond that, where a suitable camp site, sheltered from the north-west, was selected. Getting coaches so far was in itself a notable achievement reflecting great credit on Captain Anderson and his co-driver (and, of course, the horses), but in the wider context it was of no great value. It was already obvious to surveyors and engineers that most of the Cass-Bealey section of the route offered the road builders few difficulties except at the Black Range.

The party's plans were for Harman, Browning and Johnstone to go up the White River, while Armstrong and Cahill would further explore the pass from the Waimakariri which Cahill had discovered so recently with Browning. With those plans finalised, on the afternoon of Thursday, April 6, the entire party walked up to the Waimakariri-White junction, a distance of about 6km. From there, with FitzGerald's blessing, the explorers went their separate ways.

Harman, Browning and Johnstone made a camp almost immediately. Next day they crossed the river and tackled the Taipo-iti stream, which promised access to the main divide. The steep climb, often hard against beetling rock walls, which in spring would be at the mercy of snow avalanches, was safe enough in April and soon brought them to the summit of what was later named Harman Pass (1326m). Crossing over they descended into all kinds of trouble in the headwaters of the Taipo River, a tributary of the Taramakau. Finding themselves "among frightful precipices and mountain torrents" they wisely retraced their steps, although Browning, adventurous as ever, was all for continuing.

Meanwhile Armstrong and Cahill were having a closer look at their pass (1265m), which had a difficult approach and had already been rejected by Edward Dobson. Both these passes were in reality only alternatives to the same destination reached by Arthur's Pass in rather less distance and they had the disadvantage of greater height.

The Picnic Party's disappointment was heightened by the knowledge that they were but confirming what Dobson had already proved—that there was no suitable pass from the upper Waimakariri. The only course remaining seemed to be to go home.

Then disaster struck. The possibility had always existed that with so many novices trying conclusions with moderately difficult mountain terrain, sooner or later one or other of them would get into trouble. That moment came on the loose-rock slopes of "Browning's" pass. Armstrong, scrambling down a particularly bad patch high above the Waimakariri, dislodged a boulder which in turn released a stream of rocks from above. One of these passed so close it tore the swag from his back, but others scored more direct hits. Knocked unconscious, crushed and bruised, he was shortly found by Cahill, on whom the burden fell of getting his dazed and injured companion down to camp over very rough going.

How he contrived to do this showed (in FitzGerald's words) "what a strong and resolute man can do in the hour of sore need and to save the life of a friend". Back in the tent the pair spent a troubled night. Cahill rose before dawn and hurried downriver to the coaches, leaving Armstrong lying in the tent beside the stream.

The coach party had been augmented a day or two earlier by the arrival of the Goldney brothers and John Marshall from Cora Lynn. All were enjoying breakfast round the camp fire when Cahill arrived with the bad news, much distressed. FitzGerald, Anderson and Marshall agreed to start immediately, returning with Cahill, while the Goldneys looked after the camp.

Thus began what was surely the first search-and-rescue operation in what is now Arthur's Pass National Park and probably in the entire Southern Alps.

The rescuers hurried with a horse to the White junction where by coincidence they met Harman and his party returning from their adventures in the Taipo. Together all pressed on up the Waimakariri to rescue the injured Armstrong, who was put on a litter and carried down to the White. Transferred to the horse, he reached camp about 7.30 p.m. after a painful journey. Four uncomfortable days of rough coach travel saw him back in his Christchurch home, where in due course he made a good recovery.

The Picnic Party had little of value to show for all their trouble and expense, which was considerable even with the government subsidy. From a purely exploration point of view their great achievement was the discovery and first crossing of Harman Pass, but this was of no use in meeting the expedition's primary requirement, a road to the Coast. The Government's 100 pounds (about what a working man would earn a year) showed a poor return on its investment and compared unfavourably in terms of value with the less ostentatious performance of George Dobson over a much wider field.

But their adventures made a lengthy and interesting page in *The Press,* in which the obvious conclusion was reached that there was no suitable pass out of the Waimakariri. However, FitzGerald thought there was no reason why a good hotel should not be built in the vicinity of the Bealey, from which trips to the headwaters might well repay those who were fond of sport and the luxury of blue duck soup, "and there is scenery which would be regarded as strikingly beautiful in any country in the world".

The hotel has come and gone several times and although the glaciers are not what they were, the mountains, the scenery and the occasional blue duck are still there.

During the return trip to Christchurch a messenger arrived with a note suggesting that the "Maori pass" at the head of the Wilberforce might be worth investigating. Accordingly Harman, Browning and Johnstone, conscious perhaps that the Government was still thinking of the 100 pounds it had spent, left the coaches at Lake Lyndon and struck out on foot for the Rakaia and the pass known today as Browning.*

But again they were thwarted. They arrived at Browning Pass after a 70 kilometre walk only to find a tent already there, housing two other explorers named Griffiths and Otway. After a combined reconnaissance of this steep, high and unlikely saddle, whose only virtue was that it led more directly to the goldfields, Harman, probably fed up with so much unproductive effort and expense, went home and left exploration to others.

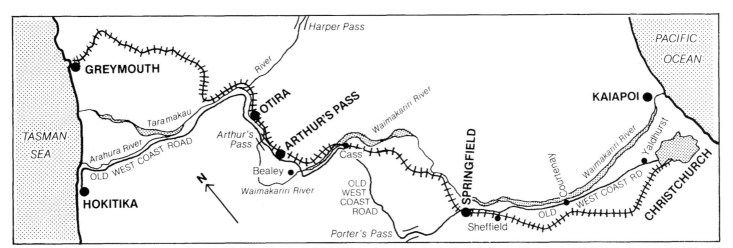

Road and rail. *This sketch map shows the routes followed by the Old West Coast Road and the Midland Railway. The principal differences between the old road line and the present State Highway 73 are between Yaldhurst and Sheffield, and on the West Coast where the coaches followed the Arahura River to the sea instead of the Taramakau.*

*Harman was so keen about finding a pass that he once travelled all the way to Moorhouse's station to interview a West Coast fugitive from the law said to be sheltering there. As E.R. Chudleigh told it, "Harman does not want to bring him to justice but to show the way he came, which was the shortest by two days of any yet known." The man probably came over a Taramakau-Poulter pass.

CHAPTER FOUR

The Road Builders

The first track over Porter's Pass into the Waimakariri sheep country was made in 1858-9 by a few men with picks and shovels and a grant of 500 pounds from the Provincial Government. A year earlier when Joseph Pearson returned from his exploration of the basin and described it to a friend, the man asked how he expected to get the wool out from such an isolated place. Well, said Pearson, he'd have to balloon it out. But of course there was no way except the long haul by packhorse down the valley and over the pass to the plains.

The unruly gash made by the Waimakariri Gorge between the Torlesse and Puketeraki ranges was too difficult and expensive a road-building proposition for the resources of the time, and the only other low-level alternative was the circuitous track through the Acheron River valley from the Rakaia, which added too much distance by far. Although it was high (945m) and often snowbound in winter, Porter's Pass* offered few engineering difficulties as it climbed over the southern flank of the Torlesse Range. While this route took the road away from a direct line to the upper stations, once the pass was crossed a long run through easy country opened up due north to the Cass River 35km away.

As might be expected there were soon demands that the track be improved and widened to take bullock wagons. The Government agreed provided the run-holders paid their share. A scheme was introduced which required the owners to freehold some of their land, the proceeds to be matched pound for pound by the Government and used for road-building.

Among others Hawdon contributed a thousand pounds, Minchin of Mount White six hundred and Mallet of Lochinvar five hundred. The road, if it could be called such, was made as far as the Cass River, but there is no record of what progress was made, if any, in extending it to such a remote station as Lochinvar in the Esk valley. Mallet was a Frenchman who soon returned to his homeland. Since his father owned a bank he might not have overly missed the five hundred pounds he paid for his road, which even yet is no more than a landrover track.

Except for a few variations, notably on Porter's Pass and in the Castle Hill region, today's road follows the original line, maintaining an average elevation of something like 600m through thousands of hectares of sheep farming lands in the great basin. Sculpting by ice age glaciers and erosion of limestone outcrops have created a fascinating landscape walled off from the west by the great bulk of the Craigieburn Range with its 20 peaks over 1850m high.† For nearly 40km the road keeps its distance from the Waimakariri, winding between isolated hills and over tussocked grasslands, but the water which flows under the bridges along the way is all Waimakariri water.

There is much to see. Between the high crenellated ridge of the Torlesse "gap" in the east and 2196m Mount Enys, highest peak of the Craigieburns in the west, stand the bold limestone towers and cliffs of Castle Hill, and beyond them the Thomas River and the Craigieburn forests, dark green in a world of ochre tussock and grey scree, snow-covered in winter.

The next river to cross is the Broken, one of those descending steeply from snowfields high on the Craigieburns which have spawned several skifields in recent years. Across the next stream, the Cave, is Flock Hill, named by Charles Torlesse because its surface is studded with limestone blocks which he thought looked like sheep. Cave Stream is so named because it goes underground for 275m before it joins Broken River.

Cave Stream flows along an almost straight limestone fault line. The road climbs beside it and round to the saddle which Torlesse named Iona, from where it descends Craigieburn cutting and takes a short run along the banks of the Craigie Burn to Lake Pearson. This is the first of several lakes which ornament the landscape hereabouts. Immediately past the lake a high point on the Ribbonwood fan opens on to a fine view of Lake Grasmere country with the first alpine peaks (on the Polar Range) dominating the background across the Waimakariri River. In the middle ground of this panorama is Cass, where the road joins with the railway, arrived here by way of the

Left: *The road to Porter's Pass climbs from the plains up a scrubby extension of the Torlesse Range. The steep top section is on the line of the original track which came up a valley hidden behind the spur at left. The pass, which is higher than Arthur's Pass on the main divide, gives access to the Waimakariri sheep country behind the front ranges. At top right is Porter Heights skifield on the Craigieburn Range, here nearly 2000m high.*

Right: *A turn-of-the century picnic party on the pass road at Hanging Rock, long since removed by road improvement.* Canterbury Museum

*Named for the three Porter brothers who took up Castle Hill run in 1858.

† Named peaks on the Craigieburn Range from south to north are: Mount Enys (named for John Enys, pioneer Castle Hill station owner and prominent in early Canterbury affairs), Mount Cloudesley (for W.J. Cloudesley, a Castle Hill Hotel proprietor), Mount Izard (for William Izard, well-known Christchurch lawyer and a close friend of Enys), Mount Cheeseman (for Thomas Cheeseman, curator of Auckland museum),

Mount Cockayne (for Dr. Leonard Cockayne, noted Christchurch botanist and the "father" of Arthur's Pass National Park), Mount Wall (for Arnold Wall, professor of English at Canterbury College), Hamilton Peak (for a Sydney lawyer-mountaineer who was a friend of Wall), and Mount Manson (for a Craigieburn station manager).

Waimakariri and Broken river gorges and the valley of Sloven's Stream, a tributary of the Broken.

Not far past Cass on a low saddle called Goldney's the traveller finally comes face to face with the big river itself, running left to right against a backdrop of mountain beech forest climbing steeply to the peaks. From here on, it is never far away; the brown hills fall behind and the mountains loom ahead. Round Corner Knob on the slopes of Mount Horrible the view changes from north to west and presents a panorama extending 24km up the Waimakariri to the snowy heights of Mounts Harper and Davie.

Halfway there the road turns up the Bealey valley and heads north to Arthur's Pass, where East meets West and the change is dramatic: the open, snowgrassed fields of the pass fall away abruptly to the rock-walled Otira Gorge and the land of scarlet rata and rain-shrouded hills.

Once across Porter's Pass *the road heads north past Lake Lyndon towards the rolling grasslands of Castle Hill country, with the snowy Craigieburn Range in the distance. There are three skifields on the section of range shown — Cheeseman, Broken River and Craigieburn Valley.*

The estimates for the road in 1865 allowed 50,000 pounds to build the 140 kilometres between Christchurch and Arthur's Pass. Of this only 39,000 pounds was spent. A meagre 30,000 pounds was allocated for the 80-90km from Arthur's Pass to Hokitika; in the event the road over this intractable, swampy and heavily-forested section cost more than 100,000 pounds and delayed the opening date by nearly six months. For much of the distance the road had to be made of logs laid in the bogs, covered with brushwood and topped off with shingle.

The economics revealed the relative difficulties between east and west and to some extent the drama of the great task. They also indicated how hurriedly, even recklessly, the project was begun with only the sketchiest of engineering assessment and costing. Admittedly there was great public pressure, the essence of which was distilled by *Punch in Canterbury,* a satirical journal of the time, in these lines addressed to the Provincial Superintendent:

Hushabye Bealey! O'er the hill-top,
When the road's made, in office you'll stop.
When the road isn't made, people will bawl,
"Down with the Government, Bealey and all."

And three months later there was this advice for Secretary of Works John Hall, who carried a heavy political and administrative responsibility for the project:

Make the road, Johnny, my dear Johnny!
Make the road, Johnny, my little man!
Anywhere, anyhow, over the mountains,
Do it as quickly, my boy, as you can.

Never mind the cost! As Philip Ross May wrote nearly a hundred years later, the highway was "a reminder of the unreasoning enthusiasm of those people in Canterbury who believed that a road would level the Southern Alps, convert

Hokitika into a suburb of Christchurch, and direct the gold trade through the provincial capital". All the road levelled, he added, was the provincial treasury.

Public Agitation *for a road to the West Coast resulted in several cartoons being published in* Punch in Canterbury, *which delighted in portraying the* Standard *newspaper as a boozy old hag, who in this cartoon is making sure Secretary of Works John Hall points his telescope at her choice of route.*
Alexander Turnbull Library

Heading west. *A traffic officer's car looks sheep-size as it hustles along State Highway 73 through smooth Castle Hill country, along much the same route as that used by early explorers and runholders nearly 130 years ago. But when Joseph Pearson led the way in February, 1857, he was 16km east of here, struggling through the Waimakariri Gorge.*

Part 1: Over the Pass

On the morning of Tuesday, April 4, 1865, when Edward Dobson moved up the Bealey with his engineer's eye appraising the prospects for road building in this almost virgin valley, the immediate tasks were to establish headquarters at Camping Flat, take levels, get a track cut towards Arthur's Pass, and plan work for construction gangs. The weather was overcast with mist hiding the peaks as the miners, still following, straggled up the riverbed. They were there only because an opportunist Dunedin printer had prematurely sold them a map showing a Waimakariri route to the Coast. While Jack Smith organised his men, the Dobsons searched out the route used by Arthur and Edward a year earlier, and with George's more recent experience of it they were soon on the pass. Here they sent the diggers on to fight their own battles in the gorge. That night Edward Dobson wrote in his journal:

Arthur's Pass differs from the other passes in the width and length of its summit valley, and the gentleness of the ascent which is very easy. The summit is strewn with large blocks of stone, in a confused manner, rendering it difficult to say whether their position is due to slips or to glacial action. As we descend on the northern side, however, the evidences of glacial action become very clear; there is a large, swampy flat which has been a lake in former times, the valley being dammed by a lateral moraine brought down by a glacier from a tributary valley in the west. Further down, the main valley is again blocked by an immense pile of loose rocks overlying a mass of mud and shingle with which the valley seems to have been filled at a very early date, and of which a good section is exposed at the head of the upper Otira gorge. Still further north the valley narrows and becomes a mere gorge, the sides of which are sheer precipices many hundreds of feet in height, all further progress being impossible, except along the river bed. Returned to camp at night after a fatiguing day, fully satisfied with the general character of the pass, although many serious difficulties presented themselves on both sides of the ascent.

Edward Dobson's first task was to select the best way to get from Camping Flat below the Bealey Gorge up to the relatively open and undulating pass. How to get down from there into the Otira Gorge and through its narrow, rock-walled confines he put to one side in the meantime.

On April 5 George Dobson left his father to his own devices and returned to the Poulter to investigate a pass from the west branch of that river, his last piece of unfinished business in that area.* Meanwhile Dobson senior, after two or three days trying to force a route up the east side of the gorge, switched to the west side when he sighted some open ground there. On the cold, showery morning of April 9 he pushed through the wet bush to investigate and found not only a good route but a place where the river could be conveniently bridged. This was the day the injured Armstrong was being rescued from the upper Waimakariri, and Dobson was no doubt pleased to have a line to the pass settled before FitzGerald could arrive to help.

As it happened FitzGerald never did get to Arthur's Pass, but he organised the next best thing. Immediately he was back in the *Press* office he summoned a reporter who could both ride and scribble and sent him off at a gallop to discover exactly what Dobson was up to in the Bealey.

When the proposed bridle track over the pass grew to assume the status of a dray road, and in turn a coach road, is not clear, but at some stage a road became the thing to have. People in Christchurch were stirred by reports of decisions taken and progress in the making, even (remembering FitzGerald's departure) coaches wheeling their way almost to the goldfields.

The *Times* called it "the most exciting topic of the month" and announced that two large parties of workmen under contractors E.G. Wright and Wm. White were starting immediately to work on the road. *The Press*, not to be outdone, called on the Government to "get on with it, spend the money, and get the road pushed through so that the escort can be got running and bring the gold to Christchurch instead of Nelson". The timing of this exhortation could not have been worse. Next day the first escort arrived back from the gold fields with no gold—a harbinger indeed. After the arduous trip by Hurunui

*Another 65 years were to pass before the discovery was made that George Dobson had missed one of the available Waimakariri passes, the Taruahuna at the head of the Edwards River, but the oversight was of no consequence as it led only into the gorge-ridden Otehake.

Works department headquarters *at Camping Flat (Arthur's Pass) in 1865—a sketch attributed to Edward Dobson.*   Canterbury Museum

Saddle to the Coast and back, both horses and men were exhausted, their efforts a failure.

On April 10 in the Bealey wet weather was setting in. The nor'wester came moaning over the pass bearing increasing showers, but it was Monday morning and there was work to do. Jack Smith got the men started and, by keeping them at it despite the rain, managed a passable track to the Bealey ford that day. But the weather worsened and work had to be abandoned. Edward Dobson retired to his tent to catch up on reports and correspondence.

It seemed to him a long way from Christchurch, this shadowed forest valley among the high mountains, far beyond the plains and uplands. The bush slopes, dripping with moisture, disappeared into the rainclouds; the river was rising and dirty. It was rough country for civil engineers. Nearly a month had passed since he left home and in that time much had been accomplished—the valleys explored, the pass chosen, the road started. He took up his pen and a small sheet of paper and wrote closely on both sides, with afterthoughts scribbled in all the margins until there was no room left.

"Dear Hall," the main part of the message to the Secretary of Works began:

I expect George will meet me at Grasmere this week on his return home. There is now not a single pass out of the Waimakariri to the north and west that has not been examined by either one or both of us. I have cut a four-foot wide track at a trotting gradient from the foot of the pass across the saddle, and am going down into the riverbed of the Otira as fast as 30 good axemen can cut their way through the dense scrub.

With the exception of a bridge over the Bealey, the work for the formation of a dray road is of an ordinary character from the foot of the Bealey to the head of the Otira Gorge. Through the Otira Gorge there will be about 90 chains of heavy rock cutting, but there is no real difficulty about the whole matter provided the necessary funds can be obtained.

Bealey Gorge. *A scene in the Bealey Gorge which would look no different today from when Edward Dobson first studied both banks for the easiest road route.*

These words would be comforting for the Secretary, waiting in Christchurch for news of the expedition, but the future was not as bright as that. Many months would pass, long drawn out with rain, hail, snow, frost, floods and a hundred as yet unimagined hardships and difficulties—and the heroic toil of a thousand men—before Canterbury had its road to the west.

As to funds, the bill would be not less than 145,000 pounds, plus heavy maintenance costs from the outset. This exceeded expectations by enough to stagger the stoutest pioneer. In return Canterbury would gain a much-admired engineering feat and the most thrilling coach ride in the country; but also what one critic termed "a monument to the supreme folly of those who guided the councils of the province when it was constructed".

But all this was in the future. Meanwhile a messenger was waiting to carry Dobson's letter to Christchurch. Although there was little space left on the tiny sheet, he found enough to be generous to the amateur explorers: "I am sorry to hear of the unsatisfactory termination of FitzGerald's expedition," he wrote. "I had previously examined the western sources of the Waimakariri and taken a set of levels which showed the impracticability of getting a road in that direction."

A whole week of miserable weather now set in. The cold, sleety rain swept down the valley and there was new snow on the heights. All this time, no matter how adverse the weather, George Dobson was exploring in the west Poulter, making visits to or crossings of both Worsley and Minchin passes and assuring himself that there were no possibilities there. He rejoined his father on the 13th and next morning chained a line from the top of the pass. Then he rode to Grasmere to set out the cuttings for Goldney's Saddle.

George Dobson photographed shortly before his death.

This was probably George Dobson's last assignment in the Waimakariri, which makes it time to say goodbye to that energetic and resolute young explorer. Within the space of a few weeks he crossed Walker Pass and explored in the Otehake headwaters, made two second crossings of Arthur's Pass and the first of Goat Pass, and completed a thorough investigation of all the Poulter branches and the passes leading from them into the Taramakau River.

His 200 kilometre (120 mile) marathon in the week his father was busy at "Browning's" pass was exceptional by any standard, and covered an immense area of rough, largely forested, and unexplored mountain country. With his faithful companion Matt Russell he tramped up the Poulter, crossed to the Taramakau in Westland (probably by Foy Pass), explored the Otehake from the west (and again had to sleep on a cliff in a crow's nest), and pushed up the Otira and the Rolleston until the weather stopped him. Returning to Canterbury he made the second crossing north-south of Arthur's Pass, continued down the Bealey and Waimakariri to Cora Lynn for supplies, then immediately turned about and marched 20 kilometres up the Waimakariri to the White junction. There he inspected the approaches to Harman's Pass, went still further up the Waimakariri to "Browning's" Pass, and finally returned to Bealey with the main party. Much of this was done in wet and stormy weather.

Fighting his way through sodden bush and bouldery gorges, struggling over high saddles, and fording rivers often dangerously in flood, George carried on his young shoulders the burden of proving the Waimakariri passes, a task he discharged with commendable professionalism. His wide-ranging and original explorations make it surprising that his name is nowhere to be found on maps of Arthur's Pass National Park, and suggests there is scant sense or justice in the way names are given to geographical features, which so often seem to glorify inconsequential nobodies. Some day this defect could be remedied, but meanwhile park lovers admiring his brother's monumental column on the pass may care to view it in truth as a family remembrance.

Something should be said also for Matt Russell, George's unfailing companion on all his journeys, who must have carried a fair share of the uncertainties, dangers and triumphs of their combined enterprise; and also for his father Edward, who at some risk took more than one gamble with the unknown and who brought to the expedition a mature judgement in planning and execution.

By a fateful circumstance George Dobson is best remembered for the manner of his death. About a year after his Waimakariri adventures he was murdered by the notorious Sullivan gang while walking alone on the Arnold River track near Lake Brunner, mistaken for a gold buyer. At first he laughed at their mistake, saying, "Did you think I was a banker? Here is all I have, about six pounds." But the gang dared not risk leaving him alive to report their whereabouts, so killed him there and then. The little town of Dobson, near Greymouth, is named in his memory, and his monument stands there.

There was no premonition of this on the afternoon of April 14 as George rode down the Bealey River, possibly for the last time, bound for Grasmere. The familiarity of these beautiful valleys and mountains among which he had spent so much time in

The road *leading down to Arthur's Pass village, probably taken in the 1920s and indicating that for 80 years of its existence the highway had not progressed beyond what was required for coaches.*

Alexander Turnbull Library

recent weeks could by now be giving him deep satisfaction. He had come among them a stranger; now they were old friends. The weather chased him down the Waimakariri and somewhere there on the broad riverbed he might have met FitzGerald's special reporter from *The Press,* riding determinedly upriver with the rain in his face. That gentleman was not in luck's way. His inspection of the pass and the gorges coincided with stormy weather, but he made the best of it, and like a good newspaperman completed his assignment and rode back to town, still in the rain, to ensure that his copy was ready for Monday morning's newspaper.

In view of the heavy rain which had fallen for a whole week with only one short interruption, the Otira River must have been in flood when the Consulting Provincial Engineer walked over the pass on April 17 and camped for the night in the gorge. It was his first close look at the place and the sight must have been depressing. While he was studying it a messenger arrived with despatches from the Secretary of Works advising that George Thornton, the assistant Provincial Engineer, was on his way to take charge.

Dobson immediately returned to Camping Flat and began setting out Smith's contract for a dray road from there to the head of Otira Gorge — that is, from Arthur's Pass township, up and over the pass, and down to approximately Candy's Bend where the road enters the gorge proper, a distance of about 6km. The price was 3264 pounds, arrived at by the usual Dobson method of estimating a reasonable figure and telling the contractor he would probably do all right at that. It was a system of mutual trust which usually worked to the satisfaction of all parties. But this time Smith lost 800 pounds on the deal. He later petitioned the Government for relief from this loss, caused, he said, by contract variations, weather, and the feeding of needy travellers. He was awarded a hundred pounds.

When Smith had been at work for six weeks he had increased his work force from 29 to 119 men, and his horses from six to eight, but still had only one two-horse dray. He must have added greatly to his equipment later, because by the end of August 14 drays were recorded as being "lost", presumably worn out on the job. Construction projects in the 1860s had not the advantage of modern engineering know-how, with its giant bulldozers, scrapers and other construction paraphernalia which today can change the landscape with apparent ease. These were the years of labourers with picks and shovels and wheelbarrows, when a two-horse dray was the ultimate in dump trucks.

Edward Dobson's days at the pass were about to conclude, but he still had to write his official report on the area. Described later as "a masterly summary", it earned him a bonus of a hundred pounds from the Provincial Council. Shortly he would be reappointed to his previous position as Provincial Engineer, carrying with it the final responsibility for the road, but his immediate obligations on site were at an end. By April 25 he was back in Christchurch. Waiting for him were arrears of work at the railway tunnel, which some wag hoped hadn't gone crooked in his absence. Numerous public works were pressing and it soon

The "White" Bridge *in Bealey Gorge, between Arthur's Pass village and the pass itself. So-called because it was painted white. The motorist in this photograph of 60 years ago is driving a Model T Ford.*
Alexander Turnbull Library

became clear that Thornton, too, couldn't be spared for any length of time.

George Thornton left Christchurch on April 18 and reached Porter's Pass the following day, where he found about a hundred men standing around doing nothing. He soon organised them into improving the track down Starvation Gully on the far side of the pass, where a creek meandered among the swamps. Further on men set to work on Dry Creek, and further on again to making a cutting at Goldney's Saddle. On the way he met Dobson returning to Christchurch, and together they decided that all Smith's men should be moved up to Camping Flat to speed up construction of the road over the pass. It was agreed that the sections should be re-allocated and the contractors made responsible as follows: From Kowai River over Porter's Pass and on to Craigieburn Cutting: William White. From Craigieburn Cutting up the Waimakariri and Bealey valleys to Camping Flat at Arthur's Pass: E.G. Wright. From Camping Flat over the pass to Candy's Creek at the start of Otira Gorge proper: J. Smith. From Candy's Creek through the gorge and down the Otira River to the Taramakau River: E.G. Wright. Wright later undertook the troublesome Rocky Point job some distance down the Taramakau. Wm. White, the man who built White's Bridge over the lower Waimakariri, did not play a very active part in the proceedings, leaving supervision mainly to his son, Wm. White junior, and his foremen.

Thornton, never one then or later to agree easily with his immediate superior, was quick to make major changes to most of the plans Edward Dobson had formulated. He was also a man after the Provincial Treasurer's heart. He proposed taking the road 500 metres further up the Bealey Gorge and across the river with a bridge costing only a fraction of that proposed by Dobson. The new line would save about 4000 pounds. He would also ignore a tunnel under the moraine bank that Dobson had been considering and take the road down the west or true left bank of the Otira, a further saving, he estimated, of 10,000 pounds.

But in the gorge itself there were no alternatives. There, as Thornton had to admit, the river was "a mountain torrent rushing between huge boulders varying in size up to 100 tons". He could see no way through except by making the road at a safe height above flood level, taking advantage of old terraces and cutting through or over the projecting spurs, and bridging the river when the spurs were too bold and precipitous, carrying the road alternately on either side as advantage offered.

He was disturbed to find that some boulders in the gorge, weighing perhaps 10 or 15 tons, had been shifted in recent times by floods. The premonitory fear which came with this observation would be realised in due course, not once but many times over the years. He drew a map showing how he would get the road down the left bank of the Otira, but he was not there long enough to build it before he was recalled to Christchurch.

Exceptional Rainfall *near the Main Divide has at intervals caused severe damage to the road in Bealey Valley. Here unruly Halpin Creek makes a nonsense of its bridge.* National Park Archives

Thrice Solved

Three engineers in succession stood on Arthur's Pass in the autumn of 1865 and wondered how best to get the road down into the Otira Gorge; and all three reached different conclusions.

Edward Dobson, first on the scene, wanted to build a tunnel through the great pile of rock which long before his time had fallen from the precipices of Hills Peak and blocked the valley. This, he said, was the best way to get the road on to the spur leading down to the gorge.

His successor, George Thornton, would have none of this. The road, he decided, should go down the west bank and over a high bridge on to the spur. (See map.)

The last of the three, Walter Blake, considered both these propositions to be impractical. He said the tunnel wouldn't improve the gradient and would come out at a most unsafe place. As to the west bank, he couldn't get a grade of less than 1 in 6.3, which he thought too steep. So he went the only way left: up the rock barrier, round the great slip, and down to the gorge by a series of zigs and zags.

Since then untold thousands of coach, motorcar and tourist bus passengers, crossing the pass for the first time, have held their collective breath as they climb over the last barrier and stare down the Zigzag to where, far below, the turbulent Otira plunges into its lower gorge. Some, like Lord Jervois, have preferred to get out and walk; others, contemplating the pain of a return trip, have taken the boat to Melbourne. Men like George Urry whose job it was for years to help fix this somewhat transitory highway whenever it came to pieces, and sometimes had to add another zigzag to get above the worsening slip, thought that of the three Thornton had the right idea. One of the original routes for the railway was to be along the west bank and over the saddle into the Rolleston River where the power pylons go. But nothing is easy in this country.

The answer to the Works Department's staffing problems was found in its own ranks in the persons of two draughtsmen-surveyor brothers, Walter and Edwin Blake. They were quickly promoted to be Road Engineers and charged with setting out and supervising construction of the road. They, more than anyone else, were to bring it to a successful conclusion under the overall direction of Edward Dobson and other engineers, and with the combined efforts of the contractors and the men who laboured for them through that terrible winter. There were times when the difficulties, compounded by incessant rain and flooded rivers, nearly brought the project to a halt. And before it was over, the Westland section almost broke Edwin Blake.

It was Walter Blake, not his brother, who handled the preliminary work on the West Coast. He was sent there with a small gang in February when the gold rush first exploded, primarily to upgrade the Hurunui Saddle track and then to explore the Taramakau valley for the best route to Hokitika.

This was real frontier country for Walter Blake. Even the names of prominent geographical features hadn't been settled. Arthur Dobson's "Arahura (?)" had become Oreirei, then the Oteira, and finally the Otira. The next tributary down the valley was the Hopeakowa, a brawling torrent which felled many an impatient fellow whose haste outweighed his caution. In local parlance it was a devil of a river.

The Maoris couldn't get their tongues round that word but they produced an equivalent which sounded like taipo, and Taipo it became — the Devil river! Nobody remembered or knew that taipo was already established in the Maori language and

meant goblin or elf, neither of which was likely to sink aquatic gold-diggers. Walter Blake spelt it Tipo or Typo. The Taramakau was often spelt Teremakau and jokingly referred to as Tether-my-cow, while, until late April when the Nelson postmaster fixed it for all time, Hokitika was known as Okitiki.

Walter Blake decided that the road should go along the Taramakau valley, in the bed or on the wooded terraces of the south bank, as far as Rangiriri, from where it would cross a belt of bush five or six kilometres wide to the Waimea Creek, take an almost direct line from there to the Kaiwhaka and on to the Arahura River, thence through the scrub on the south bank of that river to the sea and along the beach to Hokitika. Apart from a couple of terraces in the Waimea it was fairly level going all the way, but much of the ground was heavily forested and swampy.

For his good work in fixing the route, Walter was complimented by his superiors and recalled to Christchurch. For much of the journey home he had for company Secretary of Works Hall and Engineer Thornton, who had been over on an inspection trip. As he rode down the Waimakariri with them he learned that he was to take charge of the eastern section of the road, from Kowai to the Otira valley. He would be replaced on the West Coast by his brother Edwin.

Walter Blake rode over Porter's Pass on the last Sunday in May, weighing up the situation (as Dobson and Thornton had done before him) with the eye of the new man in charge. Much of what he saw failed to please, and unless there was to be a dry winter he could see trouble ahead. He hastened to tell White's foreman to get on with shingling the track before the winter rains came. In fact the winter turned out wet and the heavy traffic of supply wagons so rutted the road over the pass and on to Lake Pearson that where possible they had to be driven over the adjacent tussocks to make way at all.

At Arthur's Pass he concluded that Smith wasn't pushing the work along energetically enough, and for a while there was talk of giving his contract to Wright. Smith went to town and recruited more men, increased his equipment, and from then on there was no further serious complaint.

Mid-June saw Khull & Jones opening their new store at Bealey town on the flat near what is now called Klondyke Corner, where sections were advertised at forty-eight pounds apiece. There were few takers.

The clear, frosty weather expected during the winter months of 1865 failed to eventuate. Instead there was much rain and more snow than usual. By July 1 work had almost come to a standstill, but directions were going out from Christchurch that among other things the path had to be readied for the first transalpine mail run. The mail was to be carried by coach as far as possible and then by horse, canoe, or on foot for the remainder. E.R. Chudleigh, who was staying at Castle Hill with

Icicles *festoon rock faces as this modern car climbs towards the pass through Westland's mist and rain — conditions similar to those that prevailed for most of the time in the winter of 1865 when the road was built across Arthur's Pass.*
The Press, Christchurch

Snow Creek *in the Bealey Valley is another menace at times of heavy rainfall. In December, 1979, flood waters had greatly lessened when this picture was taken by M.J. Aplin, but the flow is still strong and damaging.*

his friend Charles Enys, reported the first mail coach going through on July 4. Enys had to lend them a horse.

Labour troubles made their appearance about this time when some of Smith's men were down in the Otira Gorge building footbridges at the river fords. This was cold and unpleasant work, splashing about in the freezing water getting adzed logs in place and bolting them to the rocks; perhaps putting up with abuse from passing diggers because the crossings weren't ready for them. The men came marching out of the gorge and refused to have any more to do with it. Blake made new arrangements with contractor Wright and the footbridges were ready when Charlie Flowers came through with the first mail.

In the gorge the thunderclap of gelignite explosions reverberated in the hills as men with hands clapped to ears blasted the roadway out of solid rock. They showered the river-bed below with broken metal and shattered the icicles which for much of the winter festooned the sunless depths. Somewhere above them other men with picks and shovels were benching out the diagonals and hairpin bends of the Zigzag.

Walter Blake treated Thornton's ideas for getting down into the gorge as Thornton had Dobson's. His plan was to take the road down the spur in a series of spectacular zigs and zags. With modifications and extensions forced by nature's whim this is still the route, but it will always have something of a temporary flavour about it.

Stories of the hardships being suffered by the road gangs on the pass began to filter back to Christchurch. *The Press* did its best to make wheelbarrow navvies look like heroes in the eyes of its readers. In a July editorial it said:

It may be a consolation to us to gather from the history of the past that whenever Providence has designed a people to a great destiny it hardens and trains them in youth to great achievements by surrounding them with great difficulties and giving them great tasks. What the mountain passes have been to Switzerland, and the encroaching ocean is to Holland, these Alps of the Middle Island are to Canterbury, and our people are called from the comparatively easy and level life of the plains to grapple with the spirits which preside over the mountains, crags, glaciers, and torrents.

Vicarious participation in the enterprise might have squared a few shoulders in Canterbury drawing rooms, but if the intention

was to stiffen the resolve of workers on the snowswept pass the newspapers should have given some account of the actual hardships or the immense difficulties of the task. Throughout the construction period almost nothing was printed to convey to the population in general the trials the men were enduring.

Instead both papers continued to belittle the Arthur's Pass project and strongly advocate the merits of Browning's Pass up the Wilberforce. *The Press* said it would not be at all surprised to see a railway running to both sides of Browning's Pass within a year or two, with passengers and freight being hauled to the summit using power generated by an adjacent waterfall! *The Lyttelton Times,* as always unalterably opposed to the Waimakariri route, described it as "this road with two mountain chains to cross, a troublesome path through the upper Waimakariri, a glacial moraine which one engineer says should be tunnelled through, terminating in a chasm which has yet to be circumvented in some manner not yet known".

Good progress was being made, however, in spite of adverse weather and hostile newspapers. By July 1 horses could pack supplies as far as Candy's Bend. Trudging over the divide pass in mid-July came a large official party — Mr Hall, Mr Dobson, the Rev Mr Buller, Mr Drummond, Mr MacPherson, Mr Shearman (Commissioner of Police), and Sergeant Beatty. The first two were there to inspect the work, to assure themselves that Smith was on schedule (the three contractors were always Mr White, Mr Wright, and Smith), and to let to Wright a contract for the Otira Gorge road, which at that stage was still only a bridle track.

That it was an effective bridle track was already proved during their visit by an event which must have made them wish they had continued on their horses. It happened that as they approached Arthur's Pass from the east two men named Corke and Thompson were leading their horse up the Otira valley from the west. Some deserters from the gorge job assured them the track was passable, and next day they made history by arriving at Bealey with the first horse to cross the Southern Alps. The official party passed them on the way.

Dobson and Hall were concerned with the apparent lack of progress on the West Coast section of the road, and took what steps they could to hurry things along. Reporting back to the Superintendent ("I have the honor to be, Sir, your Honor's obedient humble servant''), Hall rose-coloured his observations and expectations — there was only half a mile of soft ground in the whole distance (nearly all the bush section fell into that category), Smith would have the cart road to the summit finished in six weeks and Wright the gorge section by September's end, and the whole road should be open for coach traffic by mid-November. (It was March before coaches could get through to Hokitika.)

He and Dobson returned from the Coast via Browning's Pass, a formidable tour de force for two middle-aged men in the depths of winter. At least they showed that *they* were not afraid to "grapple with the spirits which preside over the mountain crags". They recommended that Browning's Pass be developed as a stock route rather than a road.

In July Walter Blake had 450 men working on his Kowai-Otira section, strung out along 100km of road, and he was a busy man. "I have had to set out and look after the whole for some time," he wrote, "not getting any assistance before the end of August. The contractors and myself had our hands full. What with bad weather and good accounts from the goldfields, wages had to be raised. All kinds of stores were dear, and very often scarce."

A portion of Blake's work involved keeping up supplies to the front line. Until the track over Arthur's Pass could take horses regularly, all the materials for work on the pass and in the gorge had to be packed in on men's backs, usually in rain which frequently turned to sleet and snow as winter tightened its grip.

Back from the West Coast, Commissioner Shearman described it as "one vast goldfield", and predicted that the coming summer would see 50,000 men at work on the diggings. The returns showed that 405,000 pounds worth of gold had been gained to date. In anticipation of increased passenger traffic when the road opened, Cobb & Co. landed 21 new coaches from America, and advertised a direct Christchurch to Hokitika service — passengers travelled 140km by coach and walked the rest!

When John Hall returned he criticised the road over Porter's Pass and said it should go up the northern side of the leading spur, a work which was completed a few years later. Better still, he considered, was the possibility of taking the road through the Waimakariri Gorge, which would shorten the distance by 9.5km and avoid Porter's Pass altogether. But when Edward Dobson had one of his men, F.N. Gale, survey the route, the cost was found to be prohibitive and the proposal was shelved. The chief obstacles, as the railway builders found in due course, were Staircase Gully and Broken River, both of which would require expensive bridges. The total cost of the 35km road from the Kowai to Craigieburn (Flock Hill) was estimated at 60,000 pounds. Dobson recommended instead the new line up Porter's Pass at a cost of about 3500 pounds.

Now the weather set new records in hostility. Walter Blake reported that work was possible only on occasional days. "We

Home At Last

Two of the men who worked on the Canterbury section of the West Coast Road were named Stevenson and Carson. When they left for the back country they arranged for their wives and families to share a house on the outskirts of Kaiapoi. After about six months of back-breaking toil on the road, swinging picks and shovelling spoil throughout that frightful winter, the time came for them to return home. Saving money in the upper Waimakariri was easy — there was nothing much to spend it on — and they brought back with them a considerable sum with which to begin life anew on the plains. They looked forward to a warm welcome from their spouses.

But the women would have nothing to do with them. Seeing two rough, bearded strangers approaching across the fields one afternoon, they fled inside and barred the entrance. The men hammered in vain on the door while their wives cowered inside, fearing the worst. Only with much shouting and declaration of good intent were they able to establish their identity. Eventually the wives, persuaded at last that all was well, opened the door to a joyful reunion with their husbands, barely recognisable after such a long and arduous sojourn in the mountains.

have had heavy rains, hail, thunder and lightning, and last night (August 16) the heaviest fall of snow for the season." Materials for the Bealey bridge were assembled and construction was about to start. The greater part of the Zigzag was benched out and turning points made instead of level platforms at the sharp bends. Blasting was now at a forward state at all difficult points in the Otira Gorge and the dray road was rapidly materialising, he said.

Jack Smith and his men, working mostly on the pass, had the worst of the weather, exposed as they were to the full fury of winter's storms. The gradients for this section had to be laid out at a most unpleasant time, when the snow was unusually deep. The men often spent the whole day clearing it away, only to find next morning that all their work had to be repeated. Retaining walls in the Bealey Gorge were built with boulders taken from the riverbed, which at the same time improved the waterway. Men were paid 14 shillings for a six-hour day on this job — an unheard-of rate of pay for labourers then — "as so few men would stand in the icy river to do the work".

The first week of September, thought by many to herald the coming of spring, was beautifully fine; the sunshine put fresh heart into everyone. But the respite was short-lived. The rain and snow returned, worse than ever. Men working on the benched track in the gorge could thumb their noses at the flooding river rushing past below them, but up top the roadmakers had to contend with great flows of water from the hillsides along the whole length. Work was often impossible and progress was minimal. A man seriously injured by a falling boulder had to be rushed across the swollen rivers and on to Christchurch hospital.

Hazards of travel *on the West Coast Road.* **Left:** *Rough Creek at Arthur's Pass was certainly rough on this motorcar of the 1920s caught by rising flood waters.*
Right: *Many a motorist had his plans turned upside-down. This man is probably watching his engine's sump pouring oil on troubled waters.*
Canterbury Museum   Weekly Press

Paddy's Bend, *high above the Waimakariri between Corner Knob and Cora Lynn, is still as dangerous and troublesome as it always was. Here modern machinery clears a slip which closed the road in the early 1980s. About this time a motorist was killed when his car skidded and left the road for the river below, and much earlier King Cobb himself, Hugh Cassidy, nearly met the same fate. As John Rountree, the coach driver, told it in his memoirs: "One night while going round the Why Mack cutting there was a rock down in front of him, wedge shape. The coach capsized, lay on the road with the top hanging over the side. Cassidy got a good shaking and the horse was crippled."*

In today's world of workers' rights, pay and privileges, it can be wondered what persuaded men to continue with this job when steady work was to be had nearer home, or the wheel of fortune on the goldfields promised a good turn. Some worked at it for more than six months, often wet through for days and nights on end, enduring the constant rain and snow, sometimes on short rations, unpaid for days too wet for work, and for wages only marginally higher than elsewhere. As Edward Dobson said later, "No pen can describe the sufferings endured by both man and beast during that terrible winter, exposed to sleet and snow and bitter frost, hardly lodged and scantily fed."

A great many deserted, of course, but those who remained must have found compensation in the companionship and bravado of their fellows, conscious that they were all working together on the most testing construction job in the country. Perhaps there was also a sense of being a part of colonial progress, or an extraordinary 19th century loyalty to the job, or perhaps just a stubborn determination to see it through, whatever the odds.

In early September the most exciting news was that three men had returned to the city with over 100 pounds weight of gold between them. A fresh rush set in. Idle bystanders derived much amusement from standing on the Victoria Street bridge watching new chums preparing to leave, packing their assorted belongings into drays. In a week three different parties, each of about 70 men, left on the long journey to the Coast. They must have faced fearful hardships, because there was heavy snow along the whole route. The road between the plains and Arthur's Pass was barely useable and Cobb & Co. were hard-pressed to handle their share of the traffic. When heavy rain fell later on the pass, a tarn there called "Lake Wretchedness" rose 10 feet above normal and the road had to be rebuilt round it. In the gorge the water was frequently up to the bearers on the bridges.

Whatever controversy lingered on concerning the road was refuelled on September 23 when a correspondent of the *Times* signing himself "Gaultier Berger" declared that it would cost fifteen pounds a ton to transport goods overland from Christchurch to Hokitika, compared with only five pounds a ton from Melbourne. "The idea of supplying the place from this side is madness," he wrote. The *Times,* by now resigned to the Otira route, replied with a long editorial in which no attempt was made to refute Berger's figures; but in a great many words the newspaper gave all the right reasons for building the road, the gist of which was that narrow considerations should not obstruct the long-term benefits of a highway joining Canterbury to the West Coast. "The road was not for gold alone."

By now Bealey was a thriving town of houses and tents with 120 residents. There were streets named Albion, Erin, Caledonia and Cambria running east and west, and St. David, St. Patrick, St. Andrew and St. George running north and south — a mixture calculated to provide the right address no matter where in Great Britain one's loyalties lay. Sawmillers were busy in the bush preparing timber for dwellings. Two policemen were resident, as was a highly-paid doctor named Stedman (succeeded in December by a Dr. J.S. Caro), whose salary was provided equally by the road contractors and the Government. Khull & Jones had earlier added an accommodation house to their store.

Upon this scene, on October 8, burst the large and jovial figure of Julius Haast, the Provincial Geologist. He came driving up the Waimakariri in his dogcart and over the pass to Wright's camp in the Otira Gorge — the first man to take a wheeled vehicle across the Alps. He was accompanied by H.L. Holmes, the Provincial Meteorologist, his friend John Enys, and some spare horses and men. The dogcart had to be left at Wright's, from where Haast continued his journey on horseback to the coast and back to Canterbury by Browning's Pass, which he thought impossible for a road.

Although there were many parts which would be sub-standard for months to come, the big push to get the dray road built over Arthur's Pass and down the Otira was plainly nearing its conclusion. Realising this, Walter Blake hastened to put 120 men on the Paddy's Bend cuttings, widening the bridle track there, west of Corner Knob. Some of the bluffs high above the Waimakariri were precipitous, and building the road round them was a difficult and dangerous undertaking.

Smith, contrary to all earlier fears, completed his section over Arthur's Pass on schedule, while in the Otira his co-contractor Wright was fast reaching a similar conclusion. Walter Blake detailed all this with some pride in a despatch sent to John Hall on October 25 in which he said:

By the foregoing information you will see that the West Coast Road may be said to be open for traffic as far as Mr E. Blake's camp at the junction of the Otira and Taramakau tracks. There is now no obstacle to drays going through. Taking into consideration the rough weather that is generally experienced in the high ranges combined with the difficulty of getting supplies and making roads in mountainous country, I consider the contractors have been very energetic in pushing their works to get them so near completion in so short a space of time, it being now scarcely three months since the road over the main range was commenced.

This was unquestionably a great achievement, but several months would pass before the whole road was complete and the coaches dashing into the main street of Hokitika. As John Hall realised belatedly the Bealey was a trifle compared with the Taramakau. Walter Blake could look with pride and satisfaction on what he and his men had achieved in the Waimakariri, but his brother Edwin would be fighting a near-lost battle in the West Coast bush for a long time yet.

One of the roadmen *whose task it was to keep the West Coast highway open poses sturdily before his ramshackle hut at the bush edge in Bealey Valley. That same bush supplied the firewood he needed to warm the chill of what must have been very long, cold, and lonely nights.* Canterbury Museum

Part 2:
Roughing It on the Coast

Except for brief fine spells, the forested hills of Westland were draped with rainclouds for most of Edwin Blake's time there. He was a Canterbury man, accustomed to firm terrain and minimal rainfall, and found it hard to acclimatise. His problems were enough to depress any man, even one invested with his brand of sincere determination.

For a start there was supply. Everything needed for the work had to be carried laboriously over Hurunui Saddle and down to his camp in the Taramakau, or up the valley from the coast. The poor work-worn horses used for this task, short of feed and often up to their bellies in mud, gradually deteriorated until they fell exhausted by the wayside. Their carcases littered the upper valley tracks. A horse could not carry as much feed as it could eat, in addition to its load, from Waitohi to Blake's camp and back again. The only alternatives were to pack supplies on men's backs or rely on Maoris and canoes on the river—a method which saw many a precious load capsized and lost.

Blake made frequent trips to Hokitika to buy stores but the gold rush was fuelling inflation and prices were always higher than on his previous visit—on one occasion by 25%. Stocks of food in camp were often threatened by mobs of starving diggers travelling one way in hope or the other in despair. They descended on his camps like locusts and devoured everything edible.

Another worry was labour, for which there was stiff competition from the diggings. Prospects of quick riches on a nearby goldfield crumbled many a good man's work discipline; his itchy feet did the rest. In desperation Blake fixed rates of pay which would have made Christchurch labourers water at the mouth, but the disproportionate number of very wet days when no work could be done, plus John Hall's unyielding "no work, no pay" edict, eroded most if not all the advantage.

Still another concern was the shortage of reliable and experienced contractors. Blake was hard pressed to get even a bridle track ready for the proposed mail service scheduled to start on July 1. On June 15 he wrote to the Secretary pointing out that most of the work was too formidable to be contracted for "by men who have only worked as they have been told".

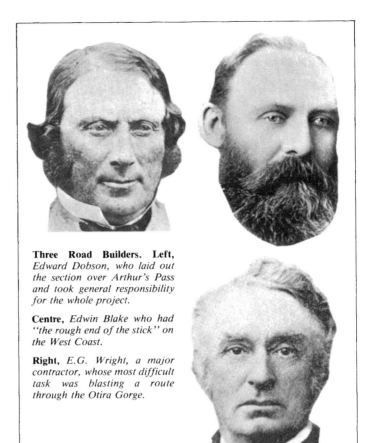

Three Road Builders. Left, *Edward Dobson, who laid out the section over Arthur's Pass and took general responsibility for the whole project.*

Centre, *Edwin Blake who had "the rough end of the stick" on the West Coast.*

Right, *E.G. Wright, a major contractor, whose most difficult task was blasting a route through the Otira Gorge.*

They were not up to the task of organising road-making through such rough, heavily-timbered country, where there were "so many awkward creeks, large rocks, no end of dead trees, and roots that stand several feet out of the ground".

The fourth difficulty was the weather. Frequent heavy rains stopped work for days on end, flooded rivers, and made travel hazardous. Blake soon learned to live dangerously. One of his letters concluded: "Could you send another map of the country below the Taipo. I had to swim the Taramakau twice on Friday and everything in the shape of paper got wet."

That letter was some time getting away by messenger because the rivers were still up and rising. Blake kept adding postscripts

In the Lower Otira Gorge *the road had frequently to be supported on logs tied into the face when rock removal was too difficult for pioneer road builders. Some of this road is still "one way". Note coach wheel tracks in fresh shingle.*
Alexander Turnbull Library and Canterbury Museum

52

Repulsing the Ruffians

Edwin Blake was so beset by trouble on the West Coast that in September, 1865, he threatened murder unless he got police protection. He and his men were continually fighting with ruffians for possession of their food and shelter; one very wet night a mob rushed him and commandeered his tent. In desperation he wrote to Secretary of Works John Hall declaring that if nothing was done soon he *"would have to be accountable for some dead men"*.

This dramatic threat brought the immediate appointment of two policemen, but no end to the supply problems which had always plagued Blake on the Coast. Hall ordered that every Monday morning two drays loaded with flour, bacon, sugar and other essentials be sent, and when the drays were unloaded they were to be used for shingling the road. The depot at Arthur's Pass would also be fully stocked to cope with an expected influx of diggers from 17 Melbourne ships arriving at Lyttelton.

But Hall's instructions coincided with exceptionally heavy falls of snow all along the route. The drays could get no further than Porter's Pass, so Blake's famine continued. He went foraging for flour and managed to borrow some from Wright's camp in the Otira. With this he kept his gang going on short rations for another month until at last the loaded drays came over the passes.

as he waited: "Monday: thunder and heavy rain, no one can leave camp." "Tuesday: raining in torrents, river very high." "Thursday: thunder and rain continuing, river a sea, short on provisions." "Friday: still raining ... turning to snow."

Before the weather lifted, five of his best men had decided to move on. The picture was depressing—Blake in his tent in the black, rainswept wilderness, writing might late into the night so that the men leaving in the morning might take his letter with them: "I am rather run for time. It is now 3 a.m. and I am a little the worse for wear for a day or two. I must leave off, no candle in camp, and the slush lamp I have is so bad that I really cannot see."

Hall, perhaps realising that Blake was close to breaking point, replied immediately with words of encouragement. "The Government is much pleased with your proceedings," he wrote, suggesting that more men be put on if that was possible. From Hokitika a few days later Blake wrote to say that good men were as scarce as everything else in that hostile environment. "I have not succeeded well in getting men," he wrote. "The diggings are rather brisk at present and my prices don't seem to suit. I shall take back a few and I dare say may be able to make up with callers." Poor Blake, standing in the rain beside the track soliciting passers-by with a 12-shilling a day offer in one hand and a shovel in the other!

Returning to his Taramakau camp after one visit to Hokitika, Blake struck six days of unceasing rain and was forced to swim three swollen creeks, a rather chilly procedure in late June. His packhorses were "done up" after weeks of constant work and no corn, and he proposed to get the stores transported by canoe as a last desperate measure.

In July John Hall and Edward Dobson arrived to see what could be done better, but apart from instructing Blake to employ all the men he could find at good wages the visit had little result except in the matter of a bridge over the troublesome Taipo River, for which they promised to call tenders immediately. Returned to Christchurch, Hall could only assure the Provincial Council that the contractors were doing their best in the exceptionally difficult circumstances. They were listed as follows: Otira to Taipo, Edwin Blake; Taipo to Kaiwhaka, Armitage and Anthony; the next seven miles, McClintock; the remainder to the sea, Alexander Aitken.

From this it might be thought that Blake was already at work on his section but he was two months away from that, busy "setting out" for the other contractors, keeping everyone in food and shelter, and wrestling with the labour shortage. "The news from the diggings is beating us," he wrote on August 20 as

more of his best men left. But help was at hand. On the Victoria Street bridge in Christchurch a sign was hung advertising vacancies for road-building construction labourers, apply Works Department, Government Offices, Durham Street.

Applicants for these positions were given some rations and a pound note and told to report to Edwin Blake at his Taramakau camp. Some of them must have wondered where that was, but they set off bravely to walk the 190km or so across plains and mountains, buoyed as they went by the prospect of earning 12 shillings a day.

By this means in the space of a week or two the labour famine became a feast. Suddenly Blake had 120 men on his payroll, but he was far from pleased with some aspects of that. "About five in every seven that come from Christchurch are useless and are only eating good men's rations," he wrote back with some urgency. "I am so overdone with men that I have been obliged to send a lot of needy hands back to Christchurch. I have given 15 of them a pound each to go back. Many of them I know of old, and if I had not one hand here, I still would not employ them."

This brought a sharp response in Christchurch, where one J.E. Walker wrote to the *Times* to say that he and some companions were among those who had gone to the Taramakau, only to be paid to go home again. It had taken them 13 days to make the journey there and back. His landlord, said Walker, was looking to this employment to pay his rent arrears, and now he was to be turned out of house and home.

The *Times* bristled with indignation. The Government's action was incomprehensible, it said. It was so fond of dilating

Wallace's Point *in Otira Gorge—an engraving from the* Illustrated N.Z. Herald *of June 28, 1876. The scene may have been the result of the disastrous 1874 flood during which the river was dammed by a slip, and when the considerable lake thus formed burst through, it swept away most of the road and bridges. The remains of one of these bridges shows at left, while travellers cross on a temporary structure.* Alexander Turnbull Library

upon its poverty, yet seemed to have enough money to pay men to go all that way and back again, and all for a lark. Of course the *Times* overlooked the labour shortage in Canterbury, where Walker and his friends could easily have made the wherewithal for their rent had they been worthy of their hire.

As it happened, the unpredictable ebb and flow of men to and from the goldfields fixed the labour problem without help from head office. "Men are rushing up here from the diggings as fast as from town," wrote a somewhat bewildered Blake on August 31, continuing:

There must have been 200 last night. What could I do with such a crowd? I got rid of a great many this morning, but now I am dead beat again as I have got all my stores eaten to the last mouthful when I thought I was getting a little ahead with them. The packhorses have just come in with tools; I must race them back again for stores. I don't think I will be able to keep going, but I will try until I hear from you. The weather is atrocious, with continual rain, and [the men] all arrive without tents. I will not trouble you with any more complaints. I am ashamed of these. I rather expect you will be sending me a reprimand or someone to supersede me, but you can send no one who will be more honest or determined to do their best ... such a mess as I am in with mud, men, and grumbling you will have seldom seen or heard.

But, he added almost as an afterthought, the work was going well. And indeed there were improvements. By early September, Blake could let several contracts to working parties. He badly needed a surveyor and George Dobson wasn't available. The substitute sent turned out to be a dud and the men refused to work with him. "They are nearly all leaving," he had to write yet again, adding his usual postscript that it was still raining.

But that was only temporary. The springlike fine weather of that first week in September cheered everyone. Soon Blake could move his gang upriver and start on his own Otira-Taipo section of the road. He found it a relief to be staying at last for long periods in his own camp, "after having to be everywhere at once owing to the men always commencing work at my heels while setting out the track. If the weather would improve I would hope to do six miles of road in a month."

But of course the weather didn't improve. If anything it worsened. The Taramakau rose higher than ever, and another man drowned in the Taipo, a shoemaker from Northampton named Joseph Adams. Poor Adams, there was nothing like the devil river where he came from. The continual cold and damp were forcing some of the older workmen to leave "with the rheumaticks".

Came October with more rain and floods. Blake's men continued to grub, hack and saw their way through the sodden bush. And now there was another death—a tree fell unexpectedly and killed John McGrath, one of his best workers. The accident was caused, Blake thought, "by the men being wet through and loaded with mud, they cannot move as quickly as they otherwise would". Demoralised by this misfortune the gang sheltered in their tents while Blake made a rough coffin and waited for the Sergeant of Police to arrive.

But the sergeant couldn't get across the river and McGrath had to be buried without the formalities. The sad little ceremony somehow survived the deluge. Two days later yet another man was drowned in the Taramakau, but his two companions managed to escape the river's clutches. All told six drownings were recorded in one week.

A quick inspection trip to the Arahura showed Blake that the contractors below him were making better progress than he was. As October came to an end, he pushed on with what he called "double power", determined not to be the one to delay the official opening. "I am making the road of timber and metalling over it. I don't fear them [the other contractors] if I can get out of the Otira bush as then I will have a good bottom in most places and the rain won't affect me so much."

Almost every week brought its flood now. Except during the heaviest downpours the men had learnt long since to work on in rain. On November 7 Blake thought the river was higher than he had ever seen it before. The boat at Taipo was washed away and lost, and people on opposite banks stared at each other for two days. A week later the mailman couldn't get through, and still another man drowned. Traffic coming east included the usual

Flood Devastation. *This etching from Reid's* Rambles on the West Coast *was probably made after the 1874 flood, and clearly shows how thoroughly the Otira Gorge road was washed away, leaving only some of the logs fixed in the rock walls as supports for the roadway.*

quota of hungry men returning from the diggings. Blake fed some of them if he thought they needed it badly enough.

And so, step by muddy step, the work went on. Drays with supplies began to come through the Otira Gorge. They were quickly unloaded and pressed into service to carry metal for the road. He finally got out of the "cursed bush" and on to open and firmer ground, and his "incessant turmoil and muddle" began to disperse. The rush of people on the track eased off from that first week in October when 500 men and one solitary woman passed through. In Christchurch the works staff scurried round and hired a dozen extra teams and drays and sent them over. One day in early December the toilers on the road stood aside to watch the Gold Escort come prancing through on its first and only run to the Coast. The weather improved for a while and Christmas was coming.

But then on Tuesday, December 19, the cursed rain started again, heavier and more constant than ever, and continued almost without pause all that week. By Friday the rivers were running bank to bank and shortly, as Edwin Blake described it, "from hill to hill, washing away islands and bringing down timber at an incredible rate". On Saturday the downpour increased further and by Sunday every creek was a raging river and every waterfall a sight to see. The mightiest flood the Blake brothers had ever known came sweeping down from the mountains, "rolling 10-ton boulders along", according to Walter, "like so many marbles".

This was the great Christmas Day flood of 1865 which, far down the Waimakariri, swamped Kaiapoi Island and threatened Christchurch. All hands in the gorges scrambled to safety and watched awestruck while the torrents swept past with a thunderous roar, as much caused by the rumble of hidden boulders carried down in the flood as by the fury of the waters. When after several days the rivers returned to normal, in some places nothing remained of the road they had toiled so long to build except where it was above flood level or benched out of solid rock. Three bridges in the Otira Gorge were wrecked beyond use and one in the Bealey (which had been built 3m above supposed flood level) had disappeared altogether. It was a salutary lesson for Canterbury road builders in mountain country.

George Dobson's prophetic words in his first report that the road would have to be rebuilt after every flood had come true already. A fresh contract had to be written for E.G. Wright to carry out this reconstruction, and another to make the cutting round Rocky Point in the Taramakau. Meanwhile all contractors pressed on with flood repairs and then through the summer months with the work of completing their sections of the road. On February 6 a man named Archer arrived in Hokitika with a dray carrying two women and two children and his possessions. He had come all the way from Invercargill.

The great dray road was open at last.

The first coach to complete the journey from Christchurch to Hokitika arrived on the afternoon of March 15, 1866. Driver William Crawley's sole passenger was none other than William Sefton Moorhouse, Canterbury's second superintendent. How he came to be there, a week ahead of the official "first" coach, with the road barely ready, was never explained. At Waimea Hill where workmen were still making a cutting, his journey came to a halt. Moorhouse disembarked and addressed the workmen, whereupon they gave him three hearty cheers, took out the horses, and carried the coach bodily to firmer ground.

Moorhouse, who represented Mount Herbert on the Provincial Council, had also been nominated for Westland, and he was present to further his candidature in the forthcoming elections. On arriving at the Shakespeare Hotel at Hokitika he addressed such electors as gathered to listen, but faltering, had to apologise for his fatigue resulting from having come so far that day. The fact that he was the first to arrive by coach gave his presence an extra lustre which may have helped defeat his opponent, William Shaw, proprietor of the *West Coast Times,* by 202 votes to 162.

A smaller coach, carrying mail and driven by John Knox, arrived two days later, and a few days after that the official party came through. This included Superintendent Bealey, Provincial Engineer Dobson, Secretary for Works Stewart, and Commissioner of Police Shearman. "The brilliancy of their exploit," said the *Times,* "was somewhat dimmed by their having been preceded by Mr Moorhouse, but as Mr Bealey was something of a rarity in Hokitika, his appearance there would be a wonder in the streets."

In an address delivered later that year, Edward Dobson said:

The Otira road is a remarkable work; whether we consider the grandeur of the scenery through which it passes, the geological interest of the Alpine district which it traverses, the engineering difficulties attendant upon its construction, or the hardships manfully endured by those engaged on the undertaking, it is in every way a work reflecting great credit, not only on the Canterbury province, but on all New Zealand.

Westland County Council, *always opposed to the notion that it should pay to maintain the West Coast Road, set up this tollgate at the entrance to Otira Gorge to help finance the work. "Every horse, mule or other animal" was charged at the rate of two shillings and sixpence (about $8 now). The tollkeeper pictured here was W.C. Wells, with son Johnny, a bright lad who collected ferns for his father to dry and sell as fern books to travellers. The* Press *took strong exception to the tollgate, which it said was illegal, and in 1883 the Upper Waimakariri Road Board called on the Government to remove it from "a road maintained by Colonial revenue".*
Alexander Turnbull Library

Gratifying "Christchurch Vanity"

West Coast tempers ran hot in 1865 over the building of the Christchurch-Hokitika road. The Coasters expressed themselves as perfectly satisfied with their established connections by sea, and saw no need for an expensive highway across the Alps, especially when they were expected to pay for what everyone knew was by far the most costly part.

In the spring of that year advertisements appeared in the majority of New Zealand newspapers (apparently inserted by the Canterbury Provincial Council) inviting the commercial world to conduct its business with the Coast through Christchurch. The road, claimed the advertisements, was open for 105 miles and the remaining 50 could be performed on horseback without difficulty.

This statement, said the *West Coast Times,* was a lie, otherwise why had the mailman to walk most of the distance, carrying 40lbs of mail on his back? In addition a gold escort was proposed — "another costly toy for the gratification of Christchurch vanity". And on top of the absurdity of constructing the road, the Christchurch public was currently advocating "an additional monument of folly and extravagance—a railway!"

Time passes. Today 750 vehicles a day on average travel the road across the mountains, while the railway carries half a million tonnes of freight a year, mostly coal for export from Lyttelton but with a useful proportion of general freight going both east and west. With its high scenic value, the popularity of the road will no doubt increase if and when the Ministry of Works completes the massive task of raising the highway to Class One. This work could include extensive reconstruction of the Zigzag section and certainly the blasting of a two-lane passage through the solid rock of the lower Otira Gorge.

Michael Cassius, representing West Canterbury on the Provincial Council, entirely disagreed. A Hokitika merchant whose stock-in-trade included gelignite, he was well placed to give eastern complacency a blast. The people of Westland could never forget that road, he told the council, since it would be impossible to delude them into the belief that they had derived any advantage from it other than being graciously permitted to put their hands in their pockets to pay for it. The laughable and utterly ridiculous returns which appeared from time to time, showing passenger traffic between East and West, proved beyond a shadow of doubt the fallacious hopes that had been raised by the road and the outrageous mistake which had been made in constructing it.

But William Rolleston, lately Secretary of the Executive and soon to be Superintendent of Canterbury, was not impressed by such talk. "After listening to the member for Westland," he said, "one felt how true the Scriptures were, for the further you go West, the more convinced you are that the wise men came from the East."

By this time the people as a whole seemed unconcerned with the road's completion and even less with the verbal sniping which attended the event. The newspapers were filled with election notices and reports, and while two columns were needed to detail the annual Canterbury-Otago cricket match, the official opening of the Great West Highway, that golden road to riches and that remarkable work to be admired by all New Zealand, rated only a few inches. Now that it was clear no gold was coming to Christchurch public interest had evaporated like mountain mist on a fine anticyclonic morning.

This transalpine road, eventually to become State Highway 73, has been closed many times since the 1865 Christmas Day flood, sometimes for long periods when repairs were more in the nature of complete reconstruction. Such occasions are too numerous to list, and invariably tell the same tale of torrential rain in the mountains — often combined with melting snow—of bridges damaged or demolished, rock slides blocking the way and traffic disrupted, followed by expensive repairs or restoration.

After the 1874 flood, for example, travellers had to ride horses over the pass from Bealey to Otira for months because of the enormous damage in the gorges. The deluge which fell in the Southern Alps during Easter of that year brought down several big slips which made a dam in the Otira Gorge. Behind this a lake formed which finally burst through the barrier and swept down the narrow canyon carrying all before it, including two bridges and virtually all the roadway except where carved from solid rock. One bridge survived only because it was immediately buried in silt and debris. The line of road was strewn with great boulders and pieces of rock, some two metres high, which had been carried down like so many pebbles.

This was four times in eight years that the road had been wrecked. A growing body of West Coast opinion held that it should be abandoned as too expensive to maintain for the traffic it carried — "a coach runs to and fro twice a week carrying mails and a dozen passengers or so, and a wagon or two pass through occasionally with Canterbury produce for the Westland market". But although Canterbury agreed the road had been an expensive mistake which could only be blamed on the gold fever of the time, it could not accept that the route should be closed.

Between the moraine bank and the top of the Zigzag where the road treads a perilous path across the great slip, engineers have had to take it higher up the mountain slopes in search of more secure ground, and then add still more to the Zigzag to get down again. It is a precarious place, threatened above and exposed below. The other bad trouble spot is at Candy's Creek on reaching the rock gorge, where maintenance of the road and bridge is a never-ending concern.

If the Zigzag is abandoned some day in favour of the west bank, future travellers would be able to look back across the valley and marvel at where the present road descends. Above the whisper of hurried rubber on bitumin their imaginations might let them hear the squeal of brakes on iron-shod wheels, the crack of the coachman's whip, and the "clip-clop" of the horses coming down the old Zigzag. Travel was real adventure then.

This amazing highway even yet holds but a tenuous grip on the mountainside. The great rock bastions of Hills Peak tower above to the sky, a thousand metres up, where live the mountain gods so brashly thrust aside in 1865. They are indifferent lords of earthquake, deluge and avalanche, and unfortunately they can call the tune any time they like.

In 1986 it was announced that the Main Highways Board and the Ministry of Works were considering several alternatives: whether to leave the road as it is, improve it to Grade I, reconstruct the Zigzag, consider the west bank, or abandon the route altogether in favour of Lewis Pass. There have also been suggestions that a rail shuttle service through the tunnel be substituted for the pass section of the road.

"Threatened and Exposed". *An aerial view of the most precarious section of State Highway 73 over Arthur's Pass. From right to left (travelling from Canterbury to Westland) are Pegleg Flat, the "Moraine Bank" up which the road climbs to get round the Great Slip (at the foot of which runs the Otira River) and the Zigzag leading down into the gorge. The grade going down the Zigzag makes it one of the steepest main highways in New Zealand.*

National Park Archives.

CHAPTER FIVE
The Gold Escort

Symptoms of yellow fever afflicted Canterbury for some years before the Great Gold Rush of 1865 sent temperatures skyrocketing. In 1863 there were such strong rumours that *The Press* began prodding the Provincial Government by declaring that immediately a gold rush materialised it should do two things: (1) establish a police escort to bring the gold to Christchurch, and (2) make a road across the Southern Alps with the least possible delay. As the West Coast was then still part of Canterbury the reasonable expectation was that riches discovered there should come east.

So when news of the gold rush reached the city two years later, on the Saturday morning of February 25, 1865, there was no hesitation about sending a posse of mounted police to the Coast on what was thought would be a most lucrative mission. The decision itself was not a difficulty — that lay in the nature of the rough and little-known country which the troopers would have to traverse. Between Christchurch and the Hokitika goldfields stretched the almost impenetrable barrier of the Alps, over which the only known route was a roundabout one from North Canterbury up the gorges of the Waitohi and Hurunui rivers to Hurunui Saddle and down the long and difficult Taramakau River to the coast. It was year's end before the path up the Waimakariri and over Arthur's Pass could be used.

The Commissioner of Police himself, Mr Shearman, mounted on his best horse, led the first Escort. Bystanders in Papanui and Kaiapoi, in that first week of March, raised a cheer for the men as they rode through, horses groomed and buttons polished. A week later they were on the West Coast half way between Lake Brunner and Greenstone Creek, "in a very miserable plight for want of forage for the horses, and on account of the exceedingly bad road which they had travelled". A great part of that "road" was marked by the sketchiest of foot or bridle tracks and for long distances there was no track at all where bouldery riverbeds offered the only path.

Hokitika was producing about 3000 ounces of gold a week when Commissioner Shearman and his men came looking for their share. The banks had already established what they considered a safe and reliable channel for its despatch — by ship to Nelson. They were not impressed with the commissioner's requests or his assurances. It had already been reported that the Escort "appeared to have come to grief on the way over by taking the wrong road, having turned off at Lake Brunner instead of keeping down the river", while another Hokitika correspondent marvelled that they had managed to reach the coast at all considering the "horrible" state of the Hurunui track, "with horses and men continually succumbing to the fatigues of the journey". He added that their affairs appeared to be at a standstill. "They will most likely never be troubled with any gold from this place whilst the steamers are running to Nelson with such punctuality as they are at present."

This was a disappointment. Perhaps the Government had not anticipated the banks establishing themselves so quickly on the goldfield, or their connection with Nelson by sea. The commissioner was forced to accept their decision but he salvaged something from the visit by evaluating the district's needs in the way of police supervision and maintenance of law and order. (The miners were as hard-looking a bunch as might be encountered anywhere but oddly true to a rough code of their own, and not above dealing out an equally rough justice to those who transgressed.)

It was mid-April before the Escort straggled back to Christchurch, rather the worse for wear. Word of their failure had preceded them and the acclaim they might have expected after all their trials was not there. Some called the trip a wild goose chase and some a token gesture by a Government which

should have known better. Others on both sides of the Alps agreed that the bankers were not to be blamed for declining to trust their gold to such a meagre convoy, riding such a dubious trail.

William Rolleston *failed in his efforts to loosen the grip of Nelson bankers on West Canterbury gold. He established the Mount Algidus sheep station (made famous later by Mona Anderson's books) and was said to be a first-rate "bullocky" who made his stubborn charges behave by swearing at them in Latin. Samuel Bealey persuaded him to enter politics and he became Canterbury's last and longest-serving superintendent (1868-1876). Named after him are Mount Rolleston, Rolleston River, Rolleston Avenue in Christchurch, and Rolleston Township.*

While Commissioner Shearman had been twisting arms in the field, Provincial Secretary William Rolleston, hastily embarked on the first available ship out of Lyttelton, was wooing the bank managers in Nelson at the receiving end of the golden chain. In the inner sanctums of the banks of New South Wales, New Zealand, and Union of Australasia he argued Canterbury's case without success. Plainly satisfied with existing arrangements, they were unhelpful and procrastinative. Only one of their number thought a change possible; if trade switched from sea to road, the flow of gold might follow.

The Secretary had to return to Christchurch with little to show for his journey, but the government, still heeding popular demand for a road to rainbow's end and an escort to ride it, already had explorers in the Waimakariri's furthermost reaches looking for a better pass than the Hurunui. Hope was not abandoned, merely deferred. "Wait till the road is completed," trumpeted *The Lyttelton Times,* "then we shall have the gratification of recording that the gold which is now in the hands of the various bank agents and diggers must come to Christchurch, as it is evident that no more will be risked by the sea routes."

Such optimism was infectious, yet no one seemed to have paused for a minute to question how Christchurch could benefit without a vigorous two-way trade across the divide, and whether this could be conducted by road at anything like the freight rates offered by sea. The passage of time was to show that wagons couldn't compete with ships for the transport of gold or anything else of consequence.

The Government pressed on, however, convinced that if they made a good road up the Waimakariri and over the hills to Hokitika a more elaborate and better organised Police Escort must succeed. Six months later as its plans were maturing, the new Provincial Secretary, Edward Jollie, tried again with the bankers. The new Escort, he promised, would carry the bullion in safe keeping and free of charge, for 50 miles by pack horse and the rest of the way by wagon (that being the existing state of road construction), and by wagon all the way within a few months.

The bank managers were no more co-operative than before and seemed now to be preoccupied with the danger from rivers, a subject they had raised with William Rolleston. He probably didn't know much about such things at the time and assured them there were only two rivers to cross. The New South Wales bank manager kept niggling about this. "I understand", he wrote to Jollie, "that you state the only river crossings on the

The Gold Escort *resplendent in their new uniforms. Most of them ended up as policemen on the goldfields.*   Canterbury Museum

entire route are those of the Taipo and Bealey, that both are inconsiderable, and that boats are available in case of need at both places.''

Thus questioned the Secretary raised the number from two to four. "The Bealey is very small," he wrote, "the Otira has to be crossed only once and is also small, the Taipo on which a boat will be in use when necessary until the bridge is built, and the Arahura which is not often flooded and is easily forded." He made no mention of the Waimakariri, the most likely to unnerve a cautious banker. In the long run the omission made no difference — the gold was never put to risk in the Waimakariri but continued always to go by sea to Nelson or Australia. Perhaps the bankers thought the overland route too devious, like the Secretary's explanations.

In August, irked by the slow pace of road-building and escort establishment, *The Lyttelton Times* fired off a blast at the administration:

It is now months since a meeting was held urging the Government to establish an escort. An effort was made, in obedience to this demand, and it is needless to say, ended in a miserable failure. And now again, we are promised an escort in the course of another month or so, some weeks after it is known that private persons have come through with pack horses . . . our Government is totally incapable of realising the importance of the occasion, and our people are too lethargic to raise themselves and compel attention to their wants.

John Hall, Secretary for Works in 1865, was probably right in his published belief that a Government which denied this popular demand would not have lasted long. Three diggers who walked into Christchurch about then, swagging 1800 ounces of the precious metal, were a satisfying example of how things should be done, and a small counterweight to the news that in July 22,400 ounces had been shipped out of Hokitika, gone to Nelson or Melbourne or God knew where — anywhere but Christchurch. Action and enterprise, someone shouted — those were the things most needed at a time like this!

Well, said the active and enterprising coach firm of Cobb & Co., we will bring the gold safely to Christchurch every fortnight for 800 pounds a month (plus some extra costs which would bring the bill to 15,114 pounds per annum, and establishment expenses of another 5000 pounds). The Government turned them down — its own plans were too far advanced. Premises had been secured for men and horses, tenders were called for staging posts at Kowai, Craigieburn, Bealey, and Otira, and applications were invited from "young men anxious to take part in an employment which promises much variety and excitement".

About 35 horses would be needed at first, it was estimated, and more later "as so many would be knocked up on the journey". By September 4, 21 had been bought at prices averaging 40 pounds each, all said to be the best available, although Robert Rickman, a North Canterbury member of the Provincial Council, described them as "such a lot of screws as he

had hardly seen before", and thought half would never reach the coast, and the other half never get back.

But when the men made their first mounted appearance in a parade near the Police Barracks a newspaper commented that they were "a fine, smart-looking corps, well-mounted, presenting a dashing and military appearance". It was noted, however, that the men's boots and pantaloons had not yet arrived, and for the present they would have to parade in ordinary black trousers. No one seemed to be having their anticipations dimmed by a despatch from a West Canterbury correspondent who wrote that people in Hokitika were furious at the thought of the Escort, reported to be costing the province 13,000 to 15,000 pounds a year, which the bankers referred to as ridiculous, as all the gold could be so easily shipped out of Hokitika. On the other hand a recent armed robbery on the goldfields was expected to make people there think again about the advantages of police protection.

On September 26 an Escort wagon left Christchurch laden with stores for the Bealey with two or three men aboard to form the police depot there. It was not a happy trip. Near Springfield one of the wagon wheels seized up or in the terms of the time "became fried". While the driver attended to this mishap the horses started and the wagon was upset. Part of the forecarriage was smashed, the pole broken, and one of the lamps damaged. The expedition had to return to town — "an inglorious end", one newspaper called it.

Despite this throughout October and November the Escort, growing more splendid every day, practised in Bruce's paddock near the barracks and fired off their rifles in the sandhills at New Brighton. *The Press,* contemplating the expectations aroused by this public display, thought the great difficulty was the insecurity of conveying treasure safely through the forests. In part of a lengthy editorial it said:

A simple solution has been suggested: if a small redoubt large enough to hold two men were erected in an ordinary American wagon, the sides being made of iron, and both sides loopholed for musketry, it will be found that the weight of such a structure would be quite within what such a wagon would carry. Two men could be seated within a bullet-proof chamber. If the wagon were attacked, the horses might be shot, and the driver, but the robbers could be shot from the vehicle the moment they showed themselves outside the bush. With such a conveyance it would not pay any gang to attack the escort unless there was a fair chance of getting the gold within a reasonable time, then clearing out with it before they were interrupted. We give the idea to the Government and to the public for what it is worth as a solution to what is a very difficult problem.

This was too much for *The Lyttelton Times,* never slow to score a point off its contemporary. In its next issue came this comment:

One of those brilliant and impracticable ideas which occasionally see light in the columns of *The Press* was given to an admiring public on Saturday morning. "If the wagon were attacked, the horses might be

58

A southerly storm *sweeps angry clouds over the Craigieburn Range as a last sunburst lights Broken River and the main highway bridge.*

Right: *Three historic sheep runs share the shores of Lake Pearson—Flock Hill (formerly Craigieburn) in the foreground, Grasmere at left, and the "new" Craigieburn at right. This picture, taken from above Flock Hill homestead, looks north to Sugar Loaf (centre) and peaks of the Polar Range (left). At left the West Coast Road skirts the lake, and the Craigie Burn crosses the foreground.*

Below right: *On a rougher day the nor'wester brews some heavy weather above the ruffled lake.*

Below: *Flock Hill's home paddock is almost the homestead's front lawn. Hamish Innes turns from his sheep for a moment to admire the view.*

Above: *Mount Wall dominates this view of Craigieburn Forest Park at the head of Broken River. A car-park for visitors to the forest centre shows at left. Above that is part of the Cheeseman skifield on Mount Cockayne, and the road to Broken River skifield zigzags up the last bush spur at right.*

Below: *The road climbs over "Parapet" spur, ignoring the old route round the "Point" at right. Ahead are the mist-shrouded Broken River headwaters and skifield, and at right, above the point cutting, is the road to Craigieburn State Forest visitor centre.*

shot, and the driver." We strongly recommend the bandits to remain *perdus* until night, when they would have immense fun in smoking out the troopers from the iron redoubt on wheels which *The Press* has built. Let the Government have the peripatetic iron redoubt constructed, and copying the treatment of Perillus, who made a brazen bull, and was the first of its victims, let the inventor of the plan be sent with it as *driver*.

With this by-play out of the way, the public was pleased to note that good progress was being made with the Escort buildings along the route. By mid-November relays of horses were going forward to these stations. Questions about the composition of the operation were answered with these details: Present strength: Officers, 1 mounted; sergeants, 1 mounted; constables, 4 mounted, 6 foot; drivers, 1 escort, 1 forage; total strength, 14 men. Horses, 12 saddle, 6 pack, 12 draught, total 30. Wagons, 3 escort, 1 forage. Miscellaneous items included coaches, kits, swords, saddlery, oats, harness, hay, blankets, mattresses, bedsteads, pants, spurs, gold-boxes, handcuffs and carrots.

The great day came on December 5 when the Escort, all preparations finalised, jogged forth on its journey up the Waimakariri and over to the Coast. There were four constables, an inspector, and a sergeant. They mustered at the stables and marched to the riverside opposite the Provincial Chambers. Here they had their picture taken by Messrs Mundy and La'Mert. The escort van was a light American one, painted crimson, picked out with yellow, drawn by four grey horses. A small crowd assembled to view the photographic process and to witness the departure of what was described as "a smart body".

The Escort arrived at Bealey at noon the next day and left again at 2 p.m. for the Coast, being next reported by Edwin Blake, supervisor in charge of construction of the western section of the new highway, cantering along the road he was making through the Otira bush. They arrived in Hokitika on Friday, December 8. *The West Coast Times* had this to say:

Yesterday afternoon the town was taken by surprise by the appearance of a cavalcade of mounted constables, with a goodly number of attendant pack horses, proceeding down Revell Street to the camp. The anxious enquiries of the public as to the meaning of this unwonted spectacle elicited the information that the imposing troupe consisted of "the Escort", which a paternal Government has sent all the way from Christchurch across the intervening range to take charge of the Westland gold, and carry it to the East Coast for clearance and export. When it gets as far as Lyttelton, we believe it is to be shipped to Nelson; and as most of the steamers from Nelson for Melbourne and Sydney call at Hokitika en route, our gold will have the opportunity of performing a pretty considerable circuit, preparatory to its finally leaving these waters. Simple-minded people will find it hard to understand what the profit will be in exposing the gold . . . to accidents by flood and field of the overland passage — to say nothing of the new field of enterprise opened to adventurous bushrangers.

The following Tuesday the *Times* was able to report with some jubilation that the Escort had left town, "taking with it the following quantity of gold: 000,000 ounces". For this there had been, at who knows what cost, an establishment of 11 men, 42 horses, five stations, and four wagons. The editor hoped Messrs Mundy and La'Mert would be on hand when the posse arrived

home to take another picture to go with the first. The irony of the Escort's unprofitable visit was emphasised by a so-called admirer who was said to have presented it on departure with six pennyweights of gold so that it could not be said their effort was without some success.

Nelson needed no persuasion to join in the general derision. The *Examiner* of that city called the Escort a costly piece of folly which had succeeded exactly as had been foretold. The would-be gold bearers had arrived in Hokitika, after all that training and expense, only to be met with jibes and ridicule. It understood the force was to be employed in a police capacity on the Coast, where it would be useful, and it was a fortunate Government which could so easily convert a blunder into a virtue.

On Wednesday, December 14, the Escort was back in Waimakariri country. A telegram from Bealey heralded their return: GOLD ESCORT ARRIVED HERE AT TEN THIRTY THIS MORNING FROM WEST COAST WITHOUT ANY GOLD AND LEFT FOR CHRISTCHURCH AT ONE TWENTYFOUR. When this message arrived at the Provincial Chambers, much concern was generated at what public reaction would be to such disappointing news. A fiasco such as this could not fail to rebound on the Government. Secretary John Hall hurried to compose a statement for the newspapers which would appear simultaneously with the Bealey telegram.

There was not the slightest doubt, he said, that those persons who would be most severe on the Government for establishing the Escort would be those who had been most clamorous for it. The hopes given by the banks had not been realised to the extent expected; but the effort should not be given up at once just because nothing was brought back on the first trip. If the expense, which had been 10,402 pounds so far, had been in vain, at least it would convince those who had been clamouring for an Escort that indeed it was not needed. If such was the case, the men and horses could form a body of mounted police, and the buildings sold for what they had cost. But still the Government proposed to give it a fair trial before finally abandoning it.

An advertisement appeared in the Hokitika *Times* on January 1, 1866, advising that the "Overland Gold Escort" would leave Hokitika for Christchurch twice a month, reaching there in time for the Australian steamers. But the Escort never rode again in that capacity. On January 20, Mr Shearman was instructed to transfer the corps to the West Coast, there to be used as a district escort and for the protection of persons and property. No doubt the young men who had joined the force looking for "variety and excitement" found plenty of both on the wild West Coast. In February the Craigieburn station was let to Joseph Hawdon for 75 pounds a year, and later Cobb & Co. took over the one at Otira at 25 pounds a year. The other two, at Kowai and Bealey, were used as police stations.

The Great Gold Escort Fiasco was for a while a subject of much speculation and criticism but once the Canterbury public had recovered from the disappointment and humiliation of the episode, little further interest was taken in the West Coast or even in the road which the Government was so expensively constructing in that direction.

CHAPTER SIX

Mailbags and Morse Codes

"Neither snow, nor rain, nor heat nor gloom of night stays these couriers from the swift completion of their appointed rounds," wrote Heredotus, referring to the couriers of Xerxes. How well this described the fleet-footed messengers who first carried Government despatches across the Alps. These energetic young men were paid to deliver important messages to Mawhera (Greymouth), Okitiki (Hokitika) and other outposts on the West Coast by whatever means and paths they could find. Although growing fit and fast on the trail they still took a fortnight to get to Hokitika and back, and longer if the rivers were in flood.

When the gold rush hit West Canterbury in February, 1865, one of the most distressing problems for East Canterbury, where the administration lay, was the communication gap between Christchurch and the Coast. How was the Government to exercise control over this distant, unruly, but suddenly wealthy dependency when it took so long to get a letter there and back?

So little was known, so much unknown. Urgent questions, unanswered, furrowed brows in the Durham Street offices. How much gold was being won? How many diggers were on the fields? How successful were they? And, most important of all, what was happening to the gold? By the time the answers to these questions came to hand they were already history, but from all accounts the rush was gaining momentum at an alarming rate, while in Christchurch the long silences were filled with frustration—and they were far from golden. Something had to be done to speed communication across the Alps.

About mid-March the Provincial Council tossed the problem to the Christchurch postmaster, indicating that he should get to work and organise a weekly mail service. That gentleman figured the cost could be at least 1200 pounds a year, which was enough to set the idea to one side for a while. By the end of May, with contractors preparing to push the road over Arthur's Pass, the Government decided to call tenders for the conveyance of mails weekly between Christchurch and Hokitika (travelling time not to exceed four days, weather permitting). The coaching firm of Cobb & Co. won the six-month contract at 700 pounds. Later, having discovered it was further to the West Coast than they thought, they asked for and were given another 350 pounds.

John Hall, the Provincial Government's Secretary for Works, determined that the first regular mail should go through on July 1 although for much of the route there was as yet no track for the mailman to follow. June days were peppered with notes to the Blake brothers, supervising engineers for the road, entreating them to smooth the mail carrier's passage. Men were put into Otira Gorge to adze logs for makeshift bridges. Further west Edwin Blake, who already had a heavy workload trying to cope with Westland bush, floods and weather, had to rustle up a couple of Maoris and a canoe so that the more intractable sections of countryside could be by-passed on the rivers.

Charles Flowers, who carried the first regular mail from Arthur's Pass to Hokitika through 1865's frightful winter, could add to what Heredotus wrote about rain and snow. He had to contend as well with flooded rivers, forest, gorge and bog. Further, long sections of his "appointed round" lay in riverbeds which ran bank-to-bank in flood, forcing him into the bush to fight his way as best he could through the dense undergrowth. He was a paragon of endurance and devotion to duty whose motto surely was "the mail must go through".

The Maoris were to be paid 9 pounds a week between them, canoe included, while another Maori and his horse to ride the beach between the Taramakau River mouth and Hokitika was to cost 3 pounds a week. When the canoe upset and tipped the occupants and mail into the river, the Maoris were asked to

build a better one, but they took so long about it that the through coaches overtook them before it was finished. However, Blake's first priority as July 1 approached was to "get a track made for the mailman as speedily as possible, and render all assistance to the person or persons carrying the mails".

The Secretary was aware the whole project might fail in the Westland forests, or the mailman and his canvas bag disappear altogether in one of the rivers. On June 27, putting his fears on paper, he asked Walter Blake, who was based at Bealey, to "have a man ready . . . who can go with the mailman to Hokitika, shewing him the direct road inland [from the Taramakau across to the Arahura] recently traversed by Mr Blake. If possible the two Maoris should be held ready for this service; the Government will pay them . . .".

The July 1 start was postponed until Tuesday, July 4. At 2.30 o'clock on that morning a light two-horse wagon from the Cobb & Co. fleet left the Christchurch terminus in High Street bound for Willis's accommodation-house at Kowai Bush (Springfield) with the first transalpine Royal Mail. Decree dictated that this was not to exceed 14 kilograms or 1500 letters, but on this occasion it weighed only three kilograms. The letters were tied into bundles of 50 tightly wrapped in water-proofing, and the bundles were packed in another waterproof wrapper and placed in an ordinary canvas mail bag. On many a future trip the mail ended up in the river and was soaked through despite the wrappings—the newspaper at Hokitika recorded having to dry out its despatches in the oven before they could be deciphered!

But on this first journey as far as is known the mail reached its destination in good shape, although its passage was far from smooth. John Knox, one of Cobb's top drivers, took the coach to Springfield and over Porter's Pass to Craigieburn, where fresh horses were waiting. Accompanying them was Captain Morgan Anderson, in charge of Cobb's operations. The road from Kirwee on was little more than wheel marks in the tussocks and the Captain, who had been over the ground a few months earlier with FitzGerald's exploration party, acted as guide. One of the horses went lame on the way and John Enys of Castle Hill lent them a replacement. That evening they made Khull and Jones's accommodation-house at Bealey, after a long and tiring day.

Next morning, Wednesday the 5th, Captain Anderson, having gone as far as he knew the road, returned to Christchurch. The man with the mail, presumably Knox, along with others who had availed themselves of Cobb & Co.'s so-called Christchurch-Hokitika service, pressed on up the Bealey valley as far as they could take their horses, probably to the top of Arthur's Pass where contractor Jack Smith and his men were making the road. There, around midday, they met Charles Flowers and handed him the precious mailbag. By then it was snowing and raining, as was so often the case in the winter of 1865.

Flowers was a remarkable fellow who had been accommodation-house keeper and ferryman at the Rakaia River main south road crossing. Possibly caught up in the excitement of the gold discoveries, he had sold out at Rakaia and joined Cobbs as their West Coast mail carrier.*

Making his headquarters at the Taipo River, he built another accommodation-house and ferried passengers over the river at two shillings a time. Naturally on such an uncertain mail run there were plenty of adventures, including once rescuing a man who had been washed off his horse in the Otira River.

On that first occasion, after saying goodbye to the Christchurch party on the pass, he had a rough trip down the Otira Gorge to

---

*It was a fortunate decision. Six months later the Christmas Day flood completely swept away the house at Rakaia, leaving only bare ground.

contractor Edward Wright's camp. Next morning, with the rivers rising, he pressed on down the Otira and into the Taramakau valley and faced the long and perilous 65km journey to the coast. His progress would be greatly affected by the degree of flooding in both the Otira and Taramakau, and it seems unlikely he reached Taipo that evening. In flood the Taipo was the most dangerous river of all to cross.

Somewhere there Flowers was to meet his two Maoris with the canoe. The rendezvous may have been a difficult one, to such an extent that the canoe ride down the Taramakau may not have started until first light on the Saturday morning, the fifth day. The exceptional speed with which the remainder of the journey was accomplished — 32km down the river and 24 along the beach to Hokitika, all by early afternoon — was within reason. The river section through the Taramakau Gorge on the crest of a flood would be fast and exciting, perhaps taking only two or three hours. And if the third Maori had the horse ready at the river mouth, another hour or two along the beach would see Flowers riding into Hokitika soon after lunch. The elapsed time, Christchurch to Hokitika, was 4½ days. Given good conditions it could have been less.

There was no question of using the short cut mentioned by John Hall, across the Waimea to the Arahura. The track then was only a series of blaze marks through the dense and waterlogged forest. Blake had already gone down the Taramakau in a Maori canoe on June 20 and established this as the best way to reach the coast.

The first return mail, leaving Hokitika on July 10, had an even more hazardous journey. The weather was still bad and the rivers up. After an easy horse-ride along the beach the canoe trip up the swift-flowing Taramakau was a nightmare. It took Flowers and the Maoris three days to accomplish what on the downward trip had taken only a few hours. Progress against the current was painfully slow and achieved mainly in the shallows near the shore. In places in the gorge, where there was no shallow water, the canoe had to be inched upstream against the current by the most vigorous paddling. At one point a capsize threw occupants and mail into the river — Flowers must have taken the precaution of tying the bag to his person, or in the yellow flood it would certainly be lost.

Eventually he could leave the canoe and his Maori friends and begin walking again, but the bad weather continued, with heavy rain often turning to driving snow. On reaching the flooding Otira it says much for his resolve that he continued, especially when he had to cross the river 27 times and the last time had to swim. The water temperature must have been near zero, but as hypothermia hadn't been heard of then he pushed on with stamping a path through snow to the top of the pass. Nobody was there to meet him and he had to continue down the swollen Bealey River to the accommodation-house, after what can only be described as a journey of heroic proportions. The practice of mailmen meeting at Bealey was subsequently adopted as being more acceptable for both parties than standing about in the cold on the pass.

Flowers abandoned the canoe after that experience and used horses to ride overland from Greenstone Creek near the coast. Thus he was able to keep to a more rigid schedule and soon the mail was going each way in four days or less. He would leave Hokitika on Monday evening (after collecting late letters at a lucrative half crown each), and reach Bealey on the Wednesday evening. Another day saw the mail in Christchurch. In a few months, as the road progressed, he rode the whole distance, using the Waimea short cut, soon to be the coach road. The Christmas Day flood put him back on his feet again, literally, when (so he reported) about 24km of road was destroyed.

In March, 1866, the highway to Hokitika was completed. The coaches drove right through in two days and Charles Flowers' duties as mailman came to an end. The residents of Hokitika gave him a complimentary dinner and a cheque for 50 pounds in recognition of his exceptional service.

His successors, the coach drivers, almost immediately began to fashion their own saga of high endeavour on the mail run,

By the road. *A couple of telegraph posts on the road to Arthur's Pass appear at right in this picture of the Craigie Burn as it babbles and bubbles its pretty way down valley to swell the waters of Lake Pearson, with Purple Hill for a backdrop.*

extending over nearly six decades until the railway finally settled all the uncertainties with the efficiency of regular timetabling. Driver Burton was a suitable man to follow in Flowers' footsteps. He arrived at Otira one Tuesday evening in July, 1871, in the face of hurricanes of wind and snow which blew the handrails off the Otira footbridge, unroofed the police barracks and overturned the coach while it was standing in the hotel yard. Similar violent weather kept everyone immobilised through Wednesday but on Thursday, Burton, troubled about his responsibility to the mail, strapped the letters to his back and set out on foot to cross the pass. He found the bridges in the gorge gone, and most of the road, but with a pole managed to ford the river where necessary and, stamping a path through the snow on the pass, splashed his way down the Bealey. According to him it would be a month before the crossing was fit for horses, let alone coaches.

Not so successful at getting through, but not for want of trying, was Hugh Cassidy, who took over Cobb & Co. soon after Lee Cole, the original owner, left New Zealand. Cassidy got the coach bogged down in soft snow one August day in 1878 on the Zigzag nearing the pass, so he unhitched the horses and with a smack on the rump sent them back to Otira. Then he shouldered the mail bags and attempted to force a trail through deep snow across the pass, but after about 8km wading waist deep in places and guided only by the telegraph poles he gave up the attempt and groped his way back to Otira.

On the Canterbury side of the Alps the mail run across the plains and up the Waimakariri valley was much easier and therefore less eventful, as right from the start horses could be ridden all the way. Later, against gales, flooded rivers and deep snow on Arthur's or Porter's passes, there must have been innumerable occasions when coach drivers fought grim battles against the elements, but these are poorly recorded. It can be certain they maintained the tradition that "the mail must go through", even though circumstances defeated them on at least one occasion. The Rev. Charles Clarke, describing a coach trip to the Coast, recalled that near Taipo a man on horseback rode up to the driver and holding up some tattered fragments of paper announced he had found the mail bags which were swept away with the coach in the flood of May, 1876. That was possibly the only time the carriers on the Christchurch-Hokitika run failed to see the mail to its proper destination.

A delightful little postscript is provided by an entry in the diary of E.R. Chudleigh, who often stayed at Castle Hill with his friend John D. Enys. On April 16, 1869, he wrote:

I must mention a wonderful dog here. When the river is high, this dog has the letters strapped to his back in an oilskin. He goes over the river and then on a mile and a half, gives up his letters, and returns with the answers. He is a large, rough collie, hailed as "Postman".

It would appear that "Postman" the dog was possibly more reliable than some of his two-legged carriers. On December 27, 1865, James Clarkin, whose responsibility it was to take the mail from Springfield to Kowai Bush, had to write to his employer, Edward Jollie, the Provincial Secretary, confessing that in trying to cross the Kowai River when it was "up", he had slipped and been swept away, and in the mishap was "compelled to let the Bundle go". As one of the letters was from Mr Jollie himself, Clarkin wrote that he "would be obliged if you could send another one". When it came to swimming flooded rivers with the mail, "Postman" might be said to have had the edge on his human contemporaries, even the redoubtable Charlie Flowers.

The Electric Telegraph

The sorry tidings of the first telegram from Bealey to Christchurch were delivered to an address in Addington on the afternoon of October 12, 1865. There they were conveyed to Mrs Charles Clegg, a mother of two children — her husband had just been drowned, the message said, swept from the leading horse of a dray crossing the upper Waimakariri River. The tragedy had happened only that morning opposite the tent of George Bird, the telegraph engineer. He had sent three men immediately to recover the body while he hastened to send the news along the electric telegraph line just completed over 140km of plains, hills and valleys. It was a sad but dramatic demonstration of the new marvel of instant communication.

George Bird was manager of the Christchurch-Lyttelton telegraph when he received the call from the Canterbury Provincial Government to construct a line from the city to Hokitika. The Colonial Secretary in Wellington had turned down the proposition that Central Government undertake the project, and the local authorities had rejected the offer of a gentleman named William H. Drew that he build it for the revenue over four years to be followed by Government purchase at 90 pounds a mile. Instead the Provincial Council decided to proceed with the job itself. As it happened the Southland Provincial Council owned a quantity of surplus telegraphic materials which were for sale and Bird's first assignment was to travel to Invercargill and finalise a deal there.

He accomplished that satisfactorily but ran into trouble getting his purchases transported to Hokitika. They included

732m of insulated wire, 80km of main line wire, insulators, glass cells, and even a bottle of mercury. Eventually he got them all to Bluff and on to a ship named the *Omer*, but when she arrived off Hokitika on June 29 the weather was so rough it took a week just to get Bird ashore. The cargo had to go on to Nelson, and it was August before it returned. The engineer's waiting time was occupied mainly in searching for a route by which he could string his wire, and pondering how he could get several tons of material distributed along it. There were no roads or tracks, the whole locality seemed to be one impenetrable forest, and he could find no better way than by dray along the beach and up the Taramakau River by canoe. The Maoris, who owned the canoes, were wisely unwilling, and Bird (who knew nothing of the interior) decided to ship himself to Lyttelton and tackle the project from that end.

Back in Christchurch he wrote to Wellington immediately for 160km of No. 8 telegraph wire and 350 insulators, 25 tonnes in all, for which John Jebson tendered 8 pounds a tonne for distribution along the route from Selwyn to Arthur's Pass. (From Christchurch to Selwyn the existing main south telegraph posts were to be used.)

The supply and cartage of poles was the most expensive part of the project. These had to be not less than 76cm long, 20cm diameter at the butt, tapering to not less than 12cm at the top, and could be cut in specified timbers (mainly black beech) from any of the Crown land forests along the way. There were three contracts. The first was of 46km from Selwyn to the Kowai

Highest Telegraph Post. *For years this double post on Porter's Pass was, at 3100ft or 945m, the highest in New Zealand. It was a welcome sight for exhausted male coach passengers who often had to climb the pass on foot if the loading was too heavy.*
Inset: *John Jebson, pioneer Sheffield farmer who played a major part in erecting the telegraph line to Hokitika. The poles came from forests along the way and most rotted away within the decade.*
Canterbury Museum.

River, 10 poles to the km, taken by Jebson at 448 pounds. The second section, 45km from the Kowai to Craigieburn, and the third, 40km from Craigieburn to Arthur's Pass (both at 11 poles to the km) were taken by William Seabright.

This individual, who signed his name with a cross, was a much sharper man with an axe than a pen, and had the whole of his 1252 pound contract for nearly 1000 poles completed by August 31. These were delivered in lots at 400 metre intervals along the route ready for gangs to set them up in holes at least 150cm deep. Bird's first troubles came with these labourers. He was told to pay them a shilling an hour, but after starting the job they struck for an extra threepence an hour, plus provisions, a guaranteed supply of wood and water, and a camp cook. They lost the battle, were sent packing, and for good measure had their names removed from the charitable aid list.

At this point, John Jebson and his gang came to the rescue, taking responsibility for erecting the line, he said, only because every man that Bird engaged refused to be involved on any terms, and in the emergency he was the most likely prospect to get the work done. He contracted to erect the poles from Selwyn to Arthur's Pass for 450 pounds, plus 240 pounds to string the wire, but claimed to be losing on the deal, through no fault of his. It appeared that Seabright had delivered the poles along a route indicated by George Bird but when the work came to be done it was found the line taken was impracticable. As Jebson later complained to the authorities, for nearly 80 kilometres

Jebson must have had a willing team working for him, for by mid-October the line had reached Bealey, and on the 18th the telegraph office there was open for business, hours 9 a.m. to 5 p.m., charges on application. It was not expected that Bealey would do much business but it was an essential link in the maintenance chain. One of its uses on many future occasions was to warn Kaiapoi of floods coming down the Waimakariri. To mark the opening, Bird sent this wordy telegram to Alexander Lean, Assistant Secretary for Works:

IT RAINED HERE FROM THREE PM ON SATURDAY UNTIL SEVEN PM MONDAY VERY HEAVY WITH MUCH THUNDER AND LIGHTNING STOP IT COMMENCED SNOWING AT DAYLIGHT THIS MORNING AND IS SNOWING NOW STOP THE RIVERS ARE VERY HIGH BUT FALLING STOP THE COACH MAY PERHAPS GET OVER TOMORROW MORNING STOP I FORDED THE WAIMAKARIRI THIS MORNING BUT IT WAS IN A VERY SAFE PLACE STOP G BIRD

At Bealey, of course, Bird had to face up to the problem of the Waimakariri and how to get the line across nearly 2.5 kilometres of riverbed in which there was no safe place to sink a pole. He solved this by excavating a "paddock" in the shingle, four metres square and about one metre deep. Four sleepers 4m x 30cm mortised together in the form of a double cross were placed in the bottom of the "paddock", and a pole 9m x 30cm was stepped into the centre and supported by four stays. When everything was bolted together and the hole filled with shingle, it made a fairly stable "cone". Four of these were placed across

Telegraph Construction Camp *at Bealey in 1882 during a major reconstruction of the line. Note side of mutton hanging from a tripod at left.* Canterbury Museum.

poles had to be manhandled "over mountainous valleys and river utterly inaccessible to horses and drays", and 12 tonnes of material had to be carried on foot "through bush, scrub, etc., in country so difficult it was about impossible to execute the work". He put in a bill for an extra 252 pounds, but C.C. Bowen, appointed later as adjudicator, awarded him only 160 pounds.

In the circumstances, the poles went up at surprising speed, averaging 8 or 10km daily. On August 24, wiring commenced from the office in Heywood and Company's premises in Worcester Street, facing Cathedral Square, and was expected to proceed at much the same rate. Work was held up for a while by shortage of supplies when the ship *Mulloch*, ferrying materials from Lyttelton to Heathcote, stranded on the Sumner bar and involved Bird in protracted haggling with insurance companies.

The No.8 wire was strung over enormous distances when required, yet it endured for years in spite of snow loading and fierce local winds. The greatest distances were at the Porter River (562m), the Valley of the Seven Springs (667m), and Broken River (1067m).

the riverbed and the wire stretched from bank to bank in five spans varying in length from 221m to 624m.

But because the poles were too short the wire was strung at excessive tension to keep it above water level and so broke frequently in floods and gales. The 1865 flood tilted one cone downstream, causing a break. Eventually Bird replaced the No.8 wire with "homogeneous steel and iron wire of small gauge, light but of extreme tenacity", and had no further trouble.

In the Bealey and Otira valleys the engineer was concerned that there was no place where (as he put it) he could place a pole and rest assured that floods would not affect it. His fears were justified a few weeks later when the Christmas Day flood felled many of them. In the Otira Gorge, after taking the line straight down the zigzag spur, he put the poles among the big boulders in the river because the hillsides were too steep and the roadway useless. In the flood some were completely submerged, but most survived.

As with the road the most difficult section of the telegraph line was on the West Coast. John Jebson again figured prominently by contracting to supply 12 men (with Richard Jebson as foreman), and horses, tools, provisions and a cook, to erect the line along the West Coast road at 2 pounds an hour. George Bird had left a foreman and a gang at Hokitika when he returned to Canterbury but they had made poor progress. He was not surprised — in some places such as between the rivers Arahura and Taramakau, where matted roots in forest swamps broke many a horse's leg, the best way to dig a hole for a pole was with an axe and a baler.

The Taramakau had to be crossed six times, a troublesome section which in one period of 115 days put the line out of working order for nine days. Much of the West Coast work was done in atrocious weather with rivers and streams almost constantly in flood. The holes filled with water as soon as they were dug. Because of the rain only seven days were worked in one 30-day spell. Even the sea was hostile. Poles along the beach were planted too close to high water mark and for three miles they were washed out in a heavy storm. Transport of provisions and material was so difficult that a tonne of wire at 46 pounds ex store cost 130 pounds on site upriver.

Almost nowhere was Bird satisfied with the line's security. "The further I advance with this work," he wrote, "the more I am convinced of its precarious nature. Floods, falling timber, bush fires, and even strong winds may at any time render it useless, and from the impossibility of getting at the line the interference may be of long duration."

On February 6, 1866, more than a month before the road was opened, the first messages were transmitted between Hokitika and Christchurch, thus linking the previously isolated West Coast with the rest of New Zealand. The total length of the line, including an extension along the coast to Greymouth, was just under 320km, costing 11,029 pounds. In the first eight months to June 30, 5065 messages were transmitted. Revenue was 1552 pounds and expenses 1476 pounds, and the following year the figures were expected to be 6000 pounds and 3000 pounds.

Bird's concern about interruptions was proved right as time passed, for about 10 per cent of which, he had to report, the line was "out of order". *The Press,* complaining in late 1866, declared it wasn't working two days out of three. "Men have to scour the country," it said, "to discover where the latest 'break' has occurred, and to make things straight for another few hours," adding that the character of the country through which it passed was altogether unfitted for the cheap and easy system adopted.

In response to such criticism, John Hall asked Bird to get out a scheme to improve matters, but nothing was done when his estimate added up to 12,547 pounds. In January, 1868, the whole enterprise was taken over by Central Government and incorporated into the national network, whereupon it ceased to be a provincial responsibility.

Breakdowns were probably exaggerated by *The Press,* but obviously the new communication link across the Southern Alps was a fragile one. Not all the breaks were caused by horrendous disasters like the Christmas Day flood. On higher parts snow often froze on the weather side of poles and took the line to earth, especially on that loftiest telegraph post on Porter's Pass. Conversely one interruption between Bealey and Christchurch in December, 1865, searched for extensively in the back country, was found eventually not far from the city where a local farmer had set fire to gorse beneath the wires and melted them.

"A CYCLOPEAN CITY"

"Late in the afternoon we opened on a broad sunny valley, and saw on a distant hillside an assemblage of rocks, some grouped like the buildings of a Cyclopean city deserted by its founders, some standing alone, stern and grim like sentries petrified at their posts; others again looking like the tombs of a colossal graveyard, or the circling seats of a vast ampitheatre; and further still huge groups and solitary masses like the gigantic monoliths of Stonehenge. A wonderful spectacle, overspread as it was with mellow liquid lights that flooded the hilltops, lingered lovingly about the savage crags, and even trickled over into their sombre shadows." — The Rev. Charles Clarke (in R.C. Reid's Rambles on the Golden Coast) *recording his impressions of the Castle Hill limestone country, which travellers find as intriguing today as did the first explorers when they came by.*

CHAPTER SEVEN

When Cobb was King

What high hopes the gold rush fired in 1865! Every week, it was thought, would see the Gold Escort, smartly uniformed and handsomely mounted, prancing home with the bullion to the rejoicing of a people barely able to grasp the magnitude of their good fortune. And every day Cobb & Co. coaches loaded to the limit with passengers and Royal Mail, and the slower wagons of profitable commerce, would travel the new road across the Alps.

Even runholders along the route saw new opportunities and considered building hotels at suitable intervals. The Government established escort stations at Porter's Pass, Craigieburn and Bealey, while Cobb & Co. built staging posts every 25km or so along the way. A town was laid out at Bealey with surveyed streets and sections and another was contemplated at Lake Pearson. Farmers drained and ploughed suitable acres near the highway to grow fodder to fuel the horse power for all this activity.

Unfortunately the idea that the Gold Escort would be the making of Christchurch was only a pipe dream, and the gold it brought wasn't enough to pay for one horseshoe. With that, Canterbury lost interest in the West Coast and traffic through Bealey fell to a trickle. The proposed town at Lake Pearson never was, while that at Bealey diminished until all that was left was a gravestone or two and a hut to shelter flood-bound travellers. The vision of a populated Waimakariri valley retreated almost to what it was before the gold rush — a half-dozen sheep stations, a few hotels and staging posts, the occasional public works camp, and a scattering of roadmen's huts.

The financial commitment required to build the road was formidable enough, but Canterbury then found itself saddled with maintenance costs which gave headaches to provincial treasurers for years. Keeping open this lengthy and fragile highway through such difficult country required road gangs to be constantly at work. Their routine labours were interrupted at intervals by floods which swept down from the mountains and washed away bridges, cuttings, embankments, protective works, and often the road itself. Nowhere was this destruction worse than in the gorge section between Bealey and Otira, where in some years the whole 24km of highway was closed to traffic for months. It was not uncommon to see more men working on the road than passengers with Cobb & Co.

Yet, heavily subsidised with mail contracts, the coaches connected Christchurch and Hokitika for nearly 60 years. The road to riches-that-never-were remained to serve more lasting ends, as a superior stock route by which to supply the meat-hungry West Coast and as a road adequate for those who had to walk, or ride a horse, or drive a cart. But its predominant use was as the thrill-packed highway over the Southern Alps for Cobb's coaches. No passenger plucked from the security and monotony of the plains and seated aloft with the driver on a Concord leather-sprung coach bound for the West Coast could ever forget the excitements of that journey.

It began at Cobb's depot in High Street with the clatter of horses' hooves as the coach dashed along Cashel Street in the pre-dawn darkness — making a showy start before settling down to the long journey across the plains. Round hospital corner stood the first milestone of all the hundred and fifty-seven to be counted off before Hokitika was reached. The year was 1866, the first in which the coaches ran the full distance, but even then familiar landmarks of today were there — the church at Church Corner and the racecourse and its grandstand a little further on.

In the darkness the journey was redolent with sounds and smells — the creak of the great leather straps on which the coach swung, the crunch of iron-clad wheels on the gravel road, and

the smell of horses warming to their work and snorting hot breath into the cold air. If the night was moonlit the passengers could imagine that they were travelling across an open plain of sheep runs, with no visible "improvements", extending on both sides of the road as far as they could see.

The monotony of the eight or nine hours of level travelling, especially the early part in the dark, could be relieved if the driver was as good with his tongue as his whip, and could brighten the tedious miles with anecdote and reminiscence.

Cobb & Company's *Christchurch headquarters on the corner of High and Cashel streets, from where coaches left daily for points north, west and south. This picture shows the premises as they were in 1872, before Hugh Cassidy took over from Mitchell.* Weekly Press

Passengers riding on the rear outside seats tucked their rugs about them and noted the glow of dawn in the east over the Port Hills, while those in front were soon marvelling as the sunrise changed the mountains ahead from sable grey to rose pink.

Soon the coach was pulling up at Watson's Halfway House, 32km from Christchurch, where a substantial breakfast awaited the passengers. With that aboard, the journey continued, occasionally with the wide Waimakariri off to the right, on to Kowai Pass (Springfield), where the horses were changed and the road began the slow climb across the Kowai River and on to Riddell's Inn at the foot of Porter's Pass. By then it was midday and time for a three-course dinner in the little hotel before tackling the mountains immediately ahead.

At the foot of the pass the men clambered down and began walking, while the coach slowly twisted and turned up the narrow road on the shady side of the spur leading to the summit, a steeper grade than any other on the whole route. The ladies rode inside trusting to the skill of the driver to see them safely to the top. All reassembled there on the windswept, barren pass, with some of the gentlemen a little breathless, to hear the driver announce, "This, ladies and gents, is a hundred feet higher than Arthur's Pass, and that there is the highest telegraph post in New Zealand!"

Horses were changed again at The Springs near the old Porter homestead, then it was on again across the great terraces to Castle Hill and Broken River, up Murderer's Creek, past Liverpool Dick and his Black Ball store, over the saddle and down the Craigieburn cutting, through the bush to Mr Hawdon's station and the escort building. Past Lake Pearson and over the Ribbonwood lay Grasmere, and further on, almost on the banks of the Cass River, was a new hotel, and fresh relays of horses.

By this time the weary passengers were inclined to think enough was enough, but they still had to face the run over Goldney's Saddle and round Corner Knob — and the drop to the river which took the breath away. Finally at about 7 p.m. the coach pulled up at Jones's Inn on the south bank of the

Waimakariri opposite Bealey, where the horses were taken out and the passengers trooped inside to pass the night. This place was noted for its good accommodation and meals. The cook was a man who prided himself on his menu and who had a gift for what one passenger described as "ornamental cookery"—he displayed such things as imitation camellias made from turnips and leaves and was delighted if guests were taken in by the cunning of his artistry.

Discovering such talent in that unlikely place might have helped to take the passengers' minds off the concern which weighed on them all—the crossing of the dreaded Waimakariri first thing in the morning. They were all up and about well before daylight for breakfast by the light of a smoky kerosene lantern—mutton chops, naturally. Then it was all aboard and into the river.

Crossing the Waimakariri. Above: *The coach in this much-publicised painting is not the type generally used on the West Coast run, and invariably there were three leading horses.* **Below:** *The reality was much more nerve-racking, especially for those passengers perched on the top seats.*

Canterbury Museum

If the Waimakariri was low there was no trouble. The driver sought the best fords in places where the river flowed in several streams. But if it was in flood this was real adventure. Cobb drivers knew their drill, putting a horseman from the stables into the river first to test the crossing. Only then would the driver urge his team into the flood and, moving downstream with the current, splash a bumpy passage through the torrent to the far bank. There were many close encounters with disaster but amazingly no record of any fatality in all the 50 years the coaches jolted through the river.

At Bealey town across the river stood a store and an inn, and the coach from Hokitika which had arrived the previous evening. Sometimes the crossing was made in a dray, and each coach returned to its home town. About 6 a.m. began the ascent of the Bealey valley to Arthur's Pass, which included 16 crossings of the river. Here, before the steep ascent began, stood John Butler's accommodation house (in 1866 at least).

By now the outside passengers were hardened veterans of mountain travel and fully accustomed to the swaying of the coach as it splashed through the fords and climbed towards the pass. The long pull up the Bealey Gorge through the bush was enlivened by glimpses of flowers, waterfalls and mountains close

Reid's Fall. *No picture conveys better the thrills and hazards of coach travel down the Otira Gorge than this early photograph taken at Reid's Fall where the road, only partly blasted out of the precipice, is perilously supported on logs pegged into the rock face. The waterfall's name is a double-banger—it refers not only to the cascade but to a road worker who fell to his death there. Passengers high up on the swaying coach must have felt some unease lest they follow the poor man to the same fate.* Alexander Turnbull Library

above. The open, undulating drive across the pass ended with the first dramatic view of Westland from the top of the Zigzag, in itself enough in many passengers to bring on further worries about how impossible it appeared for the coach to get down into the Otira Gorge far below.

This awesome experience was certainly not to everyone's liking. Archdeacon Henry Harper, who made regular trips to the West Coast when it was part of his diocese, recalled an elderly gentleman who rode in the seat behind him stepping down from the coach at Otira, shaking himself, and saying, "Well, sir, I'm thankful we're here; nothing shall ever induce me to come down that pass again; I shall return to Australia by sea."

He still had to survive the journey down the valleys of the Otira, Taramakau, Kaiwhaka and Arahura rivers before he could find a boat to take him to Melbourne. While waiting he might have rewarded himself with some of the pleasures of Hokitika, such as a visit to Mr Bartlett's new theatre which boasted the largest stage in New Zealand. "The entrances," wrote a visitor, "are through bars thronged with customers served by handsome barmaids dressed in the finest style of fashion, and wearing much jewellery." Those were big days in Hokitika, in themselves almost enough to compensate for the coach ride over the Alps.

The coaching firm of Cobb & Co. was initiated in Christchurch by Leander G. Cole in 1863, taking the name of the famous American company. With the help of his head driver, Captain Morgan Anderson, Cole established coach runs to all main centres in Canterbury and in 1865 when the gold rush saw

Two of Cobb's 17-passenger coaches *pause (in 1904) for a photograph by James Ring near Castle Hill on the run down the Waimakariri valley, against a background of Craigieburn peaks. On a fine day the outside seats were much favoured, but in stormy weather warm and waterproof clothes were essential to survive the two-day journey.*
Canterbury Museum

thousands of men heading for the West Coast the firm laid on "specials", first to Hurunui and then to Bealey.

When it became clear the Provincial Government intended to push a road right through to Hokitika, the firm imported from America 21 coaches, wagons, etc. for the anticipated trade. As the *Times* said, "Their enterprise needs no competition to sustain it; what they can't do with coaches they will do with horses, and what cannot be done with a road will be done without a road" — a comment occasioned by the fact that while the road-builders were still toiling in the gorges, Cobb & Co. were advertising regular services to Hokitika.

These coaches ran initially to Springfield, but soon the run was extended to Bealey. They left the city at 3 a.m. and arrived at their destination on the south bank of the Waimakariri about 7 p.m. Next morning the passengers rode on horseback to the top of Arthur's Pass and walked the further 50 miles, guided by Charlie Flowers the mailman. As the road was extended so was the run, until in March, 1866, the first coach to reach the Coast rattled into Hokitika with a flourish. The popular notion of coaches travelling thus at speed behind galloping horses was a romantic flight of fancy — in fact they averaged only 10km an hour over a day's journey.

Lee Cole went back to America in 1871 when the firm was taken over by Mitchell (who was manager) and Burton. They ran into opposition almost immediately from a large, genial Irishman named Hugh Cassidy, who until then had owned a store, hotel and coach at Waimea on the West Coast. Cassidy started a service to the Coast leaving from the Clarendon Hotel and did so well that in 1873 he was able to take over Cobb & Co. and operate thereafter under that well-known name. As "King Cobb" he ran the service for nearly 50 years and died an old man just one year before the Otira tunnel finally put the coaches out of business in 1923.

Cassidy had to fight off various competitors over the years — the Midland Coaching Co. (Stronach, Cloudesley and Montgomery), Campbell Bros., Moynihan & Co., Hall & Co. — these were some of those who sought to take over the run. One of the key factors was the lucrative mail contract, which some new outfit was forever acquiring when the contract came up for tender. Cassidy gave up on January 1, 1881, and sold the coaching part of his business to Binnie & Co., but was soon back again. When Hall & Co. won the mail contract in 1912 Cassidy was reduced to carrying passengers for as little as four pounds return to Kumara, "or as much as they could afford". But whether he won by attrition or by amalgamation the end result was always the same — Cobb & Co., that romantic old name of coaching legend, continued along the West Coast Road until the very end.

Hugh Cassidy *(right), the "King Cobb" of the coaching business on the West Coast run, was an Irishman who gave up looking for gold to start a store and coach run at Waimea before taking over Cobb & Co. in 1873. He operated the run, often as driver, for half a century of the most dramatic days of travel between Canterbury and Westland. The driver at left is John Rountree.*
Canterbury Museum

As the railway slowly crept forward towards the Alps from both east and west Cassidy found his run shrinking — from Springfield to Kumara in 1880, Springfield to Otira in 1900, Broken River to Otira in 1906, and from 1913 to 1923 only the few remaining miles across Arthur's Pass.

The design of the coaches, evolved by years of trans-continental experience in the United States, at first sight produced an impression of awkwardness and impracticability. The height seemed out of proportion to the wheelbase.* Yet considering the rough nature of the travelling there are few records of coaches actually capsizing. Suspended as they were on a cradle of leather straps, they swayed a lot with a motion which led some to call them "ships of the road".

*The track of the modern motorcar is similar to that of a coach, but its height is less than that of the coach's massive rear wheels; and the occupants sit about half a metre from the ground, whereas the top passengers on the coach were nearly three metres up in the air.

Calamity at Castle Hill

(with the money in 1987 dollars)

Consider the sad case of Alexander Thomson, shepherd, who began one hot day in 1872 to walk from Rakaia to Craigieburn, where there was supposed to be a job waiting for him. The sun beat down on the dusty road and when he reached Castle Hill Hotel, then run by Frederick Harris, it was unthinkable that he should pass without calling in for a couple of beers to slake his thirst.

When he was about to leave Harris shouted him a generous slug of gin. Before long Alex was in genial mood and inclined to put off until the morrow thoughts of the hard road to Craigieburn. Instead he settled down to some convivial tippling and in his own words "became very drunk". In due course Harris and his wife put him to bed.

In the morning he woke with a raging thirst but Harris fixed that with a good measure of free grog and a hearty breakfast. Unfortunately Alex discovered that all his money was gone, about $80. What to do for more? He studied his good Crimean shirt — would Harris buy that, perhaps?

Sure, said Harris, I'll give you $20 for it.

That day Alex spent the $20 and "got really drunk". Broke again, he sold his boots to Harris for $24. When that was gone, "I became really stupid and sold one of my dogs".

A shepherd without dogs is like a carpenter without tools. Things were getting serious. As Tuesday passed all his money went across Harris's bar counter. Some time before midnight they carried him up to bed again.

Once more Alex didn't feel too good when he woke. But there was a glass of spirits beside the bed, so he drank that. Just then Mrs Harris passed the door. Seeing him awake, she returned with another full glass.

With that aboard, our man Thomson staggered out and sold his second dog, his best one, for $240. Now he had plenty of money, but no shirt, no boots, and no dogs. Something had to be saved from the wreck if he was to get that job, so he bought back the first dog for $80 and the boots for $24. Shirtless still, but at least equipped with some of the essentials, he prepared to continue his journey.

But he reckoned without Harris, who took him to the stable and showed him a sheep hanging there. Thomson's dog had killed it, said Harris, and he wanted $40 compensation. Here Alex made another mistake. He returned to the bar to argue the matter. By day's end he was still there, and much of his money was gone again.

Next day, Friday, went the same way, but on Saturday morning, broke, shirtless, bootless, and without either of his dogs, he trudged up the hill behind the pub and finally set out for Craigieburn.

That wasn't the end of the matter. Thomson must have told his story to the police, or the runholder at Craigieburn told it for him, because Harris was duly prosecuted in the Christchurch Magistrate's Court on charges under the Licensing Act of supplying an intoxicated person with liquor and accepting articles in pledge for liquor. He was found guilty and fined $2400 plus $1440 costs.

Readers might consider that excessive. So apparently did the magistrate, who decided on reflection that he had been too harsh and knocked $800 off the bill.

The rear wheels were 1.42m high, with iron rims nearly 25mm thick which wore out after only a month or two of the excessive braking required along much of the route. Foot lever brakes were worked one by the driver and one on the opposite side by a suitably strong man from among the passengers. With a full load eight people rode outside, six facing forward and two to the rear, while inside were another nine.

All were warned in advance to come well protected from the weather, which could quickly change from warm and sunny to cold and snowy. Luggage was stacked in a leather-sided "boot" and on top between the seats. Signwriters and artists contributed to the showy red-and-green decor with the words "Christchurch and Hokitika" in gold beside the magic names of "Cobb & Co." and "Royal Mail". Some coaches bore a colourful

representation of a multi-pointed stag posed against a background of forest and snowcapped mountain, enclosed in a rococo frame.

The horses in the Cobb stables, sometimes numbering more than 200, were bred on Canterbury farms with the coach trade in mind. Their working life was often less than 18 months on the West Coast run. With the stamina and intelligence which is the stamp of a good horse they soon learned to cope with their gruelling task, to be footsure and reliable on the narrow mountain roads. Newcomers were broken in between two experienced veterans, invariably yoked in a 3-2 formation — three leaders and two polers. With a proportion of light greys among them, it was a driver's fancy sometimes to place a grey between two blacks in the front row, or two greys on the pole.

Tales of coach drivers and their adventures were legion. Most relate to flooded rivers and the hair-raising crossings in which some seemed to specialise. Arthur Davies was a well-known "whip" whose only passengers on one flood crossing of the Waimakariri at Bealey were the roadman, Wilson, and a midshipman. After asking Wilson if he could swim Davies plunged the coach into the river, but in midstream the current was too deep and swift, lifting the body off the chassis and sweeping it downstream. Davies hung on to the reins and let the horses drag him out, while Wilson jumped in and swam ashore. The account fails to mention what happened to the midshipman — perhaps he went down with the "ship".

Another time Davies capsized in the Otira River trying to cross when it was too high. He was driving a Red Jacket 21-passenger coach with seven passengers aboard, including a doctor, a priest, and a Miss Ecclesfield who was travelling in the doctor's care. Inside were a Mrs Horne and her niece and another lady. Again the coach came apart but this time Davies released the horses. Noting Miss Ecclesfield floating down the river, he plunged in and dragged her to the bank, then got the

A **coach** *in the Otira Gorge braves torrential rain and a swollen river. This engraving is from a painting by John Gibb exhibited in London in 1886.*
Reproduced from "Colonial New Zealand" by permission of the publishers.
John McIndoe Ltd.

other ladies out of the stranded coach and on to dry land. When Mrs Horne was safely ashore she fixed Davies with a steely glare and said, "To hell with your soul, Arthur Davies, and the next time I come overland in your coach, I shall go by sea." Chastened, Arthur went looking for his horses, finding the two leaders away downstream standing in the middle of the river on the bodies of the polers, drowned in the flood.

On the next trip when the rivers were up Davies decided not to push his luck so far. Instead he herded his passengers into the

Otira Hotel to wait for an improvement; but their peace of mind was shattered when the proprietor burst into the room to tell them the river had broken out and was threatening to flow under the very room they occupied. They hastened to seek shelter elsewhere.

Flooded rivers, snow-blocked roads, high winds — these were all hazards of the coaching days. John Rountree, another of the legendary drivers of the 19th century, remembered that the winter of 1895 was so bad and the snowfalls so heavy that for 10 weeks he had to "pack" the mail to get it through, while 20 men shovelled to clear a narrow roadway. When conditions improved a little they were able to reach Bealey with a light wagonette drawn by four horses. On one such trip the rear wheels slipped into an old track near Castle Hill and broke every spoke in both. Rountree rode back to Springfield and just managed to get out before floods blocked the road again, but it was 12 weeks before the wagonette was recovered.

On another trip he fought a nor'west gale all the way down from Bealey, which blew the coach off the road several times near Castle Hill. On Porter's Pass he was forced to shelter in the lee of the hill for an hour before deciding to make a dash for it on foot. After roping the wheels he and the three passengers took the horses and ventured the descent. Several times they crouched to avoid being blown away, and managed to reach the stables at the foot of the hill only to find half the roof gone and the top half of the chimney collapsed into the kitchen. With no fire and nothing to eat they huddled in the lee of what was left of the place, holding the horses until the rain came about 6 p.m. and the wind dropped. Then they returned for the coach and reached Springfield about 10 p.m.

One of the passengers, a priest from Sydney, had walked on while Rountree was changing horses at The Springs. The wind picked him up, carried him along, and set him down again on the road. He said he wouldn't have missed the trip for anything.

Strange things happened at the Porter's Pass stables, as on the day John Deans and a friend arrived to find the door locked. Looking in at the window they were confronted with a large monkey staring out at them, and as neither had seen such an animal before the shock was considerable. The mystery was solved when they discovered a French circus camped nearby, the owners of which had lost their horses and while out searching had shut the other animals in the stable.

Archdeacon Harper made his first visit to the Coast in 1866, about six months after the road was opened. The coach was running late and stopped for the night at Cass instead of Bealey. Here are his impressions of the journey:

With a few exceptions of flat ground, everywhere the road may be said to be dangerous, though well made, and fairly smooth underfoot: narrow ledges cut in solid rock, with overhanging cliffs and deep precipices below; deep ravines where it is not possible to avoid very steep gradients; sharp corners on a cliff side, round which you almost lose sight of the leaders; no room for a mistake, or any hesitation on the driver's part; and yet after a few hours of it, one loses all sense of danger. During this part of the journey the district is sub-alpine, a vast stretch of good sheep country, rising as high in places as 7000 feet, well watered, but liable to heavy winter snowfall. Its inhabitants are few and very far between.

A halt is called at nine for breakfast on the banks of a formidable river, the Waimakariri, which wanders, in dry season, over a river bed more than a mile in width, and in flood time becomes one broad impassable stream. We find it fairly low, but that means half a dozen streams, deep enough to cover the wheels, rushing at great pace over such a rough bottom that, as the coach pitched and rolled like a boat at sea, one wondered it could hold together. A capsize would be no joke, for the water is icy cold, and rushing so fast that a swimmer would have but a poor chance.

The river crossed, a lovely but very dangerous, long, gradual ascent of the Otira pass lay before us. Everywhere the mountain sides clothed with mountain birch: every variety of rich fern growth and moss, nourished by the never-ceasing waterfalls which pour down from the heights above, where snow is always lying. As you near the top of the pass, the road is amongst huge masses of rock, fallen from above, and continues for nearly eight miles [sic] up and down, until it reaches the western descent; but sterile and bleak and savage enough to be the haunt of Kuhleborn himself, with his attendant gnomes and sprites,

for it is flanked by magnificent precipices of bare rock, two thousand feet above you, which are scored with channels, down which the water god comes in grand cascades; yet the whole place is relieved by a growth of Alpine flora; daisy, ranunculus, the Mount Cook lily with its plate-like leaves, and a great variety of veronica. The pass is said to be the ancient moraine of a great glacier.

Archdeacon Henry W. Harper *(above) was Archdeacon of Timaru and Westland and frequently travelled the West Coast Road. His father,* **Bishop Henry John Chitty Harper** *(right) was first Bishop of Christchurch.*

Looking down westward, you stand on the edge of the old moraine dyke; in the ravine you can trace at intervals a rushing glacial stream, losing itself in a continuous mass of trees. To make a road down this and onward was a bold undertaking, but successful. [The road] zigzags down with such sharp turns that at several corners the leaders' feet are within a yard of the edge; they curve and round about like circus horses; the road has a surface of soft, broken metal, good holding ground; the driver knows his work, the brakes grind and squeak. "Hold her now your side," says the driver to me, as I put my whole weight on it. "Now easy, hold her again," and so we get down safely, and at a good pace, which is necessary to keep the coach from swerving; and after two miles of cavernous, rugged rock-cutting, just above the roaring blue glacial torrent, every now and then besprinkled with the spray of waterfalls, we pull up at a little shanty for a welcome lunch.

Travellers were fortunate when the weather was fine and the rivers clear and blue. Heavy snowfall added a new dimension to the journey, as Archdeacon Harper discovered on later trips. Many a passenger began the journey across the plains on a warm nor'west morning, enjoying the balmy airs from an outside seat, only to reach the summit of Porter's Pass in time to see blue-black storm clouds sweeping down from the Alps in the distance — a sure sign of trouble ahead. As the coach clattered along the intervening miles and the first rain struck the driver and his seat-mates in the face, many a timid passenger, especially the ladies sheltering inside, must have offered a prayer for Divine protection from the dangers ahead. If by chance the driver was the one called John Knox, that might help with the Almighty!

On one such trip Knox arrived at Bealey to find the Waimakariri so high he could not cross, and had to wait for 24 hours. Next morning, impatient to continue, he took the ford with the river still in flood, to the alarm of the passengers, and after a precarious crossing proceeded up the Bealey, where the road was so bad that at intervals all the men had to disembark and help clear away boulders and fallen trees. At one bad slip the horses were taken out and the coach manhandled across piecemeal.

The Otira Gorge was in an even worse condition; there the road gangs were called out to clear the way. Eventually the coach arrived at the Taipo to find that river running so high that the leading horses were carried off their feet and the driver had to run with the river until they could scramble back to the bank they had just left. The coach waited there for 30 hours before making a dangerous crossing, only to find the river at Wainihinihi impassable, forcing a return to Taipo. Eventually the journey ended at Hokitika four days late.

When James Wylde, the engineer from Kaiapoi who was one of those who wrestled with lower Waimakariri flood problems,

The first Otira Gorge Hotel, *pictured about 1880. A passing tourist described it as "a dilapidated-looking structure which once fronted the road with a pretty islet opposite in the riverbed, but which now has only a narrow footway between hotel and river. Keenan, the proprietor, is philosophic about it — 'Bound to go before long', he says." Sure enough, in 1886 the river carried everything away.*

Alexander Turnbull Library

took a coach to Hokitika in 1868 he met with conditions which were familiar to so many passengers—the sudden transition from balmy Canterbury to rain-swept Westland. He wrote:

The drive up the pass was most beautiful, the sun having risen and the morning being fair and warm, but the moment we reached the summit everything was changed. A fierce driving rain met us in the face, the whole valley below us was filled with cloud and rain whilst overhead towered up the snowy peaks with one great glacier just then through the cloud. The appearance of the road at the descent ... is nearly enough to frighten anyone. The road is cut out of the face of a precipice on a zig-zag manner and at each turn it appears as though the horses and coach must drive over and be dashed to pieces. Add to this that the rain had caused continual slips ... which could not be seen until too late to avoid them and that in many places there was not three inches to spare in the width of the road and you will not wonder that we all wished to get out and walk down ... the coachman said he would stop directly, but instead of that he started off at a dashing rate and all we could do was to hold on and be as calm as we could ... I assure you I never felt a greater "sensation" in my life. It appeared almost miraculous that we should have reached the bottom of the mountain in safety, but we did so, then galloped on as fast as the horses could go through the narrow gorge of the river Otira till we reached the house where we should have breakfasted at 8 o'clock. No time however was to be lost unless we chose to be bailed up by the rapidly rising rivers, so all had to help in changing the horses as fast as possible. I darted into the house and secured a loaf of bread and then away we went again in our race against the water; every stream we had to cross increasing in depth as we advanced.

One of the drivers employed by Cobbs was a man named Stobie, who established a reputation for always getting through, floods or no floods. In July 1870 he managed a particularly chancy crossing of the Waimakariri when it was in high flood, made it over the pass in heavy rain, and approached the first ford in the Otira with confidence. But half-way over, the current lifted the after part of the coach and carried it down among the boulders. Stobie couldn't get the horses out before one drowned. The river, still rising, bundled horses and coach further downstream until everything was hopelessly tangled, with passengers and mail still aboard. He had no choice but to swim the outfit down the river, but on the way it struck a large boulder and broke one of the fore wheels. Rae, the hotelkeeper, seeing what was happening, rushed over and he and Stobie, with a passenger

named Hewitt, all up to their chests in water, got the coach to the bank and saved the remaining horses. A lady passenger, prostrate with shock, was taken to the hotel to recover.

Twice in August of that year Stobie had to swim his coach down the Waimakariri at Bealey when it got out of its depth. The second time he discovered too late that the ford had shifted; he was a long way down before reaching the opposite bank, with passengers and mails soaked. The West Coasters, long accustomed to aquatics, thought highly of Stobie and his skill in the rivers. His coach was so often afloat he was referred to in colloquial terms as "Captain" Stobie. In March, 1871, he was honoured at a function with a purse of 85 sovereigns, a handsome acknowledgement indeed of his services. When the new road was opened on the northern side of the Porter's Pass spur on October 24, 1871, he was given the privilege of driving the first coach up to the pass.

There was always an air of glorious uncertainty as passengers climbed aboard in High Street, never quite knowing what lay ahead or if they would reach their destination. Those who left Christchurch on a fine Friday morning in October, 1866, had a splendid trip across the plains, but conditions beyond Porter's Pass were so bad that the Porter River, in high flood, forced them to retreat over the pass to spend the night in Riddell's Hotel.

With a fresh start next morning, they mustered some roadmen on the way who cut a path through the river bank, enabling the coach to be driven safely across. There was trouble at the Thomas, the Broken and the Craigie Burn, and eventually they were pulled up short at the Cass to spend Saturday night in the new hotel there (by which time they should have been in Hokitika). Next morning a horseman came galloping through the rain with the mail and the news that there were floods everywhere, and the coach from Hokitika was still in the Taramakau, on the other side of the mountains.

On Sunday morning all the passengers elected to continue on horseback, using horses from Cobb and Co.'s stables. They forded the Cass River and pressed on to Bealey, made an adventurous crossing of the Waimakariri, worked their way up the Bealey, which was also running high, crossed Arthur's Pass and, just as darkness fell, reached Rae's Hotel at Otira. It was a day to remember.

70

Regal and Vice-Regal

Royalty's only crossing of Arthur's Pass was in 1920, when on May 13 Prince Edward the Prince of Wales (he who later renounced the throne and married the American divorcee Wallis Simpson) drove over in a special coach during his tour of the country. The settlements at Otira and Arthur's Pass were in a fever of excitement. Every man, woman and child turned out to see His Royal Highness board the coach at Otira and drive away up their own Otira Gorge to cross the Alps. At the reins was old Alexander Hall, doyen of coach drivers, who by then was 79 years of age. What the Prince thought of the trip was never known, but at least the coach with its geriatric driver managed the journey without mishap.

Grace Adams tells the touching story of Jack O'Kane, the roadman (from whom her *Jack's Hut* gets its name):

From the moment Jack knew the heir to the throne was to travel over Otira Gorge ... he was beside himself with excitement. The old roadman worked like a slave on his piece of road, and when the great day arrived, every inch was in tip top order. At the appointed hour he washed and changed into his Sunday suit, then taking his newly-polished shovel, he stationed himself at the edge of the road, with little Margaret [Grace's sister] beside him, her hand in his. They had a long wait — the coaches were running behind schedule — but eventually the cavalcade could be heard approaching ... Jack removed his hat and stood at attention, shovel at his side. The Prince's coach, a splendid-looking vehicle of gleaming red, was travelling very fast, the driver no doubt having been instructed to make up for lost time. The Prince, who was engrossed in conversation, didn't so much as glance up to see Jack waiting there expectantly. Grace and Guy [Margaret's parents], who'd come hurrying out at the sound of the coaches, faded quickly back into the trees, their hearts quite aching for the poor old man.

At the village the Prince found time to walk a short distance into the tunnel to chat with some of the men. Then he was whisked away on the special train to Christchurch.

The vice-regal visit was much earlier, when the Governor-General, Sir William Jervois, was taken from Canterbury to Westland during his tour of the country. When the coach was stopped at the top of the Zigzag for him to admire the view into the Otira Gorge he promptly disembarked. To the great disgust of Hugh Cassidy the driver, resplendent for the occasion in a navy-blue suit and bowler hat, who was about to demonstrate to his eminent passenger some of the finer points of his craft, Sir William set out on foot, remarking that while being whirled down the pass at nearly 20 miles an hour was no doubt splendid as an exhibition of skilled coachmanship, it was a little too fast for the scenery to make its proper impression!

Other notable pass-crossers included Richard John Seddon, the country's premier at the turn of the century, whose home town was Kumara and whose electorate was Westland. A frequent traveller on the coaches, he preferred Cassidy to drive him, and often slept most of the way.

And then the All-England cricket team made the crossing during their tour of 1877, with Cassidy driving the leading coach. They struck bad weather and floods and one of the coaches foundered in the Otira River, the cricketers having to be carried ashore one by one. For the rest of his life Cassidy treasured a very special pocket-knife given him by Lord Harris, the team's manager, to mark the occasion.

Sgt. Haddrell, *of the Bealey armed constabulary, keeps a sharp eye on his territory. One of his duties was to satisfy himself that the credentials of travellers on this sole overland link between Canterbury and Westland were above suspicion.* Canterbury Museum

On Monday morning they rode down the Otira and Taramakau valleys and finally reached the coach. But it capsized in a bad ford and broke in two, the main part going downstream with an alarmed female passenger still aboard. Luckily for her the party included a Captain Smith, who dived into the flood and at great peril to himself (so it was reported) successfully brought her to shore. She was in rather a bad way by then, as might be expected. Eventually the coach reached Hokitika about a week late.

The Waimakariri crossing at Bealey was always risky when the river was up. On one occasion in 1866 the coach, driver and passengers were stuck in the middle of the flood and had to spend the night there, a terrifying experience for all. The coach was dragged out next morning with ropes and extra horses. When the same thing happened again later, all the passengers except four Maoris were taken off by horse. The wahine in the party could not be persuaded to leave so her companions stayed and rode out the flood all night and next day. As it happened the coach had stranded immediately below the telegraph wire, which descended steeply from the south bank at that point, enabling resourceful people at the hotel to "wire" food and drink to the castaways in an improvised cradle.

The weather of course was no respecter of persons. Once the passengers included the Chief Justice, his associate and a number of others travelling to an important judicial inquiry at Hokitika. The coach arrived there eight days late, having been delayed by floods and slips on the road. It had been upset in one river, when three of the horses were drowned, the passengers had narrow escapes, and much of the luggage was lost. But the mails got through safely, and so apparently did the Chief Justice.

Nobody on that trip could have called it an enjoyable experience, but the weather wasn't always to blame. A

Five of a kind. *James Ring's camera caught this unusual shot of coaches in convoy crossing the Bealey riverbed.* Canterbury Museum

*A picnic party camping at **The Klondyke Hut,** built in 1890 at Klondyke Corner to shelter floodbound travellers unable to reach the hotel on the opposite bank. It was usually stocked with food and blankets, but all the food had gone when one man arrived. He showed his displeasure by scrawling the word "Starvation" on the hut. At a later date, probably about 1897, another man likewise found the hut unprovisioned. This was when tales of starving miners on the Klondike goldfields in the Yukon were being much publicised and after a hungry night he gave vent to his feelings by superimposing the word "Klondike" over the first inscription. An oft-told story is of the lone traveller who, arriving late at night and tired, tumbled into the bunk alongside someone already in occupation and, waking in the morning, found his bedmate was a dead Chinaman. The police sergeant had placed the body there for later removal. The hut is long gone, but the name lingers, albeit with changed spelling.* Canterbury Museum

correspondent writing to *The Press* in 1866 complained that his trouble was fellow-travellers:

The trip I made recently would have been entirely agreeable had I not been seated between two madmen, one of whom was morose and the other whimsical. The latter was certainly amusing, though perhaps it was fortunate there were no women on the coach, as one of his extravagances consisted of divesting himself of his trousers and running uphill before us carrying them under his arm, and another time he begged hard for a newspaper to light a fire in his boots to warm his feet. I would have laughed more at this comical figure but for my more saturnine neighbour whose occasional threat was to cut my throat. Also I did not dine so well seated next to him. In addition to these the company was augmented by some prisoners.

The writer thought the Government should have its own vehicles for its own purposes, and leave the public in peaceful possession of those provided by Messrs Cobb & Co. He might have been better off riding outside on one of the box seats, which in fine weather were highly prized by passengers with an eye for scenery. In 1881 a man named Pharazyn sued the coach company for twenty pounds because he didn't get the box seat as promised. He and his wife were on a pleasure trip and wouldn't have gone had they known they were to ride inside, and he demanded his money back. The magistrate awarded him five pounds and costs. However Cobb & Co. did the right thing by giving him free return tickets with box seats guaranteed.

Gerhard Mueller, whose survey duties took him to the West Coast in 1865, found Paddy's Bend, high above the Waimakariri a few miles beyond Cass, the most exciting part of his coach trip. Writing to his wife he recalled that the coach pulled up for the night at "Haughton's Sheep Station", where the passengers got "good quarters and tucker". Of Paddy's Bend he wrote:

I have never rode in a coach over such a dangerous road. It is entirely cut out of rock—the river running right underneath it at a depth varying from 700 to 1000 feet. On the left is the steep rocky mountain rising from 1000 to 2000 feet above, the top completely covered with snow, and in some places the rocks actually overhanging the road, threatening to crush men and horses, and on the right a yawning abyss, a wild mountain torrent running at 10 or more knots, and in many places quite perpendicular beneath you. The road is frightful and I consider it a shame—a scandalous shame—that the Government does not at least erect a stone wall of two feet on the side, to prevent accidents, for if anything about the coach fixings should give way, or a horse should startle, it would be death for every soul on the coach.

Mueller had sent his man Ned on ahead with a horse and his gear. As the coach neared Bealey Ned came riding up, but not on Mueller's horse. The following conversation ensued:

Ned: "Have you seen the horse, Sir?"
"What horse?"
"Your horse, Sir."
"Have you lost it?"
"You have passed him, Sir, at the Waimakariri."

"What is he doing in the Waimakariri?"
"Dead, Sir—kicked the bucket, Sir—got knocked up, Sir—and stretched out for good, Sir."

Mueller was much upset by this news, but for twenty-one pounds managed to buy the horse Ned had borrowed, and continued his journey. Apart from crossing the Bealey River 20 times, resulting in his feet being wet all day, he had no further comment to make on the road, the descent of the Otira Gorge apparently being nothing compared with the death-defying traverse of Paddy's Bend.

Like every other coach journey the West Coast run had its share of drunken and blasphemous passengers and, on some occasions, drivers too. Horses were usually changed at hotel stages, and while the ladies and gentlemen took tea and scones in the dining room, many of the men spent their florins in the bar. As the miles passed, the journey became for them something in the nature of a rural pub crawl, with extra supplies carried on to the coach or bought from grog shops along the way. In such circumstances an unescorted lady might find herself harassed in her mobile prison by bad language, ribaldry and possibly unwelcome advances.

Not that all male passengers made life difficult for the opposite sex. This refreshing tribute from a grateful father appeared in an 1879 Christchurch newspaper:

Sir,—Permit one whose daughter has just arrived by coach from the West Coast to describe conduct reflecting the highest honour to those concerned. The coach was detained at a small hut on the further side of

The Mystery of the Missing Still

Along the West Coast Road in the 1880s the subject of the missing whisky still was keenly discussed. The story involved a trader from Waimate who took horses to the West Coast for sale. In his travels he became the possessor of a whisky still. He engaged a Christchurch plumber to make a new pipe for it, but when the man presented his account the horse trader said the charge was too high and refused to pay the full amount. Piqued, the plumber informed the police, who alerted the constable at Otira to apprehend the still's owner when he came through.

Somehow one of the roadmen learned about this and warned the Waimate man, who hid the still in a gully above the Arthur's Pass road. Then he went on to Hokitika and sold his horses. The whereabouts of the still, which had left Christchurch but failed to reach Hokitika, became a prime mystery, to the extent that the police offered a hundred pounds for information leading to its discovery. The roadman, who had been nursing plans of his own for the still, decided the thing was too "hot" for him. He went to Hokitika, got drunk, staggered round to the police station, and gave them the information they wanted.

Result: The roadman got 50 pounds and the horse trader 12 months.

From coach to train. *When the Midland railway reached Bealey valley in 1913 and eliminated the Waimakariri crossing, a temporary station was opened at Halpin's Creek, about 5km from the tunnel entrance. On this summer's day the coaches, just arrived from Otira, are being readied for the return trip. The ladies in the near wagon should escape sunstroke judging by the size of their hats. In the nearer shed at right Mrs Minchin sold tea and scones which she baked every day at Arthur's Pass and carried down to Halpin's.*   Alexander Turnbull Library

the Bealey. Thunder, lightning and heavy rain were almost continuous. The two men occupying the hut, plus the driver and four male and two female passengers were shut up in this one small room for three nights and two days, and during the whole time the men were unremitting in their kindest attention to the females and not a single unpleasant word or unseemly action proceeded from any of those seven nature's gentlemen. To all of them, unknown as they are to me, most grateful thanks are rendered by: A FATHER.

Keeping the West Coast Road open and in good order, each with about 20km to look after, were such men as William Hurrell (overseer), Peter Corrigan, Billy McDonald, Bob McKay, W. Hewitt, John Murray, Candy and Jones. Noted drivers were Arthur Davies, Tommy Power, John Knox, "Captain" Stobie, Tom Rountree, Henry Campbell, Sam Eastgate, James Clark, Joe Searle, W. Rae and Tommy Mahar.

On Sam Eastgate's run between Springfield and Bealey in the 1880s the hotels were Donald's at Porter's Pass, Cloudesley's at Castle Hill, Hewitt's at Cass, and O'Malley's at Bealey. He would leave Springfield after the Christchurch train arrived about midday, and reach Bealey about 9 p.m. If the weather was bad and the creeks up, or snow lay on the road, he might get in at midnight or 2 a.m. Most coaches were licensed to carry 17 passengers, but sometimes there might be only one, or even none — just the mail. In his day there were six changes of team, at The Springs, Craigieburn, and Bealey, and beyond that at Otira, Taipo and Kumara.

Eastgate recalled one of the few accidents in which a life was lost. He was driving an extra stage across Arthur's Pass when on the moraine section above the Zigzag his coach, heavily laden, toppled over in a washout. The horses took fright and dragged the capsized coach along the road. A mother and baby were thrown out and the baby killed.

The Tommy Mahar mentioned lost his coach altogether one May day in 1876 at the Taipo River. Pulling up there for lunch, on the run from Hokitika, he found the unpredictable Taipo in high flood and uncrossable. So he parked up in "the usual place" and trooped the passengers across the wire bridge to the hotel.

After dinner Mahar was astonished to find the river flowing 20ft deep where he had left the coach, which had disappeared altogether along with the luggage and the precious mail. Also at dinner in the hotel was a sheep drover named Andy Jackson, who was driving a mob from Canterbury to the Coast. Arriving at the Taipo and being unable to cross, he left the sheep at the riverbed while he had lunch, wondering the while how long the delay would be. When he came out later all his troubles were over. The same sudden change in the river which had carried away the coach had cut a new course behind his sheep, miraculously repositioning them untouched on the Hokitika side ready to resume their journey.

The great 1867 snow stopped all coaches in their tracks. One which left Springfield on August 1 of that year broke its pole trying to force a passage over Porter's Pass and had to be abandoned there. By August 8 the snow was eight feet deep on the pass and all traffic was long since halted. On such occasions coaches would take all day to get from Bealey to Cass, and another to reach Castle Hill. In the winter of 1895 the snow was two metres deep on Arthur's Pass and traffic was stopped for months. A heavy white blanket lay across the whole country that winter, from coast to coast, followed by bright weather with heavy frosts.

Archdeacon Harper, for so many years a familiar figure on West Coast coaches, was making the trip to Christchurch when

A Hair-raising Descent

There was much reliance on brakes in the Otira Gorge, and indeed on any of the steep hills along the coach route. If they failed, which luckily seldom happened, the driver faced a grim situation. The unrestrained coach, gathering speed, would quickly push the pole horses into the leaders with only one possible result—tangle, collapse, and certain disaster. The reinsman had only one choice—to "drive like hell and make the leaders fly!" They had to be whipped mercilessly and at all costs kept ahead of the polers and the coach, while the driver summoned every ounce of skill and nerve he possessed.

A noted driver in the 70s was Tommy Power. His descent of the Otira Gorge without brakes was talked about for years. The sole passenger was a young man named Mortimer Davies, who was no stranger to horses but chose to play the role of new chum, asking Power silly questions along the way such as, "Where did the people go moa hunting?" and so on.

Starting down the Otira, Power gave a smart crack with the whip and the four horses took off at great speed. Mortimer thought this a bit risky but kept silent. Although Power applied the brake at the top of the Zigzag the pace kept increasing. Mortimer noticed the driver's face whiten.

"Hello," he said, "Brake gone?"

Power shouted back, "Yes, it's going now!"

Normally there was a brake lever on both sides of the coach, but Mortimer was concerned to find none on his side. As the coach gathered speed he shouted, "Is there anything I can do?"

"Yes," replied Power, "you hold on to the guard iron with one hand and put your arm around me and hold me—I'm going to stand up and keep the horses ahead of the coach!"

At that he stood, reins in hand, and there followed (as Mortimer Davies described it) the finest piece of driving he had ever seen.

With the four reins in his left hand, Power struck the leaders with the lash. They shot forward just in time to prevent bunching with the pole horses which were being pushed on by the ever-gaining coach. A swing of the hands and the reins were in the right hand, followed immediately by a crack like a pistol shot—a left-hander this time and the near leader sprang forward with a bound that carried it round the point of rock. And so it went: whip and reins changed hands at every bend and the maddened horses, covered in foam, knew it was a gamble with death. One stumble and all would be over; but no, they made it. The coach shot out of the gorge and bumped along the riverbed until the panting horses pulled up at the hotel. White and shaken, Power climbed down and said, "I'm done, can you drive?"

"Yes," replied Davies.

"Then what the devil d'you mean by pretending to be a new chum?" he demanded. "It was only that which made me start such a pace at the top. I'll never forgive myself."

"Oh," said Mortimer, "was *that* it!"

Power was completely played out; the strain had been too much for him. After half an hour at the hotel they continued their journey, but this time with Mortimer Davies at the reins.

---

the snow was at its deepest. Although the roadmen at Otira pronounced the pass impossible for horses or vehicles, he and Tom Rountree decided to "give it a go" in a wagonette with four horses. Some of the drifts on the pass were five metres deep, so it took them all day to reach Bealey. Next day they reached Craigieburn by noon and Castle Hill by dusk. By now they were in real "snow country", and had to proceed on foot, leading the horses through deep drifts.

Near Lake Lyndon five figures could be seen approaching—all that was left of roadman McKay's party of 12 volunteers from the Porter's Pass Hotel which had set out to meet them, having heard of their coming on the telegraph. McKay reported very heavy snow on the pass and suggested a miracle was needed if they were to get over alive. Forcing a way to the summit through deep drifts, they found no sign of the road on the Christchurch side, just an unbroken snow slope.

Through this they ploughed and stamped a path, and at last reached the welcome warmth of the inn. But McKay would allow none to go near the fire until all feet had been rubbed and warmed. The Archdeacon, with long experience of the vicissitudes of travel on that route, always wore an oversize pair of woollen socks pulled on over his boots and well up his legs, declaring they were by far the best thing to wear in the snow.

Another time, in 1868, he made a rough winter crossing in July to attend the diocesan synod meeting in Christchurch. At Otira he and five other passengers, including a rather lightly-clad French cook, were advised that there was too much snow on the pass for the coach to continue, so horses were secured and the party set out in single file to ride and walk over to Bealey. Luckily it was a fine day without wind. In places the track was hard and frozen, in others the snow deep and the horses floundering. But they reached Bealey in good shape, and had to

At the Pass. *The scene at the old Arthur's Pass railway station when the coaches handled the traffic over the pass. Passengers must have been numerous this day, for extra cups and saucers have been set out on trestles on the platform. The bridge over the Bealey River leading into the tunnel just shows at far right.*

Alexander Turnbull Library

decide whether to continue another 15 kilometres to Cass. As the road was buried in snow drifts, all elected to ride down the frozen Waimakariri, but a cold fog which came up at dusk saw them lost on the way. After anxiously wandering this way and that the Archdeacon recognised Jupiter, the evening star, through a rift in the fog, which provided sufficient divine guidance to steer the party to the hotel, reached about 9 p.m. The French cook was frozen stiff in his saddle and had to be carried in a sitting position into the hotel and rubbed with snow while he roared with the pain of returning circulation. The Archdeacon noted that the bottles on the shelves were cracked, leaving the frozen beer standing unsupported, like so many cold brown statues without overcoats.

The extreme cold of the winter months in the mountains was not only hard on drivers and horses, but also on the men working on the roads. In July, 1873, during a particularly cold winter, a gang of roadmen camped in the Bealey valley struck temperatures well below zero for days on end. In a storm two of them collapsed and had to be rushed to Christchurch hospital, where both died, probably from hypothermia. The others were cared for in the police barracks at Bealey, where they sat wrapped in blankets with their feet in tubs of hot water until recovered. At that, one said he'd had enough and walked the 70 kilometres over Porter's Pass to Springfield.

Along the lonely road to the West Coast the coaches at intervals caught up with and passed the occasional wagon loaded with freight — units of an historic transport system which survived for decades until the railway took over. On their wheels much of the primary produce and other merchandise required on the West Coast or at sheep stations on the way was conveyed from the Canterbury horn of plenty, and consignments of timber, coal, and wool from the Coast and the tussock country brought back. No doubt the wagoners had their share of adventure and misfortune with flooded rivers and roads blocked by slips, but they appear to have left few records.

Among the earliest of these was George O'Malley, an Irish lad who came out to New Zealand in the early 1860s and was still only 19 in 1866 when he saw the potential offered by the new road over the Alps. He bought a wagon and five horses and began carrying supplies to the diggings, and soon was leasing Castle Hill farm from Enys brothers and growing oats for feed for his teams and selling the surplus to Cobb & Co. for their coach horses. He also undertook contracting work for the Upper Waimakariri Road Board and on occasions attended to road maintenance on the highway. O'Malley did well, took a trip to Ireland, bought a property in Kirwee and became a prosperous farmer.

Another who had a long association with transport in the Waimakariri valley was John Milliken. Like O'Malley he rented the Castle Hill farm to grow oats, and his fleet of wagons hauled most of the valley's wool for years. He also retired to go farming, bought the Brooksdale and Castle Hill stations, and died a rich man.

From 1900 when the railway from the West Coast reached Otira, Cobb & Co. and their opposition, Hall's coaches, had to maintain large stables there, with up to 120 horses and 20 coaches at peak periods to cater for the railway passenger traffic. A line of 15 or more coaches would be drawn up at the station ready for the train to arrive and disgorge its human freight, luggage and mail. The little station buzzed with frenzied activity as all hurried (if it was a fine day) to secure outside seats for the thrilling drive over the pass. It must have been a great sight to see the long line of coaches snaking through the gorge and up the Zigzag, whips cracking and horses straining. At Arthur's Pass the convoy met the train from Christchurch, snorting up the Bealey grade to expire with a steamy sigh at the station in the village. When Guy and Grace Butler found themselves among the 250 people riding the coaches over the pass on Boxing Day, 1916, under a perfect summer sky and with the rata just starting to bloom, they so fell in love with the beauty of it all that they bought Jack's Hut, a surplus roadman's cottage in the Bealey Gorge, and from then on lived there whenever they could.

Tough Going. *The old unsealed Zigzag was steep, rough and subject to frequent slips — the leading coach in this James Ring picture is about to cross one.* Canterbury Museum

The Hotels

When Edward Dobson and his sons were frequent travellers into the upper Waimakariri, engaged in survey work or exploration in the Alps, there were already several hotels or accommodation houses along the way offering meals or a bed for the night. By December, 1865, the expected traffic bound for the gold rush on the West Coast had spawned a chain of 13 hostelries between Christchurch and Arthur's Pass (compared with six today), and in addition there were shanties and grog shops scattered along the highway wherever their owners thought a thirst might generate.

On horseback or in a coach the journey was a long one, and for weary foot travellers the more hotels there were the better. According to most authorities these establishments were in order along the Old West Coast Road (or the Coal Track as it was known in earliest days) and from Sheffield on Highway 73, as follows:

TAYLOR'S HAREWOOD HOTEL

The present Yaldhurst Road was called Harewood Road originally, hence the hostelry's name. It was built in 1865. The name Yaldhurst was said to be that of a horse owned by a friend of the licensee. The present Yaldhurst Hotel occupies the site.

THE MINER'S REST

Built by Reuben Cook in 1863. Originally known as the Malvern Hotel it had 11 rooms, stable, coach house, water well, and 50 acres of land. The place had deteriorated by the mid-seventies and had outlived its usefulness by the time the railway came through.

WATSON'S HALF-WAY HOUSE

The first hotel on this site, at the junction of Old West Coast Road and Halkett Road, was built of cob by Charles Watson in 1864. It was midway between Christchurch and Sheffield and was a popular breakfasting place for those travelling west. The old hotel was soon succeeded by the building illustrated, which survived until it was demolished in 1970 to avoid further spoiling by vandals.

Watson's Halfway House.

WHITE'S COURTENAY HOTEL

This was one of the earliest accommodation houses on the route (possibly the earliest), and was established in 1861 to service the Courtenay-Dagnam ferry across the Waimakariri at this point.

The original house was run by Charles White in the old Ledard homestead which he had bought a year earlier. The new premises were erected in 1864 and still stand. They were a popular stopping place in the early days, as references confirm in the chapter *The Explorers*.

MALVERN ARMS HOTEL

Built in 1865 by George Willis, doyen of the district's early innkeepers, near the intersection of West Coast Road and tracks leading to Racecourse Hill, Homebush and Cabbage Tree Flat (between Sheffield and Annat). Coaches usually stopped here and the hotel flourished until the railway reached Sheffield.

Convinced that Sheffield would be the railway terminus for many years, Willis built a new hotel there and transferred the

Malvern Arms licence to it. (This building was demolished not so long ago). He leased it to one Michael Flanagan, who left in disagreement over the lease and built his own pub a few doors along the road (the present Sheffield Hotel). For a time the two establishments traded in opposition.

SPRINGFIELD HOTEL

George Willis established the original hotel in 1863, when it figured largely in the accounts of travellers going over Porter's Pass into the Waimakariri country. Until 1870 when the name Springfield was adopted for what had been called Kowai Pass, the hotel was known simply as Willis's. In May, 1865, J.H. Bailey succeeded Willis and built a new hotel, the first on the

present site, which burned down (it is said) on January 5, 1880, the day the railway reached Springfield. Its replacement, the present hotel (pictured) was bought by W.J. Cloudesley in 1895. A lively entrepreneur, he enlarged the hotel to 40 rooms, built a hall next door to hold 500 people, and kept coaches to take tourist patrons to choice local picnic spots.

There was another hotel in Springfield built by Lauret Neilson about the turn of the century, a large, 18-roomed edifice opposite the domain.

PORTER'S PASS HOTEL

After the "new" road up Porter's Pass was opened in 1871 a hotel was built on the flat beside the Kowai River. The earlier Riddell's Inn, the first in the locality, was near Thomas's homestead in the shaded little valley where the old road started for the pass (straight ahead instead of turning right to begin the climb). Early coach passengers had dinner at Riddell's before attacking the mountains. The old road is still there as a curiosity for occasional trampers.

D'Arcy's Accommodation House and Staging Post at The Springs

Canterbury Museum

The Second Porter's Pass Hotel

CASTLE HILL HOTEL

The original accommodation house and stables were close to The Springs, near the present turnoff for Porter Heights. They were built of slabs and wattle-and-daub by a man named Michael D'Arcy, probably in the mid 1860s. This was a staging post for the coaches.

Fred Harris took over in 1871 and built a new limestone-block place opposite the present Castle Hill Village, and was succeeded by Thomas Douglas. In 1881 W.J. Cloudesley, who had been manager at Cass, began his 14-year tenure, which included adding a second storey to the building. The coal supply for the hotel was from an open seam close by on the banks of the Porter River. In 1903 Castle Hill had 20 rooms and had become a popular place for visitors wanting a holiday with plenty of scenery and fresh air, huge log fires, and Mrs Cloudesley's famous scones. (These were also popular with passing coach travellers who took morning or afternoon tea there.)

Before and after the fire.

The stone for the hotel came from blocks lying at the base of Castle Hill itself, carted the 2km to the site and assembled by a stonemason named Davies. The hotel was gutted by fire on September 17, 1904, and never re-established. All the hotels beyond Springfield—Riddell's, Castle Hill, Craigieburn, Cass and Bealey (3), have disappeared almost without trace.

CRAIGIEBURN HOTEL

Little is known about this place which apparently had a short life. It is recorded by a bold, square dot on J.N. Gale's 1865 map as being at the corner of the two straight sections of the road between Flock Hill station (or Craigieburn as it was then) and Lake Pearson, at the point where Gale drew the proposed Waimakariri Gorge road joining the existing highway. Another

reference was in *The Press* of January 2, 1866, reporting that "Hawdon's accommodation house at Craigieburn was accidentally burned down", and in the same newspaper of May 12, 1866, William Wilson, describing his coach trip to the Coast, says, "a spacious stone building is reached, which was intended for an inn, but is now used as a manager's residence or some other private purpose in connection with Mr Hawdon's station". In her book *Coaching Days,* Mrs McLennan refers to "the spacious inn there; in 1865 the proprietor was John Ashton".

CASS HOTEL

This hostelry stood on the north-east side of the highway about 400 yards short of the Cass River, and a little closer to it than the

Road Board office. It was built in late 1865 by L.G. Cole & Co. (Cobb's coaches), doubtless to compete with the one at Bealey. It may have decided Joseph Hawdon not to continue with his establishment at Craigieburn after the fire. Cass Hotel itself was burnt down—the date is uncertain but there is a reference to it *not* being there in 1906. According to McLennan there were 16 rooms in the building and generous stabling at the rear. The earliest licensee appears to have been Alfred Baker in December, 1865. Eight others followed during the next 14 years, including the redoubtable W.J. Cloudesley in 1879. For some time the premises were used for meetings of the Upper Waimakariri Road Board, and one of its members was at one time the licensee.

BEALEY HOTEL

This last and most memorable hotel in the Waimakariri country was situated on the south side of the Waimakariri opposite the Bealey valley, into which the road turns after crossing the Klondyke Bridge. This was a pleasant, sunlit site well above the river with excellent views up both Waimakariri and Bealey valleys to the snow-covered heights of the Alps a few miles away.

The first accommodation in the area, on the other side of the river where the Bealey township was laid out in 1865 on the flats now known as Klondyke Corner, was no more than a calico shanty offering a rough bed, a simple meal, and a glass of grog; and the proprietor was Everard Jones or his partner Khull or both. In the rapid development of the area as the roadbuilders began work, Khull & Jones were soon in business more substantially with a store and accommodation house. As that eventful year of 1865 progressed their establishment became an integral part of the Christchurch-Hokitika route, catering for the flood of diggers arriving by coach to begin their long walk over Arthur's Pass to the goldfields, and for the hundreds of labourers working on the road.

The famous Bealey Hotel *on the south bank of the Waimakariri opposite the Bealey valley. This was the traditonal overnight stopping place. The picture shows the simple L-shaped building standing almost unchanged from when Everard Jones built it in 1865. Behind the hotel some bush has been felled for firewood. The Waimakariri River (right) had to be crossed almost immediately by west-bound coaches.* Canterbury Museum

No colder or gloomier place in the middle of winter could be imagined. In consequence by July the Provincial Council was inviting interested parties to build a hotel on the sunny south bank; preferably someone who would also operate a ferry at the river crossing. Jones took up the challenge, sold his Klondyke complex to a man named Grant, and organised from Christchurch the timber and iron for a new building and a boat or punt for the ferry.

But the pace of development outstripped his finances. Although work was started in September, and the punt was reported to be on its way, a month later construction remained at a standstill and the council was advised that Jones had made an assignment of assets to his creditors. They must have agreed to let him carry on because early in 1866 he was offering "superior accommodation" in the simple, L-shaped corrugated iron building by then established as a recognised stop for the coaches.

Some time later the Klondyke premises closed and gradually the various concerns sited there — the telegraph office, the police barracks, the cottages for roadmen and others — were moved

This picture of the hotel in 1887 features a clerical gentleman on the verandah, possibly Archdeacon Henry Harper, whose diocese at that time included the West Coast. The building, by then owned by James O'Malley, is substantially unchanged. Alexander Turnbull Library

Right:
On a stormy day six coaches are battened down against the rain while their passengers shelter in the hotel. The year is 1892 and O'Malley has added an extra storey to one wing of the building, increasing the number of bedrooms to 25.
Alexander Turnbull Library

Below:
It is the turn of the century and O'Malley has given the hotel a coat of paint and a new title, "Glacier Hotel", carved into the fascia board above the porch. Note that in comparison with earlier pictures the hillside bush is completely cleared. This hotel burned down in 1910.
Alexander Turnbull Library

across the river to the more salubrious south bank location. Piecemeal additions were made to the hotel to cater for increasing traffic.

In 1882 one of the best-known Bealey publicans arrived, an ex-sergeant of police named James O'Malley. Impressed with the area and confident that traffic across the Alps would increase, he had timber and iron brought in by traction engine to upgrade the original building and add another storey. While on the job he thought up a new name, "Glacier Hotel", even though the nearest glacier was 16km distant.

The year before he arrived, his namesake George O'Malley (no kin) had cut a track for the Upper Waimakariri Road Board to the White River glaciers about 24km up the valley, and the new publican was entrepreneur enough to advertise them as good reason for people to spend a week or two at his improved hostelry. He kept a handyman at the hotel to act as guide, often a roadman named Murray, and suitable horses for parties to ride up to view the impressive upper Waimakariri scenery including

of course the glaciers, which in those days were worth travelling all that way to see.

Interest in mountain attractions was keen in the latter part of the 19th century, and O'Malley's pub must have been a lively place for a holiday with scenery, fishing and shooting and the almost daily arrival of coaches laden with travellers en route to the romantic west. When the river was up, crowds accumulated there waiting to cross. One account tells of over 100 people bedded down on mattresses spread around the large dining room. There were 34 rooms available, of which 25 were bedrooms. Outside were large stables, for this was also a changing post for the coach horses.

The scene in the morning was a busy one, with ostlers hurrying about their business yoking up the five-horse teams, the luggage being brought out and stacked away on the coaches, and the passengers, replete with bacon-and-egg or mutton-chop breakfasts, settling anxiously in their seats for the river crossing and the exciting trip across the pass and down the Otira Gorge.

Fred Cochrane *was mine host at the Bealey Hotel for a decade from 1928. Before that he was a cafe proprietor and hotelier in Christchurch, a caterer at Tuatapere, a tearooms owner in Timaru, a land agent, and after leaving Bealey ran the supper-rooms in* The Press *basement in Cathedral Square. Most of his revenues at the Bealey came from hauling motorcars across or out of the Waimakariri before the present bridge was built in 1936. At right he tows a sedan car and its five passengers through the flooded river. This service cost a pound (perhaps $50-$80 today). But the owner of the three-seater above, who plainly has attempted the crossing under his own power and failed, would have to pay five pounds ($250-$400) to have his vehicle rescued — or see it swept away to total loss.* Jack Cochrane

If perchance their driver was old John Rountree, he might be persuaded to entertain them with tales of early coaching adventures; though his Waimakariri and Taramakau always became "Why Mack" and "Terrymacoo", they remained a legitimate background for many a well-told yarn.

O'Malley often went up to the glaciers with parties of his more notable guests. Once while visiting the Kilmarnock waterfall in the White valley he took the opportunity to hide a bottle of brandy among some rocks near the foot of the fall. Either he had tired of carrying it or thought it should be kept there for emergencies. The legend of the brandy bottle at Kilmarnock grew with the years, and many a passing tramper (including the author) wasted time searching for it. The only tangible result of the incident was that the waterfall took on the name of the brandy, whereas it was supposed to be called after Lady Jervois, wife of the then Governor-General.

In his later days at the Bealey O'Malley also had the two hotels at Otira — he was said to be the only man who held three hotel licences simultaneously. When he left Bealey is not clear, but in 1910 the first of the fires which were to plague the establishment burned the old hotel to the ground. About the same time the railway, pushing ever further up the Waimakariri, reached Cass. Within the next few years it would bypass the Bealey Hotel and isolate it from the main flow of passenger traffic, like Castle Hill and Cass before it.

Also in 1910 the local road boards were amalgamated to form the Tawera County Council, and as one of its first problems concerned the loss of the hotel and the responsibility of the licensee to look after the river crossing, the council rebuilt the hotel on a lesser scale, with a small bar, a dining room, and a few bedrooms. When the railway reached a temporary station at Halpin's Creek in the Bealey valley, and the coaches no longer drew up at the door, the hotel's main business dwindled to helping a few vehicles across the Waimakariri ford and providing for the occasional passer-by who needed a drink, a meal, or a bed for the night.

This was the hotel which Fred Cochrane took over in 1928 from the previous licensee, one Cox. Fred was one of the more flamboyant proprietors, a man who seemed either to be admired or hated but never ignored. Musterers and mountaineers enjoyed his company and he theirs, but plainly there were many people he couldn't stand. His temper flared quickly. David McLeod tells a believable story about a motorist who pulled up opposite the pub and gave Fred the reasonable expectation of selling a drink or two. But the man spent a long time photographing the scenery and then prepared to leave. Fred, who had been watching all this, could contain himself no longer. Grabbing a shilling from the till, he rushed across the road and thrust it into the man's hand, saying, "Here, if you're too bloody mean to have a drink in this pub, have one in the next!" The story gains point knowing the next pub, at Otira Gorge, was owned by Cochrane's son Jack.

Albie Cochrane, *who lost his life when the second Bealey Hotel caught fire, is seen here ferrying Tom Newth's Dodge car across the Waimakariri on the transporter built for the purpose by his family.* Stan Conway

Trade must have been especially lean throughout the Depression years. Motorists were few in those days, and it was a brave one who ventured along the West Coast Road with its succession of unbridged creeks, the Waimakariri to contend with, and the dangerous crossing of Arthur's Pass in the days when the Zigzag was more like a shingle-slide than a main highway.

An occasional tourist came and stayed for a while to admire the scenery and take walks in the bracing mountain air; or perhaps a shooting party. But the pickings were lean, and the Cochranes were glad to have the revenue from the ferry service.

Motorists were advised by notice-board not to attempt the Waimakariri crossing on their own, but to engage the services of the hotel-keeper, who kept a team of horses ready to tow cars through the river for a fee of one pound (about $60 today). When the river was low the more adventurous travellers might essay the crossing under their own steam, of which they made plenty if the river proved too deep and they got stuck. They had the choice then of leaving the car to its fate or paying Fred Cochrane a penalty fee (often five pounds if he thought they looked affluent enough) to have their car rescued. That was more than a week's wages for an ordinary tradesman.

After a few years of this, Fred, whose dark eyes flashed with anticipation whenever he was engaged in one of these confrontations, gained a reputation which to many made him seem not much inferior to Old Nick himself—the "Bandit of Bealey" was a title used in Automobile Association circles. With profits from the ferry business he built a most efficient travelling platform, on which the cars were mounted for the crossing. In normal conditions the job was a sinecure, but when the river was in flood it required courage and skill. Business boomed as the road was slowly improved and motorcars became more numerous but in 1936 the bridge across the river wrote finis to the last of the Waimakariri ferries.

The following year the Tawera County Council, which owned the building, decided to put the tenancy up for lease. The result was that the licence went to a well-built young local musterer named Reg Ferguson. He was recently married to a good-looking girl, Thelma; together they made a fine couple, and the whole district wished them well.

So Fred was "out". To celebrate his departure after nearly 10 years in the hotel, he threw a final party. The guests came from far and near and a good time was being had by all when suddenly there was a shout of "Fire!". In a few minutes the building was ablaze from end to end as the horror-stricken party-goers rushed to safety. Last out was Cochrane's second son, a likeable young fellow named Albert, his clothes in flames. He was quickly wrapped in a blanket and loaded into the family car to be rushed to hospital in Christchurch 90 miles away.

But on the Goldney Saddle the car broke down. Someone ran a mile or two to Cass and phoned David McLeod, the Grasmere station-owner, who brought his car and loading poor Albie into the back seat set out as fast as the road would allow over Porter's Pass and on to Christchurch. It was to no avail—the badly-burnt young man died next day.

As the son was being rushed away, the father was having a heart attack beside the lonely road on Goldney's Saddle. He and his wife were taken to Grasmere to be cared for by Mary McLeod. For 12 months following the tragedy, Fred, now recovered, ran the Otira Gorge Hotel for son Jack, who was developing the family cartage and contracting company.

Reg Ferguson found himself with a publican's licence but no pub. The Tawera Country Council, its obligation to the ferry crossing at an end, was not interested in rebuilding. For two years while Reg battled to get something organised the business was run from the old post office down the road, known locally as the Dew Drop Inn, where the tiny counter served as the bar. Eventually McLeod and others, with the help of a liquor wholesaler, built a small hotel on the old site. In this Reg and Thelma resumed their roles as mine hosts of a real establishment, and he boosted his earnings by mustering on nearby stations.

But fire and tragedy were not finished yet with Bealey. One fine day in 1946 the young couple went shooting on the hills above the hotel, each equipped with a rifle. However it happened, Reg Ferguson lost his life that afternoon in a tragic shooting accident. And in 1963 the last of the Bealey hotels suffered the same fate as its predecessors; it too burned to the ground.

Today the site is a pleasant picnic spot, high above the river, surrounded by beech forest, where a passer-by may pause to dream of the days when the coaches clattered up the road to halt for the night and, fresh-loaded in the morning, set off across the wild Waimakariri for the pass.

The final words of this chapter belong to Mona Tracy, an author with a special affection for the road across the Alps. In a 1936 magazine article she wrote:

Imagine the pageant which once passed Bealey—the coachloads of bewhiskered men and crinolined women, the diggers who tramped across the Alps with their packs on their backs and the lure of El Dorado in their eyes; the laughing girls off to seek their fortunes in the goldfields dancehalls; the dejected diggers returning with their golden dreams crushed; the packers, the pedlars, the parasites, the swaggers, the down-and-outers. Sometimes, standing by the Waimakariri at Bealey, I have wondered if ever, in the whole of New Zealand, there is a road so romantic as this; or a more motley company of men and women than that which once came by Bealey, paused to rest the night at its hostelry, and passed on again next day, beckoned into Westland by a finger dipped in gold.

The Bealey Hotel *built in 1911 by Tawera County Council. Fred Cochrane presided over its last years before it burned to the ground on the night of his farewell party in 1937.*
Canterbury Museum.

The last. *Reg Ferguson (standing by the petrol pump) was first licensee of this last Bealey Hotel, built in association with local runholders David McLeod and John McAlpine and a liquor firm. Its fate was that of its predecessors, destroyed by fire, in 1963.*
Thelma Jacobsen

CHAPTER EIGHT

The Sheep Stations

The early sheepfarmers, many from Australia, made big changes when they came to Canterbury during the first decade of the province. With their blade shears they cut a wide swath through the intended pattern of English agriculture and gave it instead a strong pastoral background, based not so much on ploughs and wheat as on merinos and tussocks. In the Waimakariri they were men like Joseph Pearson, Marmaduke Dixon, Joseph Hawdon, the Porter brothers, Goldney brothers and the Minchins. With others they established their flocks on the plains alongside the river, or back in the valley among the mountains.

The new colony was supposed to be a slice of England transferred in toto to the antipodes. Men of substance were to buy estates and form an agricultural aristocracy of the South, supported by working farmers, artisans, tradespeople, shopkeepers and servants, each to his own and all for the commonweal. Finance was to come from the sale of land, hopefully 500,000 pounds' worth by the time the First Four Ships left England in 1850.

In the event only a fraction of this goal was in sight when the ships sailed into Lyttelton Harbour, and the association's resident agent, John Robert Godley, had to be persuaded that the settlement's immediate future must rest as much on wool as on cropping. Accordingly he sought and obtained permission to alter the regulations so that the vast pastoral lands of Canterbury might be brought into useful production. Their place in the original plan was such that they were administered by a "Waste Lands Board".

Competition for leaseholds of the best and most available of this land was divided among three groups: the "Pre-Adamites", settlers who were in the province before 1850 (surprisingly they numbered about 900); sheepfarmers from Australia called "Shagroons", or "Prophets" because they prophesied ruin for the agricultural development plan; and "Pilgrims" who came from England in the first years of organised immigration. The Australians were discouraged by years of drought in that country and came looking for a greener alternative. They gave Canterbury's fledgling pastoral industry a valuable injection of capital, stock and experience.

The "waste lands" were allocated on a rough-and-ready system of first come, first served. A prospective runholder would search out an unoccupied place and apply for it at the Lands Office. If there was no prior claim it was his. The would-be wool baron then set out with bullocks and dray, tools, household necessities and a tent to set up his "station" from which to work the run. He had to stock it within nine months or forfeit the lease. By the close of 1855 all the plains and front hills had been taken up and in another 10 years there was scarcely a tussock in Canterbury not spoken for.

As time passed there were significant changes. The best land on the plains was converted from sheep to crops, either by the runholder or by small freeholders who bought blocks of their choice out of the runs. This development saw the settlement take on something of the shape originally planned for it, and with the pastoral industry making a worthwhile contribution Canterbury began to know periods of great prosperity. Many "Prophets" and "Pilgrims" shared in the good times, though few of the latter knew much about practical sheepfarming when they arrived. But they put away their top hats and pulled through somehow, greatly aided by good managers and shepherds. These were often Highland Scots who quickly adapted to their new environment.

Part 1: The Hill Country Runs

Lochinvar, Castle Hill, Cora Lynn, Grasmere, Craigieburn, Avoca, Mount White—these romantic names of upper Waimakariri sheep runs enhance the aura of mystery and remoteness surrounding their location beyond the front ranges. Most were caught up in the stirring events of 1864-65 when explorers were looking for a way to the West Coast and the road was pushed across their boundaries towards Arthur's Pass. The gold diggers came marching through and the half-century run of the coaches began. But when that excitement was over the loneliness returned.

Living there has been smoothed by electricity and the modern motorcar, but otherwise work on the big stations is much as it always was. The great ranges impose their disciplines. Sheep still have to be cared for and mustered in from the high tops for drafting, dosing, shearing and dipping. Winters are as snowy as ever and summers hot. It will always be a life of extremes for lean, hard men—and their lean, hard dogs.

In descending order from the main divide the runs on the upper Waimakariri and its tributaries (Hawdon, Poulter, Esk, Broken, Porter and Kowai) were (until 1917) as follows:

SOUTH BANK		NORTH BANK
Cora Lynn		
Grasmere	*Beyond*	Riversdale
Craigieburn	*Porter's*	Mount White
Avoca	*Pass*	Lochinvar
Castle Hill		
Brooksdale		
Mount Torlesse	*Front*	Woodstock
Ben More	*Ranges*	

The traveller from Christchurch meets the hill stations as he approaches Porter's Pass, with Ben More on the left and Brooksdale on the right. From Lake Lyndon to Dry Creek the road runs through Brooksdale country, changing at the creek to Castle Hill. Broken River is the boundary between Castle Hill and Flock Hill.* Further on, Lake Pearson shares its shores with three stations, Flock Hill, Craigieburn and Grasmere, all of which also have frontages on the Waimakariri. From the lake to Cass River the road is through Grasmere station, and from Cass to the Bealey, through Cora Lynn.

At Goldney Saddle, beyond the Cass River Bridge, a shingle road leaves the highway at the point where the traveller gets a first glimpse of the Waimakariri. This road crosses the river and accompanies it for 25km downstream through the sprawling 50,000ha Mount White complex comprising the original Riversdale, Mount White and Lochinvar runs, bounded by the main divide and the Dampier and Puketeraki ranges and drained by the Hawdon, Poulter and Esk rivers. Still further down the Waimakariri, beyond the gorge and the Broken River junction, lie Avoca, Mount Torlesse and Woodstock runs, completing a 120 km roundabout up the road and down the river, beginning and ending near Springfield, and embracing a sheep and tussock world 50km wide and 65 km long.

When Joseph Pearson struggled through the Waimakariri Gorge in February, 1857, he must have been pleased to see the land ahead of him opening out to such a vast spread of tussocked flats and gentle hills. This was what he was looking for—good

*A boundary change in 1917 saw a new station, Flock Hill, created from the old Avoca run and part of the original Craigieburn.

Above: *Mount Binser is central to this photograph taken from a Puketeraki spur above the upper gorge. To the right, behind Whale Hill, lie the Mount White homestead block and the Poulter River headwaters, while to the left the Waimakariri valley leads towards Cass and the Sugar Loaf, the road and railway. The tiny speck far below on the sunlit river at left is a jetboat.*
Photo by Pat Dolan (Mannering & Associates.)

Right: *Duke Dixon and his jetboat head into the shadow of beetling rock cliffs.*

Below: *Another jetboat enthusiast, Bevan Tulett, snapped Zane Findlay at a club outing with these two fine salmon he hooked in the gorge.*

Summer...Winter. *Lake Pearson lies 600m above sea level midway between east and west coasts, and accordingly the extremes of climate are greater than on the plains.*

Above: *The northern reach of the lake, here dressed in late summer finery, mak* *strong call to travellers to halt awhile.*

left: *But in winter's harsh garb the scene is vastly different. The lake is actually ...n here, beside remnants of the old road — the view much as coach passengers saw ... years ago.*

Above: *Willows rimy with hoar-frost embellish the lakeside looking south to Broken Hill.*

Below: *A Midland line train threads a tunnelled course along high terraces above the river as it approaches Staircase Gully viaduct.* N.Z. Railways photo.

Left: *The view upriver from Mount White Bridge, where the Waimakariri is narrowed to a single stream by the Hawdon fan.*

Below: *Road and rail meet again at Corner Knob beyond Cass, where the Waimakariri runs close by. Towering above morning mist over the river stand the snow-clad Dome (1939m, right) and satellite peaks.*

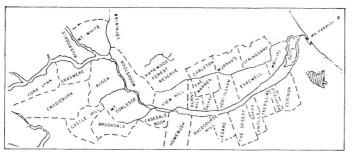

This map *shows approximate boundaries of sheep stations occupying Waimakariri country in the 1860s.*

sheep country for his Australian friends, and there was plenty for all — 40,000 hectares at least, perhaps double that. The fires he lit to burn off the scrub and accumulated tussock debris of centuries were so large some people in Christchurch thought it was an especially lurid display of *aurora borealis*.

The map he drew on returning to View Hill showed the Waimakariri River as a dominant feature, threading a broad path through the proposed sheep runs. He marked down Hawdon for 8000ha centred on Lake Grasmere, some of which was across the river on what was later part of Riversdale. Aitken was to get 8000ha, half centred on Mount Binser and the remainder on the south side of the river opposite Poulter junction. Pearson pencilled himself in for 12,000ha extending north from Broken River and intersected by Sloven's Stream. The fourth holder was to be Thomas Woolaston White with 4000ha in the fork of the Poulter and Esk rivers. White was a neighbour of Pearson on the plains.

William Guise Brittan, Commissioner of Waste Lands, approved of and signed Pearson's map, but when the licences were issued later in 1857 the runs as he had drawn them had been changed, and some of the people as well. Pearson and Aitken appeared to have withdrawn and their allocations were taken over by Hawdon. There may have been an element of prearrangement in this. Hawdon thus assumed control of nearly 30,000 hectares, comprising most of today's Flock Hill, Craigieburn, Grasmere and Riversdale runs. But he was no stranger to big country — before coming to New Zealand he had owned much greater tracts of land in Australia. The licence for

White's run was issued in the name of Edward Corker Minchin, after whom Lake Minchin was named. It would seem his brother Frederick was also involved. Of Edward Minchin it was said he was "a handsome, athletic man, and one who could handle a quarrelsome fellow in fine style, without any bounce or pretence, and a fine wrestler".

There was no access to any of this country except by scrambling over what was later named Porter's Pass and riding on slowly over the tussocked flats between the high ranges. The sheep had to be got across a succession of rivers — Kowai, Porter, Thomas, and Broken, and for some the much more formidable Waimakariri.

On arrival at what was considered a suitable place to locate the "station", tools and stores were unloaded from the packhorses and tents were pitched. Next day, while the shepherd introduced his flock to new pastures in unfamiliar country, the squatter and his men rode to the nearest bush to cut timber for a hut and a post-and-rail yard for the horses.

Succeeding weeks were devoted to building a homestead from materials at hand — cob (paddled clay mixed with chopped tussock) plastered on to beech or manuka laths and covered with wood slabs, and a roof thatched with snowgrass on laths. The builders were unaware that mountain beech quicky deteriorates when exposed to the weather, requiring early replacement with more durable timber or (when it became available) corrugated iron. In later years Castle Hill stone made a more permanent building alternative.

Although there was a thriving live sheep and cattle trade with the West Coast when the road was opened (in 1866 4000 sheep and 25,000 cattle were driven across Arthur's Pass to feed hungry diggers), farming economics were more generally based on wool from the sheep's back. A run required well-grassed lower country for the merino ewes, hoggets and the rams, preferably with some paddocks for growing good pasture, hay and root crops. Enough safe blocks of rough grazing were needed for the main wether flock in winter, backed with extensive areas on the higher ranges for summer pasturage.

Hawdon built his place beside the Craigie Burn above Lake Pearson, named the run after the stream, and engaged Joseph Pearson as manager and a man named McRae as head shepherd. Another station was built at Grasmere for his son Arthur, who was to manage there. The Minchins established their station near Pete's Stream about 10 kilometres up the Poulter River, which is about as far from civilisation as a

Fine sheep country. *Four upper Waimakariri views: (1) Castle Hill flats backgrounded by the Torlesse Range. (2) Wide tussocked flats in the upper valley of Sloven's Stream with the railway at right and Craigieburn station marked by trees at centre; Bullock Hill at left; Sloven's-Broken River junction lies 16km away to the south. (3) The West Coast road bisects Grasmere, Polar Range on left skyline, then the Pyramid, Hawdon valley and Cass Hill. (4) Grasmere tussocks lead down to the Waimakariri and across the river to high terraces and bush on Mount White run to the 1800m heights of Mount Binser.*

homestead could be in those days. It was unlikely that either family (Edward Minchin's sons William and John ran the Poulter property) was in residence until the spring of 1858. Torlesse makes no mention of them when he explored their domains in February of that year.

As was often the case with early runholders much reliance was placed on experienced shepherds, one of whom customarily became head shepherd and possibly manager. These capable and practical men attended to the day-to-day running of the station, while the runholder himself might be found residing in his town house or on a plains property not too far from town. There he had time to indulge his other interests, from idling at the Christchurch Club in Latimer Square to pursuing a career in local politics.

There was good profit in wool in those early days, when a runholder might expect a return of 25% on his investment. Sometimes there was even greater gain in the acquisition, improvement and sale of properties for capital gain, which is the likely explanation for most of the rapid changes of ownership which characterised many of the early stations. Another factor in this respect was the isolation of the upper Waimakariri, which did not suit everyone.

Work was hard and living primitive. On the other hand just being there among such grand surroundings was compensation enough for some. In those pioneering days there must have been much that was profitable, agreeable, and worthwhile. It would be a decade or two before Grasmere drove its owner to drink and Mount White's to suicide.

In the winter of 1858, not long after Hawdon and the Minchins had taken up their runs, the three Porter brothers appeared to the south of them at the 14,000ha Castle Hill block in the V of the Craigieburn and Torlesse ranges, a place with good natural boundaries in the Porter (south) and Broken (north) rivers. The brothers built some kind of a station at the junction of the Porter and Springs Creek near where the present Porter Heights ski-field road leaves the main highway. From here the original track is said to have followed an entirely different route from that of today, crossing the Broken much lower down and traversing a valley behind Flock Hill (the one with the limestone "sheep"*) to join the present road before it reaches Craigieburn saddle.

As the 1850s became the 1860s the occupation of runs beyond Porter's Pass was completed with the issue of licences to William Thomson for Lochinvar, the largest run of them all, and to the Goldney brothers for Cora Lynn. They were furthest from the track which by then was slowly becoming a useful if not always discernible connection with the outside world. In 1859 the sledge track by then completed over the pass enabled the wool (said to be already 5000 bales) to be brought out. This track slowly extended up the valley and improved until in 1865 the gold rush saw it hastily converted into a highway fit not just for bullock teams and wool wagons, but for coaches bound for the pass across the Alps.

Lochinvar, the remote Esk River station, had a ring of derring-do about its name, recalling Scott's hero bursting in upon the fair Ellen's bridal feast and sweeping her away on his horse. William Thomson's son John had the horse but certainly not the fair lady when he and his three companions drove a mob of cattle up the bed of the Esk in 1860 to stock the run. It took them 2½ days from Avoca, itself a long way from anywhere. When it was time to drive them out again, the easiest way was reckoned to be over the top of the Puketeraki Range to Hawarden in North Canterbury. Legend has it that one of the drovers was frostbitten on the way.

In 1860 when the Goldneys took it up, Cora Lynn was about as isolated as Lochinvar. The only access then was to take to the Cass and Waimakariri riverbeds and keep up the river until more open ground was reached past the bluffs. The run extended westward up the south bank of the Waimakariri for about 20km, far beyond the Bealey, until the last traces of feed were lost in the bluffs high above the Anticrow River. The Goldneys built their station on the extreme eastern end of the run, across the Cass River from Grasmere.

*When one gets among them, they are as big as houses.

Because of their position as last outpost on the soon to be developed main route to the West Coast, the Goldneys found themselves playing host to numerous visitors and travellers passing through. Arthur Dobson stayed there in 1864 while discovering his pass, and one of the Goldneys made the first crossing with him. Later when the track was sufficiently advanced for foot travel over the divide they and the Hawdons were plagued with gold diggers and swaggers looking for quarters and meals. Sometimes up to two dozen or more "free" lodgers, tired and hungry, were fed and bedded down for the night before moving on with high expectations or otherwise, depending on whether they were coming or going.

By 1879 the number of sheep on the top six runs in the Waimakariri had grown to 68,000, and by 1895, before the disastrous snow of that year, to 92,000. From then on numbers declined as a 20-year period of depression afflicted all runholders until World War I came to their aid with better prices for both wool and meat. By that time sheep numbers were down to 45,000. In the Great Depression wool prices fell to only 7d a pound (1932) and remained low until demand during World War II brought more stable markets. It was war again, this time in Korea, which saw wool climb to 150d a pound, when some exceptional bales actually achieved the golden figure of a pound for a pound.

By 1960, when the Catchment Board was preparing to retire up to two-thirds of some runs as a conservation measure, sheep numbers had fallen to 42,000. At the same time the virtual elimination of introduced pests, which competed for pasturage, and the introduction of aerial topdressing and improved fencing resulted in better grassland quality and carrying capacity, with a resulting increase in stock units.

The high country runs are mostly held under pastoral leases which are granted for a term of 33 years with perpetual rights of renewal. In 1873 the Crown granted Canterbury College an endowment of 26,000ha comprising the Grasmere and original Craigieburn and Avoca runs. The Crown took over all other leases when the Provincial Government was abolished in 1876.

CASTLE HILL

The three Porter brothers who first took up Castle Hill run in 1858 were sons of a London landowner who visited New Zealand only briefly. One of the brothers, Alfred, appears to have been the sheepfarmer, managing Rokeby station on the Rakaia and renting it on terms before going to Castle Hill. The other brothers were a lawyer and a civil engineer. After holding the run for six years they sold in 1864 to John and Charles Enys and Edward Curry for 11,920 pounds. The Porters left behind them the rough homestead on the Porter River, some yards and sheds, and their name on the river and the pass.

John Enys, the foremost of the new owners, was one of the more interesting characters among the district's pioneers, and a rarity in that he kept a diary. (Apparently this was an old Enys custom, for among his ancestors at Enys Place in Cornwall was one whose journal in the time of Queen Elizabeth included this entry: "Today we saw the Armada go up the channel.")

The Enys brothers, *John (left) and Charles (right), who took over the Castle Hill run in 1864 from the Porter brothers. Known as "Buckets in the Well" because one or the other was always away in England. John had wide educational and scientific interests, while Charles was a gifted painter and crack shot. At centre is their friend Edward Chudleigh, who frequently visited the station and enjoyed working with the sheep.*

Trelissick. *The Castle Hill station buildings sited north of the present Castle Hill Village. When James Milliken bought Flock Hill he moved most of these buildings there.* Alexander Turnbull Library.

The Enyses made good use of the abundant limestone outcrops on the property by blasting and sawing large blocks lying near the base of the cliffs. If a block was too big a hole was bored with an augur, and gunpowder poured down it and exploded. Suitable pieces were then sawn into shape. With this material fireplaces were built, and a station house on the flat in front of Castle Hill, where it still stands. The homestead, which Enys called Trelissick, was erected in 1865 of pit sawn timber, further north across the Thomas River, and in that year the brothers bought out Edward Curry.

They also built a sheep dip near the Thomas. It was made of cut stone and the fireplaces were laid on a bed of coal. (There were in those days five large coal seams within 16km of Trelissick.) As a precaution against scab the sheep were dipped in a mixture of tobacco and sulphur boiled together and used hot.

The Enys brothers made many trips back "Home", and when Charles was in England in 1868 one of John's closest friends, E.R. Chudleigh, came to stay. He kept a more informative diary than his host, and among the entries is one which gives a detailed description of mustering at that time seen through the eyes of a comparative new-chum. The gang camped five miles from the station at the base of Mount Torlesse in order to make an early start:

We were all up at 3 a.m., had breakfast and off. Four of us went to the top in three hours and had a glorious view. It was too cold to stop long, so McLennan (the head shepherd) and I started along the top and reached the appointed rendezvous at 11 o'clock. Those at the foot collected the sheep with their dogs as we drove them from the top and sides. We all had a great feed and then a small sleep and at about 2 p.m. we went off to muster another part of the country. We got back to camp about 6 p.m., had tea, and turned in.

Breakfast was had by 5 a.m. The ground was alive with blowflies; the meat full of maggots, and the blankets not covered with a mackintosh were covered with blows. We were off again and by 9 o'clock had the sheep at a river we wanted to cross, the yards being on the other side. We were two hours crossing. The sheep would not go in. We took them up and hurled them in, but no, back they came again and, breaking into small mobs, rushed past men and over dogs in a most determined way, but they gave in after a two hour fight and crossed. The sheep were fairly beaten and so were we, for as soon as I had a bath and a good dinner I slept for three hours.

John Enys's many and varied interests and activities suggest that the life of a station owner in his time was not too onerous. No doubt McLennan was a good man, enabling the master to be away for much of the time. As a Justice of the Peace he was often called on to preside over inquests and inquiries or to serve on the Bench. He was a member of the Road Board, the County Council, and the Provincial Council, chairman of the Museum Committee, a member of the University Senate and of many other organisations concerned with the public good. In addition he was a foremost authority on moths and butterflies, a keen fisherman, and an amateur botanist and geologist. When not engaged in these activities he would be entertaining a succession of distinguished visitors at Trelissick, from Governer Grey down. And, as mentioned, he was often away in England.

His much younger brother Charles had quite different interests. He was reputed to be the best shot in New Zealand, and his prowess on the billiard table at the Christchurch Club astonished his fellow members. He once bought a pistol to shoot birds — he said it was too easy with a gun.

Until he could stock the local lakes and rivers with trout, John's enthusiasm for fishing had to be restricted to catching eels; one day in 1867 he caught 25 in Lake Pearson. That same year the first trout ova were brought to Canterbury, and next year were introduced to provincial waters. Enys was to the fore with this in the many rivers and lakes of the upper Waimakariri. He watched their progress with intense interest, and after a time entries like these began to appear in his diary: "Caught first trout at Grasmere, kept 3 ate 1." "Rode up to Mount White, saw trout spawning." "Caught first trout with fly."

Evening by the fire. *William Packe's 1868 painting of Charles Enys and J. Philpott in the main living room at Trelissick shows the slab timber construction, simple furnishings and generous library which combined to make living in the back country tolerable. Some homesteads managed a piano as well.* Alexander Turnbull Library.

Valley view. *Castle Hill run is central to this view, with one of the rare "straights" on S.H.73 passing through the station. The limestone quarry on Castle Hill itself is prominent, with Thomas River bush and Craigieburn Range beyond. Whitewater Stream descends at left to join Porter River. Snow in foreground is on the Torlesse Range's highest eminence, somewhat confusingly called Castle Hill Peak (2000m).*

Still there. *The most visible of the very early station buildings in the Waimakariri valley is the limestone cottage at Castle Hill, built in the mid-1860s before the Enys brothers shifted to Trelissick. Of the three main buildings the one at right has survived and is still in use today.*
Canterbury Museum.

The brothers each had a special cat. One was called Firebell because it woke the cook one night when the kitchen caught on fire. Charles allowed his cat to drape itself round his shoulders when he was at table and help itself to titbits from his fork. John's sat more sedately on his knees. The brothers, as might be surmised, were bachelors.

Winters at Castle Hill were not without their seasonal pleasures. The Enyses built a pond at Trelissick for ice-skating, a pastime also pursued at Lakes Lyndon and Pearson. In warmer weather they enjoyed boating at Lake Pearson, when they could fish comfortably and shoot down the occasional black teal. And in February, 1871, John did something he must have been contemplating for some time — he splashed through the underground passage of Cave Stream.

In 1890 Charles in New Zealand and the eldest brother in England both died; John inherited Enys Place and went "Home". But before leaving he took his favourite cat to friends in Christchurch and made sure it was settled before he sailed.

The station was placed with an agent and leased first to A.G.Stronach, then briefly to Julius Herman von Haast, a son of the museum director, and finally to Lewis Mathias before it was sold in 1901 to John Mackenzie. John Milliken, who had

the next-door station, Brooksdale, bought it in 1908, and son James came on the scene in 1912. Subsequent owners were W.B.Clarkson & Co. (1921), G. and J.Frizzell, R.Blackley (manager for Clarkson's), Mrs J.Stringer and Mrs B.E.Tait (1952), the same combination minus Blackley (1960), Castle Hill Run Ltd. (D.S.J.Reid) (1968). and from 1976 to 1987 S.M.J.Smith, V.M.Smith and A.M.Smith. Max Smith would be better known as the chief engineer for the Waitaki hydro works. The present owners are the developers of Castle Hill Village.

CRAIGIEBURN

A great block of country extending from Broken River to Lake Pearson, and from the Waimakariri River to the Craigieburn Range, comprised the original Craigieburn run, first taken up in 1857 by Joseph Hawdon. In Australia he had driven the first cattle from New South Wales to Melbourne and Adelaide via the Murray River, and explored north-west Australia with Captain George Grey (later Sir George, a New Zealand governor and premier). It is said that Hawdon made a fortune, which would have been greater had he stayed in Australia, since one of his runs in Victoria became the site of the town of Dandenong.

He was married for a second time in 1856, to a young wife, and settling in New Zealand began what was to be a lively and agreeable period in his life. He bought a town house near the western end of Salisbury Street in Christchurch, predicted all kinds of prosperity for Canterbury, and later served on the Legislative Council until his death. The Hawdon River and

The Enys Snow Gate *was designed to operate when snow on the ground made conventional gates useless. A writer who inspected it in 1880 wrote: "It is a queer-looking apparatus, the posts to which the gate is hung bearing some resemblance to a double gibbet, with a rope dangling from either side. Pull one of these ropes and the gate rises [above snow level], describing an arc as it passes between the two high posts, and drops down either side of them." The gate was known locally as "the Enys kea trap". In this picture the West Coast Road can be seen as a vertical white line to the right of the gate, with Castle Hill Hotel showing immediately above the foot gate. The Enys homestead, Trelissick, lay along the road leading right, and the new Castle Hill Village is being built on the flat at right.*
Canterbury Museum.

Lake Hawdon were named after him and Lake Marymere after his wife.

Craigieburn was an attractive run for a sheepfarmer sickened by Australian droughts, with a large proportion of easy country, but Hawdon probably spent little time there. He had efficient managers in Pearson and McRae and in addition his son Arthur was at Grasmere next door.

The coming of the West Coast Road in 1865 brought dramatic changes to Craigieburn, as the homestead was near the road where it emerges from the gorge of the Craigie Burn, near the present Flock Hill station. The Dobson boys made it their headquarters while surveying in the district, as did Jack Smith and his road-building gang. When the avalanche of Coast-bound footsloggers began, all demanding food and shelter, Hawdon took immediate steps to ease this burden by building a hotel below the station at the bend in the road halfway down to Lake Pearson. This was a spacious stone

Craigieburn homestead. *The original house in Joseph Hawdon's day, one of a number of paintings by Charles Enys. The stream which brought down the shingle ran in the gully behind the house.* Canterbury Museum.

building which unfortunately was gutted by fire almost as soon as it was opened, about Christmas, 1865. It must have been rebuilt promptly, because early next year it was reported as being in use as a manager's residence for the station. There is almost no trace of it today.

Craigieburn had more than its share of murders and accidental deaths. When the Duke of Edinburgh was visiting New Zealand in 1869 one of the young gentlemen in his company, Algernon Fitzhardinge Kingscote, came to stay at the station. While walking through an open door into the dining room carrying a loaded gun the butt struck the door frame, the gun exploded, and he fell dead.

The demands of travellers often led to friction with station people. An example was the confrontation between the Craigieburn cook, one Peperell, and an Irishman named Levell who arrived with two bulldogs demanding meat and bread. The cook refused him anything but flour and took up his gun when Levell threatened him. Levell was killed in the struggle and the cook was charged with murder. Fortunately for him the jury found "no bill".

Nearly demolished. *The old Craigieburn homestead (at what is now Flock Hill) pictured here after heavy rain triggered a shingle slide which came near to flattening it completely. But the shingle was shovelled away and the old house still stands.* From Hamish Innes.

Cave Stream, which provides idyllic picnic spots near the highway as it approaches Craigieburn Saddle, and flows down to Broken River through its famous limestone tunnel, enjoyed more name changes than curves in its course — Buchanan's Creek, Deadman's Creek, Murderer's Creek and Blackball Creek were some. Two of these derived from the murder of a man on a nearby travelling-stock reserve. Neither murderer nor victim was ever identified, but some Chinese were suspected. The tale grew with the years, the most popular version being that a man named Granger (possibly a later hotelkeeper at Sheffield), on going to the creek for a drink found himself staring a dead Chinaman in the face, lying just beneath the surface. The deceased, supposed to have been carrying a large swag of gold from the Coast, was murdered for his loot — but he was the wrong man; the one with the gold went over Cass Saddle.

Hawdon continued with Craigieburn and Riversdale until 1867, when he sold to the Campbells — Michael, Douglas and Hume. Michael withdrew in 1871. For a time most of the runholders' wives in the district were Miller girls. John Cochran of Mount White married Fanny Miller, while his brother James of Lochinvar married a sister, and Douglas Campbell yet another. Douglas Campbell went back to Scotland in 1872 and for a year or two the run was managed by Reginald Foster of Avoca station, who was also chairman of the Road Board.

Bruce of Cora Lynn had a hand in the run for a few years until in 1881 it was taken over by the Loan and Mercantile Company. Subsequent owners were Jones and Stronach and Edmund James; then in 1906 it was bought by Frederick Savill, for whom David Manson was manager. When the railway came through in 1910, providing superior transportation to that on the neglected road (by then no longer used for coaching), Savill abandoned the old homestead by Lake Pearson and built a new one close to the railway opposite Lake Hawdon, a decision later occupants must have regretted as the road improved and rail services declined.

In 1917 a big change completely altered the configuration of Craigieburn. The leases for the historic run, which were in the hands of Canterbury College, came up for review. The run was

The Milliken family *was associated with three Waimakariri sheep runs. Seated, from left, Robert, Lillian, John (Brooksdale and Castle Hill), Elizabeth, James (Flock Hill), Minnie; standing, Les, Ivy, Jack, Vina, William, Gladys; in front, Myrtle and Albert. Milliken senior was also the district's chief transport contractor until the railway opened.*

From the air. *The upper Waimakariri from above the gorge entrance with Craigieburn run country facing the Waimakariri at left and Mount White station at right. Esk River enters from lower right in front of Whale Hill, with Poulter River valley beyond. Mount Binser stands above the hill and Peveril Peak is at far right. On the horizon are main divide mountains.*
Catchment Board.

divided into three and put up for auction. Joseph Studholme and W.K.McAlpine secured the block extending from Lake Pearson eastwards to the Waimakariri, which included the homestead Savill had built. James Milliken, a son of John Milliken of Brooksdale and Castle Hill, got the other two, for which he re-established the homestead on the old site beside the Craigie Burn and named the run Flock Hill.

FLOCK HILL

The early history of Flock Hill, therefore, is essentially the history of the original Craigieburn run. When Milliken came in 1917 there was possibly some feeling about names. As mentioned, in Savill's time the operating base for Craigieburn was moved from the main road five or six miles across country, and the block containing the new homestead was given the venerable title of "Craigieburn", even though it no longer had much connection with either the stream or the mountain range of that name.

Priorities in such matters may have been influenced by the dominant runholders of the time, Studholme and McAlpine, who already had Mount White and Riversdale and were about to take up Grasmere and the "new" Craigieburn. In this situation Milliken was a relative outsider whose only option was to accept some alternative. He chose "Flock Hill", or had it chosen for him, after the eminence above Cave Stream where (as mentioned) scattered limestone blocks are supposed to look like flocks of granite sheep. The end result was that Flock Hill station stood on the Craigie Burn, and Craigieburn station on Sloven's Creek.

Milliken moved into the old Craigieburn homestead, part of which had been built by Hawdon in the 1850s. (It is still there, a survivor of years of occupation by shepherds and shearers, and

near destruction by a shingle slide.) He took most of the Trelissick farm buildings from Castle Hill and re-erected them at Flock Hill and after a while built himself a new homestead on the present site. He was a big, powerful man whose feats of strength are legendary and he fitted easily into the run's broad acres — it extends for nine kilometres along the highway from Broken River to Lake Pearson, and for 24km from the Craigieburn Range to the Waimakariri, on which it has a frontage of about 16km.

In 1948 Flock Hill was taken over by Gerald Urquhart, one of the well-known sheepfarming family and another big and immensely strong man, who after a few years married Doreen Pickens, equally well-known as a mountaineer. They farmed together until Gerald's death in 1973 after which Mrs Urquhart continued with her sons David and Ross for another nine years before selling in 1982 to Hamish Innes. The Urquharts introduced two novelties of the time — commercial deer farming and holiday accommodation for visitors. With an eye to the growing needs of skiers bound for the Craigieburn fields, the present owners, Hamish and Philippa Innes, plan to expand the accommodation part of their activities.

THE "NEW" CRAIGIEBURN

Of all the near hundred owners who have farmed upper Waimakariri sheep runs, one name stands out for accomplishment and continuity of association now encompassing four generations. That name is McAlpine, which appeared on the scene in 1910 when Joseph Studholme and Walter Kenneth McAlpine took over the big Riversdale-Mount White-Lochinvar complex.

Walter McAlpine was an aggressive, determined Scot with a temperament to suit the vast scale of his tussock, bush and scree territory. He was ready at any time, it was said, to settle disputes with his fists if necessary. His wife Gwendoline was a fitting companion — a good walker, horsewoman and rifle shot who enjoyed the back country. When the college leases were auctioned in 1917 McAlpine extended his interests across the Waimakariri from Mount White to include Grasmere and the new Craigieburn run, and took up residence in the less isolated homestead beside the railway.* In 1920 he began a retrenchment by giving up Lochinvar, in 1924 Riversdale and Mount White, and in 1927 Grasmere when the partnership with Joseph Studholme ended. He then concentrated his interests on Craigieburn and on property in North Canterbury.

His son John grew to manhood in time to battle (with typical McAlpine vigour) against the hard times of the Great Depression, closely associated in the struggle with David McLeod of Grasmere. Like his father he developed a keen interest in local politics (both served on county councils and as chairmen of Lyttelton Harbour Board), and in the 1940s became Member of Parliament for Selwyn, and subsequently Minister of Railways, honoured later in life with a knighthood.

Craigieburn is still in the family, run by Fenton Westenra and his wife Louise (McAlpine). It is an attractive station, intersected by Sloven's Stream and based on the homestead opposite Lake Hawdon, with frontages on Lake Pearson and the Waimakariri opposite Poulter valley.

Left: *Walter Kenneth McAlpine.* **Above:** *The Craigieburn station on the railway established by Frederick Savill. The house burned down and the McAlpine family records were lost in the blaze.* **Right:** *John Kenneth McAlpine (later Sir John).*

*Subsequently destroyed by fire, as were Flock Hill homestead and all the hotels beyond Porter's Pass — Castle Hill, Craigieburn, Cass and the three at Bealey. The homesteads at Flock Hill and Craigieburn were both replaced with handsome new buildings.

GRASMERE

Arthur and Sarah Hawdon, *who farmed Grasmere until 1876 and had to leave with nothing when Dalgety's stepped in and took over. She was the former Sarah Elizabeth Barker, daughter of Dr and Mrs A.C.Barker, the first child born in Christchurch following the arrival of the First Four Ships, in a tent it was said, and christened from a pie dish. Their unhappy marrige bore two children, one of whom died in a mental hospital and the other of cholera in Kashmir. Arthur Hawdon, described as "an ill-tempered boozer", when remonstrated with by a family friend for paying more attention to whisky than his wife, was said to have offered to "sell her for a fiver". In later life Sarah Hawdon was a frequent contributor to publications under the pseudonym of "Tent-born".*

David McLeod farmed Grasmere and Cora Lynn for more than 40 years, from 1930 through the Great Depression and the Second World War and on through the more prosperous 1950s and 1960s. He wrote such popular and entertaining books about them that for many readers they are among the most familiar of Canterbury sheep stations. Grasmere, as mentioned, was one of Joseph Hawdon's 1857 acquisitions and was the home and workplace of his son Arthur, who was manager there until 1876. That was about five years after father Hawdon died, long enough for Arthur to so mismanage the place that he had to forfeit it.

Arthur Hawdon served on the Upper Waimakariri Road Board, which for much of its life met rather sociably along the road from Grasmere at the Cass Hotel. His other claim to fame was that in 1872 he married the beautiful Sarah Elizabeth Barker, eldest daughter of Dr A.C. Barker, whose early photographs of Christchurch are so highly prized today. Dr Barker was reported to be pleased with the match, but probably changed his mind later.

Like its neighbours Cora Lynn and Craigieburn, Grasmere was often a base for engineers, surveyors and workmen who built the West Coast highway across these stations in 1865. When Edward Dobson, his son George, and explorers Browning and Cahill came through in March of that year they made Grasmere their home for a time. And it was to there that the Dobsons, wet, cold, miserable and beaten, returned after their abortive trip into the Otehake wilderness. No doubt Arthur Hawdon did his best to warm them with a stiff glass or two.

The original Grasmere homestead, across the road from Lake Grasmere, was built in 1858. It was a simple two-roomed slab hut which served Hawdon for the term of his bachelor days. In

The Grasmere homestead *which Arthur Hawdon built in the decade 1858-68. The timbered chimneys are an interesting feature of the old house.*
Alexander Turnbull Library.

Dr A.C.Barker *visited his daughter late in 1872 and took this photograph of his new son-in-law posed against a background of Grasmere station buildings and snowy Craigieburn peaks.* Canterbury Museum.

1872 he enclosed this in an enlarged house faced with limestone blocks to give it a semblance of dignity and permanence for his new bride. One hundred and twenty-nine years later some of the original construction is still there — the oldest such relic in the valley still in daily use.

Near Grasmere, towards the Cass River, stood the Cass Hotel, the Road Board office and library, the coaching stables, the temporary shacks of railway construction gangs, and later the railway station with its refreshment rooms nearby. There was also a post office which was closed and re-opened at least five times, manned for years by the redoubtable "Robbie" (Mrs Grace Robertshaw). Race meetings and sports meetings were held on the Grasmere flat, and even a race ball in the Road Board office (eventually removed and made into fishing huts on the shores of Lake Pearson; the others have disappeared without trace).

Like all the stations Grasmere has had a succession of owners down through the years. After Dalgety and Company's 22-year term (with Fortesque Dalgety as manager for a time) it was sold in 1898 to John Sim, then to Sealy Rutherford in 1903. In the lease auction of 1917 Rutherford lost out to Studholme and McAlpine, who already owned Riversdale and Mount White. They held it for 10 years before selling to Taylor and Faulkner in 1927. This partnership, which already had Cora Lynn, sold both stations in 1930 to David McLeod, whose youthful enthusiasm for his "Kingdom of the Hills" anaesthetised the pain of the Great Depression. McLeod continued, for a time with his partner Orbell, until 1970, after which a son, Ian McLeod, carried on until 1978 before selling to Dugald Harcourt.

Grasmere today. *One of the gabled rooms at left is part of the original building. For his new bride in 1872 Arthur Hawdon built an additional gabled room and faced both with Castle Hill limestone. The remodelled portion at right belongs to a later period. Note forest changes and gully erosion behind the house compared with the 1872 picture.*

The Cora Lynn homestead *built by Thomas Whillians Bruce after he bought the station from the Goldney brothers in 1867 — a painting by Charles Enys, with peaks of the Black Range forming an impressive background.*
Canterbury Museum.

CORA LYNN

Cora Lynn (or Coralin as it is shown on early maps) is the top run in the Waimakariri, the valley of which hereabouts lies east and west. The run's eastern boundary is on the Cass River, and the western boundary used to embrace distant alpine heights dominated by Mount Gizeh.

The run was taken up by the Goldney brothers, Francis and George, in February, 1860, and is said to have been named by them after a locality in Dumfries, Scotland. They were merino breeders who held stud sales in Latimer Square opposite the Christchurch Club, the sheepfarmers' "home-away-from-home" in the city.

Their primitive homestead was on the west bank of the Cass River not far from Grasmere, and most of their domain was remote from the station because of the great bulk of Mount Horrible and the difficulties of access round Corner Knob where the Waimakariri ran hard against the cliffs. Some time later when the road was established round the Knob the station was moved to its present site near Broad Stream and a house, woolshed and stables erected. The Goldneys applied for an accommodation house licence in 1865 but never went ahead with it.

Cora Lynn *had not changed much in 1887 except for the addition of a corrugated iron roof.* Alexander Turnbull Library.

Because of its precipitous nature the section of road round the Knob and Paddy's Bend was the last to be completed on the way to Arthur's Pass. When the road was finally opened in 1866 the advantages for Cora Lynn became obvious, since it was then the nearest station to the lucrative stock markets on the Coast goldfields where diggers with big appetites were hungry for good meat. Two men who were already involved in this trade were quick to buy Cora Lynn when the Goldneys decided to sell in 1867 (possibly because of their losses in the big snow of that year). They were John Macfarlane and Thomas Whillians Bruce. It did not concern them greatly that Cora Lynn was bad snow country. Macfarlane was able to fatten the stock at

Thomas Bruce and John Macfarlane, *who bought Cora Lynn primarily to fatten stock for the West Coast market. Macfarlane soon withdrew but Bruce carried on alone until 1889.*

Coldstream, his property near Rangiora, rest them at Cora Lynn, and hold them at Inchbonnie until he judged the West Coast market to be at its best.

But after three years of this Macfarlane, who had his troubles elsewhere, sold his interest to Bruce, who then began alone his long (23 years) ownership of the run. Mount Bruce, overlooking the station, and Bruce Stream are named after him. Besides Cora Lynn, Bruce owned Riversdale on the opposite side of the Waimakariri, and for a time had an interest in Craigieburn. He was an original member of the Upper Waimakariri Road Board when it was formed in 1871 and served several terms as chairman. He was described as "a polite, natty little man" and a terror when roused, known all over Canterbury as "The Little Angel", who "washed his hands with invisible soap" while conducting a conversation.

Bruce survived the difficult eighties better than some of his neighbours, but succumbed at the end of that decade when the Loan and Mercantile Company assumed control of his runs. The company held them until 1902, then (along with Mount White and Lochinvar) sold to F.J.Savill. In 1903 when his lease of Cora Lynn ran out it was taken up by R.McKay until 1907 when he sold in turn to Sealy Rutherford. The new owner was already installed at Grasmere and so began Cora Lynn's 60-year association with that run, each balancing the other in the provision of summer and winter country.

In the heyday of railway construction about 1910 Cora Lynn hosted a considerable township at the Mount White turnoff. Here there were two stores, a police station, a school, draper's shop, butcher, blacksmith, Paddy Crowe's boarding house, the Public Works headquarters, and a number of houses and shacks. Almost no trace of any of these establishments is to be found today.

Nimmo's General Store, *opposite the Mount White turnoff, in the days of vigorous railway construction in the valley. It was said to be equipped with a septic tank, and the story went that when this gave trouble its performance was improved by drilling a hole beside it and exploding therein a plug of gelignite.*

Taylor and Faulkner bought Cora Lynn from Rutherford in 1922 and added Grasmere in 1927. From 1930 the two runs were worked together by the McLeods until 1978, when they were sold to Dugald Harcourt, who within a few years sold Cora Lynn to George Logan and Oliver Newbeggin — and so the runs were separated again, as they were in the beginning.

MOUNT WHITE

Not a great deal is known about the Minchins, Edward and Frederick, who with John Aitken first took up the Mount White country across the Waimakariri between the Poulter and the Esk. Aitken soon sold his share to the others. The Minchins were not at the station a great deal, leaving its day-to-day running to Edward's sons William and John, whose father lived in a large house in Shirley-Richmond on the site of the present Churchill Courts hospital.

The first Mount White homestead *beneath White Hill built by Thomas Woolaston White in the early 1860s, from a painting by Charles Enys.*
Canterbury Museum.

A.R. (Ronald) Turnbull, *(left) who in 1920 extended his farming interests in North Canterbury to the Waimakariri by taking over the lease of Lochinvar, the largest of the sheep runs on the river. With assistance from two uncles he also took on Mount White and Riversdale in 1924, and the three stations, farmed as one, have been owned by the Turnbull family ever since. The family is mainly domiciled in Timaru, where D.C.Turnbull & Co. Ltd. is one of that city's long-established commercial and shipping firms.*

Frederick J. Savill, *(right) (1874-1965) was a notable Waimakariri runholder who at one time had more of the valley's acres under his control than anyone before or since. In 1902, at age 28, he took over Cora Lynn, Riversdale, Mount White and Lochinvar and in 1906 the original large Craigieburn run as well. Coming out as a young man from England (where his enterprising father was a co-founder of the Shaw-Savill shipping line) Frederick entered the sheepfarming business as a cadet at Orari Gorge. Coincidental with his Waimakariri activity he held the large Hakatere run, giving him 135,000ha to look after, but later his name was most closely associated with St.Helen's at Hanmer.*

After only a year or two the Minchins sold the run to the man who was to have been the original owner, Major Thomas Woolaston White, of the Warren, on the Oxford plains. Like the Minchins he visited the station infrequently, leaving most of the running to a head shepherd and his younger brothers Taylor (17) and John (15) while he lambasted the Provincial Council about the poor condition of the road over Porter's Pass. White built a new homestead near Lake Letitia, which some say was named after the Major's wife and some after Letitia Bowen.

The Minchins continued to hold the run as security after they sold to White in 1860, and when he failed they took it back. This was probably about 1864, because later in that year Frederick Minchin was informing the Government that as he had paid

some money towards a road to the station he was expecting better progress with the project than was evident so far. The present track, he said, was "perfectly impassable for dray traffic", which was upsetting, since he had bought a wagon in expectation of being able to cart his own wool that season. The Minchins contributed six hundred pounds towards the road. In a bid for self-sufficiency in their isolation they actually grew wheat on the Poulter flats and built a small flourmill there.

The road existed long before they left in 1870. The buyer was John Moore Cochran, then aged 36, who brought his wife, the former Fanny Miller, to live there below White Hill. For a time Ernest Grey had a share in the station. Cochran suffered heavy snow losses in 1878; the depressed wool prices in the years which followed so worried him that on May 24, 1884, he took a gun and shot himself.

Next year the Loan and Mercantile Company took over Mount White and held it for 18 years. During their term much emphasis was placed on breeding horses for the commercial market, and the Coronet (Mount White) brand was eagerly sought in Christchurch when the annual draft came over Porter's Pass and went under the hammer at Addington.

Getting the wool out of Mount White in the early days was a long and arduous business. John Milliken of Springfield for years carted the station's clip with three wagons each carrying 25 bales. He used to ignore the bridge over the Waimakariri near Cass and instead shortened the journey by splashing across the river opposite the station to join the main road. One time when there was a moderate flood in the Waimakariri he drove in, but finding it deeper than expected tried to recover by taking the horses round to the back of the wagon to pull it out. While he was doing this the outfit capsized and sailed away downriver, wool and all..

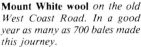

Mount White wool *on the old West Coast Road. In a good year as many as 700 bales made this journey.*
Canterbury Museum

Above: *Mount White station about 1906. The weatherboard building in the foreground is still there. Behind it stands the original homestead depicted in the Enys painting.* Weekly Press.

Right: *Ray Marshall, present manager of Mount White, typifies the men who run high country sheepfarming in the upper Waimakariri today.*

In 1902 Loan and Mercantile sold the station to Frederick Savill, along with Cora Lynn, Riversdale and Lochinvar. Together they formed a great block of pastoral hills and flats along both banks of the river — to ride from one extremity to the other was a journey of 80 kilometres. As Savill also bought Craigieburn in 1906 he was then holding over 80,000 hectares of Waimakariri country and shearing 40,000 sheep.

In 1910 ownership changed to Studholme and McAlpine, and in 1924 to A.R. (Ronald) Turnbull and his uncles, D.C. and R.T. Turnbull. The three runs (Riversdale, Mount White and Lochinvar) are still owned by the largely absentee Turnbull family of Timaru.

Among upper Waimakariri stations the Mount White complex is "the big one" — last and loneliest, but far from least. Its 50,000ha are bounded to the south by the big river, in the east by the Puketeraki Range, to the north by the Dampier Range, and in the west by Bull Creek, the East Poulter, Mount Brown Stream and Arthur's Pass National Park. The Riversdale part is largely tussock flats facing the river and extending back to high bush faces, while the Puketeraki country is mainly sunny, open basins and long spurs, where mustering can be a five-day job. In the Poulter Valley bush-bound flats extend up the river for about 30km. This sheepfarming empire exceeds in area all the stations on the west or main highway side of the upper Waimakariri.

The original homestead built beneath White Hill by Major White in 1860 disappeared long ago, but the second still stands, a rambling wooden building overlooking the lake nearby. Lower down the slopes towards the river stands the new homestead with all modern conveniences built by the Turnbulls in 1977. Jim Thompson was manager for 26 years until in 1946 he collapsed and died in the stable yard. Among his successors were "Shorty" Edge, Peter Newton, Ron Bell, and now Ray Marshall.

Snow time. *An early photograph of the old Mount White woolshed in winter. An elevated wooden flume brings water to drive the big wheel at left, which would be connected to a chaffcutter.* From Jack Ede.

RIVERSDALE

Riversdale, the top station on the north bank of the Waimakariri, is a large L-shaped block extending from Douglas Creek (across the river from Cora Lynn homestead) down the Waimakariri to the Poulter River, and back to the unoccupied country of the main divide. It has little history of its own since it has always been run with other stations — with Grasmere in Hawdon's day, with Craigieburn under the Campbells, with Cora Lynn in the 1880s, and since then with Mount White and Lochinvar. There was a house and a woolshed at one time on the flats near St. Andrew's Stream which were occupied until 1937 but have since disappeared. In the coaching days attempts were made to grow oats on the flats for the horses and at one time a small dairy farm was started, but these enterprises were shortlived.

LOCHINVAR

With 26,000 hectares Lochinvar was (before incorporation with Mount White) the largest of all the Waimakariri stations, and the most distant, occupying the sprawling watershed of the Esk River discharging into the main river just above the gorge. It was bounded on the east by the Puketeraki Range (beyond which lie Lees Valley and the Ashley River), and on the west by the Poulter and Cox rivers.

Lochinvar had a flurry of early owners, from William Thomson in 1858 (possibly in partnership with Joseph Pearson), through Sefton Moorhouse (the Provincial Superintendent), R.M.Morten, Cracroft Wilson, and the Frenchman, Mallet. Some time later, probably in the late 1860s, ownership settled down with the arrival of James Cochran, a brother of the John Cochran who bought Mount White.

As mentioned elsewhere the Cochrans married sisters. James built a slab hut on the Lochinvar flat, about 24km beyond Mount White, from which to work the station. While his wife came to share this mean accommodation at times, most likely she stayed a good deal with her sister "next door".

Either way it would be a lonely life for them, but nothing like that endured by Mrs Cox, the wife of a Dundee man, J.W.M.Cox, who in 1880 pushed into unoccupied country eight kilometres past the Lochinvar hut and established himself and his family at Bull Creek. He built a rough house of sorts in the angle of the East Poulter and the creek, and tried to make a living there running cattle and sheep. He even set up a dairy and was said to backpack its products over the Dampier Range to Hawarden, where he exchanged them for flour and other necessities. Certainly Mrs Cox and the children would be pleased to see him back! It was poor country and snowy, and after a time he was forced to go. Traces of his occupation have been found at Bull Creek — an old milk can and a child's shoe — and the wild cattle in the valley were thought to be descended from his herd.

In fact those wild cattle came to be a problem on Lochinvar and men had to be contracted to shoot them. It was while out after them that Edward Chapman, of Springbank, was fatally shot and had to be brought out on a "bush hearse" — a forked branch of a tree with a litter rigged in the "V", dragged along by the trunk.

When James Cochran lost his brother in 1884 both Lochinvar and Mount White were taken over by the Loan and Mercantile Company and worked by them until 1902, by Savill until 1910, and by Studholme and McAlpine until their tenure ran out in 1917. As they held other leases they were barred from re-applying and for a time the place was unoccupied. Then James O'Malley tried his hand at it but soon sold (in 1920) to Ronald Turnbull.

Turnbull built a house near Nigger Hill, about 16 kilometres in from Mount White, and installed Jim Thompson there to run the place. Once again there was a lonely woman on Lochinvar, for he took his wife and young family with him. It was a rough house built of pit-sawn timber, believed to be the last in Canterbury made that way. Four years later when Turnbull and his uncles took over Mount White, Thompson and his wife moved to the rather less isolated homestead there.

J.W.M.Cox, *the man who tried to establish himself in the remote headwaters of what is often called "Cox's Poulter". One of the mysteries of his distant homestead site is that an 1867 map shows it as having been freeholded long before he arrived on the scene. When Cox gave up he became the butcher at Waikari.*

AVOCA

Hidden away from sight (unless one travels by rail), and indeed the most inaccessible of all the Waimakariri stations, is Avoca, which fronts the river between Staircase Gully and Broken River, and extends inland about five kilometres to a boundary with Castle Hill station. Historically it has a split personality, because the original Avoca lay north of Broken River and had been enlarged in 1904 by the addition of a block on the south bank taken from Mount Torlesse run. In the 1917 reshuffle northern Avoca was incorporated in Flock Hill.

The old Avoca was taken up by Charles Harper, a son of the Bishop of Christchurch. He shore his sheep on the property and brother George packed the wool out on bullocks, three sacks each, then sledged it over Porter's Pass. Harper sold to Foster and Moore in 1864, and there have been many owners of both stations since then, the longest tenure being that of J.Kidd from 1926 to 1948. The station buildings face Broken River opposite Sloven's Creek. In 1987 the run was taken over by Malcolm and Alana North, of Christchurch.

Avoca Coal Mine

Early settlers in the Waimakariri basin were quick to take advantage of the numerous deposits of coal which were a feature of the district. Most of these were speedily exhausted, but at Broken River not far above its junction with Sloven's Stream more extensive deposits were found. A lease was granted to William Cloudesley, of Castle Hill Hotel, and others, but little mining was done except to satisfy their own needs.

A subsequent lease was taken out in 1915 by Frances Redpath (a member of the well-known Redpath family of Christchurch engaged in varied commercial activity), and a company formed known as Mount Torlesse Collieries (Broken River N.Z.) Ltd.

Coal trucks *on their way up the inclines at Avoca coal mine, en route to the Midland railway and a ready market in Christchurch.*
Canterbury Museum.

Production began in 1918, and during the next nine years 72,501 tonnes of coal were extracted. The best year was 1920 with 15,770 tonnes, when the company employed 58 people, of whom 44 worked underground. Coal was trucked by tramway for five or six kilometres to the Midland railway at Avoca, and was described as a high grade lignite, hard and fairly bright, with low sulphur content, high ash, exceptionally high fixed carbon, and high calorific value.

However on May 23,1924, fire broke out in the mine's return airway, starting from a fall in the old workings above the existing tunnel, and from then on the mine was plagued with fires and diminishing returns, until in 1927 it was closed. The curious may still discover numerous signs of this activity at the site.

The other main mine in Waimakariri country was at Springfield, run by the Springfield Colliery Company from 1876 to 1940. In a good day the mine delivered up to 100 tonnes a day of coal, while the nearby pottery works turned out large volumes of fireclay for bricks and field tiles.

Part 2: The Front Stations

Although sheep have been a lucrative source of revenue for plains farmers for many decades, in most people's minds they are more closely identified with the high country. There is about the hill stations a quixotic image of runholders, shepherds, musterers, packhorses and dogs working shingled heights in summer and raking snow in winter.

There are in the Waimakariri front ranges, however, a cluster of historic runs which enjoy the best of both worlds — their owners live at the edge of the plains, with a good view of them from the verandah on a clear day, but their work takes them out the back door and into the ranges. In this category on the north bank of the river is Woodstock, while on the south side are Mount Torlesse, Brooksdale and Ben More.

WOODSTOCK

Woodstock is shown on early maps as taking in all that land extending from the Esk River to View Hill boundary. The upper section was heavily bushed and has since been incorporated in Oxford State Forest, leaving the more open country in the lower gorge and on the flats further east.

Originally Woodstock was divided into three blocks, the top one being occupied by David Kinnebrook, who built his hut well up the lower gorge at or near the site of the present Kinnebrook Hut. He died in a snowstorm in 1865 while out on his lonely acres. He had taken his son of four or five years with him and when caught in the storm wrapped the boy in his heavy coat. The lad was found alive by rescuers but was never quite normal afterwards. He was brought up by a local family but one day wandered off and was never seen again. Years later when the river changed course and the big rock which gave its name to Rockford near the Kowai junction became accessible from dry land a skeleton was found on its top, presumably that of young Kinnebrook.

Kinnebrook's block was taken over by William Foster, a former sea captain who built his home by the river three or four miles from the end of Woodstock Road. He also put up a woolshed near the river but always said the place was so inaccessible he would have to float the wool out on rafts. Some heavy snowstorms and a flood which took the woolshed ended his sheep-farming days. There is in the area a Kinnebrook Creek, a Foster Creek, and a Mount Foster by which to remember these sturdy pioneers.

During the early years the lower parts of Woodstock had innumerable owners. In 1872 the three blocks were incorporated into one run and in 1902 Richard Dixon bought it at auction. It is still farmed by his nephew, Marmaduke Spencer Bower and his sons.

Woodstock station *nestling at the foot of the Torlesse Range foothills is closest of all to the Waimakariri, which runs right to left immediately beyond the homestead.*

MOUNT TORLESSE

In the 1850s the runs fronting the south bank of the Waimakariri above Racecourse Hill were in turn Homebush, Easedale Nook and Patterson's. In 1860 Joseph Longden and Robert Deane bought Easedale Nook from the Percival brothers and divided it in two, Longden taking the part which he named Mount Torlesse.

Edward Curry, who was associated with the Enys brothers in the purchase of Castle Hill, managed Mount Torlesse for Longden, who went back to England in 1864, dying there the following year. Curry bought the station for eleven thousand pounds when it was auctioned in January, 1866. He was a successful sheepfarmer, a devoted family man, and was described as taking on much of the work round the station not normally done by owners. But he was a hard taskmaster, and few employees stayed with him for any length of time. John Enys is credited with calling him "our disgusting partner", but didn't say why.

Across the river. *Major Percy Hawkins Johnson and his wife, the former Catherine Dixon, extended the Dixon influence across the Waimakariri when in 1904 they bought Mount Torlesse station, which like Woodstock opposite is still farmed by descendants of the old pioneer.*

Curry sold Torlesse in February, 1868, to Thomas Anson and John Kerslake, and in their time Patterson's 2000ha run was added. George Patterson had no road access to the property, but kept a punt at a crossing near Woodstock. In 1929 Col. E.B.Milton described him as

...a devout, simple-minded, lovable man. The scene enacted each night in the slab-walled, earthen-floored hut assuredly could not be reproduced in any Canterbury backblock homestead of today. George Patterson seated at the head of the rough boarded table, reading aloud by the light of two tallow candles from his great family Bible. Around him his staff and schoolboy guests listening to the inevitable chapter before they went off to their bunks. The dim, primitive interior, the solemn voice of the old man, the deep note of the river, left an indelible impression on the mind that to this day has not faded, though fifty years have passed.

After Kerslake and Anson, successive owners of Mount Torlesse station were J. and J. Brett (sons of Col. de Renzie Brett), D. and D. Matheson, and the Loan and Mercantile Company (with Thomas Douglas as manager). In 1901 G.L.Rutherford became the owner, staying until 1904 when the Johnson family began its three-generation ownership of the property. Major Johnson's wife was Catherine Dixon from Eyrewell, and after selling to her brother the quarter share of that station she had inherited, the couple bought Mount Torlesse. Their son R.M.D. (Peter) Johnson took over in 1926, and his son Richard is the current owner.

BROOKSDALE

Brooksdale station (originally Brookdale) lies to the right of the main highway for much of the way from Springfield to Porter's Pass, and on both sides of the road as far as Dry Creek, sharing

Mustering novelty. *Woodstock put an early model jetboat to practical use in the lower Waimakariri Gorge for the annual muster. Packhorses are readied for the five-hour journey which the boss and his dog (photographed here in a shallow side stream) disposed of in 30 minutes.*

its boundaries with Ben More, Mount Torlesse and Castle Hill runs. Robert Deane sold it in 1872 to Hopkins and Anson, and they in turn to Dugald Matheson in 1873. The Loan and Mercantile Company took it over in 1882 and sold in 1901 to John Milliken, who was in business in a big way carting wool from the upper Waimakariri stations. No doubt the coming of the Midland railway influenced his decision to abandon transport for sheepfarming. He later bought the adjoining Castle

Hill station. Milliken died in 1920, having done well, and Brooksdale was then managed by his son Les. The present owner is Maurice Milliken.

Until the railway *went through, Porter's Pass was the "high stile" over which all supplies for and wool from the Waimakariri stations had to be hauled. This wagon is completing the last pitch up Starvation Gully to the summit.*
From E.Cotter.

BEN MORE

Much of Ben More, on the left side of the road approaching Porter's Pass, drains into branches of the Kowai River. In Chapter Three, *The Explorers,* mention is made of Edward Dobson and party, embarking on their 1865 journey to the Waimakariri headwaters, spending a night at Thomas's homestead at Porter's Pass. This was in the days when the road went up the south side of the spur. Both the hotel and the Ben More homestead were in the valley of the old road but although the author can remember seeing traces of both, none remains today. Ben More had a cluster of owners in addition to Richard Thomas — Archibald Macfarlane, Robert Maxwell, Elliott and Jackson, James Thomson, the Hommersham brothers, Orfeur Parker, Mathew Weir, George Rutherford and Dugald Matheson and son were some of them. The present owner is Roger James.

Part 3: The Plains Runs

The greatest success story of all Waimakariri runholders belongs not in the mountains but out on the plains, with a Lincolnshire immigrant named Marmaduke Dixon. Coming to Canterbury in 1853 he took up 6500 hectares of light land on the north bank of the river, which in time he and his family by sheer hard work and enterprise built into a farming empire extending 60 kilometres along the river. Somehow Dixon found time as well to involve himself widely and effectively in provincial and local politics and community affairs, and on the side was something of an authority on astronomy. Of all the original Waimakariri settlers his family is the only one (now in its fourth generation) still farming by the river.

Marmaduke Dixon was a good example of an Englishman chancing his arm in an entirely new career on the opposite side of the world and making a good fist of it. He had spent the earlier part of his life at sea and knew nothing about sheepfarming, but was probably helped a lot in the initial stages by the Australian "know-how" of his friend John Murphy, who had bought a run immediately across the Eyre River and who no doubt persuaded Dixon to settle where he did.

Dixon's descendants include such diverse people as his son Marmaduke J., a co-founder of the New Zealand Alpine Club and (with George Mannering) the first New Zealander to reach the icecap of Mount Cook; his granddaughter Olivia Spencer-Bower, the noted painter; and great-grandsons M.J.O. ("Duke") Dixon, who pioneered commercial jetboating in the

Waimakariri Gorge, and Simon Spencer-Bower, who is among the country's top aerobatic airmen. Others have been prominent in river control authorities: his son Richard, grandsons Marmaduke Spencer-Bower and Peter Johnson, and great-grandsons "Duke" Dixon and Richard Johnson, both Catchment Board chairmen.

Many of the qualities of this interesting family reflect the old pioneer's adventurous and innovative ways. His struggle to make something of his drought-prone, scrub-covered acres was an epic one. When he took up Runs 83 and 93 between the Waimakariri and Eyre rivers he built himself a whare called "The Hermitage" and settled down to a life of unremitting toil. Tired of sledging water from the Waimakariri, he dug a well 26m deep, but it turned out dry — the only water it produced must have been tears of frustration. For a start he climbed up laboriously with each bucket of shingle, but as the well deepened he invented a gadget which enabled him to hoist the bucket to the top and empty it by manipulating ropes and pulleys.

Dixon stocked the run with 3000 sheep bought on terms from John Hall (later Sir John), who was a fellow passenger on the voyage from England. In summer when the Eyre River ran dry his stock had to be pastured within reasonable distance of the Waimakariri and its life-giving water. But through these and many other difficulties he survived and prospered sufficiently to build a new homestead closer to the Eyre, and return to England to be married. A sad loss during this period was a fire which

The Dixons. *Centre, Marmaduke Dixon, the pioneer of Eyrewell, who achieved success with his indifferent acres. Left, elder son Marmaduke John, mountaineer, canoeist and inheritor of Eyrewell. Right, the only available photograph of second son Richard Orme, who for years increased and managed the Dixon "empire".*

burned the old "Hermitage" hut to the ground, along with his considerable collection of books, diaries and papers.

The wells Dixon dug near the new house tapped reliable water, which prompted his wife to christen the homestead "Eyrewell". It became a popular watering place on the road to Oxford. But her determined husband, wanting more than the water a well could give, was dreaming of schemes to use the never-failing flow of the Waimakariri to irrigate his dry acres. How well he and his son succeeded with this venture is told in Chapter 13.

Considering that he started with so little, and that so much of his land was difficult, Marmaduke Dixon "prospered exceeding well". His light manuka country was not sought by small freeholders, but the Eyrewell leasehold was given to the Midland Railway company in part payment for their work on the West Coast line, and Dixon had to buy it back at 15 shillings an acre. At the same time he was able to buy the leasehold parts of Burnt Hill and Dagnam, runs above him on the river whose owners did not or could not freehold them. By 1892 he had achieved a position enjoyed by few if any Canterbury runholders — ownership of all his land, valued at over 40,000 pounds. This is an extract from a letter written about three years before his death:

My firm intention is to cut up the Eyrewell part of the property at once among my [four] children. That will give them about 6000 acres of irrigable land for each one, and the other portion [about 10,000 acres] will sell at an average of about three pounds per acre. At any rate I do not expect to have much or any debt, if I spin out this frail chord for three or four years longer, for then I think I shall have done my share of work.

The four children were Marmaduke John, Richard (who never married), Catherine (Kitty), who married P.H.Johnson, later of Mount Torlesse station, and Rosa, an artist, who went to England to study and there married a civil engineer, Anthony Spencer-Bower. She returned to New Zealand when her twin children, Marmaduke and Olivia, were aged 15.

A successful "squatter" he might have been, but Marmaduke Dixon was never thought of as such. In politics he was regarded as Canterbury's first Liberal of note, with strong sympathies for the problems of the small farmer, devoting much time to local body service and as a member of the Provincial Council working tirelessly for his community and its interests. When the Council was abolished in 1876 he became an original member of the Ashley County Council, which controlled all that area north of the Waimakariri. One of his greatest interests was the study of sunspots and their effect on the weather. His library overflowed a whole room. One of his last public services was to see the Waimakariri-Ashley Water-supply Board established to bring stock and household water to farms from Oxford to the sea, but sadly he died just before it was officially opened in 1896.

Within a few years of their father's death the sons bought most of Worlingham, their large neighbour to the west, and the remains of Wai-iti in the east. In addition Richard Dixon bought Woodstock in 1902, the station on the Waimakariri opposite Mount Torlesse where his sister was already established. By then there were only pockets of useful land on the north side of the

river from Lochinvar in the Esk country to the lower end of Wai-iti, a few kilometres from Kaiapoi, which were not part of the Dixon empire. Much of this is still in Dixon hands — Woodstock and Claxby (Spencer-Bower and sons) and Holton (Wai-iti) (M.J.O. Dixon).

Eyrewell homestead *in its palmy days, with father Dixon on his horse and Mrs Dixon and the family — Marmaduke J., Richard, Rosa and Catherine — seated round the tennis court.*

The original Marmaduke's sons, Marmaduke J. and Richard, were worthy upholders of their father's passion for hard work. In their day the remaining areas of giant manuka, some four metres tall, were attacked with traction engines, huge rollers and scrub ploughs. The big McLaren engines were said to be the largest in the Southern Hemisphere. After the elder son died, Richard (always referred to as "R.O.") took over management of all the properties. A forthright character with set ideas and a loud voice, he was nevertheless highly thought of by all who worked for him, and to keep track of his sprawling realm was said to "work all day and drive all night". He died at the age of 78, appropriately out mustering on a Woodstock block.

In descending order from the front ranges the Waimakariri plains runs (and those on its tributaries, the Kowai, Eyre and Cust rivers) were:

SOUTH BANK	NORTH BANK
Easedale Nook	View Hill
Homebush	Burnt Hill
Racecourse Hill	Carleton
Ledard	The Warren
The Desert	Dagnam
Sandy Knolls	Worlingham
Tresillian	Murphy's Run
Ashfield	Eyrewell
Coringa	Springbank
	Wai-iti

The plains runs on the south bank across the river from Dixon, especially those which had better quality land, were quick to suffer from freeholders nibbling at their edges. This process soon reduced the original holding to just another farm among many, but some notes on early owners are of interest.

The nearest station to Christchurch was Coringa, some of which is now in suburban streets and houses. The name lives on in a country club and golf course at McLean's Island. Charles Haslewood, one of the "Prophets" who came from Australia, was its first owner. He is best remembered for the manner of his untimely death in 1858. While cleaning his gun, having withdrawn the charge, he pointed the nipple at a candle and squinted down the barrel. The remains of the powder exploded and injured him so severely that he died the next day. Incidently Haslewood also took up 1,200 ha of Waimakariri Gorge country but did not live long enough to do anything with it.

Another ex-"Aussie", Edward Templar, who could write and speak four languages, was next on Coringa, and left his name on Templar's Island in the Waimakariri, and on Templeton. He was at Coringa in 1865 when the Waimakariri flowed through the station "in a broad but shallow stream" on its way to the Avon and a scary flood in Christchurch. A later owner was G.G.Stead, one of the city's notable commercial men and reputed to have been the most successful racehorse owner in New Zealand.

Allan McLean (along with his brothers John and Robertson) took up Tresillian and Ashfield, the stations west of Coringa. He was remembered for his tartan waistcoat, his Chinese servant, and for milking his cow in the open. He later moved south, bought Waikakahi on the Waitaki River, became a wealthy man, built his baronial retirement home in Christchurch, died in 1907, and bequeathed his mansion (and his fortune) to the McLean Institute to be used as a home for indigent elderly ladies. In time the establishment was moved to "Holly Lea" in Fendalton, but the old building remains in Manchester Street north, an impressive memorial to the palmiest days of Canterbury sheepfarming.

The owner of the station above Sandy Knolls, called The Desert, was Captain Dunbar Muter, who fought one of the few duels recorded in New Zealand. His opponent was C.B.Robinson, the first Resident Magistrate at Akaroa, and the dispute was about some land on the peninsula. The duel was fought with pistols in good old English fashion. Robinson fired above Muter's head, but the captain in all seriousness aimed for his opponent — and missed. He wanted another shot, but was persuaded to desist. His second was Crosbie Ward, then or later an editor of *The Lyttelton Times*.

Ledard, which adjoined The Desert on its western boundary, was taken up by another military character. This was Dugald MacFarlane who, it was said, often dined with Sir Walter Scott, and as a lieutenant at the Battle of Waterloo was reputed to have fought the engagement in one boot and a dancing pump. He had been at the Duchess of Richmond's ball with fellow officers on the eve of the battle and was called away to the front so urgently that in his haste he could find only one boot with which to go into action.

The early days of Racecourse Hill, the next station to the west, are associated with the name of R.A.Creyke, who is remembered in the street running past the University of Canterbury. With 14,000 hectares it was one of the larger places, as was Homebush, taken up by the Deans brothers in 1851 when they were concerned about the permanence of their Riccarton farm. Homebush was originally 13,360 hectares and extended from the Waimakariri to the Selwyn. The greater part of the run was freeholded in the 1870s, and since then much has been cut up and sold for closer settlement.

The remainder is still occupied by the Deans family, who with the Dixons on the other side of the river share a continuous record of family ownership from pioneering days. There is a difference however — Homebush no longer fronts on to the river, yet surprisingly it retains a visible connection. A recent check of Malvern County survey records revealed that a remnant of Deans land — a half acre on the east side of the southern approach to the Gorge Bridge — was still in family ownership. Ceded to the county, it has since been developed by the Lions Club as a picnic area.

North of the Waimakariri the scene on the plains was dominated by Eyrewell and the Dixon family, but there were nine other runs on the Eyre and Cust rivers. In addition there was the 2000 hectare Day's Run in the middle of the Waimakariri on Kaiapoi Island, taken up by George Day. The sheep on this run were soon replaced by crops as the land was subdivided into small farms, but with the river rushing past on two sides they were often flooded. Today the river runs through the middle of the island and the old north and south branches have been reduced to spring-fed creeks.

Wai-iti, the first station on the north bank proper, was described as "bounded by the rivers Courtenay (Waimakariri) and Eyre and the Great Swamp". Much of that swamp is now rich farming land. Wai-iti's most prominent early owner was a genial Cornishman named Captain James Row, described by a contemporary as "a very good old fellow". Wai-iti's 4500 ha had shrunk to 950 when Richard Dixon bought them in 1897. Today the Dixon farm continues at "Holton", about four kilometres due west of the motorway bridges, where Geoffrey

The Shearing Gang. *A Burnt Hill "blade" gang poses for the camera. The woolshed behind them is built of slab timber with thatched roof repaired here and there with new-fangled corrugated iron. Joseph Pearson stands at left (in hat) and the boy in front of him is probably son William Fisher Pearson, later Member of Parliament for Oxford.*

Dixon, a nephew of Richard, has been succeeded by his son, a fourth generation Marmaduke Dixon.

On the Eyre and Cust rivers but without direct frontage to the Waimakariri there were four stations — Springbank, Murphy's, Carleton and The Warren. Their fortunes were varied. Big money was made out of a place like Springbank (William Kaye, who sold it in 1853, was reputed to have taken back to Australia with him a sum exceeding what today would be a million dollars). On the other hand Carleton and The Warren all but ruined ex-Indian Army officers like Henry Coote and Thomas Woolaston White, whose former occupations apparently left them ill-prepared for farming sheep.

Beyond Oxford was View Hill station, with most of its higher country in dense forest so that essentially the usable part of its 8000 hectares was on the extensive terraces and flats fronting the Waimakariri on both sides of the Gorge Bridge road. It was from View Hill that Joseph Pearson, living there after taking up the run for Aitken, launched his journey of exploration up the Waimakariri Gorge in 1857. After a number of owners following Aitken had been and gone, the run was bought by John Richard Gorton in 1873.

Pearson was of course one of the grand old men of Waimakariri sheepfarming, and historically associated with the four stations west of Eyrewell in addition to his discoveries beyond the gorge. Soon after arriving in New Zealand in 1851 he took up Burnt Hill, so named because one of its characteristics is typical volcanic rock. In 1877 he bought Dagnam, more than doubling the 3000 hectares he had at Burnt Hill, and then in 1873 added Worlingham (5870 ha), the next run again, which made him a neighbour of Dixon at Eyrewell.

In the Midland Railway land sale Pearson freeholded about 2800ha at Burnt Hill, but over the years (as mentioned) the Dixons bought both Dagnam and Worlingham and added them to Eyrewell. At various times before this both runs had other owners, including at one stage an American from Massachusetts named Thomas Curtis who became first superintendent of the Lyttelton Fire Brigade. The first lessee of Dagnam in 1853 was a gentleman with an impressive name, Crackenthorp John Wentworth Cookson. His account of the miseries which sometimes befell pioneer runholders is well described in this note (he had already survived a long and dangerous crossing of the flooded Waimakariri in order to reach his broad acres):

After travelling through drizzling rain all day we reached towards evening the site of my future hut. Making a temporary shelter with the boards we brought, and placing some on the ground to lie on, we went through the same process as before and at length got our fire to burn, for, as it had been raining all day the operation was even more tedious than in the morning. Next day we set about building a hut, which took us about a month. In the meantime we put up a mia-mia to sleep in, the dimensions of which were seven feet long by four feet wide, constructed of cabbage trees, with the butts resting on the ground, and the heads tied together; as it was only three feet high we had to crawl to bed.

Cookson and his two men, a cadet and an Australian aboriginal named Black Jack, lived in their cabbage-tree hut for a month until they got a proper hut built. According to D.N.Hawkins in his *Beyond the Waimakariri* they existed entirely on potatoes, sour flapjacks and black tea. Cookson soon sold to Joseph Pearson.

Administrating the Never-Never

For some years after upper Waimakariri sheepfarmers took up their runs the district behind the front ranges was an administrative no-man's-land. When provincial authorities set up the Oxford Road Board they must have waved a hand airily towards the gorge and said, "All that's yours, too." But Oxford had its own problems on the plains, so the country beyond the gorge remained in limbo, outside their scope or comprehension

in terms of road building or maintenance, populated mainly by Australians and Scots shepherds, and requiring passage through Malvern territory even to reach it.

The Mount White and Lochinvar squatters, whose runs were miles from the lonely West Coast Road and separated from it by a big river, complained bitterly about the injustice of being rated by Oxford when work on their meagre access tracks had to be done at their own expense. The Campbells of Craigieburn joined the Minchins and Cochrans in May, 1868, to petition for the whole territory to be removed from Oxford control and included in the Malvern Road District.

But Malvern didn't want them either. The upshot was that a boundary alteration in 1870 gave autonomy to this orphan country with the formation early in the following year of the Upper Waimakariri Road Board. The inaugural meeting was held on February 13, 1871, in the Cass Hotel, when the following runholders were elected: Reginald Foster (Avoca), chairman; John and Charles Enys (Castle Hill), Arthur Hawdon (Grasmere), and Thomas Bruce (Cora Lynn). Prominent sheepfarmers not included were Robert Campbell (Craigieburn) and John Cochran (Mount White), creating an unusual situation in that the region north of the river, where most of the roading work was needed, had no representation. It was two years before this anomaly was removed with the election of Cochran to the board.

The new Road Board appeared to get along without funds for that first year except for Government grants for West Coast Road maintenance. Then a very high rate of sixpence in the pound was levied, cut back to threepence next year, and to one penny in 1875. Even at that the board usually had several thousands of pounds in the bank on fixed deposit. Yet in spite of this affluence it was 1883, 12 years after formation, before access to Mount White was properly facilitated with the construction of bridges over the Waimakariri and Poulter rivers.

An interesting proposal in 1880 was to spend a hundred pounds on a track down the Waimakariri Gorge to Oxford. The Oxford Road Board kept to its part of the project, but what happened to the upper section is not clear except that in the following year a reward of five pounds was offered to anyone who could find a route for a bridle track to the Oxford boundary.

In 1883 it was decided to buy a plot of land at Cass and build an office. Previously the board spent some money on the old Escort station at Craigieburn; and for many years preferred the advantages of meeting in the Cass Hotel, the licensee of which was for a time a member.

At one time or another nearly all the runholders in the valley, and a few others, served on the board. John Enys played a major role in its affairs until he left in 1890 to live in England. He forgot to resign, and when two meetings had gone by without leave or apology it was recorded that by these deficiencies he had forfeited his seat. By then he was far away and occupying a quite different one — the family seat in Cornwall. (Enys would have so many clubs, committees and boards to resign from he must have overlooked the one nearest home.)

It is never clear from the board's minutes how the West Coast Road was maintained during the 40 years of the Road Board's existence. At its second meeting in 1871 the board agreed to a request from the Provincial Government to undertake maintenance and supervision of that part of the road within its boundaries, provided sufficient funds were made available and the boundary altered to include Porter's Pass. Yet subsequent references to the road are almost non-existent, although several times over the years the Bealey section was almost completely demolished by floods. In 1874 it was reported that coach passengers "had to be conveyed on horseback seven miles into the Otira Gorge, the gorges of the Bealey and Otira being impassable, the road being completely destroyed in both".

Somehow, by somebody, repairs on the grand scale required by such disasters were carried out, but no mention of such activity ever appears in the minutes of the Road Board. Monuments to its work remain to this day in the Mount White Bridge across the Waimakariri and the Poulter Bridge.

Otherwise almost all traces of the board and its work have vanished, and that includes the 1871-88 minute-book. (Fortunately a copy exists thanks to T.N.Beckett, author of "The Mountains of Erewhon", and has been deposited with the Malvern County office.) In 1910 the Upper Waimakariri and Malvern road boards were amalgamated to form the Tawera county, which has since been merged with an enlarged Malvern county. The road, being a state highway, is maintained by the Ministry of Works.

"Many a Glorious Morning"

In words that could only be written by one who has "been there and done that", David McLeod in one of his books describes the pangs and pleasures of a musterer's pre-dawn climb to his "beat" on Cora Lynn. It is reproduced here with his generous permission:

We slept uncomfortably on the uneven ground, and were up and away before it was light. The spur above the camp rises steeply at first, catching the climber before he gets into the rhythm of his stride and the steady lung-filling which makes the difference between ease and agony. With the chill of early morning upon him and the tussocks hardly visible in the half dark, he stumbles up the almost perpendicular face, cursing the day he decided to be a musterer. All around him and his companions the screen of dogs scramble about, loosening stones to roll upon the climbers and snarling at each other whenever they happen to meet. After a few hundred feet the exertion makes him stop and take his coat off and the short breathing space eases the thumping of his heart and the constriction in his lungs. After that the climb seems easier, but it is nearly a thousand feet before he reaches the first break in the slope and comes out on a ridge. Here a man drops off to take the "second to the bottom" beat and two men climb on.

Above this it's practically all shingle — good walking on a ridge, with the weatherworn stones firmly embedded and not sliding under the feet. The sky has lightened with the dawn, the feet no longer stumble over half-seen rocks and tussocks and the first glorious touch of pink has turned the pale grey crest of the Craigieburn Range to mother of pearl. With that breathless moment a dawn wind always seems to come, wandering from some unseen hollow of the hill where it has dreamed the night away, waiting for this moment. The climber's sweating brow cools at its touch and a magic elixir seeps into his lungs and renews the failing oxygen in the blood. His stride lengthens and the agony of the valley is forgotten in the ecstasy of the mountain top.

Big Night, Big Day

Peter Newton, later a prolific writer on high country life, who was a shepherd, head shepherd and manager at Mount White, records the occasion when the boys on the station, short on social life, decided to attend a dance at Springfield. They left home at 4 p.m., rode their horses 30 kilometres to Cass, and boarded a train there for the 60 kilometre journey through the gorges and tunnels to Springfield, where no doubt they impressed the young ladies at the dance. At 2 a.m. they caught another train back to Cass and rode home for breakfast and a spell "in the sack" after what surely was their longest night-out ever.

On another occasion Newton and his friend Reg Ferguson, possibly with nothing better to do on the day, crossed the Esk River, climbed to the top of the Puketeraki Range (1800m) and walked the tops until they ran out of range. Descending through interminable forest and across farm land they finally reached the Waimakariri River near the Kowai junction, waded the ford, and trudged across country to Springfield, where they could at last line up at the bar for a well-earned beer. Their journey was 30 kilometres as the crow flies, possibly double that on the ground, and involved 1500 metres of ascent and descent.

On Mount White Road. *Typical Waimakariri tussock uplands feature in this photograph of Mount White and Lochinvar country. Two main tributaries flow left to right across the picture, Poulter River in the foreground and Esk River at the foot of Chest Peak (1936m), highest point on the Puketeraki Range.*

Exit the Hot Shop

On the lonely road past Mount Binser leading to Mount White station, there stood a hut with the intriguing title of "Hot Chop", which still appears on most maps of the district. Why "Hot Chop" is something only the distant past could explain. It was built by the upper Waimakariri Road Board about 1883 for one of its workmen on a site near Hot Chop Creek. The late Sir John McAlpine, whose father once owned Mount White, said that when Andy Montgomery was roadman and lived there, his wife, a hospitable soul, invariably whipped up a batch of scones if she saw anyone approaching in the distance. Travellers grew to welcome such unexpected kindness, and Mrs Montgomery surely must have enjoyed the company. Because of this the name changed to Hot Scone Hut, which in turn was shortened to what Sir John and other "locals" called it — the Hot Shop.

What happened to the old hut with the quaint name? Although a fairly derelict affair in later years, it was still popular with shooters out for a weekend's sport. The Mount White musterers took a dim view of this, as permission was seldom sought, and one night, finding it so occupied, they decided to pull it over with a rope and a Model A truck. The old hut rocked a bit, but that was all. Later a new generation of Mount White "hard shots" did the job properly — they drove a Land Rover clean through it!

The First Big Snow

Generally speaking runholding was not a very profitable affair, a contention supported by the frequency with which the stations changed hands. Owners sold mainly because of low returns, and buyers bought because with eternal optimism they knew better how to do the job. There were good times when wool prices were high, and there were bad times when financial returns and heavy snow fell together.

On July 30, 1867, while many runholders in the Waimakariri basin were just finding their feet, snow began to fall from the north-west and continued unabated for 80 hours. By then it was a metre deep at Castle Hill homestead and enormously more than that on the higher country. Intermittent falls continued until August 8 when there were still three metres on Porter's Pass.

When the annual muster was held in December only 7500 of Castle Hill's 10,000 sheep remained and 300 lambs instead of 2000. This disaster coincided with a slump in wool prices of about one-third. The Enys brothers had some money advanced on the security of the wool clip, and found themselves having to repay this. Three years passed before they recouped the losses, and theirs were not as bad as for some runholders in the valley. Craigieburn, Riversdale and Cora Lynn all changed hands that year.

The year 1867 was the first in which exceptional snowfall was experienced in the upper Waimakariri. Subsequent memorable falls were in 1878, 1895 (when the road over Arthur's Pass was closed for three months), 1903, 1918 and 1945.

CHAPTER NINE
The River Port

"But Lord! What a sad time it is to see no boats upon the river," wrote Samuel Pepys in his diary in 1665. He was talking about the Thames, of course, but his remark could well be the lament of any Kaiapoi old-timer leaning on the bridge and dreaming of the days when up to 20 vessels were crowded into the river at one time and the bullock wagons stretched along the length of Charles Street waiting to unload at the wharves.

The history of the Port of Kaiapoi, on the North Branch* of the Waimakariri River, goes back well beyond the First Four Ships and their 1850 arrival in Lyttelton Harbour to the time when the Maoris, newly aware of the value of dressed flax, loaded up their largest canoes and paddled them down the river, over the bar, and round to Port Cooper where the Sydney traders anchored.

In the spring of 1848 two white men appeared on the banks of the Waimakariri. They were Walter Mantell and Alfred Wills, sent down from Wellington by the New Zealand Company to look into the purchase of a large part of the South Island. Mantell was impressed with the river's potential as a navigable port. He borrowed a canoe from the Maoris so that he and Wills, who was a surveyor, could make an adequate assessment. Unfortunately the seas were too rough for soundings on the bar, but it looked feasible and so did the channels leading to good North Branch anchorages eight or nine kilometres upriver.

A couple of sawyers, White and Hay, who were associated with early survey work, were also in the Waimakariri in 1848.

They rowed a boat "about four miles" up the North Branch and into the Cam and further on still to the Maori Bush and Church Bush. Among other things they built the first house north of the Waimakariri, for Charles Torlesse, the surveyor, at Kaiapoi.

But the real practical pioneer of the navigable Waimakariri was Alfred Rhodes. With four others he sailed a large sealing boat over the bar and up to Kaiapoi with stores and instruments for the survey parties starting work there in 1849. And later he repeated the feat several times. He explored the lower reaches of the river thoroughly and was first to demonstrate that Kaiapoi could be made a viable point of entry to North Canterbury, long before there were any roads into the area.

This was soon seized upon by others with an eye for the development of the extensive regions north of the river. One of these was William Norman, manager for the trading firm of Cookson, Bowler & Co., for which he established premises on the Cam River at its junction with the North Branch near the site of what was later the Woollen Mills. He brought out from England a cottage in sections. The cost of transporting it from London to Kaiapoi must have been more than it was worth, but the fact that it arrived at all at least demonstrated the effectiveness of the sea connection between Lyttelton and Kaiapoi.

Soon goods of all kinds were being unloaded at the Cam, which could take vessels up to 80 tonnes. They lay close in against the banks, making unloading easy. For years supplies

Kaiapoi Harbour in 1862 *from a painting presented to the borough by a descendant of James Baker, an early Kaiapoi farmer presumed to be the man standing on the jetty. The produce being loaded was bound for Australia and the Bendigo gold rush. Two local historians, Don Hawkins and Patricia Ward, combine to suggest that the building in the foreground is the "wattle and daub" hut built in 1851 by the ferryman, Alexander Baxter, on the site of the present Borough Council property.* Kaiapoi Museum

*Renamed the Kaiapoi River in 1959.

The Emma Sims, *one of two new auxiliary screw schooners built in Australia for John Sims, which arrived in Kaiapoi in 1898 to a boisterous welcome. Here, gaily decorated and crowded with visitors, she sits at the wharf immediately below the town bridge.* Kaiapoi Museum

were landed there and put on bullock wagons waiting to make the long journey to sheep stations as far north as Hurunui. On the return trip the ships carried wool and produce to Lyttelton.

As the 1850s progressed Kaiapoi blossomed as a trading port of some importance, with a church, school, courthouse, merchants' offices and stores. The population was greater than Lyttelton's and at one time was only 53 less than in Christchurch. In 1853 when talk of the "Gladstone settlement" at Kaiapoi was in the air, Henry Sewell was convinced that Christchurch had reached its peak. "Newcomers won't settle there," he exclaimed, "witness the *Minerva* people, they are all off to Kaiapoi."

Nothing came of the Gladstone project, but the little boats kept breasting the bar and sailing up the river. Up to 100 of them made Kaiapoi a regular port of call, servicing the growing number of settlers spreading north and west over the plains and into the hill country.

George Day of Sumner was the first of the regular traders. With his schooner *Flirt* he began a monthly service early in 1852, with the occasional chartered trip as required. Much of the impedimenta of early settlers was transported in this vessel plying between Heathcote and Kaiapoi.

Some pilgrim families, their resources stretched to the limit, made the journey the hard way, manhandling their meagre possessions over the Bridle Track and along the rutted trails leading into North Canterbury, Sometimes it took them all day just to get everything across the Waimakariri.

The more affluent had their household effects lightered round Godley Head to Heathcote to await one of the *Flirt's* scheduled voyages. George Day was an expert on both the Sumner and Waimakariri bars and with favourable winds and tides could coax the little schooner to make the trip in three or four hours, from Heathcote out over the Sumner bar, across Pegasus Bay, into the Waimakariri and safely to anchorage in the North Branch. With luck a wagon could be hired there to complete the long journey by sea and land, from "Home" somewhere in Great Britain to whatever virgin plot of tussock was to be the family's new antipodean address.

From those early days in the '50s the development of Kaiapoi as the port of North Canterbury was rapid. Wharves and stores appeared along the riverbanks, bridges built across the river had to be equipped with swing sections to allow the passage of vessels, and first attempts were made (with a couple of brushwood baskets on poles) to give masters something by which they could line up their craft for the run over the bar. Often these markers were not of much use as the bar was constantly changing. The Waimakariri had a typical lagoon at the mouth, running parallel to the shore but separated from it by a long sandbar. The river joined the sea by an opening through this barrier which shifted to and fro at the whim of storms and

floods, but which generally was about two kilometres south of where it is today.

Smaller vessels often carried only the master at the tiller and a boy at the foresail and jib. When they were lined up for the crossing it was a case of hang on for dear life while the spray broke over them, and the breakers and their own sail power carried them through the gap and into the calmer waters of the estuary. The later 1850s saw the introduction of small steamships on the coastal run, affording much better control for captains and crew. One of these was the 45-ton *Planet*, which was enough of a novelty for *The Lyttelton Times* of the day to print this graphic word-picture of the 75km voyage from Lyttelton to Kaiapoi and back:

The little steamer *Planet* has made her maiden trips to the Waimakariri and the Heathcote during the week. Her departure for the former river was delayed for one day in consequence of the tides not being suitable for crossing the bar on Monday. The next morning however she left the jetty a little before eight o'clock, with a considerable number of passengers and their luggage. Several immigrants just arrived by the *Roehampton* took the opportunity of transporting themselves in this convenient manner to Kaiapoi; and others, both ladies and gentlemen, embarked as on a pleasure trip. The day commenced with a strong breeze from the eastward, and rain, while everything was thickly covered by fog. In fact the weather was as unpropitious as it well could be for the trial trip. The *Planet* steamed on against all obstacles with great success, and, crossing the Waimakariri bar without touching or stopping, arrived at Fraser's wharf in just four hours from Lyttelton. Here she landed her passengers and cargo. The next morning she was loaded with sixty-eight bales of wool, but a large number of passengers offering, many of whom, as before, were ladies, fourteen bales were taken off, and the vessel proceeded down the river about half-past ten o'clock. As on the previous day the weather was thick and rainy and a strong easterly breeze was blowing, so that a high sea was running on the bar. The weather altogether was so unpropitious that sailing craft all ready to start had been detained in Lyttelton harbour since the previous Saturday, and the *Uira* had been lying in the Waimakariri unable to come out although ready for the three or four previous days. The *Planet,* however, went steadily at the bar, without stopping, and crossed it safely though bumping once or twice. About half-an-hour had now elapsed since leaving Kaiapoi and the remainder of the trip was completed in four hours more. Mr Tregear, late of the *Flirt* schooner, acted as pilot both ways. We understand that the bar of the Waimakariri is in a bad condition at present, the channel being undefined and very shallow, so much so that even at the top of the tide and in tolerable weather vessels seldom come out without touching. Twelve hours must therefore be consumed in the river. The same evening the wool was delivered on board the *Glentanner.*

The thought of the cocky little *Planet* plunging headlong into rain and rising seas, and bumping recklessly over the bar, brings a degree of awe mixed with admiration for her master. Apparently caution was not a word he wrote often in his ship's log, and the plume of smoke billowing from her shiny funnel must have been his declaration of faith in the absolute superiority of steam over sail. His passengers, including those daring young ladies — surely they were *young* ladies — must have shared to some extent his trust in the *Planet's* invincibility. Shades of the *Titanic!* Many another vessel trying conclusions with the Waimakariri bar was not so fortunate, whether driven by steam or sail. There was a growing list of ships that went

On a full tide. *Three of Joseph Sims' fleet at his wharf, from left* Rock Lily, Huon Belle, *and* Emma Sims.

ashore, some on sandbars in the channel, and some which missed the entrance altogether and stranded themselves on one spit or the other, often with disastrous results.

The 1870s were the high days of the Waimakariri's port. The 1800 bales of wool exported over the wharves at Kaiapoi in 1861 grew to over 5000 by 1870, and bushels of grain from 10,000 to 334,000. In addition there was a steady export trade in numerous smaller items — flour, vegetables, cheese, bacon, butter, oatmeal, bran, sheepskins, grass seed, peas, tallow, flax, and in 1870 even 2350 bushels of beans and 10,000 dozen eggs.

And the ships didn't sail up the river empty. The settlement of over 600,000 hectares in North Canterbury, first on large runs and then in smaller farm units, created an enormous demand for all kinds of goods and services ranging from a few sticks of furniture and bags of coal for town and village dwellers to the expanding needs of hundreds of plains farmers and sheep station owners. The great building and fencing boom was in full swing when crates of roofing iron, boxes of nails, barrels of cement, coils of wire, bundles of standards, and sawn timber exceeding half a million feet a year poured on to Kaiapoi wharves for transportation further north. Other imports included casks of sulphur and sheep-wash tobacco for the sheep scab epidemic threatening North Canterbury flocks. Even the telegraph poles for the line to Blenheim came up the North Branch.

An interesting pen picture of those busy days was given in a 1928 interview* by Thomas Heney, who came to Kaiapoi in 1859:

I have seen drays and bullock wagons stretching from the Kaiapoi Shipping Company's office right along to the bend in Charles Street at Anderson's bakery, waiting to unload produce on to the wharves. Included in such a string of vehicles was a dray from Oxford in which were yoked a bullock and a horse in double harness. The wool came in right from Waiau, also grain from Amberley and Oxford and intervening districts. The sheep were driven over the cliffs in the early days after shearing, when the scab was so bad as there was not sale for mutton. Or the carcases were boiled down and the fat was shipped away with the wool. There were some fine bullock teams. One team which I used to admire belonged to Messrs Rhodes and Wilkins, of St. Leonard's station (near Rotherham) which was managed by Mr Davidson, the present owner. This team consisted of seven bullocks and a very large barren cow and it drew 16 bales of wool from St. Leonard's.

I have seen 26 sea-going boats in the river at Kaiapoi at one time, one of them having 350 tons of oats on board for Sydney. This was the John Bullock, a three-masted schooner. I have seen ten sailing boats and two steamers come over the bar and come in at midday on a Sunday on the tide. The bar was as good then as it is today, but no better; only there were times, as now, when the position of the bar, after a breakout, ensured deeper water.

In those early days, two steamers ran regularly, viz., the Gazelle and the Moa. The former afterwards went, I think, to Tasmania, and the latter was at Lyttelton for years. They would come in at certain periods of the tide twice in the 24 hours, working between here and Lyttelton. These boats brought coal and timber into Kaiapoi and this was distributed all over the district. Produce went out by them to all parts of New Zealand.

Alone on a wide, wide sea ...

The sea was not too rough one Tuesday morning when the s.s Moa took the bar about 6.30 o'clock on its way from Kaiapoi to Lyttelton. With that trial over, the master relaxed and looked round for his "first mate", a black retriever bitch named Fan, his constant companion on all his travels.

But Fan was nowhere to be seen, above or below deck. Yet she was aboard coming down the river. It was never learned how she came to slip overboard, but somewhere off the river mouth she must have started swimming after the rapidly-disappearing Moa heading south-east across the bay toward Godley Head, 25 kilometres distant.

Fan was picked up off the heads about noon by the ketch Margaret, spotted by a sharp-eyed crew member, still swimming bravely after her master and ship, long since safely berthed at Lyttelton.

---

*Dictated to the author's father, another Robert Logan, who was a shorthand reporter and owner-editor of The Kaiapoi Record in the 1920s.

Serving this burgeoning import-export trade were dozens of vessels, mostly schooners, cutters and ketches. The majority were on the Kaiapoi-Lyttelton run, but some of the larger craft, as Thomas Heney described, carried North Canterbury exports to more distant parts. The paddle-steamer Lyttelton, locally dubbed "the weedcutter", began a regular service in 1861 between Kaiapoi and Wellington, while others established sea links with Nelson, Wanganui, Westland and Otago. There was no doubt that the Port of Kaiapoi played an important role in the development of trade between North Canterbury and the rest of New Zealand.

As this increased, and with it the number of ships on the river, competition grew apace among the smaller vessels for their share of the business. There was always keen rivalry to load the first of the season's wool, which occasion was marked by a quaint little ceremony much prized by captains and crews. The first bale was hoisted to the top of the mast and secured while all below drank a toast to the new season. Thus refreshed, the "lumpers" on the wharf disposed of the remaining bales with a will. (Perhaps there was a similar ceremony in later times for the first of the season's wheat, which could explain how Joe Drabble fell into the river with a full bag while loading the Kestrel. The captain stripped off and dived in after the wheat, leaving Joe to be rescued by George McAllister.)

Ardent rivals among members of the "mosquito fleet" in the mid-fifties were Captains Day in the Uira, Whitby in the Annie, Russell in the Ebenezer, and Hobbs in the Maid of the Mill.

Crossing the bar. *Typical of the small steamers which used the port in its later days is the* Tuhoe, *the Cure Boating Club's highly successful river boat (220 trips in three years, carrying over 16,000 passengers, from the wharf to just short of the bar). She is seen here heading out to sea en route to Lyttelton for annual survey.* From T.M.Ayers.

Each of these men knew the shifty Waimakariri bar like the back of his hand, and the contests between them were always a good talking point on the wharves. When trade was brisk one would slip out of Lyttelton in the gloom of early morning to race across the bay and be first to sail up the river. As likely as not the challenge would be to come in on the flood tide, load smartly, and sail out again on the ebb. Long familiarity among these skilled seamen eventually led to the practice of taking the bar at any tide, and this inevitably resulted in an increase in the number of strandings on sandbanks in the estuary or the river. But in most cases these were only a matter of waiting for the tide to float the vessel undamaged into deeper water.

The first total wreck was probably the 17-ton cutter Iris, which in August, 1866, arrived off the river in darkness with a heavy load of timber. After beating about for awhile the master decided to give the bar a try, but the ship bumped badly, lost her rudder, and was swept on to the south spit. The sea did the rest, and her cargo was delivered somewhat unconventionally, strewn along the beach.

This mishap broke a long spell of trouble-free navigation. Within a few months the Akaroa ketch *Thetis* was caught in a sudden wind change while leaving the river and like the *Iris* she also ended up on the south spit. A fast unloading job saw her cargo saved but the vessel filled and sank. In the next year at least five other ships came to grief on the bar, but while an occasional cargo was lost or damaged, all were somehow refloated and towed up to Kaiapoi for repair.

Not all the hazards of the harbour were at the bar or in the estuary. The need for some means to dredge the North Branch channel was talked about for years because of the sand and shingle banks that kept forming there. In 1866 the schooner *Spray* had to spend the night on one of these. Coming free in the morning with the flood tide she sailed upriver to pass through the town bridge, but unfortunately the tide which had been her salvation was now her undoing. Her mast, riding high, fouled the telegraph wires, and before anything could be done she swung violently against the bridge, holed herself and ripped away some of her rigging.

In that year the first "harbour master" was appointed, a Swede named John Petersen who lived in a hut near the mouth. His duties were to tend the moveable beacons, stake out the channel, and when required act as pilot. These improvements seemed to have some effect, at least until April, 1870, when the 47-ton schooner *William and Mary* was wrecked on the bar, and next month the 17-ton ketch *Folly*. On that occasion two lives were lost and there was further agitation to make things safer. A semaphore post was placed on the sandhills, south of the entrance for the benefit of vessels coming in. Captains of outgoing ships still consulted Petersen.

In September that year Belcher and Fairweather's 157-ton paddle steamer *Sturt*, one of the largest vessels using the river, was on its way out towards the mouth with a ketch in tow (steamers often helped sailers through the breakers), when she was ordered to stop and disconnect the tow rope, then almost immediately sent on her way. But by then she was in shallow water and soon stranded. An engine defect kept her there and next day she broke her back. The loss was serious and probably accounted for Petersen being replaced by George Day, the veteran of the port's earliest days.

But the march of time was catching up with Kaiapoi's port trade. Not far upriver from the North Branch junction contractors were hammering hardwood piles into the shingle for a bridge to carry the Great Northern Railway into the land beyond the Waimakariri. In 1872 the line was opened but when the first train rolled into the new Kaiapoi railway station local residents greeted it with stony silence. They knew it sounded the ultimate death knell of their port and with it their prosperity. Yet their fears were premature. Although the railway was extended rapidly to north and west, into the country on which Kaiapoi relied for much of its business, the port continued to prosper for another 40 years because the economics of sea transport remained in its favour.

There were many problems, however, in maintaining a good service. One of these was that most Waimakariri water was now going down the South Branch and could no longer be depended on to keep the North Branch clear. The need for a dredge became imperative. In 1876 a Waimakariri Harbour Board was constituted, and although poorly funded managed to scrape together enough finance to buy a dredge — but not enough to operate it regularly.

A local merchant named John Sims, who imported large quantities of coal and timber, declared his faith in the port as a better proposition for him, at least, than the railway, and he had the capital and drive to justify his faith. He chartered the schooners *Croydon Lass, Edith Reid, Jessie,* and *Falcon* to bring in his cargos and developed a general transport business which, beginning in 1877, prospered for several decades until the start of World War I. The port came alive again. In the 1880s Sims added the *Janette, Huon Belle, Owake Belle,* and *Rock Lily* to his fleet.

John Sims, *the ex-bushman entrepreneur who set the port of Kaiapoi alight in the 1870s by chartering and purchasing numerous vessels for his fast-growing import-export trade. He enjoyed conspicuous success except for the inevitable loss of some of his ships on the Waimakariri bar and elsewhere.*

He had his troubles, of course, as would be expected of any ship owner operating in such chancy waters. The 58-ton *Jessie* was trapped on the bar and wrecked in 1882; the 41-ton *Janette* foundered off Cape Campbell in 1886; and the *Owake Belle* came to an unfortunate end on the bar. She was approaching the opening before a light easterly when she lost the breeze at a critical point and drifted on to the beach. Her captain, Ted Mallash, thinking the ship safe enough where she lay, came ashore with the crew and walked to Kaiapoi. But in the night a gale sprang up and by morning the rising seas were pounding her to pieces.

A big flood which came down the river in 1885 cleared out the channel in such splendid fashion that the Harbour Board sold off its dredge to a gold mining concern. Its replacement, the *Hinemoa,* was not a great success and came to an unhappy end when she was carried away in another flood and lost at sea.

John Sims seemed undeterred by misfortune; he went to Australia and ordered two new auxiliary-screw schooners to make up his losses. The day these arrived was a notable occasion. All Kaiapoi turned out when the brand new vessels came cruising up the river, direct from Sydney. While the band played, the official party boarded a pontoon anchored at the ships' bows, the speeches flowed, and so did the champagne from the traditional bottles cracked right and left by the owner's daughter as she named them *Joseph Sims* and *Emma Sims*.

In keeping with such private-enterprise confidence the Harbour Board bought yet another dredge in 1907 and appropriately named it the *Kaiapoi*. Meanwhile the interests of John Sims and others were incorporated in the Kaiapoi Shipping and Trading Company. As business was still thriving, a small steamer, the *Wootton,* was bought in Sydney, but even then the fleet couldn't cope with all the trade offering. So an order was placed in Dublin for what was to be Kaiapoi's pride and joy, the

The steamer Kairaki's arrival *in 1909 was the outstanding event in the history of Kaiapoi's port and was greeted with jubilation by this large crowd at the wharf. Built in Dublin for the Kaiapoi Shipping and Trading Co., she had a capacity of 580 tons and a speed of 10 knots. Unfortunately in 1914 she foundered in a howling gale off Greymouth with the loss of all 17 crew.*
Kaiapoi Museum

103

181-ton *Kairaki,* a vessel specially designed for the river trade, with a draught of three metres, a speed of 10 knots, and a capacity of 580 tonnes.

Kairaki was a great success on the river and between 1910 and 1914 played the major part in moving 1,100,000 metres of timber, 1421 tonnes of coal, 822 bales of wool, 1652 cattle, 145,265 sheep, 70,000 sacks of grain and potatoes, and 290 tonnes of general cargo to and from ports in all parts of New Zealand. Her loss with all hands while on a trip to the West Coast was a severe blow to Kaiapoi, and marked the beginning of the end for the port. The *Wootton* continued to call occasionally, but in 1915 even her visits ceased.

At the conclusion of the Great War there were moves to revive the grand concept of Kaiapoi as the port of North Canterbury. In 1920 local bodies as far north as Amuri were organised into a new Waimakariri Harbour Board rating district by an Act of Parliament which also gave the board power to raise 75,000 pounds for modernisation. This was to be spent on a new training wall to stabilise the bar, new wharves, a cattle landing, a turning basin, a slip, and improvements to the river. The public was bombarded with propaganda advertising the great advantages of this development for the whole district and when the poll of ratepayers was taken the battle was won by 889 votes to 683. It seemed that Kaiapoi's port was about to rise from the dead.

But before anything could be done the whole edifice collapsed. Strong opposition developed, delaying tactics came into play, political pressure intensified, and eventually a Royal Commission was appointed to study the whole question. Their findings dealt Kaiapoi a body blow — a new Act of Parliament overrode its predecessor and reduced the Harbour Board's rating district to one local body and one only — the Borough of Kaiapoi.

This was the end. Occasionally in the years that followed a scow or two came in with a load of lambs for the freezing works, and took away a few tonnes of potatoes, but dreams of a flourishing port and a return to the prosperous days of the 1870s were shattered forever. The port faded away to the accompaniment of dark mutterings about the political clout of big wool and maritime interests which were alleged to have scuttled Kaiapoi's fond hopes.

Today the motor vessel *Tuhoe,* a relic of coastal trading, is tied up at Kaiapoi's wharf, her ownership vested in the Cure Boating Club. She has been restored and made seaworthy and has a licence to carry passengers. On high days and holidays she makes excursion trips down the river. These evoke echoes of almost 100 years ago when the little paddle steamer *Diamond* used to cast off from the same spot for trips to the river mouth, sometimes by moonlight, gaily decorated, loaded with happy excursionists, whistle blowing at the bends, and the brass band aboard playing its heart out. The crew must have been hard pressed to keep their minds on their work, and the captain could not forget one concern which doesn't worry the *Tuhoe* — he had to keep watch for cargo vessels coming up the channel, the little ships which for so long made Kaiapoi and the Waimakariri one of the busiest ports on the coast.

Port of Kaiapoi. *The view today from the main highway bridge, with the* Tuhoe *anchored at the wharf. Imagination is needed to picture dozens of similar small trading vessels crowding the river as they did last century.*

CHAPTER TEN

Ferries and Bridges

If in Canterbury's earliest days the problem was how to get yourself across the Waimakariri, a fat, jolly Maori named Tainui was the man to look for, provided you arrived at the river opposite Te Aik's pa when he wasn't away eeling. For sixpence he would cheerfully ferry you over in his canoe — or a shilling if the river was up.

By late 1851 progress had caught up with Tainui in the form of a punt and a flat-bottomed dinghy operated by one of the then-unemployed survey labourers, a man named Alexander Baxter. He was the first of several Europeans who provided good service at the river until 1863, by which time both branches were bridged.

Baxter built himself a wattle and daub hut where the Kaiapoi Borough Council chambers now stand in Williams Street and for a time operated his ferry across the combined river below the junction. But soon he found the going too tough and shifted his operation upstream to Kaiapoi some time in 1852, leaving the South Branch to the Maoris.

Next on the scene was one George Jackson. In 1853 he took over the South Branch and continued there until 1857, when the new road was built across Kaiapoi Island and Joseph Felton set up his ferry near where William White later built his second bridge. Jackson discovered he had literally been sold down the river so he disposed of his punt and retired to his hotel in Kaiapoi, the Ferryman's Arms.

There were others. A man named Dudding bought Jackson's punt and carried on until a flood washed everything he owned out to sea. Another was S.P. Smith, who built up a thriving business ferrying timber over the South Branch, operating at the junction, where he built a wharf and accommodation house. The timber was carted away to Christchurch by bullock wagon along the old Chaney's Road but when trade fell away so did Smith, even though he cut his prices to the bone in 1859.

The great ferryman survivor was Joseph Felton. Inheriting a virtual monopoly of South Branch traffic, daily growing with the expansion of settlement north of the river, he arranged affairs nicely to suit himself. He acquired a licence for his ferry house at the crossing and soon embellished this with a title, The Courtney Arms. Travellers found the punt never seemed ready to leave until they had spent something at the bar, and occasionally as opportunity offered their stay was further prolonged while Felton saw to it that the transport needs of teetotal sheep and cattle were seen to. Impatient members of the public felt very much at his mercy, and he treated them as a monopolist certainly should not. In 1858 he inserted this advertisement in the newspapers:

The punt at the New Ferry, Kaiapoi, will be taken off for repairs on Monday, 15th inst., and will be ready for work on the 24th. Foot passengers and parties willing to swim the river can cross as usual. — Joseph Felton.

Edward Dobson, the Provincial Engineer, thought the Government should spend about six hundred pounds and fix up the ferry properly and then lease it to the highest bidder. But Felton's eye for business must have matched his sense of humour, because far from being ousted he soon had two ferrymen operating the punts while he managed the hotel. Complaints about the service mushroomed. Changes in the river channel often took the stream away from the bank, forcing passengers to wade through mud and water to get aboard. Letters in the newspapers listed their grievances. A shingle bar which formed a few yards from the bank often meant the punts could not be used for three or four hours while the tide was out.

Joseph Felton, *who established his ferry upriver in 1857 and so put Jackson and his successor Dudding out of business. The newly-built North Road across Kaiapoi Island fixed the position of Felton's Ferry, near where the motorway crosses the river today.* Kaiapoi Museum

Suggestions were made in the newspapers that Felton should roll up his sleeves and get to work with the shovel and remove the obstruction. One correspondent began his letter by saying, "There exists at the present time on the river Waimakariri a serious public nuisance known by the name of Felton's Ferry", while another called on the Provincial Government to inform Mr Felton that if he did not immediately take measures for the proper performance of the service it should be removed from his control.

Felton was not fazed by these criticisms. He replied that he had tried many times to remove the shingle bar, the formation of which was beyond his control, that his punts had cost him 600 pounds each and were unequalled in New Zealand, and that he had never had a complaint yet from any of his customers, adding that he was deeply hurt by the attacks of "anonymous writers in the public prints".

The Waimakariri Ferry. *This showy horseman with the two-metre whip looks as though he's missed the boat in this Haubroe painting of 1855. According to Don Hawkins the date suggests the punt is Jackson's, operating over the lower river opposite what looks to be Kairaki sandhills.*

This 1853 sketch *by Dr A.C. Barker of the river at Kaiapoi, looking towards Mount Grey, shows the crossing where Alex Baxter operated his ferry approximately where the town bridge stands today.* Kaiapoi Museum

By 1863 traffic had built up to the point where sheer volume was causing lengthy delays. An average day that year saw the punts handling 13 bullock drays, 23 horse drays, 24 spring carts, 46 horses and their riders, 42 sheep and cattle, and over 247 passengers and foot travellers. If Felton's pocket was happy with figures like these it was doubly so when the hotel takings were added — somehow low tide on the river, when the punts were immobilised, always coincided with high tide at the bar (the one with the foot rail). But the bonanza was about to end, and the man who wrote finis to it was another publican, the one "who built a bridge but never drove a pile". His name was William White.

William Sefton Moorhouse, *who served two terms as Superintendent of Canterbury and earned lasting fame as the man responsible for the Lyttelton railway tunnel. This chapter relates how he and William White fell out over his apparent deficiencies as a solicitor.*

William White, *the silk weaver who built two bridges across different branches of the Waimakariri, and the original bridge over the Rakaia River. He owned various hotels (Kaikanui, Spreydon Arms, Coker's), and was said to have fenced off part of Cathedral Square for his horses. A great friend of William Rolleston. Described by E.J. Burke as "Snuff box in hand, with 'I hope I don't intrude' manner, keenly after business but to the eye quite unhurried".*
Jane Mears

White's Bridges (1858 and 1863)

To trace White's career as the ultimate eliminator of lower Waimakariri ferrymen it is necessary to go back a few years and change the scene to the North Branch of the river where Alexander Baxter was handling the ferry traffic at Kaiapoi. Not far south of his domain White had built the Kaikanui Hotel near the corner of Peraki Street and Ohoka Road. This tall, quiet-spoken man came to Canterbury in 1852 with his wife and two sons. He was stricken almost immediately with rheumatic fever but survived with the devoted care of his wife and the services of Dr. Barker. He was a silk weaver by trade and something of an inventor, but as Canterbury had no openings for silk weavers he involved himself instead with a number of other enterprises.

One of these was a bridge over the North Branch at Kaiapoi. It is interesting to note that this was to be located on the Peraki Street line for through traffic, on which his hotel stood (traffic eventually settled on the North Road line a block further east). The builder also planned to get Government consent for a toll system by which his costs could be met, and which hopefully would provide him with an income.

A little promotion in 1857 produced a petition in support of the enterprise signed by 56 residents, and White engaged a solicitor to prepare a private bill and act as his agent in presenting it to the Provincial Council. For this he chose a bright young man named William Sefton Moorhouse, of Redcliffs, who was a member of the Provincial Council.

The choice was unfortunate for White. According to him Moorhouse either did not know, or neglected to inform him, that Standing Orders forbade a member from acting as agent for a private bill, and from that point on Moorhouse appeared to be guilty of an astounding series of omissions and deceptions. In February he advertised in the newspapers, as required by law, advising the introduction of the bill and that copies could be seen at his office and at those of newspapers. Yet when White inquired he could find no such thing, and Moorhouse had to admit that the bill was not yet drawn but that he would see to it immediately. As to the problem with Standing Orders, he gave White the surprising assurance that he would resign his seat in the House so that he could present the bill personally.

In March when White inquired again, Moorhouse gave a further intimation that everything was proceeding satisfactorily. Although the notices continued to appear weekly, the only bill in evidence was the one from the newspapers for advertising. It then transpired that it was too late for the presentation of private bills at the current session of the House, but Moorhouse assured White there was another way—he would push it through as a public bill.

By this time White had learned something about procedure, and knew that Moorhouse was talking nonsense. Not surprisingly he severed the relationship and engaged a Mr Pritchard, who in due course prepared the bill properly and had it presented to the House. It was supported by the Superintendent, Mr FitzGerald, even though he appeared vague about where the bridge was to be built, thinking it was across the South Branch near the Seven Mile Peg. White presented his case in a petition outlining the difficulties he had experienced, concluding by saying that he had "lost all confidence in the statements of the said William Sefton Moorhouse Esquire", and

Cast upon the waters. *During a centennial celebration in Malvern County these intrepid "pioneers" get a push off on a crude ferry to show how their grandparents crossed the river.*

Above: *A large flock of merino sheep on Mount White — a photograph taken by manager Ray Marshall on the homestead block. The Waimakariri River is beyond the trees at left, with Craigieburn Range peaks in the distance. Poulter River comes in from the right, and above it stands Mount Binser.*

Right: *Lake Minchin, one of the district's seldom-visited scenic gems, was named after Mount White's first owner. It lies 40km up the Poulter.*

Below: *Looking down the rambling Waimakariri towards Mount White. The Poulter and Esk rivers join the main river from the left at either end of Whale Hill, above which to the right stands Chest Peak (1936m), highest point on the Puketeraki Range.*

Since 1936 *the Klondyke Bridge has carried traffic safely over the Waimakariri where once coaches splashed through the river and Fred Cochrane rescued stranded motorists.*

Above: *As west-bound motorists top the Grasmere straight they get a first glimpse of alpine regions ahead. The peak is Mount Scott on the Polar Range.*

Right: *And from a lookout bay on the road up Arthur's Pass this view presents itself of the National Park's dominant peak, Mount Rolleston, mantled here with winter snow.*

Below: *As the road nears Bealey, exotic autumn colour blends with the sombre tones of native bush against a background of Shaler Range peaks.*

At dawning. *Early sun lights up Mount Rolleston high above a chilly Crow River, still half-lost in night's shadow.*

begging favourable consideration of his proposal. Later in 1857 the bill was passed, giving White power to build his bridge and charge tolls for a period of seven years. At last the job could proceed, while Moorhouse went ahead with an affair of more importance to his own future — his election as Superintendent of Canterbury on October 30 of that year.

William White's troubles were not over, however. The handiest source of timber for the bridge was owned by the Maoris, who took little interest in his money. The time limit on the project was beginning to press when a chance meeting with a newly-arrived watchmaker solved the problem. Acting on a hunch he bought 10 pounds worth of old watches and offered them to the Maoris as a barter payment. The trick worked and White had all the timber he needed.

The bridge was built below the North Branch-Cam junction in line with Smith Street, some distance above the present traffic bridge site where Alex Baxter plied his ferry. No doubt that worthy watched proceedings with misgiving. The new structure was a simple timber affair for which White engaged as foreman a ship's carpenter named Hammett, and was (as a newspaper described it) "carefully and ingeniously constructed, having a drawbridge of sufficient space [6.5 metres wide] to allow any small craft to pass through; the draw machinery is strong and easily worked".

The new bridge was ready for traffic on May 31, 1858. The occasion, while a sad one for Baxter,* was a joyous celebration for the residents of Kaiapoi, who assembled in large numbers to see the two halves of their town united at last by Mr White's enterprise. Mailman Wheeler drove the first vehicle across, an old Whitechapel cart with three worthy citizens aboard, and the opening was further celebrated with a dinner at the Northern Hotel attended by 60 people. *The Lyttelton Times* commented: "The dinner was sumptuous, the speechifying characteristic and applicable, and the whole proceedings were harmonious and gratifying to all present."

Occasional complaints about the price of the tolls were answered by White with assertions that they brought in about 500 pounds a year, and this returned him only 25% on his investment, which he did not consider exorbitant considering the responsibilities and risks of the enterprise.

Nevertheless before his seven-year term was up the Government decided it had had enough of his bridge and commissioned its engineers to build another a short distance downstream, on the site of Baxter's defunct ferry service. White immediately protested, claimed breach of contract, and demanded 1500 pounds in compensation. The matter was debated at length by the Provincial Council, where Mandeville representative Robert Rickman moved that the money be paid — the bridge had been built in good faith and an undertaking given by the Government at the time that the term was for seven years. But the other Mandeville representative, Joseph Beswick, hotly opposed the motion, claiming White was making 1000 pounds a year out of the bridge and had caused the road to be diverted directly to his public-house. If anyone deserved compensation, said Beswick, it was the owner of the

punt on the river whom the bridge had ruined. The thing was tumbling down anyway, he claimed, and to use a digger's phrase, "White had worked out his claim and now wanted to jump another man's."

William White was not without friends in high places — three past, present or future Superintendents of the Province, FitzGerald, Bealey and Rolleston, were all close acquaintances. *The Press,* which FitzGerald owned, came out strongly on his side, maintaining that he was being shabbily treated after discovering that he was not adequately protected by the 1857 ordinance. But when the vote to grant him the 1500 pounds was taken it was defeated 15 to 5.

Beswick's reference to White wanting to jump another man's claim referred to the bridge builder's next move. No sooner had the Government decided to replace him at Kaiapoi than White threw another proposition into the ring — a startling plan to build a bridge over the "unbridgeable" Waimakariri South Branch near Felton's Ferry.

The Government had approached this formidable task on a number of occasions, but had always retreated in the face of problems which seemed to have no solution. A decade of enormous floods had just begun and these made the construction of a bridge capable of withstanding them something the Provincial Council and its engineers were not prepared to tackle.

At the time White made his extraordinary proposal the Provincial Engineer, Edward Dobson, was experiencing great difficulty in getting a bridge over the North Branch on the road between Kaiapoi and Rangiora. It was pertinent to ask what hope there was that a silk weaver, a rank amateur, could succeed with a task of even greater difficulty. The need for a South Branch bridge was widely recognised and accepted, and dissatisfaction with the ferry's limitations had led the Government to consider the subject on a number of occasions, but there were no precedents for coping with a wide and vagrant river subject to heavy flooding and sudden changes of course. As far back as 1858 a competition had been organised and advertised throughout the colony, soliciting designs for a bridge to suit the special problems of the Waimakariri. Fourteen entries were received from eminent engineers and sent on to Auckland for judging by a Colonel Mould, R.E., who chose one designed by Henry Whitcombe, of the Canterbury survey staff.

The Lyttelton Times had seen the entries before they went to Auckland and was impressed with their quality and ingenuity, but was concerned nevertheless that the wandering Waimakariri posed a problem with which Colonel Mould was probably unfamiliar. "A man who contracts to build a bridge over the Waimakariri will not have fulfilled his engagement if it turns out that he has only constructed a viaduct over a dry shingle bed," said the *Times,* reflecting on the river's propensity for changing its course with every flood.

Perhaps this was enough to weaken the Government's resolve. Henry Whitcombe's bridge was never built, and the Waimakariri was left to the much relieved Mr Felton — at least until August of 1862, when William White finally persuaded the Government to let him go ahead. A second White's Bridge Ordinance was passed, giving him another seven-year lease on toll fees. Again with Hammett as foreman he went to work on the new venture. What followed was one of the strangest episodes in the annals of Canterbury engineering.

By mid-June of 1863 White had seven spans of the new bridge completed and members of the public were looking forward to the day when at last they could cross the river dryshod and without annoying delay. But at this point James Wylde, then assistant Provincial Engineer, stepped into the picture and noted that the time limit for the work imposed on the builder had expired. He inspected the work and informed White that the bridge, as far as it went, could not be passed for public use because of shoddy construction — among other things some of the piles had split, there were bent braces, and the joists were made of unsuitable timber. "The workmanship is of the roughest and most slovenly description," he reported.

The Courtney Hotel *which stood opposite Felton's Ferry (and later White's Bridge) across the South Branch. Names here are tricky in that the licensee when this sketch was made was C. White, apparently no relation of the bridge builder, and there was also a White's Courtenay Hotel 35km further up the river.* Kaiapoi Museum

*D.N. Hawkins records that "the end of Alexander Baxter, Kaiapoi's first settler, came in an appropriate fashion. He was observed one evening rowing downstream from the Northern Hotel towards the lights of his hut, but was never seen again. The boat was washed up out on the beach, but old Kaiapoians liked to believe that somewhere out on blue Pegasus Bay Baxter was still rowing on".

The battle for the bridge. *This old (1868) and tattered illustration depicts the original White's Bridge over the Waimakariri's South Branch. It is the focal point here of an exercise by Canterbury Volunteer Artillery in which 230 men fought for possession of the bridge before an audience of 2000 spectators. According to a C.V.A. history by Guy Bliss, the gunners tired of waiting for the expected assault, and for every 5 min delay added another handful of gravel to their blank charges, forcing the cavalry to retire in confusion. A substantial two-storey addition has been made to the hotel compared with the sketch on the previous page. In the 1874 flood, when the entire river flowed in the South Branch for the first time, the bridge was entirely submerged and the water was a metre deep in the hotel.*

Canterbury Public Library.

This was a bombshell indeed, though in the event it blew Wylde much higher than the bridge. His opinion was fully backed by his indirect superior, Edward Dobson, who wrote to Provincial Secretary Tancred on August 12, 1863, as follows:

Sir,—I have the honour to report that W. White has failed to complete his proposed bridge over the Waimakariri ferry within the times named in his contract dated 2-8-62.

I have further to report that the portion of the bridge which has been erected is so badly constructed as to be unsafe for public traffic and that I should therefore recommend that Mr White be instructed to remove the whole of his work and to reinstate the banks to their former state.

I have the honour to be, Sir, your obedient servant,
EDWARD DOBSON, Hon. Prov. Engineer.*

There was in all this, of course, some element of professional pique with White now that his "impossible" bridge was actually nearing completion. The thought of such a difficult and important engineering problem being solved by a silk weaver turned pub-keeper, with such a frail and spindly contraption, was about as much as the professionals could take. But there was commonsense in the design, which ensured that flood waters could pass safely beneath the decking with the least possible obstruction.†

Wylde and Dobson reckoned without the full consequence of the public outcry which arose immediately their decision was made known. The community north of the river—farmers, townsfolk and station owners—had all been impatient for the day when they could finally dispense with Felton's autocratic ways and indifferent service. To be denied their bridge before they had even crossed it was too much to take. They urged White to press on and finish the job regardless, and this he did. Immediately the last yard of approach had been shovelled in place the public streamed across, cheering as they went, and thumbing their noses at Felton mournfully contemplating his idle punts. He had one consolation—those in the mood to celebrate at least did so in his bar.

But White could not collect tolls without a permit from the Provincial Engineer, and pressure on that gentleman began to grow. The subject was argued at length in the Provincial Council executive meetings with no result except that White was ordered to close the bridge in the meantime. This only served to increase public impatience. *The Press* stepped in and endeavoured to bring sweet reason to bear on what had by then become the topic of the month. "Now what is the history of this affair?" it asked equably, and continued:

Mr Dobson originally recommended that the bridge should be built at the seven mile peg, because the river there having come to its greatest possible width was no longer washing away its banks. The bridge was not built there because the work was considered to be a too costly one. Whilst the matter was still in abeyance Mr White says, I will build you a bridge for certain tolls across the river at the present ferry, on the line of the North Road as at present laid out, made, and used. The Provincial Council entertained his proposition and after debate resolved to adopt that course. Mr Dobson was consulted. Not long ago Mr Dobson wrote a report to the Government recommending that as Mr White had not completed his work within the time contracted, he should be required to remove the bridge again and make good the banks as he found them. The idea of Old White being required to pick up a bridge some hundred feet long* before it was opened for traffic and cart it away again was so ludicrous that no one could imagine the motive for such an eccentric recommendation. But Mr Dobson's career has been studded with little crotchets of this kind, which sorely shake reliance in his judgement, and impair his professional usefulness.

According to the White family archives the impasse was solved in no uncertain manner by the Provincial Superintendent, Mr Bealey, who arrived in style, drove over the bridge, and declared it open. James Wylde having been dismissed or persuaded to resign, his place as assistant Provincial Engineer was filled by the appointment of George Thornton, sometime District Engineer, and no admirer of either Wylde or Dobson. His first official duty was to make a thorough examination of the new structure, after which he declared it safe for public use and authorised the collection of toll fees.

All obstacles now having been cleared away, White's Bridge entered on its useful career as an essential link in the Main North Road. With this (and his victory over envy or timid conservatism) William White became something of a folk hero in North Canterbury. None was more enthusiastic in praise than the sheep station gentry. An advertisement inserted in *The Press* of February 26, 1864, read:

WAIMAKARIRI BRIDGE

Many residents in the north of the Province think it due to Mr Wm. White that some Testimonial be presented to him for his intelligent enterprise in projecting, and perseverance in successfully bridging the Waimakariri. This great public convenience speaks for itself.

The undermentioned gentlemen invite the cooperation of those who agree with them in the propriety of a Testimonial and will gladly receive subscriptions.

    J.T. BROWN, Mt. Thomas.   G.H. MOORE, Glenmark.
    A.H. CUNNINGHAM,   T.S. MANNERING, Birch Hill.
      Fernside.   R. RICKMAN, Kaiapoi.
    M. DIXON, Eyrewell.   R.L. HIGGINS, Cust Valley.

*Dobson, Canterbury's first Provincial Engineer, appointed in 1854, held that office in effect for 14 years. But from January 1861 to October 1865 he discharged whatever general duties were required of him in an acting, honorary or consulting capacity while he was occupied as Railways Engineer building the Lyttelton tunnel.

†In the 1868 flood all bridges in North Canterbury were damaged or swept away except White's.

*The bridge was actually 600ft (183m) long.

These joined with many others at the Mandeville Farmers' Club ploughing match soon after, when the bridge builder was presented with his testimonial and a gold watch and chain to mark their appreciation.

Yet not everyone who had to cross the river was pleased that Joseph Felton's stranglehold had been inherited by William White. As time passed, fresh grumblings were heard abroad. At a meeting at Rangiora, Mayor Henry Blackett reckoned White was taking 3000 pounds a year in tolls, more than enough to build a new bridge every year. He wanted to know why the Government didn't build its own bridge over the South Branch, as it had done earlier on the North Branch. In another direction Edward Dobson, who could never view White's Bridge without a shudder, worked out a flood protection scheme and a new course for the river which would leave White and his bridge high and dry, but nothing came of it.

Lesser protests came from 1865 gold-diggers heading north to the Hurunui Saddle and the West Coast, some of whom threatened to throw the tollkeeper into the river. But none was more truculent than one John Murphy, a farmer of Kaiapoi Island, who refused point-blank to pay up and, when the tollkeeper took the horse's reins to turn it back, jumped out of the dray, grabbed him by the throat, and threatened to throw him off the bridge. Moreover when the keeper's wife came to her husband's aid Murphy took her by the throat too. A special constable named Thomas having arrived on the scene, Farmer John proposed to throw *him* in the river as well. Eventually Murphy was brought before the court and fined four pounds.

In 1872, after the seven-year lease had expired, the bridge was taken over by the authorities and another span added. The professional antagonism to White's "unsafe" structure had by then dissipated. Arguments about its stability were answered by the bridge itself, which remained unimpressed by anything the river could do. However, its frugal builder had not planned far beyond the terms of his lease when he selected timbers for the job, so that by 1876 much of the native woods used were rotting and a replacement had to be considered.

Details of the new bridge which replaced White's and carried the same name are not easy to come by. It was opened in January, 1878, and consisted of 15 spans of 10.6m each, all in timber, the piles being of ironbark. It was probably initiated by the Canterbury Provincial Council but finished by central government after the provinces were abolished. No mention of its construction appears in any of the public works reports for the period save one brief announcement of its completion. The contractors were Evans and Butt, and as soon as their task was finished the historic old White's Bridge close by was demolished.

EMPIRE BRIDGE (1903)

The Dobson family's association with the Waimakariri surfaced many times over the next 50 years in connection with bridges, irrigation and power schemes, and the next bridge on the Felton's Ferry site was designed by Arthur Dudley Dobson. This was the Empire Bridge, opened in 1903. Although by then Dobson had become Christchurch city engineer, the terms of his appointment allowed him to supervise this work. A Howe truss bridge, it was 167m long with a 6.5m roadway, built of ironbark with turpentine piles. The builder was A. Pearce of Kaiapoi, whose price was 6560 pounds.

Led by Sir Joseph Ward, a large group of dignitaries assembled one day in June, 1903, for the opening ceremony. At almost the last minute it was realised the subject of their attention still had no official title. A hurried conference to one side produced a number of suggestions, one being "Empire", to which there appeared to be no particular objection, and so it was. Sir Joseph cut the ribbon and a couple of traction engines were driven across to prove it safe for public use.

THE GIRDER BRIDGE (1863)

The vagrant ways of the Waimakariri must be considered when discussing the subject of bridges in 1863. At that time the river was unable to make up its mind which side of Kaiapoi Island it should flow — into the North Branch where Edward Dobson and his provincial engineering department were building the Girder Bridge on the direct route to Rangiora, or the South Branch where William White was at work. It was Dobson's misfortune to have the river increasingly favour the northern channel, rendering entirely unsuitable the short, low and heavy iron-girder bridge he had designed. His failures with this venture earned him much unfavourable criticism. After one flood *The Press* commented that the bridge was "condemned and rebuilt three times, and now condemned again", and was inclined to think that private money was being better spent than public, since White's bridge on the South Branch appeared to be quite indifferent to floods, no matter how severe.

The Girder Bridge replaced a flimsy wooden structure possibly built by Charles Torlesse in 1849, which had been carried away by a flood.*

Sir Joseph Ward, *deputy Prime Minister, declaring the Empire Bridge open for traffic. A strong clue to its location lies in the fact that the short "exit" road from the motorway to the old North Road is called Empire Road. All three bridges up till then (and Felton's Ferry) were sited a short distance west of the motorway opposite the "Exit" sign.* Weekly Press

The Empire Bridge *was the second replacement for White's original bridge over the South Branch. It was dismantled when the river was diverted into Wright's Cut in the 1930s and the present "old main highway bridge" was built.* Weekly Press

*The lower Waimakariri River has changed or been changed so much that the location of earlier landmarks is often blurred, but the site of the original Girder Bridge may still be found. Christchurch motorists en route to Rangiora who leave the motorway at the second exit beyond the Waimakariri, marked "Ohoka - Kaiapoi South", will soon find themselves on Island Road, passing a cemetery on their right. Immediately round the next bend there is a small bridge which spans all that is left of the old North Branch channel. This is where the Girder Bridge stood. A second small bridge further on spans Ohoka Creek, and is followed shortly by the Skew Bridge over the Main Drain. This was dug to drain the Ohoka-Rangiora swamp. Among other things it carries the flow of the Cust River, which used to empty into the swamp. All are tributaries of the Kaiapoi River, which occupies the original North Branch channel through Kaiapoi town and flows into the Waimakariri near Kairaki.

Left: Edward George Wright, *who built Kaiapoi's "Swing" Bridge in 1863 to replace White's original North Branch bridge. This was Wright's first major contract in Canterbury, from which he went on to become one of the province's leading public works contractors.* Right: The Swing Bridge, *so-called because the centre span swung round to let ships pass, stood on the site of the present town bridge. The span at left carried away in the 1868 flood. The scaffolding at left probably marked the beginnings of Hansen's Buildings which stood beside the bridge for many years.*   Kaiapoi Museum

Dobson's concept of iron girders for bridge work was new to Canterbury and had local bridge-watchers doubting whether the piles would be strong enough to carry them. A newspaper correspondent signing himself "L.M." was bitingly critical of both the bridge and its designer. It would soon be in deep water, he declared, "and while I am amused at the Engineer's pluck, I am disgusted at his impudence as a public servant in throwing dust in the eyes of our Representatives".

He was right, as it happened. Not long after the bridge was opened on June 11, 1863, a flood carried away the superstructure, leaving the piles standing alone in the bed. When the water went down workmen had the job of recovering the precious girders from the mud. The event gave another correspondent the chance to agitate for a better site, "one which would not require users to wade up to their middles to reach the bridge".

Rebuilding, for which the Provincial Council allocated a thousand pounds, was completed in October 1864. At 88 metres the new bridge was more than twice the length of its short-lived predecessor. It was also a metre higher — but still not high enough. The Christmas Day flood of 1865 submerged it completely. When the water subsided two or three days later the critics were disappointed to find the bridge still there. But the approaches were gone, and the addition of another nine metres of girder was considered advisable. The Mandeville and Rangiora Road Board, whose responsibility it was, appealed to the Provincial Government for financial help. Since it was their brainchild in the first place, that august body could hardly refuse — but not, they warned, to a greater extent than 500 pounds.

When the extension and new approaches were finished the travelling public enjoyed only six months of uninterrupted use before the November, 1866, flood arrived. Scoured by turbulent waters, the piles at the northern end sank under the weight of the girders and all heavy traffic had to be prohibited.

Again repairs were made and this time a protective groyne was built above the site. In the 1868 flood, recognised as the worst ever in Canterbury, the bridge was submerged yet again but surfaced in good shape. The groyne was considered to have done its work and damage to the approaches was minor. The total Waimakariri flow was probably less in 1868 than in 1865, and the volume in the North Branch would certainly be less because much of its water was going down the new canals on Kaiapoi Island and into the South Branch.

Two Amberley contractors, Thomas and Hill, replaced Dobson's troublesome Girder Bridge in 1879 with a long wooden truss structure which had no girders but still retained the name. As it grew older the cross planking on the deck worked loose and clattered explosively every time a motor vehicle drove across. On frosty nights the noise could be heard in Kaiapoi. It grew louder with the years, as the water flowing beneath grew less, until eventually the old monster was silenced and replaced with the present efficient single span — one which, thankfully, is seen but not heard, and is quite adequate for crossing the stream meandering quietly where once nearly all the Waimakariri flowed.

THE SWING BRIDGE (1863)

As already mentioned, while White's No.1 bridge on the North Branch at Kaiapoi still had a year or two to go before his seven-year lease on tolls was to finish in 1865, the Provincial Government decided to build a new one downstream approximately where the main highway bridge in the centre of town now stands. The main objection to White's seems to have been that it was no longer in the right place and traffic had to detour to use it. And of course there were the tolls.

The new structure was designed to incorporate a centre span which could be swung away to allow the passage of ships up and down the river, Kaiapoi then being a thriving port for coastal shipping — hence the name "Swing Bridge". Plans were drawn by the Government's engineering department under the supervision of Edward Dobson and a contract for some heavy ironwork let to Anderson's Foundry in Christchurch. The bridge itself was built by Edward G. Wright, an English-trained civil engineer — his first public works undertaking in Canterbury. He later became the largest such contractor in the province, responsible for many of its railway and roading works.

By mid-June of 1863 construction had been started, which meant that work on three major bridges in the district was under way at much the same time — Girder, White's South Branch, and Kaiapoi's Swing. By mid-November reports said that the new bridge, "the largest work of its kind yet erected in New Zealand", was nearly ready, and expected to be of great benefit to the town and indeed to the whole settlement.

But it seemed impossible for the course of true bridge-building to run smoothly in North Canterbury. Apparently Wright's price was 180 pounds above the sum provided by the Government, perhaps for some embellishments added to satisfy local requirements. This amount was promised by Kaiapoi subscribers but when the bridge was completed at year's end there was no sign of the money. Wright promptly advertised in the newspapers that although the bridge was ready for use, it would not be opened until those gentlemen who had pledged subscriptions paid up, the 180 pounds involved being supplementary to the Government grant of 2000 pounds.

A later photograph *of the Swing Bridge shows Hansen's Buildings in place. The building in centre, showing between the two stores, is the Pier Hotel, then (as now) situated in Charles Street.*   Weekly Press

The response was nil, whereupon Wright advertised again that until the subscriptions were forthcoming the "swing" would remain open for ships but on no account for road traffic. Whether the money was paid, or even part of it, is not known, but after about three weeks he gave in and threw open the bridge for both road and river. Meanwhile the Provincial Council accepted the tender of one William Crooke for the toll franchise, at 400 pounds. Soon the town's latest acquisition was reported to be working "exceedingly well and capable of being readily opened and closed by one man".

About this time the Municipality of Kaiapoi was the recipient of a handsome bell donated by William Wilson, a member of the Provincial Council. The Kaiapoi authorities determined that this should be placed in the toll house, which prompted the weekly journal, *Punch in Canterbury,* to note that the public and the bell could now be tolled together.

Two years later the bridge was found to need repairs, expected to cost about 70 pounds, and later there was trouble with the massive key and capstan gear which worked the swing section. The Christmas day flood of 1865 gave the structure a severe shaking, and it had more of this in 1866 when in two separate incidents large vessels ran foul of it. Then in the 1868 flood the northern span broke away and went out to sea.

For some weeks the travelling public had to depend on punts and rowboats again while a contractor named J. Bowmaker built a temporary span and the council lent a sympathetic ear to a recommendation from local engineer Wylde that an entirely new structure be built, preferably without an opening span. In July, 1868, plans were adopted and a contract let to R. Wright for 1246 pounds. The Provincial Government granted 600 pounds on condition that the tolls were abolished, but the council was opposed to this.

During the following year Wright's contract was annulled and Bowmaker re-engaged at 960 pounds to replace his temporary span with something more substantial. When he was finished the swing section wouldn't open anyway and so ships were unable to work the wharves above the bridge.

One of the Beswick brothers, prominent in timber and shipping, took umbrage at this and threatened the council with legal action unless it opened up the river immediately, claiming damage to his business interests. Council shrewdly countered with a notice pasted on the bridge to the effect that it was closed indefinitely for repairs. For good measure they sent a copy to Beswick. He was so enraged he swore to raise an army of supporters in Kaiapoi and demolish the bridge forthwith; if he couldn't raise them in Kaiapoi he would get them in Christchurch.

Eventually Beswick was persuaded to fight in the courts rather than on the bridge. He sued for 500 pounds damages, won the case, and was awarded 175 pounds. But the council appealed and had the decision overthrown. Ultimately the only real beneficiaries were the legal fraternity. The old bridge, properly repaired, lasted another 17 years until the elegant but unworkable Iron Bridge replaced it and ended forever all further navigational disputes on Kaiapoi's shrinking river. Toll charges on both White's and the Swing bridges were abolished in 1874.

This railway bridge *had to be built after the river took to Stewart's Gully about 1880. It was situated 1½km below the present one, and was built with a slight curve. Truss bridges of this type were common throughout Canterbury for both road and rail.* Weekly Press

THE RAILWAY BRIDGES (1872)

In 1871 the railway was being pushed north and the first major obstacle was of course the Waimakariri River. It then ran north-east from near the present railway bridge more directly towards Kaiapoi, joining the North Branch (or Kaiapoi River as it is now) near the freezing works. A site for the railway bridge was chosen two kilometres below the present bridge, and in June, 1871, the Canterbury Provincial Government started construction to a plan produced by its chief engineer, George Thornton. The contractor was William Stocks, of Dunedin (who later built the Gorge Bridge). The railway structure had 19 spans of 10.6 metres with five-tonne iron girders mounted on Australian ironbark piles, and a total length of 191 metres.

No other section of railway in Canterbury traversed such uncertain ground as that between Chaneys and Kaiapoi, built as it was across sandy bogs and old river channels and with a capricious river ever ready to shout "Washout!" in the ears of harassed engineers. The fault was partly theirs as far as the bridge was concerned, for at 191 metres it was too short and constricted the river's flow during major floods.

Over the years tens of thousands of pounds were spent in the area on groynes and stopbanks trying to keep the unruly Waimakariri at bay. Larger floods broke out above Chaneys and invariably washed out some of the permanent way, if that is what it could be called. Occasionally trains were at risk. Once two boys discovered a flood had scoured out the line and made a deep hole. Realising a train was due they ran back along the line and, signalling desperately with their handkerchiefs, managed to stop the engine before it reached the washout. They became heroes of the day and were rewarded with fifty pounds each, a fortune to a small boy.

In 1879 the resident railway engineer, Henry Lowe, wrestling with the many problems of the area, thought he saw a solution which would take the pressure off both Kaiapoi and the railway. He recommended that a channel be cut through the farmland of James Stewart and his sons to provide an overflow in flood time. By coincidence or with a little help from its friends, the Waimakariri obliged by making its own channel about where the

Tragic Train Accident. *When the 1905 flood washed out the railway line this is what happened to the Kaiapoi train as it steamed north towards the Waimakariri rail bridge. When the engine plunged into a washout the front carriages telescoped and killed two men. One of those who died was R.J. Alexander (pictured), headmaster of Kaiapoi school.* Weekly Press

engineer thought it should be, and thus "Stewart's Gully" was born.

In Lowe's scheme a few extra spans would be needed at the south end of the railway bridge to accommodate the water flowing in Stewart's Gully, but when the river adopted the new course in toto he had to build a complete new bridge. As usual this was too short at 158 metres. Most people knew this and so did the river, which soon forced an extension to 247 metres. This structure, handicapped by the unstable nature of the ground, skirmished for years with unmanageable flood waters. At times piles were undermined, at others approaches washed away. It was estimated that between 5000 and 6000 tonnes of rock were used to keep the river away and the bridge open. On the occasion of one flood the midday train for Christchurch had only just cleared the bridge when a considerable length of the southern approach collapsed and was swallowed up by the river. At times for a week on end the service had to be maintained by trolleys shuttling between trains at each end of a washout.

In these circumstances a simple train journey from Christchurch to Kaiapoi was fraught with uncertainty. On Friday, June 23, 1905, there was a strong nor'wester, very warm for the time of year, and next day the Waimakariri was in full flood. As usual it had broken out and spread over the land so that the midday train was soon splashing through a strong but shallow stream as it progressed north of Chaneys through the protective groves of silver poplars. Noting this, three passengers, R.J. Alexander (the headmaster of Kaiapoi school), J. Richards and G. Clothier stepped out on to the carriage platform for a better view. Just as Clothier turned to resume his seat the engine plunged into a washout and the train was wrecked. The carriages where Alexander and Richards were standing telescoped and they were killed instantly. Clothier was partly trapped and both his legs were broken.

Since those unfortunate days the bridge has been replaced yet again, this time in 1957 some distance upstream and alongside the old main highway bridge.

When the railway went through in 1872 the North Branch had also to be bridged. The first train crossed there in July of that year. This structure, fortunately, never suffered the interruptions and frustrations which so bedevilled that over the South Branch.

THE "SWING" FOOTBRIDGE (1874)

Because the main bridge in Kaiapoi was plainly unreliable in flood time, and to give children in particular and pedestrians in general a safer crossing, about 100 residents petitioned the Provincial Council in 1873 for a footbridge some distance upriver on the line of Black and Davie streets. Government agreed and by February in 1874 the bridge was completed.

The construction was light and simple, with a total length of 110 metres in eight spans. The piles bore suspension posts about 2.5m high, which carried wire ropes on iron pulleys, and from these iron droppers carried the weight of the deck and its load. Clearance was 1.5m above the highest known flood.

The Suspension Footbridge *in Kaiapoi was known to generations of residents as another Swing Bridge, the original of that name having vanished and this one having the motion inherent in cable-supported structures. It is the longest-serving of all Waimakariri bridges, now 114 years old. When the raupo part of the riverbed was reclaimed the bridge was shortened by half. In the foreground is a Cure Rowing Club four leaving from their boatshed.*
Kaiapoi Museum

As time passed and the original "swing" bridge on the main street disappeared, the name was transferred to the footbridge but with a different meaning: a span of the original swung aside to let ships through, while the footbridge's semi-suspension had something of the characteristic movement associated with wire cables.

Massive. *Considering the cement had to come halfway round the world, and all the mixing was done by hand, there was no skimping when the buttresses were being built to support the Gorge Bridge.*

THE GORGE BRIDGE (1877)

That impressive, nearly 30m high, caisson-supported structure which spans the Waimakariri on the road between Oxford and Sheffield, known generally as The Gorge Bridge, is the oldest and most imposing of those which cross the main river today. The explanation for building such a grand affair in the 1870s, so early in the life of the province, was bound up in the special problems of the site, the development of Oxford as a major source of sawn timber, and the current enthusiasm for railway extension throughout Canterbury.

In addition to the main north-south trunk railway a secondary line was envisaged, running from Rangiora to Temuka via Oxford, Sheffield, and the western border of the plains. This could link with a possible Midland line and cross the Waimakariri and Rakaia rivers at their respective gorges. Eyreton, Springfield, Methven and similar connecting lines would see Canterbury literally crisscrossed with railways, then definitely the transport system of the future.

Early crossing places of the Waimakariri upriver from the Main North Road included the ford at Courtenay, the one used by the Godleys on their return from Oxford. As Christchurch became increasingly dependent on Harewood Forest timber an Oxford sawmiller, Harry Kenrick, built and installed a punt at the crossing. To get the wire cable across Joseph Pearson swam the river bearing the pilot rope. Ultimately this enterprise was abandoned in favour of Coldstream Pass (Waimakariri Gorge), where lingering foothills briefly constrict the river to a single channel, the lack of which had troubled the Courtenay ferry. Earlier there was a ford near the Kowai River junction, known as Rockford because of the big rock in the river there.

As early as 1863 there was talk of a bridge at "The Gorge", which Kenrick offered to build in return for a franchise on the tolls, but nothing eventuated. By 1870 District Surveyor E.P.

Sealy was estimating the cost of getting approach roads down the steep banks to water level at 250 pounds. Superintendent Rolleston, however, deciding the Oxford Road Board was best fitted for the enterprise, persuaded it to take responsibility for the road work and punt building with a grant of 500 pounds and some wire rope.

The Road Board got the approaches built for half the Government's estimate and decided they were doing well. But a punt? Specifications for punts implied a knowledge they could hardly be expected to possess. Provincial engineers couldn't help either, but George Thornton, by then their chief, thought Hokitika knew something about punts. A plea to the County Council there produced the requisite plans and building was soon under way.

While the Road Board carpenters grappled with the intricacies of vertical knees, transoms and stem pieces, Thornton organised a wire rope across the river and a boat to provide an interim passenger service. A Mr Martindale was in charge, who demonstrated to the engineer that crossings could be made in only 90 seconds. The flaw in the scheme was that after the next big flood the boat was nowhere to be found.

By April 16, 1872, the Road Board had completed the punts, ready for the official launching. They were really flat-bottomed pontoons, with decks and handrails, and end walls which lowered to make landing ramps. They were attached to a cable stretched between the lower walls of the gorge, above the waterline, and were propelled by the pressure of the river against a large rudder. Each could carry a laden 8-horse wagon or 200 sheep. The operator was John Wilson, known to all as "Punty", who lived in a cottage on the north bank.

The trial consisted of a dozen trips which Thornton, stopwatch ever at the ready, timed at between 80 and 105 seconds. There were free rides for all and the children had a field day. "Gog" and "Magog", as the vessels were christened, worked so well that the whole affair was pronounced a perfect success, filling a real need in the community.

But Oxford residents were not satisfied for long. Next year they wanted a bridge. The punts had been a great improvement on Martindale's boat, especially when it wasn't there, but a bridge was the thing to have. A petition to this effect, addressed to the Government, was in circulation early in the new year, contending that with drought and floods, and the river too low one week and too high the next, the working of the punts was in a very unsatisfactory state and an impediment to the district's growing agricultural and timber trades. This was signed by 200 residents.

In April, 1873, George Thornton drew plans for a bridge 52 metres long and 20.4 metres high with a central stone pillar supporting two truss spans. The Provincial Government,

The Gorge Bridge. *This interesting photograph taken about the time the Waimakariri Gorge Bridge was opened in 1877 shows the punt it superseded moored at the south bank. At right is the road leading down to the river and in the foreground stands "Punty" Wilson's cottage from where he could anticipate the needs of travellers arriving on the Malvern bank. The punts operated for five years.*   Canterbury Museum

The Day the Trains Ran. *Although the Gorge Bridge was built for both rail and road, and was opened for the latter in 1877, it was not until July 28, 1884 that the first trains connected Oxford with Sheffield. This was the scene on that occasion, with spectators crowding the bridge for the ceremony and a train from Oxford waiting to make the first crossing.*
Canterbury Museum

however, chose a much higher and grander design by Harry Higginson, a resident New Zealand Government engineer. He proposed two sets of massive steel caissons nearly 25m high, filled with concrete, on which were to rest three iron girder spans of 33m, bedded in large concrete abutments on the gorge walls. The ironwork alone weighed 473 tonnes and the concrete work required 1250 barrels of the best Portland cement.

The tenders for ironwork manufactured in England, including freight and insurance, came to 10,067 pounds. The cylinders alone cost 2587 pounds, and the superstructure 4415 pounds, bringing the total to an estimated 23,000 pounds. The tender of William Stocks was accepted to build it. Higginson (who was paid 50 pounds for his design) was consulting engineer, E. Cuthbert was supervisor, and the overseer (at 25 pounds a month) was John Snowball, who was shipped out from England for the job, recommended from London as "steady, sober, industrious, and a clever foreman and engineer".

The concept of this lofty, dual-purpose, road-rail structure was entirely new to Canterbury, and for William Stocks was as far removed from his railway bridges over the lower Waimakariri as could be imagined. The work was not without its difficulties. The river flow had to be diverted while excavations for the steel caissons were blasted from the bed-rock to a depth of at least 30cm. Men were lowered into the towering cylinders on slings, and air was pumped down to sustain them as they worked far below by the light of lanterns. Only short shifts could be worked; longer spells caused nose-bleeds among some of the men.

The first materials arrived at Lyttelton on the *Tintern Abbey* in May, 1875, and the bridge was opened for road traffic on October 9, 1877.* Stocks, whose troubles were often compounded by strong winds as his men worked high above the river, was penalised for failure to complete the job to specifications.

The railway over the bridge, connecting Oxford and Sheffield and used mainly for freight, was opened in 1884 and closed in 1930. The grades at either end of the bridge limited the length and weight of all trains on that line. Special one-day excursions from Oxford to Arthur's Pass and Greymouth, promoted by local organisations, were often so well patronised that when the train came to the slope on the south end of the bridge no amount of huffing and puffing would get it to the top. The remedy was to uncouple half the carriages and take them on to Sheffield, then return the engine for the remainder. The same procedure

had to be adopted on the return trip at the north end of the bridge. Some Oxford old-timers remembered getting home from these excursions just in time to milk the cows.

In 1947 the bridge was redecked, and in 1964 narrowed to take only one-way traffic as the alternative to large-scale re-piling work. Still later, considerable remedial work was done to the concrete abutments, and the expectation is that the venerable and impressive old centenarian of Waimakariri bridges will serve for many a year yet.

THE MOUNT WHITE BRIDGE (1883)

This bridge gives access from Highway 73 to Mount White station, the shingled road for which leaves the bitumin about 3km beyond Cass, on the summit of Goldney Saddle. For a hundred years it was used only by station people and occasional visitors, but every year now it is the scene of frenzied activity as hundreds of competitors in the annual Coast-to-Coast marathon and their many supporters gather for the start of the river section.

The bridge was built by the Upper Waimakariri Road Board and opened in 1883. A man named Peter McGrath won the contract, but somehow the arrangement fell through and the job was taken by Thomas and Hill, of Amberley (the builders of the "Girder" Bridge at Kaiapoi), who also built the Poulter River bridge nearer Mount White station. The engineer for both projects was Arthur Dudley Dobson, then in business in Christchurch with his father Edward.

This ancient structure is the "hard shot" of Waimakariri bridges. Bits of it have been replaced so often that very little of the original timbers remain. The decking undulates on the way across, according to what sort of a rough time the piles are having. There was a major reconstruction in the 1950s, when according to Peter Newton "everything was renewed except the piles", and another a few years ago when a flood nearly took the lot away. Its other notable peculiarity is that the West Coast railway comes along the south bank and passes the bridge-end with only a metre to spare, which tends to give new-chum motorists the jitters both coming and going.

*Newspaper coverage of major engineering projects in early Canterbury was minimal. Construction difficulties on the West Coast Road went almost unrecorded, while reference to the Gorge Bridge, another engineering landmark, appears to have been restricted to one small paragraph in *The Press* of October 12, 1877, advising that the bridge was "declared open for traffic at midday on Tuesday".

A Rickety Affair. *The Mount White Bridge, one of three crossing the Waimakariri above the gorge, gives access to Mount White sheep run on the north bank. This photograph looks due north up the rainy Hawdon valley. The bridge is like the axe which had two new blades and three new handles — virtually nothing remains of the original yet it looks much the same.* **Below:** *Rhonda Marshall, wife of the manager at Mount White, helps pack supplies for the station across the bridge after it was seriously damaged by floods in 1979.*

Kaiapoi's main street *looking south from the Iron Bridge. The photograph was probably taken about the turn of the century, before the library and fire station were built on the corner section at left. The business houses at right include Brown's Temperance Hotel, J.C. Roll, chemist, Mrs R. Dunn's tea rooms, confectionery etc., and the Kaiapoi Cooperative Stores. On the left are the Borough Council office and the Ready Cash Drapery.*

From D.D. McLauchlan

THE IRON BRIDGE (1885)

When the old Swing Bridge on Kaiapoi's main street came to the end of its useful life, the Borough Council determined that its replacement should be the handsomest in the country. In 1884 an innovative engineer named Otto Peez was commissioned to design an iron girder structure in the form of a low arch, 70 metres long, with four fixed spans and one draw opening which, the engineer said, could be raised in a couple of minutes or less.

Councillors were impressed. The plans and perspective drawings showed the bridge would be a fine one indeed and a credit to the town. They trimmed the specifications a little and called for tenders. Unfortunately the project was to prove a thorn in their sides, and for the town's inhabitants a source of wonder and sometimes ridicule.

What persuaded council that a bridge to open for shipping was still necessary is not clear. Many years earlier, when the 1868 flood carried away a span of the Swing Bridge and temporary repairs made the swing section unusable, councillors decided then that such an amenity was no longer needed. Yet in 1884 they proposed, at some extra expense, to have a lifting span included in the design. Perhaps they had thoughts of London's Tower Bridge, also on the drawing boards at that time; but Kaiapoi was not London, nor Otto Peez England's Horace Jones or Wolfe Barry, and the costly lifting span proved a disaster from the start.

Scott Brothers of Christchurch were entrusted with the ironwork and construction, with J. Butt as sub-contractor. Completion date was supposed to be in February, 1885, but much water was to flow to and fro under what one ratepayer dubbed "this work of art" before Mrs Richard Moore, the mayoress, could cut the ribbon. And still more before the one ship to risk it made passage through the nine metre opening span.

The public was fascinated by the progress (or lack of it) which marked the construction of this "most striking bridge in the colony," as it was hailed by one reporter. Among the bridge-watchers were some who found themselves compelled to write to *The Press:*

Sir, — We beg to express our utter amazement at the audacious statement in your widely circulated journal to the effect that the above bridge is to be opened on Queen's Birthday — unless you meant next year. We and Us, who have sat on the rail day by day and have pensively watched the progress of the work ... know that since the two men have been taken away, and the poor little boy left with all the work to do, it cannot be done on time. ... The boy yesterday accomplished a feat in cutting a piece of timber half through; he then placed a screw in position and got two turns on the nut. ... We hope for many more pleasant days in which to watch the skill and agility of the contractor's men ... and the dear little chap who is fixing up all the beautiful mechanism of what is to be so grand a triumph of engineering and bridge-building skill. — Yours, etc., WE, US & CO.

By mid-May one of the local correspondents noted that "town talk" was very busy on the matter. Nevertheless, he thought the bridge was fast approaching completion and might be ready by May 25. The only hitch was that the Mayor was away in Australia; and also there just might be some little delay occasioned by defects found in the lifting mechanism. Once they were fixed, he announced confidently, the work could be proceeded with, the bridge opened, and the old one alongside removed.

Alas! Two days later, Scott Brothers wrote to the council declining any liability which might arise for damage to vessels unable to pass the bridge, and by June 2 the council finally had to admit that there were grave defects in its design and/or construction. Councillors immediately formed themselves into a Bridge Committee and held an urgent special meeting on the next Saturday morning.

Led by the mayor, now back from his travels, the good councillors trooped along to the site with Mr Peez. There they probed and prodded, and wondered about the lifting mechanism, which refused to function properly for Peez or anyone else. It was, they decided, unworkable. The engineer attributed this to a lack of ballast in the balancing part of the

The Iron Bridge *served Main North Road traffic for over 60 years before it was dismantled and the present concrete structure erected. In the background are the Post Office and the Fire Station with bell tower and observation platform. Beyond the Post Office is the Courthouse, now the Kaiapoi Museum.*

From D.D. McLauchlan

opening girders but the town fathers were not moved. The time had come, they agreed sotto voce, to part company, and from that moment Peez was suspended from all further participation in the project.

"The date for opening the bridge remains as far off as ever," lamented the *Press* representative, J. Lowthian Wilson, who happened also to be deputy-mayor of the borough. It was he who had been presiding over the troubled council meetings in the absence of the mayor. An independent engineer from Christchurch, J.G.Warner, was engaged to carry out a thorough investigation. One result of this was a consultation with the borough solicitor to ascertain how far Scott Brothers were bound to give the council "a complete workable bridge", and to what extent the acts of the engineer pledged the council.

Meanwhile Scotts were paid another 500 pounds, the chairman of the council's works committee resigned, and some disgruntled burgesses proposed petitioning for a public meeting on the subject. They were discouraged on the grounds that this would not serve anyone's best interests. As the opening ceremony now seemed so distant it was decided to spend some money repairing the old bridge to make it last a little longer.

No doubt "We, Us & Co." found plenty to amuse and interest them in the weeks which followed. The work proceeded slowly. Council was unwilling to pay out any more money, and Scott Brothers threatened to sue in the Supreme Court to get

Pons Asinorum. *Borough councillors inspect the Iron Bridge at a time when its successful completion was still uncertain. A local wit has dubbed it "Bridge of Asses". The old Swing Bridge still serves alongside.*

Kaiapoi Museum

settlement of their account. They maintained that if the bridge couldn't be worked properly it was no concern of theirs but the fault of errors in design.

By July's end council had received legal advice to the effect that no grounds existed on which it could defend an action by Scott Brothers, and they agreed to make the payments sought. In return Scotts supplied some additions which were supposed to make the lifting spans work.

All these matters were dealt with by council in secret, so it was not surprising that the public was engulfed by a flood of rumours. One correspondent wrote that he feared the whole project was "a miserable fiasco"; urgent attention should be given immediately, he said, to taking soundings round each pile — "There has been considerable scour during the month and reports are flying round which, if only partly true, are sufficiently bad to necessitate active measures being taken at once, or the whole structure may collapse." Another declared there were two feet of water under one pile. The bridge was supporting it instead of the other way round.

Still another, hearing that the most eminent bridge engineer in the country was about to be hired, no doubt at great expense, thought his opinion would merely be what everybody already knew — that the drawbridge would not open, the piles were unsatisfactory, and the question was, who would pay the piper?

It can only be assumed that somehow Scotts managed to overcome all these problems and complete their contract because, finally, on the last day of October, 1885, the opening ceremony was staged. It was a gala day in Kaiapoi and a great crowd gathered. Scott Brothers, putting all their troubles behind them, decorated the bridge with bunting for the occasion. A feature of the ceremony was the opening of the lift spans, something which was thought to be impossible, and now was greeted with audible surprise and loud applause.

Immediately they were lowered the Kaiapoi fire engine, brasswork gleaming and smoke belching from its funnel, was driven across behind two decorated horses. Then came Mr I. Wilson's carriage, bearing the Mayor and Mrs Moore. At the centre of the bridge the carriage stopped and Mr Moore rose and made a speech, the main point of which was that this substantial structure, costing upwards of 4800 pounds, had been provided without any increase in the rates. The contractors, he added, had done their work well, and if there were any faults they were due to the designer and engineer.

"I now declare this bridge open for traffic and name it the Kaiapoi Bridge," said Mrs Moore, producing her scissors and cutting the ribbon to a second round of cheers. Seventy leading citizens and their wives then adjourned to the Middleton Hotel where the Mayor was host at a celebratory dinner.

The infamous centre spans were in the news in June of 1886 when the timber-laden vessel *E.U. Cameron* arrived in the stream one day, wanting to unload at Robins' wharf beyond the bridge. After much argument council staff were persuaded to see what could be done. Over 30 men who had assembled to watch the fun found themselves pressed into service to act as a human counterweight, and with their aid the spans were slowly lifted, to rousing cheers from all present. The *Cameron* was a large vessel, and the opening barely wide enough for her, so traffic was held up for more than an hour while she was slowly edged through the gap.

This chancy adventure must have been of some concern to the ship's master, who could have found himself marooned on the wrong side of the bridge if it could not be reopened. However when the time came another gang of willing helpers was rounded up and with the additional help of a loaded dray provided enough weight to repeat the operation. As far as is known this was the sole occasion on which the bridge was opened to allow a vessel through. The need for this convenience disappeared with the decline of shipping in the river.

Whatever the extent of Mr Peez's deficiencies as a lift-span designer, his Kaiapoi bridge was a handsome and durable affair which carried the increasing volume of North Road traffic through town for 60 years. It also survived several floods and when finally dismantled some of the spans were used for access bridges in the remote North Canterbury back country, where they are still in service.

A traction engine driver who arrived on the scene one day in July, 1886, had no lack of faith as he steered his massive vehicle on to the bridge. With the three loaded wagons he was towing, the combined weight was about 35 tonnes. An observer noted that "although the lateral motion was considerable, the deflection was inappreciable". Whatever that meant, the bridge survived. With some repairs made in 1898, the graceful old structure remained the focal point of Kaiapoi town until it was replaced in 1946 with the present plain but functional affair.

This had to be constructed on the same site without interfering too much with traffic. Half the new bridge was built alongside the old one, which was then removed and the second half built. The result was an exceptionally wide structure capable of handling all future traffic requirements.

But 20 years later the new motorway was opened, bypassing Kaiapoi, and traffic decreased immediately, leaving the town with an unnecessarily wide bridge. Having in mind the shortage of parking space in the town centre, the Borough Council

Above: The twin motorway bridges, fifth in succession to carry Main North Road traffic across the lower Waimakariri. Below: The old Main Highway Bridge (left) and the railway bridge were the first to be built in concrete nearly 70 years ago and are still in good shape.

obtained permission to use the two outside lanes for cars, thus securing for Kaiapoi something of a rarity—possibly the only main highway car-parking bridge in the country.

THE MAIN HIGHWAY BRIDGE (1930)
When the River Trust straightened the lower river new bridges were required for both road and rail, and these are still there, side by side on what is now called the old main highway. The weather, as at Bealey six years later, did everything it could to ruin the opening ceremony. The day set in late July, 1930, produced the worst snowstorm in Canterbury for 10 years, forcing a postponement. On the new day, August 5, a drenching sou'wester saw Prime Minister George Forbes sheltering under a tarpaulin at one end of the bridge to make his speech to about 500 people who had braved the storm, mostly struggling with umbrellas which looked ready to turn inside-out at any moment.

The title of the new acquisition was "The Waimakariri Highway Bridge" (when it wasn't being called White's Bridge or just "the Waimak Bridge"), and since the twin motorway bridges were built a little upriver in 1967 it has been used mainly for traffic between Kaiapoi and the city. It was the first on the river to be made in concrete, and as this is so much more durable than wood, it is reasonable to assume that the sight of the bridge-builder at work on the Waimakariri may not be seen again for many years. A point of interest is that the motorway bridges are only a few stone-throws from where William White's historic old structure stood so long ago, "tall and spindly like its builder".

THE KLONDYKE (BEALEY) BRIDGE (1936)
The last major obstacle on the Canterbury-West Coast Road persisted until 1936, 60 years after the opening, when the Waimakariri River was finally bridged near its junction with the Bealey River.* For all that time any journey on this highway was coloured with uncertainty about getting across the big river. Coaches were sometimes washed downstream, and the owner of many a motor vehicle stuck in the ford had to pay a small ransom to hotelkeeper Fred Cochrane to be rescued. Less reckless motorists wisely paid him the sum of one pound on arrival and were ferried over on a horsedrawn contraption he had built for the purpose.

The bridge project was initiated by the Coalition Government in its final year in office, in response to pressure from the Automobile Association and perhaps as a gesture of faith that the Great Depression was nearly over. It was finished about nine months after the first Labour Government took office and opened by the Minister of Works, Robert Semple, on September 12, 1936. In some ways this was appropriate, for Bob Semple was no stranger to the district. He had worked on the construction of the Midland railway many years previously, was a friend of Cochrane's and had enjoyed many a political argument over a glass of beer at Fred's bar.

It was one of those days when almost nothing went right. The affair was organised by the Automobile Association, a contingent from which chose to travel to Bealey by bus. At Springfield it broke down, but most passengers were content to cool their heels and their thirsts in the "local" while a replacement came from Christchurch. As the scattered convoy of cars approached Bealey the nor'wester grew in strength and rain began to fall. Semple's limousine almost came to grief in the Bruce, one of the many unbridged creeks, and expired soon after at the side of the road. He and his inseparable companion P.C. Webb, Minister of Mines—better known as Paddy—had to trudge through the rain for the last half kilometre.

The luncheon at Fred's hostelry compensated to some degree. Cochrane was an expert caterer and the guests sat down to soups, chicken, turkey, beef, mutton, lamb, fruit salad, jellies, trifle, ales and spirits. The occasion was not so pleasing for a contingent from the West Coast. Although the bridge had been in general use for a week or more, nobody was allowed to cross on the great day until the official opening, so they had to eat their sandwiches in the rain on the wrong bank.

*The official Ministry of Works name for this bridge is "The Waimakariri River (Bealey) Bridge". For as long as the Bealey Hotel was nearby it was invariably called "The Bealey Bridge", even though it crossed not the Bealey River but the Waimakariri. With both the hotel and the fleeting Bealey township long gone, the most prominent local feature on the map is Klondyke Corner, which has inherited approximately the original township site and is now lending its name to the bridge. But names for Waimakariri bridges, no matter how inappropriate, do not easily go away. Lands and Survey maps were still calling the lower Waimakariri's fourth bridge "White's" a century after the original was dismantled.

The Klondyke (Bealey) Bridge *by which State Highway 73 crosses the Waimakariri en route to Arthurs Pass. The photograph was taken in 1986 within a few days of its 50th birthday, looking up a rainswept Waimakariri valley with the river rising.*

By 2.30 p.m. all present at the hotel had been fed to their satisfaction, whereupon the Minister of Works set out on foot for the bridge, rain or no rain, setting an example few cared to follow. The ceremony started in showers and a half gale. It was no time for long-winded oratory, one of Bob Semple's specialties. With a few brief words he took the scissors and cut the ribbon. Unfortunately this was flapping so wildly in the breeze that the official act included one of the honourable gentleman's fingers, which bled profusely, and so the bridge was christened, some thought appropriately, with ministerial blood.

With that, the chief participants stuffed their prepared speeches back in their pockets and retreated to the pub, where host Cochrane was preparing for a profitable afternoon. But they had no time for more than a quick one (or two) before word spread that the Bruce was rising fast. In a few minutes every Christchurch-bound vehicle was on its way, leaving the bar empty except for a few West Coasters. To them heavy rain was nothing to get excited about.

The return trip was a race to beat the rising rivers. Some made it through the Bruce unaided; others had to be assisted. A nameless roadman was the hero of that crossing—nearly all afternoon he worked in the flooded river, helping push out cars, drenched to the skin. The car of the Hon. D. G. Sullivan, Minister of Railways, stuck in the Cass and had to be towed out, then further down the road at Castle Hill it gave up completely. Dan Sullivan had urgent commitments awaiting him in Christchurch; luckily seats were secured for him and his wife in a passing car. There were four cars in the Cass at one time—the leader of the convoy couldn't get its rear wheels on to dry land and effectively blocked the ford. Still others came to a halt in the Craigie Burn. It was an anxious afternoon.

No doubt the next week saw a flutter of ministerial memoranda about unreliable public service vehicles and unbridged creeks. Actually work was scheduled for the Bruce Creek bridge to be started the following week, and there was money on the estimates for others at Cass and Rough Creek. In due course they were all bridged, even the Ribbonwood near Lake Pearson, and as the two-lane bitumin extended ever further towards the west it became difficult to remember the hazards which used to bedevil that journey.

Another Wet Ceremony. *Pouring rain and flooded rivers marked the opening in 1936 of the Klondyke Bridge by the new Labour government's first Minister of Works, Robert Semple.*

Bridge of Curves. *Latest of the bridges to the built across the Waimakariri was this gracefully curved replacement for the original railway bridge near Corner Knob.*

118

CHAPTER ELEVEN
"The Great Western"

"We hope that when the snorting of the iron horse is heard in the Alpine country as the well-freighted train rumbles along the track of the West Coast Railway, the shepherd, the miner and the woodsman will think of 1884 as the year in which that spectacle was made possible," said *The Lyttelton Times* on New Year's Day in 1885. To the hundreds if not thousands of Midland railway buffs in Canterbury and on the West Coast, not to mention Nelson, that was a good thought with which to start a new year.

The newspaper was prompted to this optimism by the passing in 1884 of an Act of Parliament with a wordy title, "The East and West Coast and Nelson Railway and Railways Construction Act", authorising the line to be built by private enterprise. That must have sounded promising to the railway protagonists who had been working so earnestly for the cause. Their enthusiasm might have been dampened had they known what a long struggle lay ahead, and that as many more years would drag past as there were miles of line still to be built.

Their first great disappointment came when Sir Julius Vogel, that great friend of railways everywhere, moved in the House to have construction by a firm named John Meiggs & Sons referred to a Select Committee for consideration. His motion was defeated and Meiggs & Sons were never heard of again in this part of the world. So, alas, the expectations of the shepherds, miners and woodsmen went unrealised. They would have to be young or lucky to hear that iron horse snorting in the valleys during their lifetimes.

Meanwhile whole train loads of public agitation, parliamentary lobbying, government inertia and ill-fated commercial enterprise had to be buried deep in the intervening decades, like fill in the gullies, before in 1923 the trains at last ran between Christchurch and Greymouth. It was nothing unusual in the 1880s for railways to be more political than practical and for years the Midland was one of the most political of all; and in the eyes of many, also the most impractical.

It also broke records for time lapse between conception and completion. Fifty-six years passed from the day in 1867 when the Canterbury Provincial Council set aside 5000 pounds for preliminary surveys until opening day was celebrated at Otira in 1923. Yet the road over Arthur's Pass connecting Christchurch to the goldfields took only a year to build in 1865 until the coaches were rattling over its shingled miles twice a week to Hokitika.

Why did the railway take so long? Most of the answers to this question lie in the rugged nature of the country through which the line had to be built—along the tortuous gorges of the

The Staircase viaduct, *looking down Staircase Gully to the Waimakariri River in its gorge. At the top of the picture the Waimakariri turns right, Broken River comes in from the left. Immediately across the viaduct the railway enters tunnel number 7. The line can be followed (with a train on it) to a tunnel in the distance taking it across in the direction of Broken River viaduct.* Alexander Turnbull Library

The Romance of Rail. *The Greymouth-Christchurch express, hauled by an "A" class locomotive, leaves Cass to begin the long pull to St Bernard's Saddle and the run down Sloven's Stream to Broken River. The highway over Goldney's Saddle shows at left above the trees, and the Waimakariri River flows in the valley immediately beyond. The Pyramid is prominent at centre while at left are the higher peaks of the Polar Range.* Roy Sinclair, 1970.

Demonstration in Square. *Part of the crowd assembled in the Square for the procession in 1885 demonstrating Canterbury's determination to have its West Coast railway.*
"Weekly Press"

Waimakariri and Broken rivers, through 16 tunnels and over six viaducts, and up mountain valleys culminating at Arthur's Pass in what was then the longest tunnel in the Southern Hemisphere, bored through more than eight kilometres of Southern Alps rock.

These works involved enormous construction difficulties which brought two major firms to financial disaster, killed a number of workers, and cost a sizeable fortune.

The spectacular scenery through which the line travels brought its own troubles for the railway builders, to whom nothing is more beautiful than a perfectly flat plain on which to lay their sleepers. But for today's travellers on a Midland special this same scenery is a treat which costs only the price of a ticket, and is some of the best to be seen from a carriage window anywhere in New Zealand.

After about 60km of easy going across the plains from Christchurch the train confronts the mountains at Springfield, a small township once known as Kowai Pass. From there the line sweeps across an open terrace and over the Kowai River to Kowai Bush, joining up with the Waimakariri River at Otarama. For about 13km then it is embroiled with country which engineer William Blair described to a Royal Commission in 1883 as "very wild, very rough". His survey party tried to ride horses through it but was forced to give up.

When he was asked by the Commission if he could locate the route on the river terraces, Blair had to reply that there were no terraces of any consequence. "The mountain slopes rise from the riverbed," he said. Pressed then to say whether he would put the line in the riverbed he replied, "There is no riverbed. It runs in a fearful gorge all the way."

The mountain slopes Blair mentioned are those of the Torlesse Range which tower above the railway on one side, while on the other the Waimakariri rushes along far below in its "fearful gorge". Thus hemmed in it is forced into tunnels and deep cuttings. Trains pussyfoot over lofty viaducts as the line twists and turns, alternating breathtaking glimpses of wild scenery with the abrupt blackness of frequent tunnels. Viaduct sides are fenced to protect trains from gales sweeping down the gorges.

Beyond the very high Staircase Viaduct (Christchurch Cathedral could go beneath it with eight metres to spare), the rails desert the Waimakariri for Broken River, where they cling precariously to the north-west bank. In about 1.5km half the distance is taken up with six short tunnels, and trains can play games of "Now you see me, now you don't".

The last of these tunnels propels the train on to the high viaduct over Sloven's Creek, a tributary of the Broken, and away from the gorge country into the relatively open and easy tussock lands of upper-Waimakariri sheepfarmers. Hills called The Puffer, Bullock, Gog and Magog glide past on the long, almost straight drag up to St Bernard's Saddle. From there the line leads down past Lake Sarah to Cass, 43km from Springfield.

Here there is a change in the scenery. The hills which have kept company with the train for so long suddenly grow into real mountains. As the railway rejoins the Waimakariri the deep green of beech forest clothes the slopes across the river. Above lie the rugged peaks of the Polar Range.

Road and rail now crowd together to get past Corner Knob where the butt end of the Black Range plunges to the river, but soon the line veers away to cross on its new curved bridge and takes to the far bank along riverbed flats towards the Bealey valley. Then it leaves the Waimakariri and, with the road never far away, pushes up the narrow valley to Arthur's Pass township. There lie the station, the electric locomotives and the long tunnel leading to Westland.

Part 1:
The Years of Agitation

Today the hard-won miles of cutting, embankment, bridge, viaduct and tunnel flash past at 20th century speed to the soothing rhythm of well-bolted rail joints. But the rocky path of promotion and actual contruction of the Midland line ran nowhere as smoothly, nor did the provincial push required to get it started in the first place. It was the longest, noisiest public campaign in Canterbury's history.

"Push-and-pull" might be a more appropriate term, for there was much argument about which way the railway should go — whether it should cross the main range to the north to connect Canterbury with Nelson or reach the West Coast more directly by Arthur's Pass.

Surprisingly the agitation for a transalpine railway began even before the Arthur's Pass road was completed in 1866. While the

"Co-ops" were effective. *Most of the tunnels on the Midland were built by co-operatives—gangs of workers who tendered for the job, worked hard, and generally made good money. Here such a gang poses with their leader and a supervising engineer at the mouth of "their" tunnel.*
Alexander Turnbull Library

Pick and shovel men. *This picture shows the way the Midland line was built. Today country like this would be attacked with bulldozers and earth-scrapers, but in 1904 it had to be picks, shovels and wheelbarrows. Resident engineer J.A. Wilson (and his horse) watch as ten workers, dwarfed by the size of the face they are attacking, pause in their labours for the camera.* Alexander Turnbull Library

road builders were still toiling in the gorges railway advocates were making themselves heard. Some favoured the Hurunui and Harper's Pass, some were for Arthur's Pass, while a few hankered after the Rakaia and Wilberforce rivers and a tunnel under Browning's Pass.

On September 5, 1865, *The Lyttelton Times,* initially a vigorous opponent of the Arthur's Pass route, thought much of the road could be eliminated by building a railway to the Bealey. "Then we could carry 200 tons of goods and 400 passengers one way every 12 hours, at a speed of 15 miles per hour," claimed the newspaper. No explanation was given of where the 400 passengers were to come from. When Cobb & Co. started their through coach to Hokitika a few months later they were lucky if they got a dozen a week each way. Intending gold diggers were the most likely ticket-buyers but most of them couldn't afford the fare and had to walk.

Rangiora leapt into the fray with enthusiasm. The largest public meeting ever held there decided that "the wants of both sides of the province can be best met by railway communication" — in their view a line running from Rangiora up the north bank of the Waimakariri. Their ingenuous proposition caused the *Times* to chide its city readers:

The merchants of Christchurch and Lyttelton are evidently satisfied with the present state of affairs — "trade continues as dull as ever". They hear the Government is making a dray road which will, perhaps, enable them to do a little trade with the West Coast. If this proves a mistake, why, they will go to sleep again. While they doze, all New Zealand is hurrying to Hokitika from north and south as fast as steamers can bring them, and Australia cannot find steamers enough to bring those waiting to come. In the meantime little Rangiora calls a meeting to declare its belief that nothing less than a railway will meet the present emergency...

But others were not convinced. A correspondent signing himself "Hughes" probably spoke for many when he wrote to *The Press* in November, 1866, as follows:

This Lyttelton-Christchurch Railway seems a bit of a useless affair and this Great Southern Railway will be the death of us all. But now we are threatened with another disorder far more costly than either of the preceding ones and infinitely more foolish. This is none other than a railway from Christchurch to the West Coast. Now, sir, of all the mad schemes which ever emanated from a diseased brain, this is by far the worst, and I hope the whole colony will rise as one man to stop it. A report says the estimated cost of this railway is 700,000 pounds. I am positively sure that the line can never be made and the rivers bridged for double that sum, but suppose it could be made for half that amount, would it ever pay? Never!

Whatever Canterbury people thought of this, most were apparently not in agreement. From the day the gold rush started on the West Coast they were convinced that a worthwhile economic prize lay there for the taking and that direct communication was the key to that prize, preferably by rail. Steel tracks and "puffing billies" were unquestionably the things to have in the matter of "modern" transport.

By 1875 Canterbury railways were one of the success stories of New Zealand. They earned a profit of 185,806 pounds that year, more than for all the rest of the colony. For the carriage of passengers and freight they were the transport system for the times, and railway stations then had all the business and bustle of today's airports.

It was understandable, therefore, that the full development of economic ties between Canterbury and the remainder of the South Island should be seen in terms of railways, and that a transalpine link was essential to this conception. The problem was how to get it built.

*Members of the **1883 Royal Commission** appointed to examine the transalpine railway proposal, and to decide the best route. They chose Arthur's Pass but recommended the project be shelved because in their opinion it would not pay its way. Standing: C. Napier Bell and Gratton Grey (secretary). Seated: C.Y. O'Connor (inspecting engineer), Captain W.R. Russell (chairman) and James Wilson.*
"East & West"
(Canterbury Progress League)

The first tentative surveys were made in 1874 by T.M.Foy, an engineer in the Public Works Department, but they led to nothing. In 1876 the provincial governments were abolished. One of the last acts of Canterbury's last Superintendent, William Rolleston, was to take the Government engineer-in-chief over one of the routes and impress him with the need for the line. (Later Rolleston—as a Cabinet Minister—took a decidedly negative stance in the matter, which eroded much of his local popularity.)

By 1880 trains were running to Springfield, in the shadow of the mountains. A clergyman, the Rev. Charles Clarke, described the trip across the plains:

The little train jogged along contentedly through the level country, stopping here and there at stations like magnified packing cases*, to take a leisurely little drink to slake the thirst of its parched little throat, and then toddled on again to where the ridge of snowcapped hills cut with sharp outline the clear morning sky.

At Springfield passengers for the West Coast left the train and boarded the coach. First stop was for refreshments at the hotel across the road. Then with a flourish and much shouting and cracking of whips the coach started at a merry clip for Porter's Pass. Out of sight round the bend in the road the flourish wilted and the pace settled down for the long journey through the hills.

In 1880 a Railway League was formed on the West Coast to promote the construction of railway lines to both Christchurch and Nelson. The Government was persuaded to pass a Railways Construction Act in 1881 so that these could be built by private enterprise. Nothing came of this at the time, but the Act was to play a vital and unexpected role in later negotiations with the Midland Railway Company.

Canterbury's ambitions were focussed in 1882 with the formation of the East and West Coast Railway League. Membership was liberally sprinkled with the most prestigious social, political and commercial names of the day. Branches were set up throughout Canterbury, Westland, and later Nelson. All were committed to applying unceasing pressure on the Government but not all were agreed on which way the railway should go, by Arthur's Pass or by one of the more northern passes. In the short term construction of the railway was seen as providing employment and alleviating the current depression; in the long term as a vital key to Canterbury's prosperity. When progress appeared to stall an influential Christchurch businessman, T.O. Kelsey, sailed for England and entered into an arrangement with a syndicate to build the line across the

*The stations certainly were small. For years a joke persisted on the Midland line about the hired hand sent with the farmer's wagon to pick up a dog kennel from the railway. According to the story he came home with the station.

island by a Hurunui route, but his brief was based on inaccurate figures and nothing came of it.

To place the whole matter on a proper footing the League persuaded the Government in early 1884 to set up a Royal Commission. This impressive title evoked a popular image of elderly gentlemen deliberating at ease in comfortable chambers, but in this case the reverse was true. Commission members tramped and rode horse over every mile of a dozen alternative routes, interviewed hundreds of people, and came to the conclusion that Arthur's Pass was the way to go. But, they added, the line could not be made to pay.

This was something the League had not expected, leaving them no alternative but to apply political pressure. Sir Julius Vogel was a candidate for Christchurch North, and while a West Coast railway was never part of his public works policy, he was aware that the elections had produced a string of pro-railway candidates who could be vital to his political future. Although he campaigned from a sick bed in Wellington he was elected and so were most of the others. The new Stout-Vogel Government assumed power.

The Railway League was not slow to press its advantage. Later that year it had the new Government pass the 1884 Railways Act, tailored to suit its needs. This embodied a contract between the Crown and 10 of the League's most influential supporters by which they undertook to build the line within 10 years at an estimated cost of 2,500,000 pounds, payment to be by compensatory land grants.

There was considerable opposition to the proposal. William Rolleston favoured the railway but not the method of financing it. His wisdom was showing when he predicted that whoever started the project, the Government would have to finish it. Sir George Grey was adamantly opposed to "robbing future generations of their heritage" by tying up millions of acres of Crown land to pay railway builders. Others labelled the project "a gigantic folly", "wild speculation" and "political gambling".

But the Railway League's boilers were fired and there was no holding it back. Money was raised to send envoys to London, where hopefully they might coax financiers to risk their capital and resources on what could not be amplified by the most eloquent entreaty as much more than a doubtful and difficult prospect in a faraway colony.

An intense fund-raising drive was organised and prominent citizens pressed to become guarantors at 25 pounds a head. Local bodies made grants. Down at Addington saleyards Jack Matson, one of the most effective canvassers, was not above cutting off the fat sheep sale in its prime to harangue onlookers until they were left with no choice but to shuffle in embarrassment or reach for their cheque books.

The contract with the Government was signed on January 17, 1885, and on that same day the three nominated emissaries sailed from Wellington to lay siege to the money-bags of Europe. They were Arthur Dudley Dobson (the discoverer of the

Left: **H. Alan Scott**, *of Christchurch, who with A.D. Dobson and C.Y. Fell went to England in search of someone to build the Midland line. Scott stayed on after the others and persuaded London financiers to form the Midland Railway Company.* Right: **Jack Matson**, *one of the line's most indefatigable proponents and fund raisers.*
"East & West"

pass) and H. Alan Scott, of Christchurch, and Charles Y. Fell, of Nelson.

In London they met with mixed fortunes until they were introduced to an American gentleman named John Meiggs with whom they were much impressed. He was a member of the firm of Meiggs & Sons, builders of railways in distant lands (including a Peruvian line said to reach an altitude of over 5000m). Meiggs had never heard of New Zealand but the project appealed to him. In due course he estimated the cost at 3,860,000 pounds and the time required at from three to five years. There was only one snag — his firm would require a Government-guaranteed profit of 97,000 pounds a year for 20 years.

When these terms were released to the public of New Zealand they raised a storm of protest from North Island parliamentarians and newspaper editors, against which Canterbury hurried to organise a counter-attack. Just about everyone in the province who could hold a pen was prodded into signing massive petitions which were shipped off to Wellington at intervals as proof of southern unity and determination. Public meetings called in centres all over the province rallied supporters; whole pages of reports and correspondence filled the newspapers.

Even though figures were produced to show that the Meiggs proposition was still cheaper than Government construction, North Island antagonism increased in fury. There were even allegations of collusion between the Colonial Treasurer, Sir Julius Vogel, who championed the measure in the House, and the Meiggs organisation. When Sir Julius moved for progress, the opposition proved too strong and Canterbury was forced to watch its cherished dream railroaded into oblivion by 47 votes to 40.

Disappointment was not much alleviated by the 150,000 pounds for the line which the Minister of Public Works placed on his estimates for the following year, "to relieve the districts concerned of the sense of soreness and injustice under which they now labour", especially when almost immediately the retrenchments of worsening depression saw this reduced to a miserable 1000 pounds.

This seemed to be the last straw, but the Railway League, mustering its full strength, was not about to bow to defeat. Instead it mounted an offensive so massive as almost to suggest overtones of revolution or secession. Building on the indignation felt so widely throughout the province it organised the greatest public demonstration the colony had ever seen — a procession more than a mile long and a public meeting in Hagley Park attended by 25,000 people.

The procession included all the worthy societies and associations in the city, Railway League members, City and Borough councillors, and County Council and Road Board members. At the last minute the Lyttelton Lumpers' Union, omitted from the invitation list but determined not to be snubbed, arrived in force and was found a place between the Trade Societies and the Orphanage Band. Dozens of cyclists (a novelty then) led the big parade and the cab drivers brought up the rear. With two or three brass bands at full blast the procession marched up Colombo Street from the Square, where it had assembled, along Tuam Street, Manchester Street and High Street, and back through the Square on its way to the park. It was so long that for a time in the "bottleneck" demonstrators were going both ways, cheering each other as they passed.

At the park the huge audience, many of whom had come to town by special train, heard pro-railway speeches of great length delivered in the impressive oratorical style of the day, from such prominent League members as Messrs Bowen, Stead, Acton-Adams, Frankish, Weston, Matson and others. With acclamation they passed a resolution designed to impress on the Government the unflinching determination of Canterbury to have its railway, come what may.

One of the League's most devoted members, A.G. Howland, was in hospital at the time. From his sick bed he wrote an impassioned letter to that evening's *Star* telling the public what a torture it was to be ill on such an occasion, and that he should have been in the Square shouting "West Coast Railway!" so loudly it could be heard in Wellington.

Almost every town and village in the three provinces held indoor protest meetings as well. The Christchurch one drew an audience of 3000. A sense of injustice was heightened by the reflection that when Central Government was established a few years earlier Canterbury had brought far more to the common wealth than any other province. The new administration had to take over provincial liabilities amounting to 3,584,745 pounds, and of this Canterbury's share was only 70 pounds. On the other hand it had contributed land sales funds and other assets. There was substance to the claim that the colony generally owed Canterbury something in the region of 5,000,000 pounds — but not, apparently, its much-desired railway to the West Coast.

Meanwhile Dobson and Fell had returned to New Zealand, disappointed with the fate of the Meiggs scheme. They left Scott in London to carry on*, and shortly he struck fertile ground with a syndicate of financiers who were persuaded they should form a company to build the line — the Midland Railway Company Limited.

It is not easy to unravel the affairs of this ill-starred concern. It was registered on April 19, 1886, with a capital of 500,000 pounds, but only half of this was subscribed. The directors, aware of the political situation in New Zealand, including the obligations of the Government to the pro-railway lobby, decided to go ahead. Their anticipation was of large profits from a small outlay by the sale of appreciating land grants and eventual sale of the railway to the Government. To raise sufficient working capital debentures amounting to 745,000 pounds were issued at 5%.

The Company contracted to build 376km of railway between Christchurch and Nelson, via Brunnerton, within 10 years. In payment they would be allowed selection from 2,430,000ha of land reserved in the three provinces for the purpose, in the ratio of ten shillings' worth of land for every one pound's worth of railway completed. Locomotives, rolling stock and rails were shipped out from England and a start made under the supervision of the Company's general manager and chief

The first of the viaducts *along the Midland line was over the normally well-behaved Kowai River, a Waimakariri tributary. However on April 22, 1951, the river rose to unprecedented heights and wrecked the bridge's major span, which crashed to the bed in complete disarray.*

N.Z. Railway & Locomotive Society

---

*Scott wrote on March 13, 1885, that the London money market was unstable because of the threat of war between Russia and Afghanistan — a conflict still in the news a century later.

engineer, Robert Wilson. He was said to be an experienced and reputable engineer and a man of good business sense.

These were optimistic days, but progress with construction was painfully slow. In six years only 120km of railway was built, mainly along easier sections on the West Coast.

Part 2:
Springfield to Arthur's Pass

In January, 1890, the Midland Company finally faced up to the difficulties of the Waimakariri Gorge. By then it was becoming clear that its skills, resources and finances were inadequate to cope with the enormity of the project. A contract was let to Andersons Ltd., the Christchurch engineering firm, for the first 8.8km of line from Springfield to Patterson's Creek. The price was a little under 60,000 pounds and included bridges over the Big and Little Kowai rivers and one short tunnel. Canterbury was delighted to see some progress.

The ceremony of "turning the first sod" was performed at Springfield by one of the oldest residents, Mr Williamson. After suitable speeches, including one from John Jebson (who reckoned the line should be called "The Great Western"), all present retired to one of Mr Benham's cottages, "where the success of the railway was pledged in champagne, and where beer and sandwiches were provided in profusion for the refreshment of the assemblage". Jack Matson went home with the "first sod" in a sack; it weighed over 100 pounds.

But while this cheerful affair gave the work a good start, the shadow of financial instability soon dimmed the memory of champagne and sandwiches. While Andersons pushed on with their task the Company explored innumerable possibilities of Government help. One of these included a proposal that the Government guarantee the interest on a loan of nearly three million pounds, the amount estimated as required to complete the project. This and other requests raised hackles in the North Island, where the Auckland *Star* wrote:

The Midland Railway Company has submitted a new series of preposterous proposals to the Government. It coolly asks that the Government shall buy back for 850,000 pounds the balance of the lands which were granted for the construction of the line, pay a further 100,000 pounds for the Belgrove-Motueka line, and make other big concessions. It is high time the Government compelled this Company to fulfil its contract engagements.

The situation, by now thoroughly unsatisfactory for all parties, drifted from one crisis to another. Wilson was placed in the position of having to plead for extensions of time while he made feverish efforts to negotiate a new contract before the old one expired on January 17, 1895. Before that, in the previous year, construction ceased at Jackson's, on the West Coast, and on May 25 the Crown Solicitor, the Under-Secretary for Public Works, the Crown Prosecutor, the District Manager for Railways and the Resident Engineer arrived without prior notice at Stillwater and seized all the Midland Company's railways and works in the name of the Crown. The authority for this action

had been discovered in the 1881 Railway Act by a wideawake clerk. Formal possession was taken later of 21 stations, 80 bridges, 3 tunnels, 6 locomotives, 7 passenger cars, and 131km of railway.

The Company contested the takeover, claiming that under the 1884 Act by which it had entered the contract there was no provision for such a step. The Government, in answer, held that the powers contained in the 1881 Act took precedence. Midland, confident this was nonsense, took its case to the Supreme Court and lost, then to the Court of Appeal and lost, and finally to the Privy Council in England, where it lost again.

A Royal Commission appointed in 1901 investigated the affair and reported that in their opinion the Company and its debenture holders had on the whole been favourably treated. There was criticism of the disproportionate expenditure on such things as supervision, commissions, salaries, costs of raising capital, directors' fees, interest and incidental expenses in relation to the results achieved. The Company had spent 1,108,628 pounds during its brief existence, of which only 654,411 pounds was for actual construction and equipment of the railway.

The Courts having decided against them, Midland shareholders and bondholders were left with nowhere to go except to petition Parliament for some relief from the burden of

Robert and Mingha

Robert Wilson, the man in the driver's seat of the Midland Railway Company, was rather more than just an overpaid engineer. He and his wife Mingha appeared to have been a sensitive and affectionate couple who also shared a deep love for this country and its scenery. He thought many parts of the West Coast were too beautiful to be spoiled by the scars of railway construction, and was occasionally guilty of making alterations to the route to avoid some particular piece of scenery held in special regard. He tried to retain Maori names wherever possible and chose them for stations along the way, although many of the localities already had established English names.

This picture of his wife Mingha and a companion was taken by Robert Wilson outside Castle Hill Hotel during one of their exploratory excursions into Waimakariri country.

The Wilsons moved easily in the best Christchurch and Canterbury circles and entertained lavishly at "Compton", their home in Opawa on the banks of the Heathcote River. They made several trips along the route of the proposed railway, enjoying together the adventure of travelling in new country.

Mingha was heartbroken when her husband, delayed at the last minute by urgent business in connection with the winding-up of the company, was unable to accompany her back to England. But soon she could write, "Bob has returned and now it is really Home again. How happy we are!"

Their happiness was shortlived. In that same year Robert Wilson died suddenly, his health possibly affected by the demands and strains of the troublesome Midland company. Apart from once having held the New Zealand record for a trout caught with a fly he is unremembered here, but his wife's unusual name lives on in a Bealey River tributary.

their losses. In the absence of Mr Seddon, who was attending the Coronation of King Edward VII, it fell to Sir Joseph Ward, his deputy, to convince a largely hostile House that it should be merciful. A grant of 150,000 pounds was proposed. Veiled threats from London that New Zealand might find its standing in the loan market somewhat tarnished unless it did the right thing, and the persuasive arguments of Sir Joseph, combined to carry the day, and the poorer but wiser Midland investors got some of their money back.

The opponents of this largesse were trenchant in their criticism. It was said in the House that Robert Wilson was paid 7000 pounds a year*, and that the directors of the company received 31,000 pounds over a five-year period. A substantial shareholder in the company was one E.H. D'Avigdor, of the firm of McKeane, Robinson and D'Avigdor, which was given the first three contracts let by the company and was alleged to have been paid the enormous sum of 187,941 pounds for 29km of railway track laid over easy country.

Work on the Springfield section came to a halt when the Government seized the line in 1895. Andersons had laid the rails for a distance of 7.5km to a little beyond the Otarama station yard and completed formation to the 9.5km peg. But during the three years the line lay idle until the Public Works Department resumed construction in 1898 much of this work had deteriorated. A great deal of material had to be removed from the cuttings, and embankments needed major repairs.

Trouble with floods. *Construction was not without its setbacks. Heavy rain washed out this tunnel approach and collapsed a work shed.*
"Weekly Press"

Andersons maintained they lost money on their contract. One of the reasons for this was the huge wooden viaduct built at Patterson's Creek to backload spoil from the cutting on the north side to make the embankment on the south side. During the three-year hiatus part of this viaduct blew down in one of the district's famed nor'westers, and Bill Gavin, the P.W.D. resident engineer, regarded it as only a nuisance to be cleared away. (He would have transferred the fill on a wire cable, a big job considering there were 17,500 cu.metres of it.) The concrete foundations for the real Patterson's Creek viaduct, put in by Andersons, were still there and a fresh contract was let to Scott Brothers of Christchurch.

But again progress was slow, and continued so until all the remaining complications relating to the Midland Railway Company were cleared up. With these out of the way work proceeded more vigorously on the section between Patterson's and Staircase. Soon a large labour force was scattered along the route. These men, many with wives and families, were housed mainly in tents on the adjacent hillsides, usually near a creek which offered handy supplies of water. Near the site of Patterson's old homestead there were two settlements — one

*A simplistic comparison between Wilson's alleged salary and that of one of his tunnel "brickies" on 10 shillings a day, converted to 1986 terms, puts his remuneration at more than $400,000 a year. The figure may have included generous allowances and expenses. His actual salary in 1894 and 1895 was 2600 pounds. By comparison the general manager of New Zealand Railways at the time was paid 900 pounds per annum.

The temporary wooden viaduct *across Patterson's Creek built by Andersons Limited to carry spoil from the cutting on the north end to fill the Springfield approach. Part of it blew away in a nor'wester and the remainder had to be removed before the steel viaduct could be erected.*
Alexander Turnbull Library

down by the river with about 50 tents and one on the plateau with blacksmiths' and carpenters' workshops and a couple of stores. Here the shingle was hauled up from the opposite side of the river for the plant making concrete blocks for the tunnels. The children were catered for by a portable schoolroom holding up to 30 pupils, and an equally portable teacher and cottage. As the line progressed deeper into the interior these buildings and the workers' tents were moved forward.

A large proportion of the 200 men on the job were practical miners engaged in co-operative work. Because of the unstable nature of the country (often old morainic deposits), most of the tunnels had to be bricked from end to end, and continual re-surveys were necessary to get the best or cheapest route.

Most of the remainder of the men laboured with picks and shovels and wheelbarrows excavating enormous cuttings, filling gullies and consolidating formation work. They also were organised into small co-operatives and assigned contracts at agreed prices. If all worked well they were well paid but there was no room in the gangs for slackers. In general this system proved to the advantage of both department and men, and was maintained on many New Zealand public works until the introduction of earthmoving machinery.

Still others were engaged in the batching works where thousands of concrete "bricks" were made for lining the tunnels. In an area there might be two such works some distance apart in which gangs worked on alternate days to accommodate the drying process. As work progressed the shingle conveyors and their wire cables were moved forward to the next convenient source of supply in the rivers, while all timber was supplied by a sawmill near Otarama.

When it came to building the several viaducts the Department agreed that this was work for specialist firms. As mentioned Scotts built the Patterson's Creek structure, while those over

Patterson's Creek viaduct, *the second on the line, stands a kilometre beyond Otarama. It replaced the old wooden viaduct.* "Weekly Press"

The Battle in the Gorges ...

Pushing a railway through the gorges of the Waimakariri and Broken rivers would be a challenging project even with modern construction machinery, but in the early 1900s only one or two crude ancestors of the bulldozer and earth-scraper were available. Most of the work was done by an army of hard-working artisans organised into very effective co-operatives.

Top: *This camp and workshop stood near Staircase Gully, with the Waimakariri River below at right in its lower gorge.*
N.Z. Railway & Locomotive Society

Above left: *Staircase Viaduct under construction. Scale is conveyed by figures on skyline at right.*
N.Z. Railways

Above right: *The famous Staircase Gully cage, hauled up the ascending grade by a horse working a horizontal gin-wheel winding in the cable.*
N.Z. Railway & Locomotive Society

Right: *Workmen mixing concrete by hand for delivery down a chute to one of the bridge abutments.*
Alexander Turnbull Library

Above: *Half a hill high above Broken River on the edge of Blakiston's Creek has been levelled to make room for a workshop and blockhouse. Deep cuttings at right lead to No.9 of the 16 tunnels.* Canterbury Museum

Below left: *Broken River Viaduct under construction, hastily completed in 1906.*
N.Z. Railways

Below right: *One of the excursion crowds from Christchurch assembled for a day out at Broken River.* "Weekly Press"

Below left: *The view at Broken River in 1907 as work proceeded on the "mile of the six tunnels" towards Sloven's Stream. This plant made concrete blocks for lining tunnels from shingle hauled up the cliffs from Broken River.* N.Z. Railways & Locomotive Society

Below right: *Fashionably dressed young ladies and their escorts pose on the breathtaking Staircase Viaduct, still only partly fenced against the wind.* "Weekly Press"

Workers' huts *lined up along Sloven's Creek are dwarfed by the great steel pylons of the viaduct.*
"Weekly Press"

Staircase Gully and Broken River were entrusted to the British firm of Cleveland Bridge and Engineering Company. The one at Sloven's Creek went to a New Zealand concern, George Frazer & Co.

By 1902 three tunnels were complete and three others were well advanced, but while Scotts had most of the steelwork on the Patterson's Creek site none of the work of erecting the viaduct was started that year. This was more or less the situation when the Premier, Mr Seddon, arrived early in 1903 for an inspection. A keen advocate of the line, as might be expected of a West Coaster, he was upset that more had not been achieved in the five years since the Department had taken over.

It was clear to him that Scotts would not have their contract finished on time, and he was told that Cleveland would take at least two years to build the viaduct at Staircase Gully. He thought these shortcomings a poor advertisement for private enterprise and promised full penalties for any delays. To speed up progress he also promised another 50 men would be employed immediately, and 50 more later.

Seddon was dead before the line reached Broken River. Almost two years after his visit there were still only 150 men on the job, excluding the Cleveland people, and the Public Works Department was only just about to put in the foundations for the Staircase viaduct. This yawning chasm, 150m wide and 75m deep, was a major obstacle in the path. A wire ropeway and cage ferried men and some materials across, but horses and heavy freight had to negotiate a steep zigzag track blasted out of the canyon walls.

The foundations for the central pier at Staircase consisted of four massive concrete piles or towers for which 1500 cubic metres of concrete were mixed and poured. The aerial ropeway required to get the shingle up to the site was more than 200m long.

By the winter of 1905 the great pier was nearly completed, and 67m of ironwork was towering above the rough bed of Staircase Gully, looking (as one observer noted) "like a monster cage in which the ogre of the depths is kept". This likeness, he thought, was emphasised by the numerous blacksmiths' fires burning all about. By this time there were 280 men at work, including the Cleveland people. The line was finished to Staircase but Broken River could still be reached only by the service road, on which a suspension bridge had been thrown across the ravine to facilitate the work. When the nor'wester blew too hard this bridge had a habit of turning itself inside-out (or upside-down), so that only the most adventurous used it in more than a stiff breeze.

Events back in Christchurch were soon to result in an increased work tempo. Preparations were in hand for the great New Zealand Exhibition in Hagley Park (opposite Kilmore Street) and the Government was keen to see progress carried to the stage where visitors could include the new and spectacular Midland railway (as far as it went) in their itinerary. The aim was to run trains to Broken River so that the trans-island journey could be reduced from two days to one. Beyond Broken River a 24km coach road would be built to connect with the main road at Cass. Passengers to and from the West Coast could then make the journey in one day with only 64km in the coaches. (The railway on the western side was completed to Otira in 1900).

Instructions went out to departmental heads that this was the way it had to be before the exhibition opened on November 1, 1906. Extra men were employed, Cleveland Engineering was given the hurry-up, work went on in the tunnels 24 hours a day, and by mid-1906 the goal was in sight. In that year the Staircase

Sloven's Creek Viaduct *carried the line out of the gorges into easier country towards Cass. In the background stands Bold Hill on a spur of the Torlesse Range.*
New Zealand Railways

The headmaster *(right)* and his assistant *(left)* flank children attending the temporary school at Otarama, along with some of their parents. These families lived near the line, mostly in tent accommodation, which with the "portable" schoolroom moved west as the rails progressed up the gorges.
Alexander Turnbull Library

viaduct was finished at last, the Broken River viaduct went up with the speed of a meccano model, the formation was pushed ahead and the rails laid, the station on the north side of the viaduct was built, and the coach road carved through the hills, up the valley of Sloven's Creek and on to Cass—all in double-quick time for the official opening on October 29, 1906.

Meanwhile the Midland line had become familiar to many Christchurch people. As the various sections were opened they became popular destinations for excursion trains. At least 30 of these ran to Otarama in 1895, and thousands of people travelled

to Staircase to marvel at the mighty viaduct, and later to Broken River where the more adventurous walked on to inspect the famous "mile of the six tunnels" clinging to the precipices on the north-west side of the gorge. The Broken River viaduct itself, not greatly less in height and length than the one at Staircase, had the advantage of being located in more spacious but equally rugged surroundings, with a river beneath rather than a creek. Families of some workmen lived in tents on a flat facing this river, a gloomy place in which at least one of the little girls who slept there can remember a flood coming through the tent in the middle of the night while her parents were absent at a meeting in the village above.

With the exhibition rush over, the railhead remained for a long time at Broken River while the work proceeded at a more leisurely pace. The bottom headings were driven through the six tunnels, while further on Frazer & Co. were getting on with the Sloven's Creek viaduct, the last on the line. In 1909 this was finished but there were still two tunnels to complete. While this work was proceeding, formation was being pushed towards Cass and beyond.

The rails reached Cass in 1910 and reduced the coach journey to only 40km. The following year piles were driven for the Waimakariri River bridge, and 1912 saw this, and the bridges over Cass River and Douglas Creek, ready for use. Much of the route lay in the riverbeds of the Waimakariri and Bealey rivers, requiring heavy protective works to secure the formation against floods. Almost immediately (in 1913) these had to be strengthened after the river washed out several sections of the line.

On November 1, 1913, a temporary station was opened at Halpin's Creek* in the Bealey valley. The Canterbury terminus was now almost in sight and in the winter of 1914, not long

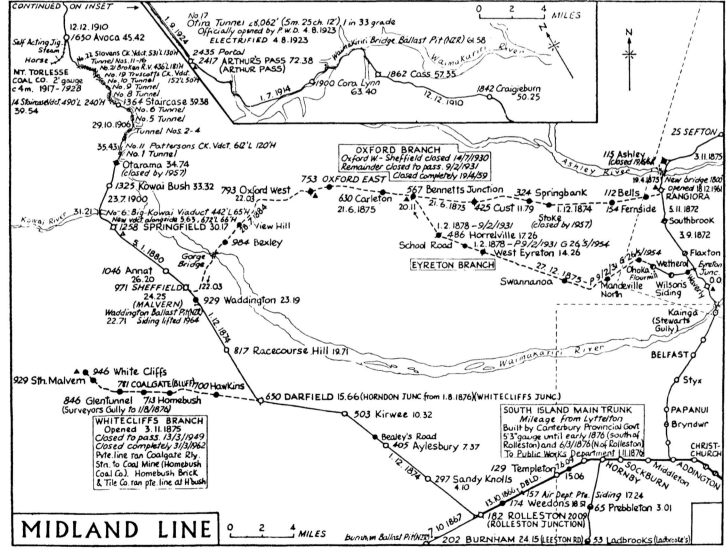

MIDLAND LINE

Midland map *has much detail for railway buffs (figures with place names are heights in feet above sea level and distances in miles and chains from Rolleston Junction).*
N.Z. Railways

*The author has always assumed that some creeks in this neighbourhood were named after roadmen, but in the case of Greyney's Creek, Mrs Catherine Elliott says that one day when her mother was driving up to Arthur's Pass the horse shied at the creek and tipped her out of the gig, breaking her wrist. A roadman helped her on her way, and later she noticed he had erected a sign at the creek bearing the words "Granny's Mistake". With time this changed to "Granny's Creek", and eventually to its present title.

Above: *The highway at Paddy's Bend provides this sweeping panorama of Waimakariri headwaters taken by Roy Sinclair. The skyline peaks from left are Gizeh, Greenlaw, Murchison, Speight-Harper and Davie. Bealey valley leading to Arthur's Pass is beyond the first spur at right.* (Roy Sinclair)

Right: *From Barker Memorial Hut in the White River headwaters, the camera looks down the White and up the Waimakariri to Carrington peak (left), with Mount Armstrong looming behind it, the Waimakariri Col, and Mounts Rolleston and Lancelot at right.*

Below: *The first Carrington Hut, looking downriver. From a painting by Bruce Banfield, one of the author's most treasured climbing companions, who lost his life while still a young man, overwhelmed by a snow avalanche near White Col.*

Above: *A view from high in the Waimakariri basin in autumn, when snow-free ranges reveal their soft colourings, ornamented here by a minor waterfall from Mount Rolleston's slopes. The distant peaks are on the Shaler Range. Note C.M.C hut lower right.*

Below: *Waimakariri headwaters peaks Speight, Harper and Davie as seen up the valley from near Klondyke Bridge. Eleven kilometres away the river valley turns right towards Carrington Hut.*

Left: *In winter the original Barker Hut was often completely buried by snow. This picture looks past the hut to the Cahill Glacier and two unnamed peaks on the Shaler Range.*
A.P.N.P. photo archives.

Below: *Striking Carrington Peak dominates this early-morning view from the still cold and sunless Waimakariri valley near Carrington Hut.*

Mountain ribbonwood, *Hoheria glabrata.*

Some of the flowers. *Arthur's Pass National Park is rich in botanical specimens, a host of which can be seen from the many established walkways near the village. Colin Burrows of Canterbury University's botany division identified these slides from the park headquarters collection.*

Southern Rata, *Metrosideros umbellata.*

Snow marguerite, *Senecio scorzoneroides x Senecio lyallii* (a hybrid).

Snow buttercup, *Ranunculus sericophyllus.*

Wet rock daisy, *Celmisia bellidioides.*

Mount Cook buttercup, *Ranunculus lyallii*

Mountain foxglove, *Ourisia* species.

Bealey Flat, *alias Camping Flat, alias Arthur's Pass—a photograph taken by James Ring about 1910 when tunnel construction was in progress. A footbridge at right leads to the tunnel entrance (not shown) and another crosses the Bealey River from the camp dining-rooms to the powerhouse at Devil's Punchbowl stream. Most of the other buildings are workmen's huts.*
Canterbury Museum

before World War I was declared, the line finally reached Arthur's Pass.

There remained then only the section across the main divide. As mentioned the line from the West Coast to Otira had been opened back in 1900. There had been nothing of note to mark that occasion. For one thing it rained all day as it so often does in Otira. The 120 people who travelled by special train from Greymouth celebrated as and where they could, mostly in the Otira hotels. They took a good look at the mist-shrouded mountains, wondered how the railway could possibly get through them, and went home again.

Part 3: The Great Tunnel

The decade during which the rail heads stood 16km apart at Arthur's Pass and Otira provided the most interesting period of transalpine travel. The coach trip across the Alps was a short but exhilarating climax to a journey already laden with scenic delights, with much more to see and experience than could be provided by rumbling along in the underground.

While the coach travellers marvelled at the wonders of the Otira Gorge, somewhere far beneath them men laboured in the mountain's interior. In the dim light of electric bulbs they bored into the rock with compressed-air drills, rammed home the gelignite, lit the fuses and ran for cover.

The road at Candy's Bend in the gorge was almost directly above the tunnel, and tourists, cupping ears and imagining they could hear the explosions, were apprehensive lest this subterranean unrest might collapse their fragile highway into the gorge. These fancies were far removed from the stark reality of life underground where the monotonous cycle of bore, charge and fire was all too real. An air drill has a fast reciprocating and a slow rotating action. This combination of hammering and chipping can bore a hole in the hardest rock, but with such a deafening clatter that men could still hear it ringing in their ears hours after they came off shift.

The business of drilling the Otira tunnel took 15 years, starting in 1908. It is 8.55km long, all on the straight, with a grade of 1 in 33, and rises from 483m above sea level at Otira to 742m at Arthur's Pass, a lift of 259m. The clear height of the ceiling above rail level is 4.72m and the maximum width 4.57m. The tunnel is lined throughout; side walls and footings are of mass concrete and the arch of concrete blocks. This was so strong that it survived undamaged through the several severe Arthur's Pass earthquakes.

The tunnel is in solid rock except for short sections at the portals. Those who expected some interesting geological revelations from the big drive through the range were disappointed, as the rock was found to be monotonously alike throughout, varying only in degrees of hardness. It lies on its edge in more or less vertical beds of greatly varying thickness,

whose strike is roughly parallel to the tunnel, jointed in all directions and badly fissured; and while explosives could be used to advantage, it proved gritty and hard on the drill-steels. Great difficulty was experienced in hardening drill-bits to stand up to the wear yet not break.

Temporary timbering was used throughout to prevent flaking of the rock-surface and fairly heavy beams were necessary in some places where faults in the rock structure were encountered. The ground was sometimes dry, commonly wet, and occasionally very wet, but the tunnel was pierced without striking any very great volume of water necessitating special methods as were required in the Simplon and other great European tunnels. The greatest flow of water was about 13,500 litres per minute, reduced to about half as the lining was completed. Most of the work was done uphill from Otira to gain the advantage of the grade in getting rid of excavated material and because of the heavy pumping required to drain the tunnel at the Bealey end until the headings met.

Usually about a dozen holes were drilled in the rock face, in which plugs of gelignite were tamped along with the necessary detonator and fuse. This had to be done in the dim light of acetylene lamps and often in showers of water leaking from the tunnel roof. When all was ready the fuses were lit with a torch made of half a plug of "jelly" blazing on the end of a stick—then a hurried scramble in the dark to a safe distance. The muffled explosions having been counted by the foreman as a safety check, all returned to the face when the fumes had cleared sufficiently.

Under favourable conditions one firing might loosen about 12 cubic metres of rock. The first job after the explosions belonged to the "prickers"—men with long steel rods who probed the walls and ceiling to bring down any loose rock which might endanger their workmates. The tunnel, following usual practice, was excavated in two sections. The lower half of the big hole called the "bottom heading" was driven in for a considerable distance, wide enough to admit trucks to remove the debris, and then enlarged to full width and the "top heading" attacked, working from a platform.

The Midland Railway Company had intended originally to lift the railway from Otira by a series of loops and switchbacks in the valleys of the Otira and Rolleston rivers, with very steep grades using the Fell or Abt toothed centre-rail system and possibly a short summit tunnel. When the Government assumed responsibility the engineers (with experience of the Fell system in the Rimutakas colouring their thinking) threw out this plan and opted for an easier ascent using conventional engines and a long (10km) tunnel. Subsequent surveys increased the grade slightly and shortened the tunnel. Owing to the mountainous nature of the country and the severe weather often experienced, these surveys were carried out under extremely trying and difficult conditions; but as was proved later, with extreme accuracy.

The Bealey River *having washed out the line, passengers cross on planks laid along the almost submerged sleepers.* "Weekly Press"

Magnificent Achievement. *Often in the worst of weather, dragging their instruments up and down misty hills through dripping bush, gangs like this completed the tunnel survey to such exact standards that when the rails met under the Southern Alps they were only a centimetre or two out of line. Their faces wear the look of men determined to do the job properly.* Alexander Turnbull Library

Murdoch and Neil McLean *of John McLean Ltd., tenderers for Otira tunnel. The Midland Railway Co. was ruined by the railway, and so were the McLeans. The brothers were married to sisters, and with warm support each for the others the foursome survived the failures and griefs of those troubled years with, it was said, never a harsh word.*

In 1906, with the railheads at Broken River in the east and Otira in the west, the Department was ready to call tenders for the tunnel. These required it to be completed within five years, by which time estimates were that the eastern railhead would have reached Arthur's Pass, enabling the line to be opened for through traffic about 1913.

In the event the great day had to be postponed for another 10 years. The reasons for this were numerous — the virtual destruction of New Zealand's largest and most experienced contracting firm; a disastrous collapse at the Bealey end of the tunnel, when men working there were endangered and one man lost his life; several other fatalities directly attributable to the difficult and often dangerous working conditions; the rise of militant unionism which "blacked" the project as "undesirable" and contributed to a chronic shortage of experienced labour; and a world war which put the brakes on for four years.

Although they considered the work might take six years to complete, the successful tenderers, John McLean & Sons, signed the contract in 1907 to build the tunnel within the specified five years at a price of 599,794 pounds. As the future was to demonstrate, both the time and the money were not much more than half what was required. At five years the rate of progress would have had to be 4.7m a day; in reality they managed only 2.5m. This would have seen the tunnel built in about nine years, with opening day in 1916 or 1917. But unforeseen circumstances and events involved the firm in heavy losses and eventually brought them to a halt. Their troubles were many — increases in wages, falling productivity and scarcity of good labour (all attributed by the contractors to union agitators*); the isolation and harsh climate of the construction sites, situated as they were close to either side of the Southern Alps; the high labour turnover (estimated in tens of thousands of men over the years); and difficult working conditions in the tunnel which made an unpleasant task even more unpleasant— all these were factors which escalated costs and slowed progress. Other considerations such as excessive drunkenness and gambling among sections of the workforce contributed to the low profile of the job in the eyes of good tunnellers who might otherwise have been attracted by the high rates of pay offered.

To what extent the McLeans were responsible for the problems which beset them is not clear. As contractors they had established an impressive reputation, having successfully completed numerous major public works in various parts of the country. They were apparently highly thought of as employers, with long experience in handling large numbers of men, both skilled and unskilled, but they were probably unprepared for the two major headaches at Otira — the inherent difficulty of the work and the degree of worker unrest and agitation.

Immediately the contract was signed Murdoch McLean left for overseas to study modern tunnelling methods and order up-to-date equipment, including the latest Ingersoll Rand air drills from New York. Meanwhile his brother Neil set about establishing the considerable facilities and accommodation required at either end of the tunnel. A house was built for

Some of the men *who helped blast out the long tunnel under Arthur's Pass.* Alexander Turnbull Library

*Among these were Bob Semple, Paddy Webb and Tim Armstrong, who were prominent in either the West Coast Workers' Union or the Inangahua Miners' Union, or both. All three were later Ministers in the first Labour Government elected in 1935. Murdoch McLean always maintained that most of his troubles started the day Semple first appeared at Otira.

Murdoch near the Otira portal in the Rolleston River, while Neil chose for himself a site among the trees alongside Rough Creek in the Bealey. Here he and his wife later hosted numerous visitors, many from overseas, who came to see the longest tunnel in the British Empire being built.

The power used for the project was generated by the waters of Holt's Creek on the Otira side and the Devil's Punchbowl Creek above the Bealey. Each developed 580 h.p., using Pelton wheels connected to dynamos. This plant worked well except when there was insufficient water because of the very occasional drought, or in mid-winter during the freeze.

The men's huts at Arthur's Pass were built on the Bealey Flat, while on the west side they went on to "The Island" in the Rolleston River valley close to the tunnel mouth, about 5km above Otira. One hundred and fifty huts were built there at the rate of two or three a day. They provided reasonable if somewhat draughty accommodation until the night of April 15, 1910, when a fearful gale arose and blew most of them away.

Starting the Big Dig. *This is the initial excavation above the Rolleston River which 15 years later connected with Arthur's Pass eight and a half kilometres away.* **Below:** *The ceremony of "firing the first shot" was held at the Otira end on May 5, 1908. Somewhere under the tarpaulin is Prime Minister Sir Joseph Ward addressing a sea of umbrellas sheltering the brave and hardy from a typical West Coast downpour.* "Weekly Press"

Gathering the remnants from down the valley and re-building them took considerable time and effort.

The cottages for married men were built in Otira close to the hillside — an unfortunate choice as it happened. One particularly wet day a shingle slide came down from the mountain and engulfed one with an unnecessarily tragic result — a man named Charlie Morris rushed back inside for his wallet and was killed when the rockfall crushed the building like an eggshell.

Early in 1908 a team of men went up the Rolleston to the survey site chosen for the tunnel and cleared away scrub and bush from the entrance. On May 5 a public holiday was declared for the ceremony of "firing the first shot", performed by the Prime Minister, the Rt. Hon. Sir Joseph Ward.

About 9cm of rain fell that day and the several thousand people expected to attend dwindled to a few hundred. Only those with firm resolve or good umbrellas made it to the ceremony at the portal. Coloured flags and bunting with which the McLeans had festooned the entrance hung dripping in the downpour as Sir Joseph said his piece, his words almost drowned by the roar of the flooding river. A delegation of notables from Christchurch failed to arrive — they were stopped in their tracks by the Waimakariri. Unable to cross, they sheltered in the Bealey Hotel and held their own ceremony there. All told it was a depressing start to the great project.

Tunnel boring began from the Rolleston end with hand drills. With the arrival of the Ingersoll Rand equipment progress was stepped up from both ends, but it was soon apparent that the rate of excavation was not what it should be. Serious trouble developed at the Bealey end when it was found that the first section was of extremely loose and unstable rock requiring very heavy timbering.

A long period of wet weather loosened the overburden and caused the timbers to give way, imprisoning 10 men. Continuing falls of rock made rescue work hazardous, but miraculously all were brought out alive, two of them after an entombment of more than three days.

Tunnel boss Jim McKeich first became aware of trouble when he heard a grinding noise overhead. Then the timbers gave way,* rock and gravel poured down, and a heavy beam hit him on the head. He was dragged out more dead than alive. His son, who was a "carbide boy" on the job, noticed that his father's false teeth were missing and a wideawake helper saved McKeich's life by thrusting a pair of blacksmith's tongs down his throat and pulling out the missing dentures. At that the victim started breathing again, but spent the next six weeks in hospital.

One of the heroes of the disaster was George Pitts, who rushed to the scene to find his camp mate, Claude Bray, almost entirely buried by timber and rock. He dug him out and carried him to safety, then returned to rescue George Beamer and another man who were buried in the same heap. Beamer was almost free when a second fall trapped them all.

Pitts ended up in the shape of a letter "U" with his arms outstretched behind him, pinned beneath a wrecked truck bearing heavily on his body. When rescuers arrived, he was still alive but the nails and skin from his fingers were missing where he had scratched away at grit and rocks threatening to suffocate Beamer. Sadly all was in vain; Beamer died later in Greymouth hospital.

Eventually all the men were evacuated except two, Doyle and Duggan, who were trapped deeper in the tunnel beyond the fall. To rescue them by trying to clear a way through the debris was too dangerous so a side entrance was excavated through the hill. While this work was in progress, using every available man, the prisoners were supplied with food, hot drinks, clothing and blankets through the compressed air pipe. Eighty-six hours later they were brought out through the emergency exit to the cheers of their waiting workmates. There was a touching reunion between Doyle and his sister, who had maintained a ceaseless vigil at the tunnel throughout the ordeal.

There were other fatalities, mainly at the Otira end, where two men were killed by misadventure while firing charges, and four by being run over or crushed by engines or trucks in the tunnel. Another was killed at Bealey when his coat was caught up in

*Experienced tunnellers were not happy with local timbers used for shoring. They preferred Oregon pine, which "talked" for some time before it gave way under pressure.

Left: **Survivors Doyle and Duggan** *after being dug out of the Otira tunnel following the disastrous collapse at the Canterbury end. They were entombed for 86 hours.* Right: **The emergency hole** *dug through the hillside above the Bealey River at Arthur's Pass to rescue Doyle and Duggan from the main tunnel.*
"Weekly Press"

some machinery.* Even the McLeans found themselves involved in tragedy, although not in connection with the work. Murdoch McLean's son Glenallan, a young lawyer from Wellington, came to visit his father one day in November, 1910. Next morning while edging forward to view the Rolleston gorge scenery, close by the house, he slipped over a precipice and was killed instantly.

In fact the whole decade was a tragic one for the McLean family. Old John, the firm's founder, died shortly before the Otira job started. Two of Glenallan's brothers were killed in the Great War, and Murdoch himself died of cancer in 1917. His death broke a very close family unit.

As time passed the difficulty in securing a skilled labour force gradually sounded the death knell of the contract as well. The job was never fully manned and many of the thousands who came and went, attracted by the high wages, were only drifters and drunkards. The booze problem was not too serious in the earlier stages when James O'Malley held the licences of all three local hotels — the Terminus at Otira, the Gorge at the mouth of Otira Gorge, and the Bealey. He was a good keeper, but when he sold the Gorge Hotel there was a change. The new man cared for nothing but liquor sales and soon a combination of heavy drinking and gambling (mainly two-up) required extra police at Otira.

The ready availability of explosives also caused the local constable much concern. Several incidents were recorded, such as the blasting open of the Otira railway safe and removal of its contents. In another a group who were offended by the smell from a neighbour's "little house" blew it up — fortunately there was nobody inside at the time. In one case an alcoholic and his drunken friends, refused entry by his wife, blew the back door and porch off his house; in yet another a resident who suspected a neighbour of stealing from his neatly sawn stack of firewood blocks bored holes in some of them and hid detonators therein, masking the holes with sawdust paste. Two days later the neighbour's stove blew out. Even the constable suffered when he grew too officious in his duties. One night when he was away investigating alleged sly-grogging someone blew the back off his house. This was regarded as a more serious offence and a locomotive driver called Brandy Jack was charged by the police, but the Christchurch jury found him "not guilty" and he returned home in triumph.

Most of the workers were a transient lot, staying only a few weeks or even a few days, then moving on again, unable to accept the hard work required of them, or the climate, or the isolation. Rainfall at Otira was close to 500cm a year and sometimes the work in the tunnel was equally wet. In the higher atmosphere at Bealey Flat the cold was often intense, with deep snow on the ground, and workers coming on shift were pleased to get into the slightly warmer tunnel.

In this time of industrial unrest in New Zealand, union organisers, many of them Australians, were singing the praises

*The eight fatalities at the Otira tunnel compared very favourably with European experience. The 14km St Gothard tunnel cost 177 lives.

of red flags and workers' rights. They organised the 1910 strike at Otira over the matter of deposits for acetylene lamps, which management claimed were being treated irresponsibly. The Bealey men considered the cause so trivial that they ignored the strike call. There was trouble in the Holt's Creek drive tunnel when the McLeans discovered it was costing 80 shillings a foot to excavate. The men were dismissed and another gang contracted at 35 shillings a foot. After expenses they made 14½ shillings a day, well above the ruling rates.

The McLeans found it difficult to understand the workers' dissatisfaction, since they were paid 10% above award. The union demanded 30% above, which would have added 150,000 pounds to the cost of the job. Labour shortages were accentuated in 1912 when Paddy Webb promised Murdoch McLean that he would do all in his power to dissuade union members from coming to Otira. An item published to this effect in the workers' paper, *The Maorilander,* marked the beginning of the end for John McLean & Sons.

The contract completion date was approaching and the company had no hope of meeting it. In February McLeans petitioned Parliament to be released from their obligations. A special committee of the House freed them on October 18, 1912.

Wetter in than out. *Workmen in the tunnel occasionally met with exceptional flows of water which made conditions uncomfortable even for West Coasters.* Canterbury Museum

134

The Great Day. *Among those present at the opening ceremony were Sir Joseph Ward (at left with umbrella), Sir Thomas Wilford (in light-coloured overcoat), Prime Minister W.F. Massey (centre), Minister of Works Gordon Coates (with coat on arm), and George Forbes, M.P., Prime Minister during the Depression years (extreme right).*
Alexander Turnbull Library

Their action was endorsed later by the House with a vote of 48 to 4, and fresh tenders were called.

The McLeans carried on until the end of 1912. They had lost heavily, not only on the tunnel contract but coincidentally on a big job with the Wellington harbour works which had also gone sour. From their homes at Otira and Bealey Flat the brothers moved to Hororata, where they had a contract to build a railway. Three years later, having discharged all its responsibilities in various corners of New Zealand, the firm went out of existence.

Not surprisingly there was no response to the call for tenders and again the Public Works Department had to step in and take over. The contractor's engineer, W.H. Gavin, continued with the job, as did many of the tunnellers. Among the more permanent residents the unity of purpose engendered by the task, and the isolation, created a strong community spirit which manifested itself in the formation of clubs and societies, church groups, etc. Without deadline pressures more discretion could be used in hiring labour and many who came during this period stayed until the finish. Gradually both Otira and Arthur's Pass became more substantial "home towns" in which their residents showed considerable pride.

When war broke out in 1914 consideration was given to suspending work on the tunnel, but the Imperial Government asked that it be continued, maintaining that if the German fleet blockaded the small West Coast ports the railway could freight the Coast's valuable coal overland to Lyttelton.*

And so throughout the war years, while their contemporaries blasted away at the deadlock on the Western Front, a small but effective task force at Otira and Bealey fired their own volleys at obstinate Southern Alps rock. They were rewarded in May, 1918, when men at the Bealey end, waiting for the dust to settle after a firing, thought they could hear faint explosions from within the mountain. As their ears were usually ringing with one or another noise, they could not be sure. But soon there was no question and by June, unhindered by the roar of rushing water which throughout accompanied work on the Otira side, they could clearly hear the drills at work.

In the following month work on the Bealey face was discontinued. Some time on July 20, having drilled and loaded the face for another explosion, the Otira men lit the fuses, fired the charge and ran for cover as usual. But this time the blast blew the other way, into the Bealey tunnel beyond. A draught of cool air came through and carried away the dust to reveal a gaping hole—after 10 years of grim toil the way through the Alps was open.

*Carrying West Coast coal across the island to Lyttelton is now the main justification for keeping the Midland line open.

The breakthrough demonstrated the amazing skill and accuracy of the survey teams and engineers who guided both ends to such exact conclusions. The floor was found to be 29mm out in level, and the walls 19mm out of alignment, while the discrepancy in the estimated length of the 8.55km tunnel was under one metre.

During the next month the headings were advanced to within a metre of each other, and the original breakthrough hole blocked up again so that the Minister of Public Works, Sir William Frazer, could fire the final shot, loaded with appropriate political symbolism. One account has it that the men performed this ceremony themselves the day before to a round of rousing cheers, and then so carefully replaced the rock that the Minister was none the wiser.

Actually the top heading of the tunnel was not completed until June, 1921. Progress was so painfully slow that a conference of local bodies set about the Government once again. A couple of strikes and a national shortage of cement did nothing to help, but finally, at 9.30 p.m. on Saturday, September 17, 1921, the last concrete was poured. To mark the occasion the local publicans shouted the men several barrels of beer. These, so the story goes, were all drunk before the concrete had set.

The firm of English Electric won the contract for the 4000 h.p. coal-fired generating station at Otira, the overhead lines throughout the section, the five electric locomotives required to haul the trains to and from Arthur's Pass and Otira, and other equipment. The price was about 313,000 pounds.

The breakthrough. *At last east and west are joined under the Alps. The story may be apocryphal but Prime Minister Massey was said to have sent the tunnellers a congratulatory telegram, adding, "At least this proves you have both been digging in the same hill."*
Alexander Turnbull Library

Opening day, not only for the tunnel but for the Midland line as a whole, came on August 4, 1923. It was hailed as the greatest event in the history of Canterbury and the West Coast, and the inter-island ferry *Wahine* brought 140 politicians and government officials from Wellington for the occasion. They and another 250 notables from Christchurch travelled up from the city by special train, marvelling on the way at the rugged grandeur of the scenery. Winter snow mantled the peaks and covered the ground from Cora Lynn on, so that every new vista was suitably framed by alpine splendour.

The train from the West Coast, arriving early at Otira, had time for a quick return trip through the tunnel ahead of the "special" from Christchurch. The Coasters were in celebrative mood but were abruptly sobered when their train, hauled by one of the new electric engines, ground to a halt in the depths of the tunnel. Had the new engine broken down? Had the power failed? Were they stuck there for the rest of the day? Panic-stricken officials, fearing all the elaborate arrangements for the opening ceremony might have come unstuck with a blocked tunnel, were relieved when after 23 minutes the lights came on again—the trouble had been a fault in the overhead wiring.

They reached Arthur's Pass only minutes before the "special" steamed in from Christchurch. Cheerful Coasters, hanging from every carriage window, gave it such a boisterous welcome that they embarrassed some of the Canterbury contingent, acutely conscious of their distinguished guests, so they were quickly

hurried away to where they came from. After a suitable delay the "special" followed, finally reaching Otira an hour and a half behind schedule.

Free lunch for 1500 people was provided at Otira, after which Prime Minister Bill Massey unlocked the powerhouse with a golden key. He and his Minister of Public Works, Gordon Coates, and a long list of other dignitaries addressed the assemblage, emphasising that the occasion was a milestone in New Zealand history and an engineering achievement of international standing. Their remarks were coloured with optimism for the success of the railway and the anticipated benefits for the two provinces which it connected.

Celebrations over, the Coasters returned home and the rest trundled through the tunnel again and back to Christchurch for the official banquet. The inter-island ferry was delayed several hours so that the North Islanders could attend, and it was after midnight before special trams took them along Manchester Street to board the train to Lyttelton. Some of the keener Canterbury enthusiasts went through to the port for a ship-side farewell, and as the *Wahine* swung away from the wharf they could relax and reflect that after 40 years of pushing and shoving at the combined barriers of yawning chasm, mountain rock, dilatory government and militant unions, not to mention a Great War, their cherished railway up the Waimakariri and through the big tunnel to the west was at last a reality.

The days of steam. *No economies of diesel or electrics can compensate for the visual excitement of a big Kb locomotive hauling the West Coast express up a Waimakariri valley, almost overshadowed by its own spectacular plume of smoke and steam.*   Roy Sinclair

CHAPTER TWELVE

The Hundred Years War

The century which elapsed between the disastrous floods of the 1860s and the relative security of the 1960s saw a succession of engineers standing on Waimakariri riverbanks wondering what to do with the river. "The very thought of the Waimakariri makes us shudder," said *The Press* in 1863, echoing the foreboding which lay like a cloud over Christchurch and Kaiapoi and all those lands in the path of what one writer called "The Great Intimidator". The first experts had to confess the river had got the best of them. For all the money he was paid for his part in Canterbury public works, W.T. Doyne could only throw up his hands and declare there was no choice but to "leave nature to work out her ends".

Nothing he said could have pleased the Waimakariri more, for rivers are born to roam. Unhappily for early settlers the Courtenay (as they called it) was still a geological youngster in its lower reaches when they arrived—still pushing out its "cone" or "fan" towards the coast, spreading out and building up the plains over the centuries on a 50km front from Lake Ellesmere northwards. When Europeans arrived the process was incomplete and the river's way of doing what came naturally was to adopt the channel which best suited the lay of the land at that particular time. Engineers were soon made aware of lingering traces of earlier courses—the Styx, Horseshoe Lake, Bottle Lake, the Avon, and the Islington channel leading to the Halswell River and Lake Ellesmere.

The "war" which was to last a hundred years was to make the Waimakariri go, not where it wanted, but where the engineers dictated.

As the bed rose the river was presented with a variety of awesome choices. It could adopt the North Branch for its main channel (which it did in the 1860s), threaten Kaiapoi, and bully small farmers on the Mandeville plains. Or it could spread out to the south, taking any of its earlier courses to upset and ruin lands in that direction. But the most exciting prospect was that which would bring the greatest distress to the greatest number—to charge down the Avon with the next big flood, sink Christchurch under mud and shingle, and contrive a new outlet near New Brighton or Shag Rock.

All these possibilities faced the solemn river-fixers, especially Edward Dobson, the Provincial Engineer, for his was the final responsibility. It was he who built the first banks and saw them swept away with the next flood, and who declared there was no real solution until the river was forced to take a direct course from the mountains to the Pacific.

That was common sense, but how could it be achieved? He suggested a new channel through the 31 sq.km Kaiapoi Island, the largest obstruction in the sprawling riverbed. This was a bold, imaginative and risky proposition which drew neither funds nor favour from his superiors. But with a combination of small-farmer determination on the island in 1867, sheer good luck at Stewart's Gully about 1880 and engineering prowess at Wright's Cut in 1930 the river was finally persuaded to run in Dobson's visionary course. The years which followed provided what was beyond him—massive stopbanks and groynes to keep it there.

The first moves towards this end were initiated, albeit unintentionally, by a Kaiapoi Island farmer and mill-owner named Donald Coutts, whose name still identifies the district where he lived. He set up his flour mill near a sluggish stream called Kaikanui (location, about a kilometre north-west from the present Belfast Hotel), tapped it for his waterwheel, and ran the discharge down a depression into the Waimakariri's South Branch. In dry seasons the supply was unsatisfactory, so he dug a water-race north-west along Maber's Road to a point on the

North Branch where the river swung sharply in his direction before veering way to the north-east.

But soon he was getting more water than he had bargained for. By 1867 the Hon. G.L. Lee is recorded as saying Coutts' ditch was washed out until it was as large as either of the two branches and carrying one-third of the river. A consequence was that Coutts and his neighbours were cut off from Christchurch, Coutts' Island was born, and another bridge had to be built to renew their access, known ever after as "The Cutting Bridge". But even before the 1868 flood the river was so out of control that the approaches were washed away, leaving the bridge standing useless in the middle of nowhere. Coutts must have wondered what kind of Frankenstein he had created.*

As it happened there were developments afoot which promised more significant and lasting changes to his environment and that of all the farmers on the island. The disastrous 1865 flood had battered them severely and prompted schemes to avoid a repetition. Much discussion resulted in a decision to dig a new course along the line proposed by Edward Dobson. This would carry flood overflows from the upper junction of the North and South branches (known as Mason's Corner) for 5km, directly down the middle of the island. Near Coutts' mill it would join the existing Maber's Road channel and discharge with it into the South Branch a kilometre or so above White's Bridge. (See maps, Chapter Two.)

The fact that the farmers themselves, financed in part by the local road board, were prepared to adopt this risky solution to their troubles serves only to emphasise how serious those troubles were. Perhaps if they could have seen a few years into the future they might have settled for the devil they knew. Contractors and the settlers themselves were hard at work providing the river with its new course when the 1868 flood arrived. It supplied immediate proof (as the Maber's Road channel had already done) that rivers seldom do what is expected of them. Soon, as each succeeding flood widened and deepened it, the "Dobson" cut was taking virtually all the North Branch flow. The flood threat to the northern half of the island was removed, the southern half became known as Coutts Island, while down at Kaiapoi the townsfolk breathed easier.

But the island farmers should have remembered what *The Press* said earlier about the Waimakariri being "a tricksy and mischievous river". As is so often the case when man interferes with nature, the side effects were serious. As flood followed flood, thousands of acres of good farm land at the top of the

"The Cutting Bridge" *(or Coutts Island Bridge) under strain from one of the Waimakariri's frequent spring floods. When Wright's Cut went through this bridge was no longer needed and was sold to the highest bidder.* Weekly Press.

---

*An inspection of Maber's Road today does little to suggest that "one-third of the Waimakariri" once flowed there, except at its southern end where deep channels persist. More than a century of farming practice may have smoothed the bed. *The Lyttelton Times* of February 14, 1868, records the North Branch as having made a channel across Kaiapoi Island down Maber's Road to the mill race, which was described as three or four chains wide and 16ft deep in places. It also says the cutting made by the island works committee was nearly completed, and both would discharge

into the South Branch above White's Bridge. The line of the Maber's Road channel in the vicinity of the Coutts' mill site is still clearly delineated on either side of today's Waimakariri, which slices through it almost at right angles on its direct course down Wright's Cut immediately above the motorway bridges.

island and along the banks of the new cut were washed away as the river took charge. The confines of an artificial channel were not for the Waimakariri, which immediately widened its new bed into the usual comfortable tangle of shingled waterways—a poor substitute for the rich cropping lands it destroyed.

In the year following the flood of February, 1868, there were a number of notable changes—not only in the Waimakariri but among those whose responsibility it had become. Edward Dobson's term as Provincial Engineer came to an end later that year, and in his place George Thornton, confident in his new role, attacked the river vigorously. By October he could report "with certainty" that the situation was "positively under control". He was convinced, he said, that the three embankments he was building in the Sandy Knolls region would provide the city with adequate protection for the future. His confidence was given substance by his early successes, which included diverting much of the North Branch water back into the South Branch some years earlier.

In 1869 the Provincial Government, not entirely convinced by Thornton's assurances and doubtless weary of river matters generally, appointed a Board of Conservators, to be concerned only with the south bank and primarily to dispose of the continuing threat to the city. For its first chairman the Council selected R.J.S. Harman, a leading citizen who was also a civil engineer, provincial councillor, runholder, land and estate agent, the discoverer of Harman's Pass, and a father of 12. The board levied a rate of one penny in the pound (0.4%) on all property in the district, with an additional penny for Christchurch and properties "immediately adjoining the known lines of overflow".

Soon Mr Harman could assure Christchurch that its future had been secured as far as the river was concerned. All the danger points had been "safed" by (1) an upper embankment near Watson's Accommodation House at Courtenay covering the Christchurch and Halswell channels, (2) a similar bank at Sandy Knolls covering another Christchurch channel, plus one immediately below to cope with any overflow which might outflank it, and (3) a bank near McLean's station to cover the low ground at the head of Styx channel. Willows were planted to protect these banks, for which Mrs Deans of Riccarton donated the cuttings.

The board was careful to remember where most of its money came from, so one sunny summer day in December, 1871, the mayor and councillors were invited to inspect what was being done to protect the city. This account, taken from a *Press* report, gives some idea of the magnitude of the works undertaken subsequent to the 1868 flood to ensure that never again would the river get into the Avon; and as it suggests the outing was not without humour.

The party assembled at the council chambers at 8 a.m., climbed aboard a four-horse coach, and were trundled out towards Sandy Knolls. After a short stop at the Yaldhurst Hotel they continued, bowling along over the stony plains and riverbeds to the house of Mr Potts, the overseer, which was on the West Coast Road about 25km from town, and three kilometres from the embankment they were to inspect. At the house the party was met by the chairman of the board, Mr Harman. After more refreshments they girded their loins for the six kilometre walk over boulders and sand, which under a scorching sun was far from the most agreeable part of the day's programme.

After walking across the "Christchurch channel", down which had flowed the flood waters destined for the Avon, and noting signs of "the terrible nature of the enemy with which the board had to cope", an inspection was made of the bank erected by the Government after the 1868 flood. This was composed of shingle topped with gorse plants; it was five metres high and about 55 metres long.

"At this point," wrote the reporter, "we missed two or three of our companions, and on looking out over the plain we saw them comfortably esconced in the lee of a sandhill. They had kept close to our worthy town clerk, who was more than once suspected of having a small flask somewhere in reserve. But our

The tiger caged. *In the foreground a main stream of the Waimakariri charges directly at its restraining stopbank; beyond that bank lies what was once the sprawling riverbed, now farmed but still marked by old channels; and in the distance (5km from the river) are northern suburbs of Christchurch.*

guide, the chairman of the board, was adamant, so after waving a mournful farewell we continued with our weary pilgrimage."

They came next to the controversial "cage" against which the whole of the river had spent its strength in the great flood. Here, in spite of setbacks, the work of the board had been very successful and the flow turned in another direction. They now reached Embankment No.2. At short intervals, wherever it was deemed necessary, willow groynes had been made, a most effectual defence.

"Returning, we find our missing friends, and now inspect what is regarded as the board's greatest triumph. Before the flood of July, 1871, two lines of boxes, made somewhat in the shape of an inverted 'V' and filled with gravel, were made to present a sloping surface to the river, thereby assisting the run of water without making a scour, and were placed near the end of the No.2 embankment, the ends having a slightly northward tendency and being faced with boulders."

But a flood in September had taken away this boulder facing and breached the No.2 embankment. The board then decided on another course. It made a line of boxes, 19 in number, each weighing 25 tonnes, protected by bags of concrete at intervals, and faced at the end with 800 bags of concrete, with a T-shaped face of six boxes jutting out into the stream, thus directing the water northwards.

The inspection party was most impressed by the magnitude of these works. Satisfied the board had the protection of the city well in hand, they straggled back to the shelter of a friendly sandhill, "where a capital luncheon was laid out", and the health of the conservators proposed and drunk in champagne.

Back at the Potts residence a testimonial was given to Mr and Mrs Potts, he for his work on the river, and she for the hospitality always extended whenever board members came that way. They were presented with a clock. Then, after another couple of toasts, all climbed aboard the coach and were back in town about seven o'clock. The mayor and councillors were well satisfied with what they had seen, and had they taken their crystal balls with them that day their optimism would have remained undimmed.

From then on the sight of Waimakariri floodwater in Christchurch was never seen again, but for nearly another 90 years the river's immediate surroundings on the lower plains, and the city's vital road and rail links to the north, were always at risk. The North Branch having ceased to be that other than in name, Kaiapoi people enjoyed the novelty of seeing their river run clear when the South Branch was on the rampage. With this change in patterns established they were convinced their troubles were over, but they soon learned otherwise.

Easter, 1874, came in early April. It was memorable for the violent nor'westers which buffeted Canterbury, and the blue-black clouds over the ranges. Not to worry, said the weather-wise: at this time of the year there's no snow back there to melt. That was true, but there was such exceptionally heavy rain on the main divide that the Taramakau River, for example, broke all records, rising a metre higher than ever before according to Westland's chief surveyor. On the Canterbury side all the

A panoramic view *of Raven Street, Kaiapoi, during the 1923 flood. At left the swollen Kaiapoi River shows behind the stopbank. Centre left behind the cart stands the Working Men's Club, and at right are the* Record *newspaper office (formerly the Mechanics' Institute) and the Mandeville Hotel.*

Douglas Jones — Kaiapoi Museum

Some men in a boat *discuss the flood in Peraki Street with a boy on a raft. At its height the water was up to the horses' bellies. At right are the old Catholic and Methodist churches.* Douglas Jones

The Mandeville Hotel *after the 1923 flood was past its worst. Staff and patrons pose in knee-deep water, with one resting a gallon jar on the hitching post.* Douglas Jones — D.D. McLauchlan

"Three men in a tub" *— well, three borough councillors actually, returning from an inspection of what was possibly the last great flood to be experienced in Kaiapoi.* Weekly Press

Waimakariri's upper tributaries rose alarmingly and another disaster was on its way.

Hundreds of Kaiapoi and North Canterbury people who went to the races at Riccarton on Easter Monday backed a loser that day, regardless of which horse carried their money. While they were enjoying a warm if windy outing on the turf, the Waimakariri was swelling to unprecedented levels. For the first time since it was built in 1863, White's Bridge was submerged, and the flood scoured out extensive sections of the North Road and about three kilometres of railway track between Chaney's and the Waimakariri bridge. Fortunately both road and rail bridges held fast, but it was many days before race patrons could get back to their homes. And for many from Kaiapoi it was far from a pleasant homecoming.

As on a lesser occasion in 1871 the North Branch ran clear even when the flood was at its height, but the satisfaction of Kaiapoi river-watchers turned to alarm when they looked the other way — the town was being attacked from the rear. The record fresh in the South Branch backed up the North Branch and once more overflowed into the streets. Sick with disappointment, residents had to watch helplessly as muddy water flooded into hundreds of shops, warehouses and homes to within 15cm of the calamitous 1868 level.

Kaiapoi Island farmers suffered severe damage and stock losses, and those along the new cut had to watch in dismay as the rogue river ate away great chunks of their fertile soil and replaced it with shingle. There was no loss of life, but several narrow escapes. The Selfoot family was rescued on a raft hastily constructed of sheep hurdles and a ladder, while lower down at the Rosser home (he was away at the time) Mrs Rosser was reported to have stood for hours in water up to her armpits before she was rescued. (For a long time afterwards, if anyone asked how high the 1874 flood rose they were told it was "up to Mrs Rosser's armpits".) Actually the depth of water in the bar of the Courtney Arms Hotel near White's Bridge was 122cm (4ft)*.

This time Christchurch escaped scot-free. The embankments built at danger points along the south side of the river, which the civic leaders had so thoroughly inspected a couple of years earlier, had held firm "although battered a good deal". They stood 30cm clear of the worst the river could do, so that the threat of Waimakariri flood water flowing down the Avon seemed indeed to have been dissipated by the commendable work of the Board of Conservators.

The second great course-straightening event in Waimakariri history was possibly engineered by the river itself at Stewart's Gully, over the final few kilometres to the sea. River-viewers on the old Main Highway Bridge today can look downstream without realising that from this same location in the mid-1870s they would have been looking across the peaceful farmlands of James Stewart and his sons, James and John. They might even have seen a train puffing across the pastures en route to Kaiapoi. The Waimakariri of those days curved away sharply to the north-east† to join the North Branch near the present freezing works, dangerously close to the borough. Yet within a few years it was established in a new and more direct course, not greatly different from that of today.

There was much speculation about how this came to be. Probably there was a depression through the Stewart farm which in earlier times might have been a river course. Severe erosion at

*This figure appears to confirm that the 1874 flood indeed submerged White's Bridge when the relative levels of hotel and bridge are compared in the picture on Page 108.

†The old course can still be identified alongside the Main North Road opposite Ashley Meats premises.

Lower Waimakariri. *The river used to flow in from the left immediately above the bridges, and to the right below them. The upper course was changed by Wright's Cut (1930) and the lower course much earlier (1880) by "Stewart's Gully", where the river still flows. The River Trust's controversial "Lower Cut" headed more-or-less towards the camera in an effort to continue the Wright's Cut direction, but proved a failure.*

the bend where the river turned north-east may have opened the way for a flood overflow to go down what always seems to have been called "Stewart's Gully". It was reported in mid-April, 1879, that "a good deal of water was going down the gully".

Meetings were held in 1879 and 1880 to form a North Bank Conservators' Board to counter the activities of the South Waimakariri River Board, and one of their requests was that the Government should dig out the channel through Stewart's farm to divert the flow away from Kaiapoi. Resident railway engineer Henry Lowe made the same suggestion in 1879, saying this would help solve the railway's problems because such a channel would take flood overflows and reduce pressure on the railway. He thought another three spans tacked on to the southern end of the railway bridge would handle the overflow in the gully. A glance at the map reveals this to be a strange observation.

Rumour always associated Stewart's Gully with dark deeds at dead of night. Did people from Kaiapoi carrying lanterns, buckets and shovels sneak on to Stewart's land to start the river on its way, to save their town from disaster? Or, as one version had it, was the ditch dug by neighbours who hoped thereby to save their own farms? Nobody knew for certain, but in 1931 James Stewart jun., then an old man, recalled that he and other members of the family used to trudge to school over dry land; then one day they found a ditch had formed which they had to jump over. It widened until a plank bridge was needed; then a punt. Each succeeding flood through 1879 to 1881 ate away the crumbling banks until by 1882 the whole river was flowing through "Stewart's Gully" and, give or take a little, has done so ever since.

Kaiapoi and the north bank conservators could not have been more pleased at this development but Lowe and his railway were in trouble. Instead of a few spans added to the bridge a completely new one had to be built. And then it had to be protected from flood damage even more vigorously than before. James Stewart remembered thousands of tonnes of rock poured into the river to protect the bridge and the railway, and two massive groynes built out from the bank. For these double rows of piles were driven, braced and bolted together, and the space between filled with rock and rubble. They took months to build but after a couple of floods stood alone in the middle of the river, impressive but useless monuments to theoretical engineering, while the wilful Waimakariri flowed on between them and his father's shrinking acres.

For half a century the Waimakariri was in the hands of river control authorities whose concern was to protect only the country to the south, and more especially the city of Christchurch. The first of these was the South Waimakariri

Board of Conservators (1869-80) and the second the South Waimakariri River Board (1880-1923). With limited resources they kept the river out of Christchurch but were unable to control overflows in the lower reaches which often damaged the Main North Road and the northern railway, along with farm lands on the lower flats. What happened on the north bank was no concern of theirs.

The river on the plains. *Eyrewell State Forest and part of Claxby farm from the air. The Waimakariri issues from its gorge to right of Mount Torlesse (centre). In the photograph below, the dotted line indicates the extent of farm land lost to the river over the years.* M. Spencer-Bower and Weekly News.

140

The River Board was helped greatly in that during all its 42 years only two major floods occurred—in 1887 and 1905. In neither case was there an overflow in the direction of Christchurch, but these and the annual crop of smaller freshes ate away at the banks and groynes, undermining concrete blocks and toppling them into the stream. The board inherited 5600 hectares of poor land extending down the river from Courtenay to Harewood Road, and much of its energy and money went into putting this in trees. The planting programme for reserves and protection works in 1881, for example, included 47 cords of willow stakes, 28,000 poplar cuttings, 9090 poplar trees, 1200 oaks, 100 ash, 1600 birch and 3450 pines. In the long term these were designed to provide a protection belt and additionally to become a source of revenue for the board.

For years it was thought that the large quantities of shingle brought down and deposited in the lower reaches came from far back in the hills, but in time it became clear that much of this had its origin in the erosion of the river's 30 metre shingle cliffs, a prominent feature of much of the Waimakariri's course across the plains. Farmers on the north bank were losing land at an alarming rate, something they strongly believed was caused by the proliferation of south bank groynes pushing the water to their side. Their protests led to the River Board sending out an inspection party, which agreed that groynes were indeed the trouble, but only those built by the Water-supply Board at Brown's Rock, far upstream, "which had set the river oscillating from side to side in its bed"—and that was the problem.

This facile explanation was scorned by the farmers to the point where they went looking for Government help, to be rewarded with the appointment of a commission to examine all aspects of the river, and ultimately with an Act of Parliament, "The Waimakariri River Improvement Act, 1922". This dissolved the River Board and replaced it with a new body, the Waimakariri River Trust.

An enormous task faced the trust, which met for the first time on May 23, 1923, while Canterbury was still mopping up after one of the worst floods in memory. It was empowered to deal with both sides of the river and with the Eyre and Cust tributaries, which in that year (as in 1868) contributed materially to the damage in Kaiapoi. The first works programme included raising the banks and preventing erosion, groyne protection, and planting wide belts of trees nearby.

In 1925, realising that half measures would no longer serve, the trust engaged as its engineer a member of the commission which had given it birth, F.C. Hay, and asked him to prepare a comprehensive scheme for the fullest possible control of the river.

Hay's No.2 Scheme, as it became known, provided for three major cuts in the river's course, closing the old South Branch, and construction of adequate stopbanks and groynes to handle a flood of 4250 cumecs. The cuts were at Wright's farm above the present motorway bridge, at Stewart's Gully to straighten the

Waimakariri as it was. *Floods in the 1920s often blocked the Main North Road near Chaney's. Here new-fangled motor vehicles are halted—but doubtless the horse and cart splashed through regardless.* Weekly Press

course there, and at the mouth where a direct run out to sea was needed to replace the lagoon channel running south behind the sandhills. To finance the initial stage of these works a poll of ratepayers had to give assent with a two-thirds majority, but controversy over the scheme waxed so hot in the newspapers that when a poll was held the proposal was defeated. One of the oft-repeated criticisms was that making rivers run straight was going against nature.

Stymied, the River Trust turned again to the government for support. The Prime Minister himself arrived and inspected the river from an aeroplane, returning to earth much impressed by the old channels he could see from above, especially those leading towards Christchurch. A new "Waimakariri River Improvement Bill" was soon before Parliament, with a provision that any future poll would require to be passed by only a bare majority. Preparations were made to go to the ratepayers again.

This time the trust had not only the government on its side—the river helped too. A flood of over 3500 cumecs, said to be the worst for 40 years, occurred on December 4, 1925, followed by another on November 5, 1926, as bad or worse, which received such vivid coverage in the newspapers that public opinion turned in favour of protection. The 1926 flood ran out of gauge in the gorge at 7.6m, put nearly 3m of water over Coutts Island and Kainga, and trapped a venturesome photographer into spending a harrowing night in a tree. Water flowed over the banks near White's Bridge for 12 hours. When the gauge on the bridge read 5m the Chaney's bank broke, at 5.1m several other breaches let the river loose, and at 5.5m it crossed the railway embankment and washed out the line. Over 800ha of good farming land was put under water.

Had the poll been held then it would probably have been carried by a big majority, but the trust was determined to play its cards right this time. There had always been a demand that Hay's schemes be considered by someone higher up the engineering tree. Accordingly the trust assembled full details and sent everything to London for some eminent engineer to study.

Doing it the hard way. *In 1930, when the first comprehensive control scheme for the Waimakariri got under way, thousands of unemployed men worked with shovels and wheelbarrows to build stopbanks along the lower reaches. But they were not enough to stop the river breaking bounds, and it was not until the 1960s that modern machinery enabled banks to be built massive enough to provide real security.* The Press

Theirs is the responsibility. *A rampant Waimakariri which broke free of its restraining stopbanks could today cause damage worth many millions of dollars. Some of the engineers charged with ensuring this has not happened since River Trust days are pictured. From left, Harold Harris, Murray Reid, Earle Dalmer, John Macdonald, Bob Poynter, the present Catchment Board chief engineer, Bob Reid, and operations manager Brian Dwyer.*

London chose Sir Alexander Gibb, a world authority on river control. He was asked to comment on the risk of flood to Christchurch, whether comprehensive control was better than partial measures, and if comprehensive, whether floods should be controlled by dams in the gorge, or by dredging the channel, or by diversions and stopbanks as embodied in the Hay scheme.

In June, 1928, Sir Alexander's report arrived in Christchurch. In all main respects it agreed with Hay. A notable exception was in the width of the cuts, which he thought should be 60m whereas Hay had opted for an economical 10m with the idea of letting the river do the rest of the work. Gibb agreed there was a distinct chance of Christchurch being flooded unless something was done.

Convinced now that it was ready, the trust gave notice in September, 1928, of its intention to hold another poll. The amount to be raised was 100,000 pounds, the Government would contribute 45,000 pounds and a new bridge, and the rest was to come from revenue. The usual criticisms surfaced again, but when the poll was taken it was carried by a majority of 629 votes.

In September, 1929, James Wright and his sons, through whose land the upper cut was to be made, sued the trust for 18,000 pounds compensation. They had presumably already been paid at Government valuation, but when judgement was given six months later they received an additional 2600 pounds. By September, 1930, a pilot channel had been cut through their farm designed to carry excess water only. The expectation was that some years and many floods would pass before the river had widened it sufficiently to take the whole flow.

Meantime the trust thought it a good idea to press on with a similar plan below the highway bridge to straighten the Stewart's Gully course and take the flow directly out to sea, but the critics, vocal as ever, declared they had been promised no more experiments with cuts until the first one proved itself. A fresh storm arose and correspondence columns of newspapers filled with wrathful indignation. The heavy guns of George Gould and *The Press* were wheeled up. The trust's old enemy, H.M. Chrystall, came out fighting, declaring that the lower cut and the manner of its birth were "laid bare as one of the gravest and most wanton offences ever committed by a local body against its ratepayers". Riccarton Borough Council was unanimous in asking the Prime Minister to introduce legislation banning all further expenditure below the railway bridge.

The trust fought back by explaining that both cuts were needed to increase grades in the lower river to move shingle out to sea and clear floods through the lower reaches at a faster rate. Nonsense, replied Chrystall, the only way the shingle would ever reach the sea would be to lower the ocean by 15 feet.*

Throughout the controversy the trust continued with excavating the 2.8km lower cut opposite the Kaiapoi River junction, from the old railway bridge to the sea, plus a 500m tributary cut to bring that river across to the new channel. The sandhills were dug away to make a new direct course to the sea and over 1000 10-tonne concrete blocks, made on site with shingle barged down the river, were set in place to stabilise the mouth.

By June, 1931, notwithstanding a strike by the hundreds of unemployed men working on the scheme, the trust was ready for

*Even today the river does not discharge shingle into Pegasus Bay. Its removal for commercial purposes, plus bank protection upstream, combine to counter current aggradation, and the present shingle "toe" peters out in the vicinity of the Stewarts Gully Sailing Club premises, some distance from the mouth. But like all similar rivers the Waimakariri in flood discharges vast quantities of silt into the ocean.

Last Meeting. *The River Trust (1923-1946) laid the foundations for today's modern control systems on the Waimakariri. This was the last meeting of the trust. Front row: H.W. Harris (chief engineer), F. McArthur, W.W. Brough (secretary) and E.T. Harvey. Middle row: W. Machin, C.W. Hervey, C.T. Aschman (chairman), W.P. Spencer, C. Morgan Williams, M.P., R.M. Macfarlane, M.P. Back row: J. McIntosh, F.W. Freeman, M. Spencer-Bower.* The Star

an official opening. A representative selection of local body and other notables was invited to Kairaki to see the final shovelsful of sand dug away and the river at last flowing straight out to sea.

But on the great day the Waimakariri declined to co-operate, due to a combination of tidal factors and low river flow. In fact the lower cut and the new mouth were both complete failures. The river continued in its old course, more or less where it flows today, but with one notable exception: the 1940 flood, helped along with some timely excavation, abandoned its Brooklands lagoon course and made straight for the ocean, forming the present mouth some distance north of where the River Trust's massive concrete blocks lie buried in the shifting sands.

In 1929 the trust had diverted the Eyre River into the Waimakariri, a move which greatly lessened the risk of flooding in Kaiapoi, and now began completing the southern embankment from Halkett to Harewood and a number of other essential works. The old South Branch running past "The Groynes" was closed off by the construction of the big Harewood crossbank at McLean's Island and numerous other groynes and banks in that vicinity, while across the river the Eyreton groynes on the north bank reduced erosion there.

But a hidden enemy was working in the riverbed itself which in time would destroy the Hay scheme's effectiveness. That enemy had an ugly name: aggradation. Over the years the gradual accumulation of shingle in the lower reaches, on average at least a metre, was in effect lowering the stopbanks by that amount and seriously reducing their holding capacity. Indeed the 1940 flood, although flowing at 500 cumecs below the design maximum, still managed to break free.

The North Canterbury Catchment Board, which assumed control from the River Trust in 1946, was faced with two major floods in its first years. In 1950, when 430mm of rain in 24 hours at Arthur's Pass produced a flood of 3087 cumecs, serious breaks occurred on both sides of Wright's Cut, and Coutts Island and Stewart's Gully settlement had to be evacuated. The great Harewood crossbank was breached in two places. Again on December 27, 1957, while people were still recovering from Christmas, the largest flood ever accurately recorded in the Waimakariri (3990 cumecs) broke free in two places, putting much of the surrounding countryside under a metre or more of water.

Journey's End. *This aerial picture from above the "new" mouth, taken at low tide, shows Kairaki settlement in the foreground and Brooklands lagoon beyond, where the Waimakariri used to flow before discharging into Pegasus Bay two kilometres south of the present mouth. Past the lagoon is Bottle Lake forest park. About a third of Christchurch spreads to the west from the seaside suburbs of North Beach, New Brighton and Sumner. Between the hill suburb of Mount Pleasant, centre, and Mount Herbert behind it, lies Lyttelton Harbour.*

It was becoming increasingly obvious that a major reappraisal was overdue. A thorough hydrological and engineering survey produced comprehensive reports from the chief design engineer (G.D. Stephen), chief engineer (H. Murray Reid), chief soil conservator (R.D. Dick) and a consultant (F.M. Henderson). As a result the board adopted what became known as the 1960 Scheme. This was submitted to the Soil Conservation and Rivers Control Council for approval and in 1962 the Government agreed to pay two-thirds of the 1,639,600-pound cost. Work was to be extended over a 10-year period with major reviews in 1976 and 1982.

In approving the expenditure the Government noted that the new scheme would continue the efforts begun in the last century "to contain one of the country's most unstable and unruly rivers over 36 miles of its course from the gorge to the sea."

The 1960 Scheme was based on a 4730 cumec flood, such as might be calculated to occur once in 100 years, with a generous margin of free-board on the main stopbanks. The result of five years of combined staff work, it recommended many major improvements, including extension of protection and river training as far up as the Gorge Bridge to reduce shingle aggradation. Liberal use was to be made of rock (known as "rock riprap") to confine the dominant flow to a channel and yet allow floods to pass freely between stopbanks to be raised in some places by 1.5m, with a top width of 3.7m to allow vehicles to travel along them.

Whereas the River Trust's area of control covered only the river and its tributaries below the gorge, the Catchment Board was responsible for the whole course from source to sea. For the first time, control could be exerted by soil conservation practices in the river's catchment areas. Experiments in reduced pastoral grazing in the mountains and aerial sowing of grasses augmented the benefits of deer population reduction. These animals had been eating out the forest undergrowth for years and causing increasing run-off in times of heavy rainfall.

Work on the new scheme began in 1963. The three largest floods since then, in 1967, 1970 and 1979 were successfully contained but together inflicted some $300,000 worth of damage to the protective works, mainly to groyne heads and plantings. The problem of aggradation in the lower reaches was mainly controlled by better bank protection in the shingle cliff areas and by commercial removal of shingle.

Unless there is a flood of enormous proportions some time in the future, Christchurch should remain safe from threats of Waimakariri invasion, yet the river remains what a Catchment Board member described as "a sleeping tiger". Thirty years have passed since the tiger escaped, but then he hasn't been trying very hard. In more than half a century no flood has come near the present danger level. The highest was in 1957 at 3990 cumecs and since then only three have exceeded 2000.

Half a century is of course only a brief interval in the Waimakariri's long history. Planners talk in terms of 100 and 200 year floods, but the unpredictable factor is an old fellow called "Hughie", the fabled weatherman in the sky, one of whose favourite haunts could well be over Arthur's Pass. In recent years he has given places like Invercargill, Nelson and South Canterbury more than one "hundred year flood", and he must chuckle at such obscure hypotheses. When he is ready he will doubtless send down the deluge, and if it measures more than 4730 cumecs in the Waimakariri the consequences will certainly be disturbing.

Christchurch people threatened by south bank overflow live and work where their troubled predecessors lived 120 years ago — anywhere along the Avon, including much of the business heart of the city. Few remember that their security depends on the whim of the weather and the massive banks which keep the river away, and some are barely conscious that the Waimakariri even exists. Nevertheless those banks are all that stand between Christchurch and a repetition of 1868 (or worse) when all Fendalton was under water and it was a metre deep in Victoria Square.

Fortunately the reasonable prospect is that the city and North Canterbury, especially including Kaiapoi, will be much better off because of the gains made in the Hundred Years War to pass floods safely to sea. That war is quiescent for the present but river engineers, like sentries on watch, still cannot relax — they have to soldier on for as long as there are cloudbursts in the mountains and the Waimakariri flows across the plains in the general direction of Christchurch.

CHAPTER THIRTEEN

The Waimak At Work

It could never be said that Cantabrians were lacking in enthusiasm when that quality was appropriate to the moment. When they wanted the road to the West Coast in 1865 their noisy clamour forced the Government's hand, and their promotion of a railway to the same destination set new records in persistence. But it was not roads or railways but electricity which drew the largest crowd ever seen at an indoor meeting in Christchurch. This was in January, 1901, in the Great Hall of the Jubilee Exhibition in Manchester Street (later the Civic Chambers). Distinguished citizens on stage (it was said) numbered between 300 and 400. They looked down on a multitude which applauded repeatedly as speakers extolled the benefits of this new and revolutionary source of power for industry and the home (not to mention lighting the streets), generated by the waters of their own Waimakariri River.

This was a time of change. The sweet smell of progress was in the air and the exhibition, celebrating 50 years of Canterbury settlement, had put Christchurch "on the map". Queen Victoria's long reign was nearing its end and a new century beckoned towards a rosy future.

One of its wonders promised to be cheap hydro-electricity. Thoughts of the great potential of Canterbury's larger rivers running to waste were easily transformed into public agitation. The meeting heard from Arthur Dobson, the engineer, how the average summer flow in the Waimakariri was all of one quarter of that of the mighty Niagara Falls — more than ample to serve Christchurch's needs for years to come. He told them the headworks at the Gorge Bridge would cost only 1300 pounds — "a very small sum". The assembled burgesses, carried along on a wave of 20th century euphoria by visions of abundant power (and glory) demanded immediate action.

Since 1888 the City Council had been considering lighting the streets with electricity. But although several business firms had installed generators in the 1890s, the council did nothing about a municipal plant until near the end of the century when it commissioned Arthur Dobson to consider the Waimakariri scheme. He proposed to take water from the river immediately above the Gorge Bridge at the foot of cliffs on the south bank where there was already an intake for Selwyn (later Malvern) County irrigation schemes. He would make several additional intakes at this point, leading into an enlarged tunnel under the bridge approach and from there into a nine km race ending downriver at a spillway and power house.

Dobson's proposal promised a good supply of electricity at moderate cost and it sailed along grandly until it struck Brown's Rock. Immediately a great collective question mark arose over the city. Brown's Rock? Where and what was Brown's Rock?

The truth of course was that this minor eminence lay about 3km below the Gorge Bridge and marked the spot where the Waimakariri-Ashley Water-supply Board had established an intake in 1896 to take water for distribution by race across the plains between the two rivers enshrined in its title. At some earlier stage when the only other requirement from the Waimakariri was for a similar purpose in the Malvern districts, the board had established a right in law to take what it needed at Brown's Rock without interference. If others wanted water they had to return it to the river *above* the bridge.

This was a body blow to the city council's plans. It counter-attacked by persuading the Government to pass "The City of Christchurch Electric Power and Loan Empowering Act 1902", which gave it authority to generate electricity on the Waimakariri and raise loans for the purpose. But even this failed to get round the rights of the Water-supply Board, which proved so formidable in defence of its aqueous privileges that it bought six columns of space in *The Lyttelton Times* so that its consulting engineer, George Phipps Williams, M. Inst. C.E.*, could explain the position to the city. Thus educated, Christchurch backed off and the whole project ground to a halt and was abandoned.

In 1900-01 the council built its first rubbish incinerator ("destructor" as it was then known) which in addition to contributing to the city's early pollution problem, produced enough steam to drive two generators — the first civic venture of a practical nature into electricity production. Nevertheless council retained an interest in the potential of hydro schemes in the back country and some time early in the new century it spent 2500 pounds on a survey of Lake Coleridge. In 1909 an amendment was sought to its empowering act to develop the lake's potential for electric power generation but in the following year Government came on the scene with an announcement that it would take over and itself promote lake power. Electricity from this source became available in 1915.

Still the city council kept the Waimakariri in the back of its mind for two good reasons: (1) because it considered Lake Coleridge would eventually be incapable of supplying the city adequately,† and (2) as a lever to keep Government power charges down. By 1922, frustrating interruptions and shortages in supply brought the council to the point where a decision was taken to engage overseas advice on a proposal to build a dam and power station on the Waimakariri, somewhere in the gorge.

Colonel Brett.

The hydro inspection party *at the Gorge Bridge. Mr Dobson is second from left, and seated at right is F.T.M. Kissell, who eventually became chief engineer to the State Hydro Electricity Department.*
Weekly Press

Arthur Dudley Dobson.

*The man who laid out the original line for the Midland Railway from Springfield to Arthur's Pass. He is abundantly remembered in not one but two mountains in the National Park — Phipps Peak and Mount Williams.

†Coleridge was expected to reach its limit at about 25,000kW. In recent years demand in Christchurch has often exceeded 350,000kW.

Charles B. Hawley, a specialist consulting engineer of Washington, U.S.A., was engaged at a fee of 3300 pounds to bring down a report.

Hawley sent out an engineer, H.V. Schreiber, who in turn engaged a local surveyor-engineer, H.M. Chrystall. In the summer of 1922-23 this pair tramped over the gorge country from end to end and even rowed a boat down the river. They chose a dam site at Otarama about 16km above the Gorge Bridge. There a pontoon was anchored in the river from which water and shingle flows were measured and the bed rock drilled to determine its suitability to carry the weight of the dam. One of the occupational hazards of this job was the wind, which blew down the gorge with such fury that a handrail had to be built round the pontoon deck to keep the men from being blown into the river.

The Mayor of Christchurch at the time was Dr Thacker, whose enthusiasm for the project was unrivalled. He saw the council having so much power to spare it could sell the surplus to the Government for an electrified Midland Railway. The lake above the proposed dam would be 8km long and would be of great recreational value, he said—a home for motor boats, sculling, regattas, and so forth, and a landing place for seaplanes. It would provide ideal picnic spots and would be the perfect place for a "recuperating hospital" where people could come who wanted rest, fresh air and good food. Dr Thacker said from 300 to 500 men were needed to build the scheme and if they worked double shifts the job would be done in about 12 months.

In early February, 1923, several city councillors visited the site, where Schreiber and Chrystall showed them round. They found a well-established tent camp with a mast and a large flag bearing the words, "Christchurch City Council Waimak Electric Power Project". The visitors were shown the site of the dam, proposed to be 30 to 40 metres high, with a powerhouse below, to which the impounded water would be conveyed by a suitable tunnel.

On the pontoon men were at work drilling into the bed rock. Three of the visitors—James and Ellen McCombs and Dan Sullivan—announced themselves members of the Labour Party and had their photographs taken hauling on the rope which worked the drill. Their visit was marred by the usual nor'west gale, which blew clouds of dust about them and was strong enough to carry away some heavy trapdoors lying on the pontoon deck. The three women in the party—Mrs McCombs and her daughter and Miss Sullivan—bravely descended the ladders leading down the cliffs to the riverbed, despite the wind. They must have had their problems.

In the main tent the surveyors explained how the Otarama dam was intended to be only the first in a series. A very large dam could be built at the head of the gorge near the Esk River confluence. This would impound a large lake with enormous potential. Then at intervals during the descent of the gorge there would be smaller dams and powerhouses. Otarama had been selected initially because it was nearest to Christchurch and easily accessible from the railway.

The initial capacity was estimated at 22,500kW, which could be doubled by extensions. The total power available from the river was said to be approximately 140,000kW from four stations.

J.C. Forsyth, who later was to become chief electrical engineer to the Christchurch Municipal Electricity Department, and then managing-engineer, described the development at Otarama as requiring the construction of a gravity-section arch dam providing an effective head of 45 metres. The whole arrangement of the dam, the control gates on it, and the intake to the tunnels carrying the water to the turbines was designed to permit the passage of maximum floods and to prevent the accumulation of shingle where it might interfere with the flow of water to the tunnel intake. Transmission was to be by a 110kV line on steel towers for a distance of 67km to an outdoor sub-station located alongside the Christchurch railway line north of Bryndwyr station. It included a span of 610m over the Kowai River.

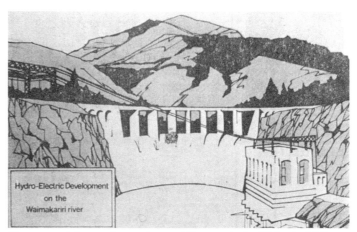

The proposed dam *and powerhouse at Otarama in the Waimakariri Gorge, which were features of the 1922 scheme to generate electricity on the river.*
The Press

During the investigation a gauging station and stage recorder were installed. Early in 1923 the department began the collection of hydrological data, including rainfall at six stations in the catchment area and stream flow measurements at Otarama. After lengthy consideration of the Hawley report, the city council decided to go ahead with the scheme. But this required an amendment to its empowering bill to cover the increased expenditure, and at this point the council found the Government stepping into the picture again, expressing opposition in principle to independent power generation.

The city council soon learned that a long and uncertain political fight lay ahead to get its own way, and when the Government offered electricity from the national grid until 1937 at a price to match Waimakariri power, the council accepted. Unfortunately the price also included exasperating power shortages and the niggling suspicion that a viable scheme and a valuable future asset had been surrendered for an easy alternative which in the end left the council with nothing.

In later days conservationists were pleased that the Waimakariri was spared. It has remained free to roam at will in its gorge unhampered by all those trappings of progress which Messrs Hawley, Schreiber, Chrystall, and Dr Thacker's council members would have imposed on it. There are still no changes in the gorge and certainly no dams, power houses or transmission lines; not even a bridge—or for that matter a recuperating hospital.

All visible traces of the scheme were removed, if not by the investigators, then by the river itself. Ralph Jenkin, who joined the M.E.D. in 1926 and was one of those who visited Otarama regularly to compile statistics, recalls that the gauging station on the cliffside had disappeared when he arrived one day to take water level readings. Since this structure was more than 6m above normal river height, its removal by a flood was in itself a rough indication of the heights the Waimakariri could reach when it was on the rampage. The cable across the river at the dam site had gone also, doubtless the victim of logs coming down the flooded river. The only sign left today of the ambitious "Christchurch City Council Waimak Electric Power Project" is one steel ring-bolt set in the rock wall of the gorge.

Although the Waimakariri is not included in existing Ministry of Energy plans, a current nationwide survey of large-scale hydro-electric potential is expected to include the river as a significant resource, so the day may yet come when the gorge area sees the creation of dams and lakes. These of course would have far-reaching effects. The flood threat to Christchurch and Kaiapoi would be minimised (except in the unlikely event of dam failure—that would be catastrophic), and water could be made more reliably available for large-scale irrigation on the plains. On the other hand the present recreational amenities provided by the river would be seriously curtailed and important salmon spawning areas rendered difficult or unavailable. Possible dam sites are as follows:

Otarama Gorge, 6km above Woodstock, 45m dam, lake extending 4km upriver from Broken River confluence.

Waimakariri Gorge, 4km upriver from Broken River confluence, 37m dam, lake extending to near Esk River confluence.

Waimakariri Gorge top end, 55m dam, lake extending 12km upriver.

Other alternatives include a dam in the Poulter River and another at the Waimakariri Gorge Bridge.

Water for the Plains

The Waimakariri used to flow through Kaiapoi, and occasionally considered the same fate for Christchurch, but what about Rangiora? Has that northern borough any connection with the big river, apart from the local "brooks" which drain into the Cam?

The answer to be truthful is a waggish one, and in the affirmative. The Waimakariri does flow through Rangiora, and moreover has been doing so for nearly a century. The explanation is simple—the water race which crosses Ashley Street near the local hospital carries Waimakariri water and is a legitimate offspring of "Old Man River", one of a network of races supplied from Brown's Rock a couple of kilometres below the Gorge Bridge. These remarkably extend the parent river's 140km length (and its usefulness) into more than 800km of well-behaved little streams distributing stock water to farms scattered over about 500 sq.km of North Canterbury countryside. Similar water extractions serve large areas of Malvern and Paparua counties, and schemes for extensive irrigation, especially north of the river, are the subject of continuing investigation.

Early settlers who took up land of the lighter type on either side of the Waimakariri naturally eyed with interest the abundance of precious water flowing to waste in the river and wondered how this could be turned to their advantage. The notion that open races could be made to work was viewed by many with scepticism. They were convinced that on light and shingly land seepage would take most of the water before it had gone far and evaporation would take the rest. Engineers discovered in due course that provided the volume and speed of water flowing in a race was controlled to strict specifications, silt in the water soon sealed the bed and scouring was not a problem.

The situation on dry Canterbury plains country in a long, hot summer bordered on the desperate. Only the wealthiest farmers could afford the expense of the very deep wells required to reach water. Others had to gather at the river to fill barrels or tanks on drays or sledges, while their women washed the clothes and gave the kids a good scrubbing.

These farmers were only too willing to listen when one of their number, a Kirwee man named Brett, who had experience of irrigation in India, assured them that water from the rivers could

Malvern stockwater scheme. *Working from a tent camp on the bleak hillside workers excavate the channel needed to carry Kowai River water to the plains.* Canterbury Museum

This memorial *to Colonel Brett stands astride the race at Kirwee.*

be brought across the plains successfully in relatively inexpensive open races. His full title was Colonel DeRenzie James Brett, a British army officer in India, who had migrated to New Zealand and bought land at Kirwee (which he named after an Indian town or district where he had served). In 1871 he persuaded the Provincial Government to undertake a survey and an engineer named C.E. Fooks examined the possibilities.

Fooks dismissed the Waimakariri as a water source because he considered getting the race up to plains level would be too difficult; and the Hawkins River because of its low summer flow. But a Waimakariri tributary, the Kowai, would be suitable, he said, with an intake above Springfield. From there to Rolleston, the planned destination of the system, was 52 kilometres, with an average fall of 7.6m to the kilometre. Another engineer, Henry Wrigg, also reported on the proposal, and finally the provincial engineer, George Thornton, studied both documents and designed a dam across the Kowai about six kilometres above Springfield, the water to be carried through a tunnel nearly a kilometre long to open channels on the south bank. Under a Canterbury Water Supply Act a sum of 22,000 pounds was raised and in 1876 work was started with Fraser Bros. as the contractors.

The dam was built on solid rock, rising two metres above water level, while the tunnel was excavated to 1.7m high by 1m wide, double bricked. The half million bricks used were made on the site, from clay dug out of the tunnel and burnt in kilns fired with Kowai coal.

At noon on December 27, 1877, the official opening was held at the sluice gates, with ex-Superintendent Rolleston presiding. The main speech was made by Colonel Brett, who predicted great success for the enterprise. It would, he said, benefit the district in which for a long time the thing they all wanted most had been as scarce as holy water, and it would be as much appreciated for home use as for stock.

On opening day only 3km of race had been excavated and there were delays in extending the system (resulting from the demise of the Provincial Government) until the newly-formed Selwyn County Council was persuaded to take control in

September, 1878. With John Webster as engineer contracts were let for the continuation of the work and its course decided. At Sheffield it was found that the railway station had been built on reserved land and the race had to be taken round the station in a concrete culvert. (But it was close at hand when the engines needed water; the system supplied the railways as long as steam trains were used on the Midland line.)

The main race was divided at Waddington, one branch going along the Coal Tramway reserve to Kirwee and the other along the main road to Darfield. Later the water reached Kirwee, where Colonel Brett, who had promoted the scheme so vigorously, at last enjoyed the fruits of his advocacy. As the supply was turned on in each new section across the parched plains thirsty sheep and cattle "lined up at the bar" to celebrate the change in their particular paddock from "Dry" to "Wet".

By 1889 the ever-increasing network of races needed additional water and so the Waimakariri was tapped at the Gorge Bridge. This was done by building an intake at the foot of rock cliffs immediately above the bridge. The water was then taken through a tunnel under the bridge approach into an open race which joined the main system at Kimberley. This scheme had several defects, one of which was that much of it ran through gravelly ground where percolation losses were severe. Another was that a great flume had to be built to get the water across Deans' gully, and another at Campbell's gully.

The new supply was completed in 1890 and proved invaluable in dry summers, especially when in 1902 floods wrecked the Kowai intake and for a time the Waimakariri had to supply the full load. Possibly because it was asked to do too much the great flume at Deans' gully collapsed in 1908. An immediate start was made with repairs but after a while they ceased and the race was abandoned.

Meanwhile the wrecked dam on the Kowai had been replaced with a new one about 1½km further upriver. Connection with the existing race required 2½km of new channel (some of which had to be blasted through rock), a large flume, and the concreting of several lengths of race skirting the tops of river terraces. When all this was completed it was found that some water could still be accepted from the old intake, and from these two sources (and from a smaller one on the Selwyn River) the extensive water-race system was supplied for many years.

But in the 1950s the growth of pastoral farming on the plains and a run of dry summers saw many properties under-supplied. A decision was taken to reconstruct the Gorge Bridge scheme and in March, 1961, water direct from the Waimakariri was again fed into the existing system at Kimberley. On most Malvern county plains farms today the value of the system is incalculable, providing essential water for stock from about 900km of water-race serving between 400 and 500 sq. km.

Such unanimity of purpose as Malvern demonstrated in these matters was not to grace the early days of water supply on the northern side of the river. The beginnings there were undertaken by private individuals who built a dam in the upper Eyre River above View Hill to serve their immediate needs. The benefits were so obvious that when extensions were proposed the scheme was taken over by the Oxford Road Board, and by 1882 it had spent 2500 pounds extending the races about 20km to near The Warren station out on the plains.

A dry summer or two revealed the unreliability of the Eyre as a source of supply, and the Road Board, and particularly its surveyor-clerk-chairman, John Dobson, began eyeing the Waimakariri. Possible intakes at Woodstock, Rockford, and the Gorge Bridge were considered, with a preference for Rockford, about 6.5km above the bridge. Under Government legislation a Waimakariri-Ashley Water-supply Board was formed in 1892, with John Dobson as chairman, in what some claimed was "a rather perfunctory manner".

On June 8 of that year some members of the board took a small drag behind four good horses for a two-day inspection junket. They looked at a possible Ashley Gorge intake, then moved across country to the Waimakariri at Rockford, where they were joined by Marmaduke Dixon and his son, Marmaduke John. Most were immediately convinced that this

Marmaduke Dixon *photographed soon after he took up Eyrewell.*

was the ideal place from which to take water, although a long tunnel would be needed. Next they went to Brown's Rock, where Dixon explained his ideas. There was agreement that the intake there would be cheaper, but being so far downriver a large part of Oxford county would receive no benefit.

Marmaduke Dixon was one of the district's best known and most colourful settlers, who had been farming beside the Waimakariri for nearly 40 years. He believed Brown's Rock would give a better and more stable water supply than Rockford and cost half as much. His word carried weight, not only because he was widely respected, but also because he alone in the community had practical experience in getting Waimakariri water on to thirsty land.

In 1891, the year before the board was formed, he and his sons Marmaduke John and Richard had of their own initiative made an intake 32km below the bridge near their Eyrewell station. From it they took a stream 3.3m wide and 0.6m deep by a canal nearly 800m long to "raise" the water to the level of the plain, installed a sluice gate to control the flow, and scooped out long races in light and sometimes stony land of little previous use for agricultural or even pastoral purposes.

Although losses by percolation were considerable at the start, silt from the river soon sealed the channels, and within weeks water was pouring on to the parched land. Not only that but in times of flood a heavy silt content was distributed, a valuable side effect on such light land.

Dixon, by then getting on in years, carried out all the design and survey work himself, using Doyne's contour maps for the levels. The intake, canals, border dykes and paddock contouring were all done with two-horse teams and scoops. This is an extract from a letter he wrote about this time for the English mail:

After the flood. *The Kowai River has a reputation for disastrous flooding, and in 1902 it wrecked the water-supply dam, requiring a replacement to be built further upriver.* Canterbury Museum

I am now going on with a small scheme on my own property quite independent of anyone else. It covers about 4000 acres. This is now well in hand and about a fortnight will see the water on the land. We have been at it about 4 or 5 weeks. We have shifted about 6000 yards of slough [outer covering or "overburden"] and got about 300 acres of land ploughed, and hope by the New Year [1892] to have well up to 1000 acres under turnips and green crops. It will not cost me 100 pounds, being my own contractor and engineer.

The effect on the land was astonishing, as a hundred farmers and other interested persons found when they attended a field day arranged by the Dixons shortly before Christmas, 1891. All present were deeply impressed by the transformation and especially by the growth on the irrigated paddocks.

This demonstration stimulated desire for a comprehensive scheme for the whole district, although in many minds there was probably confusion about the difference between irrigation and stock-water. In 1893 an influential body of ratepayers, concerned at the board's preoccupation with Rockford and their talent for procrastination, inspected Rockford for themselves and decided against it. At the next election a new board was elected with John O'Halloran as chairman. One of its first decisions was to proceed immediately with a scheme taking water from Brown's Rock. Ten thousand pounds was borrowed and by November, 1896, the work at the Rock was complete and the main race built to the Eyre River crossing 17km away.

Marmaduke Dixon did not live to see the official opening — he died in the previous year. But a warm tribute to his pioneering work was paid at the ceremony by the Prime Minister, Richard John Seddon, who admitted to considerable experience himself of water-race construction. "King Dick" turned the screws and raised the gate to send water to the intake tunnel, 76 metres long and blasted through solid rock, taking 23 million litres a day out of the Waimakariri and sending it off to destinations as yet unspecified. The engineer, G.J. Webster, was confident water would be flowing through Rangiora within four months. A large flume (later replaced with a siphon) carried the water across the Eyre riverbed.

The official opening was a gala day in the district, with a grand banquet in a marquee at the Rock. A special train from Christchurch gathered passengers en route, puffing its way through Rangiora and Oxford to the Gorge Bridge, from where

The old and the new. *The Waimakariri-Ashley water-race crossed the Eyre River by this bridge or flume which was so often wrecked by floods that in 1913 a 60m concrete siphon was built below riverbed level to provide a secure crossing.*
Weekly Press

passengers had to walk downriver to the ceremony. The official party fared better — they were ferried by wheeled transport from Oxford. As was customary on such occasions the speeches — somewhat like the Waimakariri and the water-race — seemingly flowed on forever, with tributes for all, including the Prime Minister. Replying to his particular verbal pat on the back, the main contractor, J. Thomas, confirmed that there was much more to making a water-race than digging a ditch — his contract had included over 10,000 metres of bridges and 12 of them were over 300 metres long.

On both sides of the river the systems were designed primarily to provide water for stock but before health regulations took a hand extensive use was made of the supply to serve domestic needs. There was probably reliance on a theory that water purified itself as it went. Some farmers along the line attempted to use the water for irrigation but in the main the volume in the races was insufficient and in any case consideration had to be given to the stock needs of others further down the race.

Marmaduke Dixon's scheme had an entirely different concept which provided for flooding of his land between border dykes. Almost all traces of the old pioneer's original works have disappeared with the years, but a visitor today to the Spencer-Bower farm at Claxby, bordering the eastern boundary of Eyrewell State Forest, might be excused if he was to imagine the old innovator at work there still. Certainly his spirit is.

Like his grandfather before him, Marmaduke Spencer-Bower and his sons Richard and Simon have set up an intake and brought inland a volume of Waimakariri water sufficient to service over 800 hectares of light pastoral farm land which in a dry summer would soon burn brown. Instead these paddocks, lush with growth, carry healthy-looking sheep, as one observer noted, "up to their bellies in clover".

The works are on a grand scale, with a massive control gate at the intake, a fish trap, an overflow channel, extensive canals, border dykes, and automatic water gates. Construction required the use of heavy earth-moving machinery working precisely to the survey's fine tolerances. Sufficient water was taken from the river to service a neighbour's farm as well. The cost, of course, was rather more than the original Marmaduke's 100 pounds.

The automatic gates and the border dykes are set 100m apart so that when a gate is closed the race overflows into that section until it is flooded. Then it opens, operated by a valve compressed in a closed tube by the rising water, which then continues on to the next gate. The smooth countryside, over most of which a car could be driven at speed, and which has a fall of 5.7m to the kilometre, is entirely suited to the scheme. But it has an Achilles heel. Like all braided rivers, the Waimakariri scores low points for reliability, and its unpredictable wanderings in a wide bed make the maintenance of a stable supply somewhat uncertain. So far this problem has been overcome, but the sight of Claxby

Brown's Rock intake *on the Waimakariri 3.3 kilometres below the Gorge Bridge was blasted through the rock itself and has in the main proved a reliable point of supply.*

bulldozers working in the riverbed shingle near the intake is not uncommon.

Remembering that Marmaduke Spencer-Bower took over Claxby without a farming background at a time when its 2700ha carried only 1200 sheep, it was a remarkable achievement that by 1970-71, on one-third less land, the flock had been increased to about 10,000 and the wool clip to over 300 bales. Obviously the irrigation scheme has proved its value through the dry summers and Claxby, its green pastures well protected by extensive shelter belts, has long been a good-looking and profitable place, considering what it was 134 years ago when Marmaduke Dixon first set eyes on its scrubby acres.

There are several other extractions of water from the Waimakariri for farm and domestic purposes. One of the oldest of these serves a large area of Paparua County, east of Malvern, and was originally established in 1886. The main race of this scheme has historic associations because it more or less follows one of the river's overflow channels which used to threaten Christchurch, starting near Halkett and heading directly for the city.

Darfield gets its water supply from a well in the riverbed near Bleakhouse, installed in 1969, and in 1977 a piped rural supply was installed which draws water from a gallery system in the riverbed for stock and domestic purposes for an area south of the Eyre River. A similar scheme gets its water from Cooper's Creek for farms north of the Eyre.*

Modern scheme. *Water for irrigation and stock flowing from the Spencer-Bower intake on the north bank of the Waimakariri at Claxby, near Eyrewell State Forest.*

At present about 7000ha of farm land is irrigated on the plains north of the Waimakariri, mostly by pumped groundwater spray, and as mentioned proposals to use river water for large-scale irrigation are a subject of continuing study. Consideration is also being given to a $3m proposal to pipe domestic and stock water throughout the Waimakariri-Ashley region, presumably to replace the water races and avoid their inherent pollution problems.

Siphon opened. *In 1913 these Waimakariri-Ashley Water-supply Board members and officials presided over the opening of the concrete siphon under the Eyre River. From left, Alex Moderate, George Smith (builder), H.T.Cooper, M.J.Dixon, W. McDowell (ranger), G.F.Wayland and James McCormack (secretary and ranger).*

*The Eyre River was named for Edward John Eyre, an early Lieutenant-Governor of New Zealand and a noted Australian explorer, who was once brought to trial in England on charges of excess in quelling an uprising in Jamaica while he was Governor there. He was acquitted, but here is Lord Oliver's crushing description of the gentleman: "A morose introvert; self-centred, headstrong, unteachable, whose injustices and misdeeds might be absolved on a contrite plea of invincible ignorance."

CHAPTER FOURTEEN
The National Park

Among New Zealand's protected mountain and forest regions, Arthur's Pass National Park rates highly for variety and beauty. There are many places to remind the wanderer of Robert Bridges' verse:

> *Beautiful must be the mountains whence you come,*
> *And bright in the fruitful valleys the streams wherefrom*
> *Ye learn your song:*
> *Where are those starry woods? O might I wander there,*
> *Among the flowers, which in the heavenly air*
> *Bloom the year long.*

Most of Arthur's Pass is harsher than that, but there is much to charm the senses in places where buttercups and daisies complement profuse displays of other alpine species. Within the park's borders are the striking contrasts of the Alps — tussock, mountain beech, open riverbed and glaciated peaks in the east contrasting with the densely forested, gorged, often rain-swept and predominantly sombre tones of Westland.

For 120 years the upper Waimakariri valleys, comprising two-thirds of the National Park, have beckoned explorers and sightseers to wonder at Nature's generous gifts to these parts — bush-clad hills rising to the peaks, valley scenes with waterfalls and clear-water streams, and glaciers among the mountain heights. These last, about 40 in number, are relatively small, a last northern echo of Southern Alps splendour, and while they are not what they were, their eventual return to good form is thought to be only a matter of time.

Certainly some or all of these things are found in other national parks (Tongariro, Mount Cook, Fiordland) but in none are they so close to a city of 300,000 people. The result, as might be expected, is that Arthur's Pass is a much-used playground for trampers, mountaineers, skiers, nature lovers, photographers and artists. In addition its scenery delights tourists and travellers on the 40 kilometres of State Highway 73 which run through or alongside the park. In 1883 these were estimated at about 1000 a year; in 1985 sometimes 1500 a day. They do not travel into the upper 24km of the Waimakariri but turn off at Klondyke Corner and follow the Bealey River to Arthur's Pass.

The narrow Bealey valley thus suffers the frequent intrusion of man and his mechanical aids — motorcars, tourist buses, trains, and of recent years heavy diesel locomotives pulling long rakes of trucks bearing West Coast coal to Lyttelton for export. Supplementing the road and railway are those other indications of man's presence — telegraph and power poles, steel pylons

Main street. *State Highway 73 is main street for Arthur's Pass. This view from near the Outdoor Education Centre looks due north to the pass itself at the foot of Goldney ridge.*

The Devil's Punchbowl. *This 150m waterfall, a half-hour walk from the village, is the most popular attraction for visitors to Arthur's Pass.*

taking electricity from east to west, and the collection of buildings which comprise Arthur's Pass village. Not all of these ornament the landscape; and the forest cover, for so long reduced by fire and railway construction gangs, is only now recovering something of its former glory.

The trappings of civilisation set down in this special place could not be expected to please everyone, but they are there and cannot be avoided. People who are too deeply offended must lift their eyes to the mountain tops or move sideways and pitch a tent in the Mingha or the Crow. But at least some of these things have given the Bealey a facility no other Waimakariri valley can offer — easy access for all who come to savour its alpine charms. The 10km road up the valley climbs gently enough to suit even an elderly cyclist — old-timers called it "trotting ground", meaning a grade of no more than 1 in 20. By contrast the sides of the valley, never far apart, climb steeper than 1 in 2, as anyone who has scaled them (and has enough breath left) can confirm. Several tracks lead to summits 1000 metres above the village with splendid views of nearby mountains. The streams which tumble down through the bush sparkle with waterfalls and rapids.

The Bealey valley lies to the north and therefore makes the most of the sun, when it shines. But Arthur's Pass is close to the stormy divide with an annual rainfall of 5000mm (nearly 200in) and an average temperature somewhat less than nine deg.C, so that for most people it is best as a summer place when on good days the sun is warm and the forests cool — and the flowers are at their best.

Thanks to the Arthur's Pass National Park Board and the Lands and Survey Department there is now a variety of attractions for the casual visitor. Half-day walks include the Devil's Punchbowl waterfall, the Bridal Veil Nature Walk, the Dobson Nature Walk, the track to Temple Basin and the forest track in the upper Bealey valley leading to the gorge below Mount Rolleston where avalanche snow collects in winter and earns the inflated title of "Bealey Glacier". Here, and at the head of a similar track in the Otira valley, the mountain-watcher is close by the soaring ramparts of Mount Rolleston itself.

For the more energetic the steep tracks beckon — they lead by two routes from the village to the summit of Avalanche Peak, from near the pass to the skifields, and from the valley to Mounts Cassidy, B'limit (Con's track), Aicken and further

Oasis in the bush. *Arthur's Pass township seen from the Bridal Veil Falls lookout, with Rough Creek defile and Mount Bealey at right.*

down to Mount Bealey. The upper sections of these tracks traverse country more than 1500 metres high and require stout footwear and some experience, especially in winter and spring when there is avalanche danger, but they reward the tramper-climber with magnificent views, again with Mount Rolleston as the centre-piece. At these heights a weather-eye must be kept towards the north-west from where sudden storms come; and if the clouds close in a compass and map in the pack are comforts in time of need.

Down in the valley there is also much to do. Arthur's Pass has a population of about 100 and there are shops, a restaurant, motels, a youth hostel, several club lodges, an outdoor recreation centre, and of course the cluster of holiday homes. Here too is Park headquarters and information centre where an obliging staff have a gift for putting people on the right track. In this building is a museum worthy of more than just a wet-day visit. There is a fine collection of pictures from the past and a much-admired audio-visual display which visitors watch cheek-

Three "senior" trampers *on a first visit to the upper Waimakariri, here posed before Carrington Peak, found it difficult to believe that the prominent diagonal crack on the face was a common ascent route. From left, Bert Thompson, Jack Hutchinson, Dick Innes.*

by-jowl with one of Cobb's coaches sidelined by the railway in 1923. Park rangers organise holiday programmes featuring guided walks, lectures and films. There is a large public shelter nearby, and a visit to the picturesque little alpine chapel is a "must".

While thousands travel on wheels up the Bealey valley to enjoy the delights of Arthur's Pass, others who want to get away from it all walk up the main Waimakariri bound for quiet places and unspoiled scenery. The first move to make these more distant regions accessible to the public came in 1881 when the Upper Waimakariri Road Board, prodded by its chairman, John D. Enys of Castle Hill station, generated enough enthusiasm to spend 100 pounds on a track to the White River glaciers about 24km above Bealey. A local farmer-contractor named George O'Malley took charge of construction. The track was required to be of "a substantial nature, sufficiently well-formed to allow a lady to ride to the glaciers with ease and comfort". The Road Board's action was probably inspired by a growing appreciation of the Southern Alps, especially Mount·Cook, as tourist attractions.

History does not record how many ladies rode "with ease and comfort" to see the glaciers, but there were enough to justify additional expenditure five years later on track improvement when the Road Board, the Selwyn County Council, and the local hotelkeeper put up another 45 pounds. A road foreman named Murray often guided the tourists in subsequent years. "That peak there is Mount Greenlaw," he would say, pointing to the mountain up the valley which was later named Mount Harper. An early Waimakariri climber, George Dennistoun, thought it ought to be named Mount Murray, "partly to honour the veteran, but chiefly to ensure that he did not misinform future visitors". The real Greenlaw is three kilometres away to the south.

The hotelkeeper mentioned was James O'Malley (thought to be no kin to George), who took over the licence in 1882. According to James McNeish in his book *Tavern in the Town,* O'Malley was a teetotaller and ex-police sergeant who stood six feet tall, bearded and muscular. McNeish says among other things O'Malley used to anticipate floods and cater for his marooned guests by bringing in coach loads of stage girls to entertain them.* He certainly was responsible for numbers of people going up to see the glaciers, and could be called one of New Zealand's first entrepreneurs to cash in on the tourist potential of mountain regions.

These early visitors rode horses to the White-Waimakariri junction where in the words of Alexander Pope, "Hills peep o'er hills, and Alps on Alps arise!" This 14 or 15km journey is over gradually narrowing shingle reaches between forested slopes above which tower Murray's "Greenlaw" and other peaks. The Waimakariri hereabouts differs from its companion Canterbury rivers to the south which have vast beds lying between mainly bare hills, all built on a tremendous scale. By contrast the upper Waimakariri runs in a cosier valley, well wooded for most of its length.

To the tramper burdened with a heavy pack it is far enough from the road to the real mountains, but it is only half the distance of comparable journeys in southern valleys. The goals set ahead by perspiring backpackers (the next spur, the next creek, the next ford) come easier in the Waimakariri, happily with many changes of scenery—up the Crow to Mount Rolleston, the Greenlaw Creek to Mount Harper, and the main river to Campbell's pyramid; the rocky pinnacles of Guinivere top the bush at right, Mount Isobel dominates the view up the White, and finally Carrington Peak stands alone framed by beech trees—all these come gradually into view like slowly changing colour slides on a big screen upriver.

Some of the early tourists, persuaded to stay longer, may have walked further into the Waimakariri above the White River junction. They would be well rewarded, for within easy reach there is an idyllic place in which to while away an hour or a day. It was here that Edward Dobson camped in 1865, along with Jack Smith (the contractor) and his workmen and began a track towards Campbell Pass. The beech forest is by this time thinning

*But he also says James, not George, cut the track.

Explorer, botanist, surveyor. *This 1897 photograph taken at Bealey shows (left to right) Charles Douglas, legendary South Westland explorer; Dr Leonard Cockayne, noted botanist and "father" of Arthur's Pass National Park; and George Roberts, pioneer surveyor. In 1901 Dr Cockayne persuaded the Government to gazette two proposed parks in the region, from which the present national park evolved.* Alexander Turnbull Library

with altitude, but enough remains to charm the loiterer. There is a waterfall or two on the rocky bluffs, far up against the sky, and grassy flats on which to rest or camp. With luck a pair of blue ducks may be seen on the river. And the whole is dominated by the soaring precipices of Carrington Peak, climbing sheer, huge and close for over 1000m from the river's edge.

From the White-Waimakariri junction, a delightful camping place among the trees where now stands Carrington Hut, the main river runs NNE to Mount Rolleston, while its almost equal tributary, the White, heads off in the opposite direction. Five miles above the junction, along a track still called O'Malley's, lie the White glaciers which were so popular last century. They were described thus by Julius Haast, the Provincial Geologist, after his visit in 1867:

About half a mile from the head of the valley, at an altitude of about 6000ft, a magnificent sight is offered to the traveller by a large glacier broken up into the wildest and strangest forms, actually overhanging a perpendicular rocky wall about 1000ft high, and in one spot where a small rib could form, it descends for some distance in the shape of a gigantic icicle. During our descent of the valley, we had the rare sight of an enormous icefall of a portion of this glacier, pushed over the cliff and precipitated into the valley with a tremendous noise, warning us not to approach too near its channel, where, close by, on alpine meadows, a rich harvest of plants was obtained.

In the original plans for the National Park two areas were set aside for conservation, Bealey National Park of 37,000ha and Otira National Park of 6885ha. These came into existence in 1901 mainly through the efforts of Dr Leonard Cockayne, a Christchurch botanist who had developed a keen interest in the district, which he called "a fine example of transalpine flora transition". He bought a section at Kelly's Creek in the Otira park and spent his holidays there, becoming so enamoured of the country on both sides of the Alps that he was determined at all costs to have it maintained *in statu quo.*

In 1898 Cockayne travelled up the Hawdon River, a Waimakariri tributary, to Walker Pass, and also extensively in the Poulter River valleys, accompanied by his son. They swagged in to Worsley Pass, to Lake Minchin and almost to Minchin Pass, and up the Thompson Stream to one of the saddles overlooking the Taramakau River. He was ecstatic about the charms of these valleys:

... Suddenly the wonderfully beautiful Lake Minchin burst into view. I have seen many lovely spots in the New Zealand mountains, but this lake, I really think, is the most beautiful of all. It lay solitary at our feet, its surface a mass of white-tipped waves; on its two sides mountains covered with green forest, pierced in many places by grey rock, rose wall-like for several thousands of feet; and for background was a huge two-peaked hill, snow-capped and storm-swept. A fine waterfall fell in three leaps some 200 or 300 feet from the mountain on our left, and in the foreground, in the lake itself, were two little islands,

exquisite with their covering of green Veronicas and white-leaved Olearias.

On the gravelly flat at the top end of the lake, Cockayne found Cesmisia blooms over four inches in diameter with leaves 18 inches long. Later, in the Thompson Stream valley, nearing the divide, he was entranced by a wealth of vegetation surpassing anything he had seen previously in New Zealand.

The large herbaceous Senecio was in full bloom, a white sheet covering the hillside and dazzling as does a snowfield. Here, too, was the huge buttercup Ranunculus traversii, a plant seldom recorded — soft-yellow in colour, with kidney-shaped leaves, and having 20 to 30 blooms on a stout stem a foot or more in height.

Following a visit to the upper Waimakariri and the glaciers about the turn of the century, Cockayne was more than ever convinced these beauties must be protected. He enlisted the sympathies of the M.P. for Ellesmere, Mr Montgomery, and the Minister of Lands, Mr McKenzie, and in due course the two parks were gazetted.

But considerable damage had already been done in the Arthur's Pass area and much more was to come. The greater part of the vegetation up to 4000ft had been burned off by a fire deliberately lit during the 1890 survey for the railway. The creation of reserves was a step in the right direction, but it provided no machinery whereby protection could be enforced. Throughout the railway and tunnel building period, extending over nearly 20 years, demands for shoring timbers and firewood saw nearby bush areas much reduced, and another fire in 1920, said to have been started by a drover, caused further damage. To top off this saga of despoilation was the mischief caused by thousands of excursionists brought to the Pass on special trains in the 1920s, many of whom went home with arms full of local plant life, most of which had no chance of survival. This was the catalyst which led indirectly to the control systems of today.

In 1912 the first mountaineers pushed into the Waimakariri headwaters and the peaks began to fall, but during World War I the region was rarely visited. Interest was reawakened in 1920 when Dr F.W. Hilgendorf and his son Charles began a series of Christmas holiday visits based on camps at the White junction. Discovering that existing maps of the area were both sketchy and inaccurate, the Hilgendorfs determined that for the 1924-25 vacation they would explore as much country as possible with a view to compiling a better map. Accompanied by some interested friends they spent 10 days at Camp Corner making expeditions to vantage points in the neighbourhood. Dr Hilgendorf came armed with pedometer, chain, compass, aneroid, rope, and ice axes, with a packhorse for transport.

Dr Frederick W. Hilgendorf, *professor of agricultural botany at Lincoln College and first director of the Wheat Institute, who in the 1920s led the rediscovery of Waimakariri headwaters and with his son Charles made the first raft trip through Waimakariri Gorge. At right,* **Charles Hilgendorf** *(later Sir Charles), who joined his father in his exploration and rafting adventures. He made the first ascent of Carrington Peak and was on the first Three Pass trip to Hokitika. A successful mid-Canterbury farmer, he was also chairman of the New Zealand Meat Board.*

One of the key points he set his heart on was the striking peak in the upper Waimakariri shown on the map as Mount Armstrong (later renamed Carrington Peak). The party climbed the slopes beyond Campbell Pass but stopped short of the final pyramid when Dr Hilgendorf became unwell. Charlie, then 16 years old, continued upward to make the first ascent alone while the remainder rested. Concerned about his father during the descent he hurried ahead to enlist the help of three young men from Christchurch who were camped down in the valley. As they later explained their participation was in no way a rescue exercise, for the patient recovered and was able to reach camp unaided.

The three young men were Ivan Tucker and Roger and Ainslie Chester, who had quite independently seized on the idea of visiting the upper Waimakariri. They were old school chums who often went swimming in the river near the "Groynes". One summer day while sunning themselves one of their number sat up abruptly and asked where the river at their feet came from. None really knew, so they decided on a youthful voyage of discovery. With a blanket each and stores from mum's pantry stuffed into sugarbag packs, they took the train to Cora Lynn and marched upriver. Camp 1 was at Klondyke Corner, Camp 2 at the Big Bend and Camp 3 at the White junction. From there they made day trips to the glaciers and waterfalls, and when they had their fill of scenery they went home, leaving the Hilgendorf party in possession.

On their way out the threesome met two other young men coming in. They were Gerard Carrington and Brian Wyn-Irwin, two Christ's College friends who were equally keen to investigate the mysteries of the upper Waimakariri.* Carrington in particular was concerned with the inaccuracy of existing maps, and determined to do something about it. They found the Hilgendorf tent pitched at Camp Corner and erected their own nearby. When Dr Hilgendorf and his party returned from an expedition to Harman Pass he and Carrington soon discovered each other and put their heads down over sketch maps, their interests joined on common ground.

Upper Waimakariri. *This autumn view upriver from Mottram Peaks ridge looks towards the White River junction and Harman Pass, with main divide peaks Isobel (left, 2045m) and Campbell (right, 1844m). A tiny section of White River shows below Campbell near where Carrington Hut is sited.*
John Sampson

Gerard Carrington is widely regarded as the founder of the Canterbury Mountaineering Club, but he was in fact much more concerned with exploration than with climbing peaks. In his day he was the upper Waimakariri's most dedicated advocate, devoted to the task of laying bare its secrets and focussing public attention on its scenic beauties.

He set the ball rolling in 1925 when he wrote a letter to *The Press* over the pseudonym of "Cora Lynn", which many an unknowing reader thought was a lady with a crusade on her mind. The letter drew attention to the existence of a wonderful mountain playground within easy travelling distance of Christchurch. Other correspondence followed and Carrington was invited to write a special article on the subject. The result was that interest grew to the point where the Canterbury Progress League promoted an expedition to the region so that members could see these wonders for themselves.

In spite of his youth (he was only 19 at the time), Carrington was a gifted organiser. The expedition, 16 strong, disembarked from a crowded excursion train at Bealey corner on Good Friday, 1925. As one newspaper described the occasion, "the party did not comply in all respects with the standard specification of alpinists. In some, silver threads were noted to have long since ousted the gold when hats were doffed in response to the cheers of the excursionists".

The train gone, the mostly new-chum party began the blister-raising tramp over the river shingle to Camp Corner, 15 kilometres upriver. They were G.N. Carrington (leader), S.D. Meares (deputy-leader), C.S. McCully, E.J. Marriner, H.W.

*All five became foundation members of the Canterbury Mountaineering Club.

153

Gourley, A.J. Derbidge, E. and N. Treleaven, W.T. Edmonds, L.P. Fuller, F.L. Hutchinson, C.E. Baynon, E.F. Dollimore (representing the Tourist Department), and three newspaper representatives, H.A. Martin *(Press)*, A.G. Sleeman *(Times* and *Star),* and O.A. Gillespie *(Sun).*

In the frenetic Christchurch newspaper world of the day "Scoop" Sleeman enjoyed a reputation for lively enterprise. This time he stole a march on his competitors by taking pigeons up the river and sending despatches by air back to his newspapers in the city. In this way the public read about the expedition's adventures while it was still in the mountains,

---

Great Shakes

As in any small and isolated community, a social gathering at Arthur's Pass involved practically every resident. On the night of May 9, 1929, a dance was in progress in the hall and virtually everyone in the village was there. In those days square dances were an essential item on the programme, and none was more popular than the Lancers. This vigorous affair had the hall rocking as the men, mostly big, burly railway workers, swung their partners ever higher as they reeled round to bursts of laughter and squeals of mock terror from the ladies. Those watching began to think things were getting almost too boisterous — it was one thing to *talk* about bringing the roof down, but quite another ...

The sharp jolt bulged the walls and in places the roof dropped alarmingly. Someone shouted "Earthquake!" The floor heaved and dancers fell in jumbled heaps. Then the lights failed.

Laughter turned to screams of real alarm as people struggled in the dark to escape into the open. They streamed out the doors only to be assailed by new sensations. The mountains looming overhead in the black night were alive with the thunder of great boulders crashing down through the bush. The noise was deafening. Soon everything was hidden in a pall of dust as thousands of tons of rock, loosened from the tops, poured into the valley. Fearful residents, not knowing what to do next, huddled under verandahs to shelter from the rain which had begun to fall.

It was a long and cheerless night. The men lit a great bonfire and dispelled some of the anxiety with warmth and light, but every few minutes another tremor started fresh avalanches of rock. And so it continued, all through the night, with none knowing what might happen next.

When daylight came the distraught condition of many of the residents prompted a general evacuation, and a special train was ordered up from Springfield. It came slowly up the valley, feeling its way, until track damage forced a halt a mile short of the village. Some of the more distressed women were ferried down the line by jigger; the remainder walked.

At Christchurch the refugees had to run the gauntlet of reporters from the city's four highly competitive newspapers, some of which made it seem that Arthur's Pass had been completely wrecked after its "night of appalling horror". But in the cold light of day the damage was not too bad. Most chimneys were down, some buildings awry, the road was blocked by massive slips, and the railway line needed repairs.

The greatest damage appeared to be to the mountains themselves. The centre of the earthquake was estimated to be a few miles along the main divide from Arthur's Pass, where at Taruahuna Pass a whole mountain split in two, and half fell into the upper Otehake River, completely blocking it. This peak was later named Falling Mountain.

As the weeks passed and the worst damage in the village was repaired, Arthur's Pass and the National Park returned to normal, showing only innumerable scars on the mountainsides as evidence of the great shake. There was no damage to the railway tunnel, but it was months before slips were cleared and the main highway reopened for traffic. There are many who think increased growth of shingle debris in the river valleys began with this earthquake, accentuated in later years by deluge floods.

Another severe earthquake occurred at the Pass in 1943. Jack Ede, long-time mountaineering club member who was in the club's lodge at the time, recalls the double brick chimney crashing into the lounge, fortunately without injuring him or any of his several companions.

---

following Carrington to such spell-binding marvels as the White glaciers, the Waimakariri waterfalls, and even to the top of ice-clad Whitehorn Pass.

Each newspaper vied with its rivals to bring vivid on-the-spot impressions to its readers. It was not surprising that for several days the Canterbury public was almost buried in an avalanche of words, extolling in the most extravagant terms the rosy future of the upper Waimakariri as a major New Zealand tourist attraction. An example, scribbled by Sleeman on tissue paper and rushed off to the *Times* by pigeon post:

On all sides mountain peaks look down in stately elegance, huge monsters of rock and ice. Sheer walls of rugged rock face the alpinist — nature's protection against man and his desecrations. It was a day of revelations to the expedition, and not one man made any effort to conceal the fact. The grandeur of the country beggared description, but praises rang out everywhere, for here are wonders which are seen but once in a lifetime. "I have travelled a lot, but I have never seen anything more beautiful," said one member of the expedition. "This is a place for the poet and the artist. However much we laymen may appreciate these beauties, we cannot flatter them. This is one of nature's bounties, and I am sure there is not a more beautiful spot in the world."

Al Sleeman lived up to his nickname with another "hot" story describing how Charles McCully alarmed his companions by setting out for the White glaciers on his own. When he wasn't back after an hour a search party was sent to look for him, without success. Fortunately all ended well — in due course Mr McCully loomed out of the falling snow, blowing hard on his hands, his personal adventure foiled by the arrival of a sudden storm.

The expedition's report to the Progress League recommended that a hut be built at Camp Corner, that an access track be made up the south bank of the river, that the Railway Department be asked to establish a flag station at the Bealey, and that an accurate map of the region be prepared and published. In turn the Progress League pressured the Tourist Department, but the department dragged its feet, plainly unconvinced that it should spend money on such a project. When a stalemate seemed likely, the Christchurch Tramping Club (mainly Carrington) offered to build the hut if the department would pay for the materials — it promptly agreed and opted out with a grant of 50 pounds. The vouchers came to 60 pounds, 17 shillings and ninepence, whereupon it stretched a point and gave another 10 pounds, but drew the line at the 17 shillings and ninepence.

Carrington was drowned soon after and the Progress League turned to other things; but tramping club stalwarts slowly and painfully got some kind of a hut built over the next three years. The upper Waimakariri prepared to receive not hordes of tourists, but a procession of energetic young Christchurch fellows dedicated to the rebirth of exploration and mountaineering.

Meanwhile there were developments at Arthur's Pass. Back in 1915 a Christchurch school teacher, W.A. Kennedy, had built

Inquisitive. *Keas are the alpine comedians of the park — but they also enjoy shredding tents and car windscreen rubber. This one thinks a tramper's sock could be a tasty morsel.* A.P.N.P. archives

The big attraction. *First call for most visitors to Arthur's Pass is the 150m Devil's Punchbowl waterfall, a short distance from the village. It was named in 1864 by Arthur Dobson. This picture was taken in drenching windspray generated by the fall in one of its more vigorous moods.*

Left: *Looking north along the "main street" of Arthur's Pass village after a fall of snow.*

Below: *Snow blankets the Bealey River flats in this picture of Arthur's Pass from the slopes of Mount Bealey.*

The highway *climbs steeply to sidle across the great slip below Hills Peak and then begins a scary descent into the Otira Gorge. After an unsure crossing of the slip (extreme right) the road descends the famous Zigzag, crosses Candy's Creek — a notorious trouble-spot after heavy rain — and continues (lower left) down the "one-way" section hewn from solid rock.*

Above: *As the sun rises over the Pacific Ocean, salmon anglers try their luck where the Waimakariri ends its journey from the mountains to the sea, and the fish begin theirs in the opposite direction.*

Left: *Among many activities on the lower Waimakariri is the sport of jetboat sprinting, in which competitors who are quick of eye and hand drive their specially-built boats at high speed through narrow, twisting waterways.*

Below: *Two yachting clubs based near the Waimakariri's mouth enjoy an extensive reach of tidal river for their sport, which includes friendly contests between the clubs.*

Credits. Except where acknowledged, all colour pictures are from the author's 35mm Pentax camera. The majority were taken on Kodak Ektachrome film, from which prints were made by Certus Cibachrome Productions, Christchurch. Other prints by Hanafins and Viko. Colour separations by Colortronic Litho Ltd., Christchurch. The book's design, setting, plates and printing by Logan Print Ltd., Gisborne, with binding by S.I. McHarg Ltd., Christchurch.

Jack's Hut people. *None surpassed Guy and Grace Butler in enjoyment of Arthur's Pass alpine delights in the 1920s. They bought Jack's Hut on the road approaching the pass and spent as much time there as they could. Among other things Guy sparked legislation to adequately protect National Park flora, while Grace was a talented artist whose paintings of local scenery were much admired. Their three daughters grew up with the sights, sounds and scents of the bush—Margaret's Tarn is named after one, while another, Grace Adams, wrote a delightful book on the district simply entitled* Jack's Hut.

The first Carrington Hut, *featuring the chimney that almost never worked properly in a nor'west gale, or for that matter in any gale.*

the first holiday home there, to which he brought a succession of senior pupils on educational forays. Other people of like mind followed, including Guy and Grace Butler, and when railway construction work finished in 1924 and the department offered surplus buildings for sale, several huts were purchased and set up as holiday baches. One of these, bought by Andrew Anderson, served for years as an Arthur's Pass base for his many climbing friends. The Pass was developing as a desirable vacation centre. Butler took over the workers' hostel and converted it into an accommodation house where visitors could stay. Soon there was a nucleus of permanent and periodic residents who developed a strong sense of community in the little settlement among the mountains. They organised tidying-up operations to remove some of the more unsightly remains of railway construction and began a movement to counter the depredations of the thousands of day visitors pouring in on railway excursions.

Their concern found expression in a letter written by Butler in 1928 to a number of organisations he thought would be interested. The result was a public meeting in Christchurch on April 3, 1928, which decided unanimously to press the Government for the appointment of a board to control Arthur's Pass National Park. Thus prompted, the Government decided to legislate not just for Arthur's Pass but for all such regions and came up with the Public Reserves, Domains and National Parks Act of 1928.

None of the original resident protagonists found his name on the new board when it was constituted, a circumstance which led to some bitterness at the time, and Arthur's Pass village was temporarily excluded from the park. The new boundaries also excluded the Poulter and other eastern valleys but gained in the west; in total a reduction from 67,600ha to 48,600ha. The act came into force on April 1, 1929, and the board met for the first time on October 29.

National Park Board *members on a tour of inspection view distant reaches of the Poulter River. From the Waimakariri junction to Foy Pass on the main divide is a journey of nearly 50km.* Deryck Morse

The new Park Board members were A.D. Dobson (discoverer of the pass 65 years earlier), F.W. Freeman, G. Harper, W.K. McAlpine, W. McKay, Sir R. Heaton Rhodes, R. Speight, E. Teichelmann and R. Twyneham, with the following *ex officio* members: W. Stewart (Canterbury Commissioner of Crown Lands) (chairman), the Westland Conservator of Forests, the Mayor of Christchurch and the Mayor of Greymouth. For a good proportion of these gentlemen personal contact with their far-flung domain was limited to what they could see from train or motorcar. The remote valleys and distant peaks remained for years entirely unaffected by the board's assumption of sovereignty, as did the increasing numbers of climbers and trampers who were exploring the more remote regions of the park, bringing the maps up-to-date and conquering the mountain summits. For more than 10 years board control and expenditure were centred almost exclusively on the township and immediate environs.

Charlie Warden, a village resident with an appropriate surname, was the first ranger. The board, suffering as it was (in spite of its influential membership) from severe financial anaemia, could afford to pay him only ten shillings a week for his services, so that what he did at the start was predominantly a labour of love. Even by 1933-34 total income was only 120 pounds for the year, most of which came from rents and hunters' licence fees. But still much useful work was done in the Bealey-Otira region, improving the appearance of the village, forming tracks to provide walks for day visitors and to give access to nearby peaks, encouraging the development of skiing at Temple Basin, establishing a footbridge to give access to the Devil's Punchbowl, acquiring and improving the old schoolhouse as a public shelter and hall, and building rock gardens. Much of this work was done by volunteers, especially the industrious chairman of the board's works committee, Dr Bill McKay, of Greymouth, with assistance from honorary rangers such as Bob Scott (of Scott's Track) and Bill Frazer, of Otira.

The only huts built during this period were the Carrington Memorial Hut in the upper Waimakariri (by the Canterbury Mountaineering Club) and the first ski hut in Temple Basin (by the Christchurch Ski Club), in 1928 and 1933 respectively. For this latter project the Board found 50 pounds from its meagre finances to help with the construction of a track to the skifields, and in 1931 five pounds to pay Roger Chester for reopening O'Malley's track in the upper Waimakariri. That same year Tom Beckett and Pat Bayley cut a path from the Anticrow River round the outside of the Big Bend, which removed the necessity for two fords of the main river, but increased the length of the journey. This became known as "The BB Trail", from the initials of its creators, or from the name of the bend, or (as it fell into disrepair) from the expletives of upended backpackers. Beckett could find no evidence that O'Malley had ever benched a track over this forested section.

Charlie Warden stayed with the Board until 1937, and in the next eight years four rangers were appointed to the position.

155

These included Evan Wilson, a noted climber, and Con Hodgkinson, a well-known deer culler and guide. At home in the wilds, Hodgkinson spent much of his time patrolling the more remote valleys dealing with problems of deer and chamois. In the year before his death he cut a new route up the spur of Mount Cassidy, later named Con's track in his memory.

In 1950 a new era dawned for Arthur's Pass National Park. Until then the ranger's duties were divided between the board and the Tawera County Council, and the board's assets were almost nil—in the words of one member "we owned half a man and half a wheelbarrow, but the shovel was all ours". Revenues were still pitiful, but the 1950s changed all that. A new ranger was appointed full time, a former wildlife officer named Ray Cleland, who immediately breathed new life into the enterprise. His arrival coincided with the appointment of a new secretary, Deryck Morse, a Mountaineering Club member with a wide personal knowledge of the park. Board members at this time included Lance McCaskill, a "live wire" who joined in 1948 and for the next 19 years was a persistent motivator. He was ably assisted by long-serving T.N. ("Nui") Robins, representing mountaineering and skiing interests, Ernest Adams (the cake man), representing village residents, John McAlpine, local sheepfarmer (later Sir John), George Lockwood, veteran Temple Basin skier, and an able chairman in Tom Preston, the Canterbury Commissioner of Crown Lands.

As revenues increased, the poverty-ridden earlier years were forgotten. The 1952 National Parks Act redirected all rents from the township and from Bealey Spur into the board's coffers, and a growth in regular government grants enabled capital expenditure to begin on new projects. The board's first vehicle, a Landrover, was purchased, a new ranger's house and workshops were built, "Mountain House" was bought and renovated in anticipation of additional staff, and work was started on the museum. The ski clubs extended their buildings in Temple Basin and the alpine club and mountaineering club their huts and bivouacs in several valleys. The board itself was now able to get into the hut-building business, erecting six new units in eastern valleys, and tracks generally were extended and upgraded.

In 1980 a new Parks Act set out altered policy, management and administrative roles. A newly-constituted North Canterbury National Parks and Reserves Board found itself mainly concerned with policy matters, while the Lands and Survey Department took over day-to-day administration and

Picturesque. *The interdenominational chapel at the Pass and its simple belltower, photographed against a background of bush-covered hills.*

management. Between them they were required to produce a policy and management plan for approval by the National Parks and Reserves Authority. Development of facilities and programmes for visitors, especially school children attending mountain education courses, has been greatly accelerated since the new system was introduced. Since Ray Cleland's day the chief rangers have been J.H. Sullivan, 1958-59; Peter Croft, 1959-77; and Ian Blackmore, 1977-1986.

In remote valleys much work has been done in the provision of tracks and huts. There are now about 40 huts, bivouacs and shelters, providing accommodation of varied style and adequacy. The more notable of these have been the board's responsibility; others have come from the clubs and the Forest Service. All are available to the tired tramper provided when he or she arrives there is still room.

And this, of course, is the problem. Where once a handful of keen young men spent the weekend in the upper Waimakariri, now it seems to swarm with people of both sexes and all ages bent on securing bunks in the palatial "Carrington Hotel". Sometimes the crush is too great, when the alternative for the overflow is to bed down among the bushes—pleasant enough when the weather is fine, but also a treat for the local sandflies.

One of the most valued efforts by board staff has been the provision of "escape" tracks in most valleys, enabling flood-trapped parties to exit without having to ford the main river. In other places wire bridges have been erected, a notable one being the Clough cableway at the White-Taipoiti junction.

Reasonably fit and experienced trampers can choose from a variety of beautiful and interesting valleys in which to spend a day, a weekend, a week, or even a cherished annual holiday. They find infinite variety in the great distances of the Poulter valleys (walking distance from the car is considerably more in the Poulter than in the Waimakariri). There are large forests, abundant flora, and gems like Lake Minchin. Access is via the Andrews Stream and over Casey Saddle, or by the lower Poulter, and those wanting to cross the divide to the Taramakau River have a choice of passes. An interesting round trip on the Canterbury side is to cross Worsley and Walker passes and return down Hawdon River.

Across the Polar Range from the Hawdon lies the Edwards valley, which some say is the most beautiful in the park. Taruahuna Pass at its head leads past Falling Mountain to the Otehake and thence to the Taramakau.

The Mingha valley, well-trodden these days in February when coast-to-coast endurance runners pass through, is another attractive valley worth taking at a slower pace while enjoying the walk over Goat Pass and down the Deception to Otira River.

A six kilometre walk up the main Waimakariri from Klondyke Corner brings the tramper to the Crow valley, dominated by Mount Rolleston's spectacular south face, with the Crow Icefall tumbling down from the summit rocks. There is a direct route from the upper valley over the range to Arthur's Pass, making an energetic round trip.

Anticrow hut. *A few years ago fire destroyed this cosy Mountaineering Club hut in the Waimakariri valley near Anticrow River. It was a base for climbs on Mount Gizeh and a half-way house on the way to Carrington Hut. There are about 40 huts and bivouacs scattered throughout the Waimakariri headwaters built by climbing clubs, Lands and Survey, the Forest Service and the Park Board.* John Sampson

Wooded walks *in both Arthur's Pass National Park and Craigieburn Forest Park richly reward keen trampers and picnickers.*

Opposite the Crow valley, as might be expected, is the Anticrow, which can lead the moderately experienced to the summit of Mount Gizeh without too much difficulty. This high outlier is a splendid viewpoint from which to study the upper Waimakariri topography.

And in that territory there is much to see and do. Carrington Hut is an ideal base for day trips: up the White to the glaciers and Neville Barker Memorial Hut, up the Taipoiti to Harman Pass, and the Waimakariri itself past Carrington Peak to the Waimakariri Falls. For the experienced all three can lead to further destinations across passes and cols, or to peaks like Murchison, Davie, Isobel, Carrington, Armstrong and Rolleston, while Harper and Speight can be climbed from either side, the Waimakariri or the White.

In the western side of the park where vegetation, weather and terrain are strikingly different, there is a parade of typical stream patterns extending from Harman Pass in the south to Harper Pass in the north, draining into the Taipo, Rolleston, Otira and Taramakau rivers. Practically all these give reasonable access to the main divide with varying degrees of difficulty, and cross into Waimakariri tributaries.

The diverse attractions of these valleys and mountains provide something for everyone who visits the park — the sightseer passing through by car, the nature lover looking for an entertaining ramble, the rover exploring new horizons, or the mountaineer reaching for the heights. Those who plan the more energetic of these occupations are wise if they first make contact with the rangers at Park Headquarters, where they can get helpful advice and maps which show routes, tracks and huts.

The final paragraph relating to Arthur's Pass National Park in the 1965 edition of *National Parks of New Zealand* is appropriate. It reads: "The future of this park is bright. The snowy mountains look down benignly on holiday throngs, point to the stars in times of solitude, hide in sudden storms, and divide two provinces with a barrier of beauty and nobility." That description remains anonymous, but it sounds like John Pascoe talking.

Craigieburn Forest Park

Approximately one-third of Craigieburn Forest Park, or 13,000 hectares, is situated in Waimakariri country and is easily reached from State Highway 73 at a point 110km north-west of Christchurch. The park includes the more distant Avoca, Harper and Wilberforce state forests in the Rakaia catchment,

making a total of 44,000 hectares. There is a popular visitor centre a short distance from the highway with interesting displays (on a loop road for those passing through), and a network of walking tracks ranging from 15 to 75 minutes is maintained for visitors to enjoy the immediate scenery.

The park includes the Broken River and Craigieburn Valley ski clubs on the Craigieburn Range above the visitor centre, and the more energetic can walk right up to the crest of the range, from where there are sweeping panoramic views including Mount Cook in the distant south. In winter and spring, of course, the upper sections are thick with snow and skiers. Cass and Lagoon saddles give access to more demanding tramping to the west of the Craigieburns, where there are some useful huts.

The Craigieburn State Forest was gazetted in 1898 and given Forest Park status in 1967. There have been many additions since to the original 5000ha, the Harper-Avoca forests being added in 1979-80 and the Wilberforce in 1984. The bush is dominated by mountain beech and has suffered from occasional fires, some apparently as early as 1100 AD and later those lit by Pearson in 1857. The last fire in virgin forest was in 1910.

About six or seven thousand people visit the park each year to enjoy its recreational facilities, and this number is expected to increase with the development of holiday facilities at Castle Hill, Flock Hill and Grasmere.

The Craigieburns *and a small part of the Forest Park. A sharp eye may detect an access road at left leading to the Winter Sports Club's skifield on the slopes of Mount Cockayne.*

Holidays in the Hills

The upper Waimakariri's first flowering as a holiday place came with the coaches, when James O'Malley at Bealey and William Cloudesley at Castle Hill persuaded city folk and tourists that a fresh-air vacation at their hostelries was the thing to spend money on. Apart from them the valley was the almost exclusive preserve of sheepfarmers and their hired hands, but as the years passed a holiday-home development appeared on Bealey Spur above Bruce Stream, and nearer Christchurch Flock Hill station set up accommodation for those wanting a farm holiday.

Next came the development of the skifields and with them the provision of club lodges at various levels to house the skiers. Now at Castle Hill a resort village is taking shape opposite the old Castle Hill Hotel site, where a 36 hectare block is being developed into 280 freehold residential sections, of which about 140 have been sold and 50 homes are built or a-building. The plans include an upper-limit population of 2000, with accommodation facilities, a shop, tavern, restaurant and skating rink; perhaps later a recreation club, condominium development and tourist hotel.

CHAPTER FIFTEEN

Adventure in the Gorge

The main highway keeps an eye on the Waimakariri as together they descend from Bealey to Corner Knob, but there they part company, and the river wanders off on its own for 24 kilometres of braided bed through open sheep country with a touch of alpine grandeur off to the left. From that region come the Hawdon, Poulter and Esk tributaries, more than doubling the river's volume. Then the gorge makes its grab and the water torture begins.

This goes on for another 24 kilometres of rapids and whirlpools. But the resilience of H_2O being something to wonder at, the Waimakariri comes out smiling once the rock walls are left behind, and goes merrily on its way in as good shape as ever. Not all who have ridden it with canoe, boat or raft can say that.

Above the Broken River junction the river's privacy is normally invaded only by canoes, rubber dinghies and that modern indigenous marvel, the jetboat, which can provide sightseers with all the thrills of skimming at speed over these troubled waters. Many people can thus see the gorge's scenery, which is as it should be, for this is beautiful, dramatic and sometimes forbidding country to look upon, and the occasion is an adventure to be remembered.

The original gorge gamblers took their chances long before jetboats were thought of. In whatever frail craft they set out upon the river, paddling or poling to get the best channel in the upper reaches, the adrenalin would be pumping when the white water took charge and the gorge rushed forward to embrace them. From that moment until quieter water was reached a long way downstream, their lives depended on their skills, their craft, and their luck.

First to challenge the gorge were George Mannering and Marmaduke J. Dixon, whose climbing exploits are mentioned elsewhere. They had been paddling Rob Roy canoes on the Avon and estuary at Christchurch when in 1889 they conceived the idea of coming down the Waimakariri from Bealey to Kaiapoi, a distance of about 130km. When word of their intended exploit spread among friends in the city they were strongly criticised for attempting what was considered a dangerous and foolhardy escapade, the hazards of the gorge then being almost entirely unknown.

Undeterred, they loaded two canoes on the train for Springfield and there hired a man with a horse and cart to take them to Bealey Hotel where their frail craft were launched to the cheers of staff and patrons. To gain experience they paddled about six kilometres down the river, parked the canoes for the night and walked back to the hotel.

Next morning at 3.30, after a good breakfast of ham and eggs, and under overcast skies they rode down to the canoes in the hired cart and took to the water again with more confidence than on the previous day. They learned to keep to the inside of the turns to avoid rocks, and hoped that by the time they reached the gorge their techniques would be adequate. Past Mount Binser on the left and Sugar Loaf and Magog on the right, they sped on, Dixon with a Christ's College flag in his masthole and Mannering with a bunch of mountain lilies presented to him by Mrs O'Malley, wife of the hotelkeeper.

The river was now closing in and the stream sometimes running hard against rough shingle banks as they approached the canyon itself. Rain began from the south-east and a cold wind chilled their wet and lightly-clad bodies — lightly-clad because they were prepared for swimming at any time. Then it was into the gorge. Mannering described the experience:

We could see nothing before us but a high wall of bare rock, with a mass of foam at the foot, and could not even tell until we were close up which way the river turned, to right or to left. We soon began to gain

Marmaduke John Dixon, *the sheepfarming pioneer's son, is the only man to have canoed from Bealey to Christchurch in one day, on the first gorge trip in 1889. He and his friend Mannering gained early fame as the first New Zealanders to gain the icecap of Mount Cook, then unclimbed. At right,* **George Edward Mannering**, *who canoed the Waimakariri again in 1890, led a remarkably varied life. A banker by profession he was an authority on glaciers, co-founder of the N.Z. Alpine Club, a racing cyclist (in the days of "penny-farthing" machines), an expert fisherman, accomplished singer, hunter, golfer, tennis player and photographer.*

confidence though, and by experience found the safest way to get through the rapids was to keep to the edge of the current on the inside, and between the current and the whirlpool which almost invariably accompanies every rapid near its foot.

The whole of the first part of the gorge work is of a similar character, and we frequently landed above the more dangerous looking rapids and sometimes climbed the rocks at the side to get a view a little further down. Shortly after entering the gorge I had the misfortune to have a small hole knocked in the bottom of my canoe by a sharply pointed stone, and the water coming in we were forced to stop for repairs, which were effected with the aid of some red lead (which Dixon had thoughtfully brought) and a bunch of tussock jammed against the break from the inside of the timbers.

As we proceeded, the stream sometimes widened out a little, and stretches of comparatively smooth water between the rapids became greater. The wind blew strongly in our faces, now and then accompanied by showers of rain, which added to the wetting we were constantly receiving from the splashing of the paddles and the swish of the waves, many of which rose to a height of about three feet or so in many of the rapids. Added to this, my boat taking in water from being stove in, our lot was not a particularly dry one.

Now we came to a regular cataract, which instilled into us a spirit of awe by its furious rushing, and not caring to face it — the danger of being swamped appearing considerable — we landed at its head and waded down the side guiding our little skiffs carefully between the boulders which lined its left bank. Half-way down Dixon (who had displayed the most adventurous spirit, and was leading most of the way, being bent on reaching Christchurch that night) said he thought we could do the rest all right, and jumping in led off, and down we went through one of the most ticklish pieces of the whole journey. There was no whirlpool at the foot as the river ran on straight and we went at a great pace safely into good water below.

When Mannering reached Woodstock, near Oxford, with the gorge behind him, he decided to break the journey and spend the night there. But Dixon, ignoring his friend's shouted "coo-ee", sped on down the river. At the Gorge Bridge he cadged a mug of tea from a swagger living there, and then paddled on for another 70km until eventually, about six o'clock in the evening, he reached the Harewood Road. There he thumbed a ride with a spring cart into Christchurch, attacked a good meal, cleaned up and changed his clothes, and went off to the Jockey Club ball to dance away what was left of the night. No doubt he was a wonder at the ball, if anyone believed him.

Mannering came down the next day, paddling right through to the North Branch and up to Kaiapoi. It was a wet trip, as the canoe developed another leak which required it to be beached and emptied at frequent intervals, but he reached Kaiapoi by 4 p.m.

Mannering canoed down the river a second time in 1890, with Herbert Brown, Ben Todhunter and C.H. Inglis. On this occasion they camped in the gorge for the night.

As far as is known Dixon's remarkable feat of completing the whole journey in one day has never been repeated, with or without a Jockey Club ball to top off the day.

The next recorded journey through the gorge was an entirely different affair. It was made in a boat early in 1923, not to satisfy youthful passion for adventure but as part of an investigation for a hydro-electric scheme using Waimakariri water.

The boaters were H.V. Schreiber, an American and resident engineer for C.B. Hawley & Co., consulting engineers for the Christchurch City Council's projected scheme, and H.M. Chrystall, engineer-in-charge at the Otarama camp set up for the investigation. Their boat was a flat-bottomed affair, with a sheered bow, and it behaved well throughout. One of the purposes of the expedition was to make a survey for possible dam sites.

The two men started from Craigieburn station at 6.30 a.m. and, after walking for an hour and a half in an easterly direction, arrived opposite the junction of the Esk River at the top of a 350m shingle slide of rather large and awkward boulders and descended to the river. There they picked up the boat, left after earlier survey work for a dam site in the Esk, and started down the gorge at 10 a.m.

Soon a magnificent rapid was encountered with waves up to 60cm in height and a velocity of 12km an hour, recorded (as one might expect from engineers) with careful precision. Chrystall wrote:

In the opening stages of a rapid, it appears as if the boat must be dashed against the rock face turning the stream. Meeting it, a wicked, boiling swirl close to the rock repels the boat, and transfers it to the moving current onwards to the calm reach generally succeeding each rapid. It is the most exhilarating and exciting work imaginable, and a cure for all nervous complaints.

Five kilometres into the gorge the boaters came to a rapid 18m wide which plunged into a rock wall, was turned in turbulence to the opposite side of the gorge against another wall, then descended steeply in a further rapid. The boat survived without mishap except for some shipped water, but took the second rapid stern-first. Chrystall said the only thing to do in such places was to sit tight, look at the scenery, and hope for the best.

One advantage of the boat, he found, was that they could stand up on the seat to sight the waves ahead. But then they had to cope with the glorious uncertainty of what to do about them.

Between five and eight kilometres into the gorge the bends were so numerous that only limited views were available. The scenery was superb: delicate ferns, small waterfalls, curious rock formations and towering cliffs. On a straight stretch at about six km the river rushed down a 30m-wide incline with waves 90 and 120cm high. Half-way down, the boat reared up on a large submerged boulder. They shot up in the air and balanced there, only their weight athwart the gunwale preventing a complete capsize.

"Nothing could be more thrilling," wrote Chrystall, "than shooting into rock faces at speed, apparently to destruction, only to be rebounded on a water cushion into the current surrounded by whirlpools, swirls and bubbles, in a blue depth which cannot be seen to the bottom in places."

Chrystall concluded his report with an assurance that the information gained on the trip would be useful in solving the problem of cheap electricity for Canterbury. He also thought someone should organise regular boat trips in the gorge for those seeking a new sensation.

The first was never to be; the second has been an exciting part of Waimakariri sightseeing for many years, but not in the kind of boat Chrystall envisaged.

Rock and river. *This scene in the gorge proper photographed by jetboat pioneer* Guy Mannering *shows typical rock folding overlooking one of the more placid reaches of the river.*

159

The **lower gorge** *viewed from Otarama. The autumn low-flow Waimakariri meanders through relatively open country towards the plains. Burnt Hill, and the Port Hills near Christchurch, show faintly on the horizon at right, while the Midland railway is just visible in the foreground.*

It is one thing to shoot the Waimakariri Gorge in a canoe or a boat, but quite another to attempt such a feat on a raft of timber and empty kerosene tins. Within a few years of the Schreiber-Chrystall boat trip two were made with rafts, with very different conclusions.

Charles Hilgendorf and J.W. Calder (called "Torchie" because he had red hair) were the first raft party. Their attempt was made in January, 1925, when both were young and adventurous.

The trip was an extension of the exploratory work done by Dr Hilgendorf and his parties in the upper Waimakariri. The 1924-25 holiday in the mountains resulted in the two young men resolving to try their luck in the gorge.

An 8ft x 5ft timber cage was made of 3in x 1in planks enclosing rows of sealed kerosene tins (then freely available anywhere for the asking), and given a trial in the Lincoln College swimming baths. Pronounced river-worthy, it was railed to Cora Lynn station on the Arthur's Pass line. From there the young rafters half-carried, half-dragged it to the river, loaded their possessions aboard, and began their journey.

It was not an auspicious start. Heavy rain was falling and about six kilometres down the river they ran into a perpendicular cliff which upended them into a deep pool, along with all their gear. Sir Charles recalled the occasion in a recent interview:

We had to swim for all we were worth to catch the raft, which was taking off downstream. One thing, the rain wasn't worrying us any more — we were wet through anyway. We dragged the raft clear of the river and made for the Cass railway goods shed, staying there that night, and all next day and night, lying on bales of wool and waiting for the weather to clear. But the rain lasted longer than our food, so we abandoned the attempt and went home.

"Torchie" was unable to join in a second attempt, but Charles was not inclined to let the river triumph after such a brief encounter. He recruited his father as co-pilot and a week or so later tried again. This time they were equipped with two long poles with which to fend off collisions with rock walls, a rope to lower the raft down the more difficult rapids, a cut lunch, and two train tickets. As both father and son were interested in the botanical and geological character of the gorge, they planned to spend a couple of days over the journey with an overnight stop on the way. At Staircase they would abandon the raft, catch the train back to Cass, and be "home" in time for the evening meal.

This plan worked well. For 24km downriver to the gorge the braided streams were navigated without too much trouble, except that the 30cm draught of the raft sometimes stranded it in the shallows. The gorge came up to meet them, where the whole stream was confined between cliffs, with none lost in the shingle. It was then they realised what a large river it was, with the Poulter and Esk just added, and how deep and strong and steady was the current filling the bed from wall to wall.

At two places the rapids were so swift, and the waves so high, that one or other of the crew disembarked and steadied the raft

down with the rope. Where the current set hard against a rock bluff, the poles were used to check its speed as much as possible. When the impact came they crouched low and did what they could to soften the blow. It was difficult work trying to manoeuvre such a clumsy vessel.

But between the rapids and the bluffs there were occasional placid reaches where they could lie back and enjoy the magnificent scenery before the next white water gave audible warning of its approaching menace.

The journey to Staircase was completed without mishap, with the raft virtually undamaged. A scramble up the cliffs and father and son were at the railway station waiting for the train. From their comfortable seats on the return journey they could look down on the now-familiar Waimakariri far below, over which they had enjoyed a brief but memorable triumph.

During Easter, 1926, Bryant Hobbs, a keen Acclimatisation Society man, made the trip through the gorge in a boat, accompanied by his brother. The reason for his journey, apart from satisfying a desire for adventure, was to see if salmon were to be found in those waters. The result was inconclusive but the trip itself was a success.

The Hobbs brothers made their own boat, nearly three metres long. Using three oars (two for rowing and the other over the stern for steering) they travelled from Cora Lynn to Cass on the first day, camping in an old hut that night to shelter from a snowstorm; from Cass to the Esk on the second day; and from the Esk through the gorge to Woodstock on the third. At night the boat served as a bed, filled with tussock for a soft and companionable sleeping place. At the Esk camp they soaked their porridge overnight; next morning the ground was white with frost and the porridge was frozen solid.

"Adventure in the Gorge" *for most people is experienced from the comfort of a seat on the railway. This picture, "snapped" through a carriage window, looks steeply down into the gorge to a muddy Waimakariri in half-flood.*

Bryant Hobbs *and his brother, who rowed a boat through the gorge in 1926, used it to camp in at night. Here one of the brothers greets a frosty dawn from his cosy retreat.* Canterbury Museum

Every gorge traveller who has ever rafted, canoed or boated into that chasm has felt intimidated, and the Hobbs brothers were no exception. "We had the awed feeling that we had no right to be there," wrote Bryant Hobbs later. Almost immediately their boat was nearly swamped. They had to shout instructions at each other to be heard above the tremendous noise of rushing water magnified by the rock walls of the gorge. The worst rapid was about three km above Staircase. Hobbs wrote:

The river seemed suddenly to burst free from the confining rock walls and enter a miniature crater. There its pace was checked and it spread out in a glorious pool. Gradually the pool became shallow, and though we stood up in the boat, not a glimpse could we catch of the river below. Nevertheless an increasing roar told us only too plainly what was happening. Cautiously, very cautiously, we approached and beheld the first crests of foam, but not until we were close up was it possible to see any distance ahead, owing to the great fall in the riverbed. For several hundred yards the river boiled in a wild tumult down a very steep incline. Speech was impossible and unnecessary. With one accord we ran the boat into the friendly bank, scrambled out, and by keeping a strong hold on it, let it down to the quieter water below. Looking up from below was an even more inspiring sight, the waves almost leaping over each other in their mad race down.

In August, 1926, two shepherds, Dave McLeod and Jimmie Nimmo, were riding from Mt White station to Grasmere when they noticed a strange object lying on the river bank near the Mt White Bridge. In his book *Many a Glorious Morning,* McLeod writes:

We saw on the far side a curious square contraption leaning up against the bank below the railway line, and as we came near we could see that it was a sort of raft made largely of kerosene tins fastened together and floored with planks. There seemed to be nobody near it and Jimmie and I looked at each other wonderingly. The river swirled angrily at the piles of the bridge, the water slightly milky and well above winter level. Surely nobody would be mad enough to trust himself in it on that frail and vulnerable craft.

David McLeod was mistaken. Fresh out from England, he under-estimated Kiwi audacity. Three adventurous young men would arrive shortly, launch the raft, and set out to shoot the gorge. They were Gerard ("Charlie") Carrington, John Shannon and Walter Brassington.

Carrington, in keeping with his resolve to learn all he could about the Waimakariri, had decided to raft the gorge to acquaint himself with this section of the river and to take photographs of the folding of the ranges he expected would be revealed on the way. The adventure was ill-starred from the beginning. August was a late-winter month when the days were still short and the weather cold, let alone the water. This raised a serious problem, since they needed heavy clothing to keep warm but this would be a handicap to swimming in the event of a

capsize. As it happened Carrington could not swim, a deficiency which may have cost him his life.

Like the Hilgendorfs their trip started miserably in the rain and the raft upset almost immediately, giving them a good wetting. But they gamely carried on for another 16km before camping for the night.

Next morning dawned bright and clear, but the river was high and discoloured. For some time the going was good until the gorge proper. Men on the bank shouted warnings at them, and further along pig hunters on the hills looked down and saw the strange craft far below spinning round in rough water until it disappeared behind a bluff. They were the last to see the three young adventurers together and all alive.

The water became rougher and the speed increased, and soon the flimsy raft was crashing into bluffs with growing frequency despite much hard work with the poles. With the river much higher than when the Hilgendorfs went through, everything was in greater degree more boisterous — rapids, waves, whirlpools, and inevitable collisions with rock walls. Yet they sped on without mishap until, coming down a bad rapid, they met with a series of waves up to two metres high. The last of these flipped the raft over backwards, tossing everyone and everything into the water. Somehow they managed to keep contact and climb aboard the upturned craft, riding the rapid that way until Carrington could jump off and with tremendous effort drag it on to a shingle bank. Here they lit a fire, wrung out their wet clothes and took stock of their situation.

The forbidding walls of the canyon no doubt influenced their decision not to attempt to climb out, but to continue rafting. Soon they came to a place where the river churned about them in greater turmoil than anything previously seen. The raft, carried down at speed, hit a bluff and overturned again. All three men were thrown in to the ice-cold river. Brassington managed to get aboard the raft twice while it was spinning in the whirlpool, but each time it crashed into the rock face he was thrown off. Desperately trying to escape, he attempted to drag himself up the bluff but was pulled back by the force of the current. Somehow in the water he got astride a piece of wreckage, but again smashed against the rocks and was sucked under, by now almost

Rough country. *The Carrington reach of Waimakariri Gorge, near where the tragedy occurred. Brassington was fortunate in finding a place where he could scramble up the cliffs to escape.* Catchment Board

Tragedy in the gorge. These are the three young men whose raft trip in 1926 ended in tragedy. From left, Gerard Nelson Carrington and John Stevenson Shannon, both drowned, and (right) William Walter Brassington, who escaped by the narrowest of margins. Weekly Press

unconscious. At last the current swept him out of the whirlpool and downstream, but only to fight another whirlpool and another rock bluff. There seemed no end to his ordeal. He was about to give up when he saw the water lighten overhead, managed to get himself to the surface, felt shingle beneath his feet and dragged himself on to the bank more dead than alive.

He lay there for a while shivering, slowly recovering, conscious only of the sound of the river rushing past. Parts of the raft came drifting downstream, but of his companions Carrington and Shannon there was no sign.

Although seriously weakened by his ordeal Brassington knew he must make a supreme effort if he was to survive. His situation was critical. The odds were against him in that wild, inhospitable place with the chill of afternoon already making itself felt, clothes wet through, and food gone. He was trapped between almost vertical rock walls, and knew that somehow he must escape and get help. The probable fate of his friends almost overwhelmed him. Turning his back on the river he scanned the cliffs for some way out of the gorge.

Driven by extremity, Brassington found that way. He climbed 500m up cliffs and through bush to reach more open country, then staggered through scrub and bogs until darkness overtook him. He knew the Midland railway line lay somewhere to the west. By good fortune the lie of the land led him almost directly to the only shelter for miles around—the Rosa, an isolated musterers' hut on the outback reaches of Flock Hill sheep station. Once inside he dragged himself on to a bunk and snuggled between two mattresses for warmth.

He was lucky—a winter night in the open would probably have been the end of him. Next morning he found two matches in an old box and lit a fire to dry his clothes. Then he set out for the railway line. In an hour he was standing on the edge of a high terrace looking down to where, as if by magic, the railway had materialised in the valley of Sloven's Stream, and shortly at Avoca a woman gave him some food. His woollen sweater and riding breeches were torn and caked with mud, dried blood from a head injury matted his hair, and his face was drawn and haggard. But he had survived the tragedy, the cold night, and the 10km walk from the river. Another 12km down the railway line would see him to a telephone at Staircase.

The food and a short rest revived him enough to continue. On the way he crossed three or four viaducts and stumbled through nine tunnels. There was a risk of being caught in one of these by a train, but he reached Staircase safely and rang Constable Johns at Springfield, who immediately set about organising a search party. This worked from Craigieburn sheep station with the owner, W.K. McAlpine. Among the searchers was his son John, who recalled much later that the three days he spent looking for the bodies of Carrington and Shannon were the most miserable of his life, the more so because he had been at school with Carrington. Fortuitously "Charlie" Carrington's old friends "Felix" Fenwick and Freddy Kay were at Springfield when the news came through and they were able to join the search immediately. As Fenwick still recalls it, "The fading hopes of those two days are with me yet."

It was some days before Carrington's body was found well below the scene of the accident, and a good deal later before Shannon was located. The death of such a promising young man as Gerard Carrington, at the time studying engineering at Canterbury College and whose father was dean of Christchurch Cathedral, shocked the entire community. His funeral at Springfield was largely attended. Shannon, who came from Ashburton and was just starting a promising teaching career, was also widely known and mourned.

Walter Brassington, a teacher at Christchurch Boys' High School, was soon back in the classroom, but he carried with him for the rest of his long life the vivid memories of that ill-fated raft trip. Affectionately known as "Brasso", he continued teaching at Boys' High until retiring in 1961. Fifty-six years after his narrow escape in the gorge 18-year-old Roxanne Brassington canoed the river with a 'varsity party in a craft she built herself. Like grandfather, like granddaughter.

Dr Hilgendorf wrote the following appreciation of Carrington in *The Press* soon after the funeral:

I met him only once. Several visits to the headwaters of the Waimakariri had shown that the area had been mapped almost without instruments and largely from memory or description, so I undertook, as a holiday task, the re-mapping of the area. One evening, on returning to camp at the confluence of the White and the Waimakariri, I found that a strange little tent was pitched beside ours, and from it emerged Carrington and his friend Irwin [Brian Wyn-Irwin]. They had been attracted to the region by the hot springs on the upper Taipo, to which we had that day discovered, or re-discovered, a snow-free pass [Harman Pass]. The new party and we entered into a discussion of distances and directions, and from that moment Carrington's immensely superior ability took the lead with chains and pedometer, compass and aneroid.

He must have visited the district some five or six times since then, leading party after party of old and young, and introducing them to the glories of the mountains that lie almost at our back door. He secured a Government grant for the erection of a permanent hut on the White, and had the materials almost conveyed to the site. I hope it will be called Carrington's hut as long as it or its successors stand. On every one of these expeditions he was surveying whenever the seeing was clear, climbing pass and peak in the desire of obtaining a clear concept of the tangled topography, and of straightening out the tremendous muddle that the early map had caused. And all this information he reduced to permanent record in some of the most beautiful maps I have seen. Those I have are on sheets of notepaper, hasty drafts on which to base discussions as to names and so on, but so accurate and elegant as to surpass the work of many a professional cartographer.

And he was only 20 when he died. It is less than three years since he was sitting for the Junior University Examination, and gaining his soubriquet of "598" because he obtained that number of marks out of a possible 600 in mathematics.

That brilliant youth, that obviously born leader, has gone. Was he over-venturesome? Was it folly to risk his life in that terrible gorge when the river was swollen and discoloured? I cannot think it. He had set out to know the Waimakariri from end to end, and in such a venture some risks must be taken: otherwise no one would ever move out of the rut of mediocrity.

Oscar Coberger, "Mac" Vincent and Felix Harvey figured in the next attempt on the gorge, in a collapsible kayak in March, 1933. Oscar was the best-known citizen of Arthur's Pass where he ran a sports goods shop specialising in equipment for

Whio IV and Pateke, *two well-known jetboats operating commercially on the river in the 1970s. In Bob Radley's time (1973-78) these boats carried 15,000 tourists through the gorge.*

mountaineering and skiing. "Mac" was a journalist with *The Sun,* a lively Christchurch evening newspaper. It was taken for granted that whatever trip "Mac" made into the mountains a dramatic presentation would follow in the pages of his newspaper and no doubt his interest in "shooting" the gorge was partly motivated by this. Oscar, never one to shun free publicity, would be happy to cooperate. Felix was at that time living at the Pass where, among other jobs, he helped build the Ski Club headquarters at Temple Basin.

The plan was that Felix would drive Oscar and "Mac" down to the main river and see them on their way. But the weather interfered. There was only about one dry week in the mountains all that summer. Day after day "Mac" looked hopefully towards the pass for a clearance, and tapped the barometer to see if it was rising. In the end he was reduced to the conclusion, like Mr Explorer Douglas, that barometers had little effect on the weather. On one particularly wet day which was at variance with the instrument's predictions, he was said to have taken it down to the flooded Bealey, held its face within an inch of the water, and demanded of it, "Now do you believe what you see?"

Eventually he had to return to work, and when the weather lifted Felix was promoted from chauffeur to crewman. The kayak, imported by Ernest Adams, was a collapsible affair of mountain ash held in shape with brass fittings and wing nuts, with a five-ply skin, three of canvas and two of rubber, bonded. Considering that when collapsed it could be carried in a rucksack it performed well in carrying the two men through the turbulent gorge. At one point, caught in a large whirlpool round which they paddled with growing desperation in ever-decreasing circles, the vortex threatened to suck them into the depths — at almost the last moment they managed to break free and gain safer waters.

Oscar and Felix, who had camped at the entrance to the gorge, paddled from there right through to the Main North Road bridge, where "Mac" was waiting with pad and pencil at the ready.

Evan Wilson was one of the Canterbury Mountaineering Club's top climbers who widened his interests to include canoe trips. With Dick Waldron and Joe White he navigated the gorge in January, 1934, from Mt White Bridge to the Main North Road in two days. They broke their journey with a camp at the entrance to the gorge, as Coberger and Harvey had done. Wilson and Waldron were in a canoe, with White in a small boat. The river was partly in flood and their trip was eventful. In one rapid the canoe overturned, throwing the two men and all their possessions into the water, but they resumed the journey without delay, apparently none the worse.

As they approached the Gorge Bridge a man there became greatly concerned when he saw an overcoat floating down the river. But soon Wilson and Waldron (whose coat it was) came

into view, having chased it all the way from their spill upriver. A second upset occurred within sight of the Main North Road bridge when the boat hit a steel cable stretched across the river, overturned, and gave White a final ducking.

There have been many descents of the river since those days, mostly in canoes. A different medium was used in the 1970s by a group of young people associated with Arthur's Pass, led by Stan Scott who evolved the idea of using tractor tubes with ply floors. For several summers parties of 15 and 20, sometimes including girls, came down the gorge on these craft, usually spending the first night camped in the gorge. It was a rare trip when one or another of these "rubber cockleshells" was not "flipped" in the more turbulent rapids, giving all aboard a ducking. Some described in graphic terms the experience of being caught by the pressure waves and dragged down into the depths as if by some huge unseen hand, but all emerged unscathed.

One of the more unusual trips was that of two Waimairi Surf Club members, E. Ealam and J. Campbell, who in 1964 paddled surf skis from Bealey through the gorge, across the plains, out to sea and along to their club headquarters.

Since the days of Dixon and Mannering in their Rob Roys and the Hilgendorfs on their raft, the dreaded gorge has lost much of its terror. Hundreds of Coast-to-Coast "iron men" (and women) who paddle their kayaks down the rapids every February have tended to make a gorge passage almost commonplace. As well the modern jetboat has tamed the rapids with its unique ability to storm through the roughest and shallowest water, sometimes watched in awe by rubber-rafters taking their quieter, more leisurely drift downriver. But some challenges remain — nobody has yet swum either way except the salmon.

Not that all this activity has robbed the gorge of its remote charms, some of which were evoked by mountaineer Jack Hayes who canoed it in 1935 with Ernie Rich and wrote of their camp site in a little bay beside the river:

Within an hour we had the tiny tent pitched and a good meal ready. An abundance of dry firewood lay piled everywhere. A perfect summer's night closed in upon a full moon and cloudless sky, with the air delightfully warm. Moreporks called eerily in the bush, whilst a deer rattled stones on a nearby slide. We smoked and yarned until late into the night.

And 70 years before them Edward Chudleigh was also impressed. His diary entry for July 9, 1865, read:

J.D. [Enys] and I went to the Gorge of the Waimakariri and it is as Haast the geologist says, one of the gems of New Zealand scenery. There is a glorious mixture in the whole of perpetual snow, lofty rock-bound mountains, with huge chasms renting them from top to bottom, boundless forests extending all over their bases 'til they die away in the distant gorges, a perfect picture of grandeur.

"Miss Kiwi" *was the first rubber raft to negotiate the gorge, in 1973. It was operated by Alpine River Jet Tours.* Bob Radley

The long paddle ends. *A crowd assembles each year at Waimakariri Gorge Bridge to greet Coast-to-Coasters finishing their long journey down the river. They still have to ride 70km to Sumner. Across the river is the gauge for measuring river levels.* Catchment Board

163

CHAPTER SIXTEEN

The Mountaineers

Torlesse and Tuwhai's ascent of a peak on the Torlesse Range on New Year's Day, 1849, was a long way ahead of the next climb on a Waimakariri mountain. Forty-two years passed before Arthur Harper and the Dixon brothers, Marmaduke and Richard, attacked Mount Rolleston in November, 1891, and nearly that long again before virile young Canterbury mountaineers swarmed over the peaks and passes in what John Pascoe called "The Waimakariri Invasion" of 1930.

In those 80 years explorers and mountaineers ventured only occasionally into Waimakariri valleys. The first to show interest was probably Hunter Brown, the young Waipara sheepfarmer Charlotte Godley thought looked like "a cross between a whaler and a German student." Some time in March, 1856, he tried to gain the Waimakariri basin from the plains but failed. Presumably the attempt was made by way of the gorge.

Next, as detailed elsewhere, were Pearson (1857), Torlesse (1858), Butler (1860), the Dobson brothers (Arthur and Edward Henry) (1864), and a host of others in 1865 either surveying or searching for the way to the West Coast. From 1866, of course, people crossed Arthur's Pass regularly on the coaches, but nobody left the security of the road at Bealey to investigate the headwaters until March, 1867, when Julius Haast, Provincial Geologist and founder of the Canterbury Museum, arrived on the scene.

An inveterate traveller, Haast followed all the main Canterbury rivers to their sources, but somehow left the one nearest home until last. Although he usually trailed in his wake a generous sprinkling of alien names for features which impressed him, in the matter of Waimakariri nomenclature above the Bealey he was silent, like Torlesse before him. Haast spent a day at Castle Hill studying the limestone formations and a few more at Arthur's Pass collecting specimens. At Bealey he found his "thriving township" of 18 months earlier reduced to a Sergeant of Police and a telegraphist, and had the choice of several deserted buildings in which to stay.

After two days at Camp Corner in the upper Waimakariri waiting for the rain to stop he went up the White River and enthused about the size and character of the glaciers and mountains there. Another day was devoted to exploring the main Waimakariri, when the party walked up to the falls and climbed beside them into the upper basin, passing en route the

Julius Haast, an unqualified German geologist with a taste for exploration, was brought to Canterbury to adjudicate between the Provincial Engineer, Edward Dobson, and Australian contractors concerning the hardness of Port Hills rock through which the tunnel was to be bored. He sided with Dobson, married his eldest daughter Mary, became provincial geologist, founded Canterbury Museum on a wagonload of Glenmark moa bones, held the first chair of geology at Canterbury College, was knighted by Queen Victoria, and ended his career as Professor Sir Julius Ritter von Haast. In earlier days he was referred to as "a large, jolly fellow" and an excellent companion on any expedition.
Canterbury Museum.

three small lakes discovered by Jack Smith two years earlier. On his way upriver Haast noted traces of the track cut by Edward Dobson's men toward Campbell Pass. In the upper basin he collected more specimens and then returned to Bealey.

Railway surveyors were probably next into the upper Waimakariri. There was a tremendous push in the 1870s for a good railway route across the Alps, when they looked into most valleys along the main divide. The one favoured by many was up the Taipo River, a tributary of the Taramakau, and under Carrington Peak by a tunnel about two and a half kilometres long at an elevation of 915m. In the course of this 1877 survey members made the first ascent of Mount Campbell near the White-Waimakariri junction and named it after their surveyor-in-charge, along with the nearby pass.

In 1882 when James O'Malley took over the Bealey Hotel, interest in the Southern Alps was enhanced by the arrival in New Zealand of an Irish clergyman-mountaineer named William Green, who attacked the virgin Mount Cook and nearly made the first ascent. His approach was via the beautiful but dangerous Linda Glacier, which (appropriately or not) he named after his wife. There was further interest the following year when an Austrian climber and explorer, von Lendenfeld, climbed the mountain at the head of the Tasman glacier which he named Hochstetter Dom. The Austrian improved on the Irishman — he took his wife with him, right to the summit.

Comment on the exploits of Green and von Lendenfeld included speculation as to why New Zealanders were leaving exploration and peak climbing to foreigners, one explanation being that the pioneers were too exhausted establishing themselves in the new colony to be concerned with adventure on high mountains. It was thought, however, that the next generation, of native-born young fellows, might find the time and inclination to take up the challenge.

And so it proved, but only in respect of a few. Foremost among these were George Mannering, a bank clerk, son of a farmer at Fernside, near Rangiora, and his friend "Duke" Dixon, son of Marmaduke Dixon, the Eyrewell pioneer on the plains north of the river. This pair,* in addition to paddling the first canoes down the Waitaki and Waimakariri rivers, made four or five attempts to climb Mount Cook, almost reaching the summit in December 1890.

With the exception of a few winter climbs in the foothills most of their experience was gained climbing on Mount Cook itself. Many Canterbury mountaineers have found since that it pays to sharpen skills in the more readily available Waimakariri, which can supply almost everything needed to prepare the embryo alpinist for his craft. It is a good place to get the "feel" of the

First on Rolleston. *George Mannering and Arthur Harper, in the evening of their days, enjoy a chat about early New Zealand exploration and mountaineering. Within a month of each other in 1891 both men attempted Rolleston up the long Goldney ridge from Arthur's Pass*
From Guy Mannering

*Descendants of both men are prominent in Canterbury today. Mannering's two sons, John and Guy, are well known, John as a recent chairman of the Lyttelton Harbour Board, and Guy as an adventurous and successful photographer, while one of the fourth generation of Marmaduke Dixons, initials M.J.O., was recently chairman of the North Canterbury Catchment Board, the local body holding omnipotent powers over the Waimakariri.

mountains and of that most important element, the weather. On its peaks there is an abundance of rock climbing in grades from easy to severe, while winter, spring and early summer provide snow climbing in all its many conditions. Ice is harder to come by, but enough can be found for practice.

As it was, these admirable training grounds, so accessible from Christchurch, were ignored, and this lack of experience possibly cost Mannering and Dixon the honour of being first to climb the country's highest mountain when success was so close in 1890.

It was not until next year that Dixon, accompanied by his brother Richard and Arthur Harper (another who attempted Mount Cook earlier in 1890 but who preferred exploring to mountaineering), made the first attempt on a Waimakariri mountain. Harper wrote:

We camped near the little lake right on the pass [Arthur's]. It was in November, so the weather was very uncertain and the snow right down to the road, but we made the first ascent of a small peak which we named Philistine after one of Dixon's horses, and to get a good view of Rolleston. Our attempt on that peak, however, got nowhere owing to thick fog and a snowstorm. I think we reached the lower summit. We took the leading spur [Goldney ridge] from the pass.

A month later, possibly inspired by this effort, Mannering appeared at Arthur's Pass with A.M. Ollivier and D. Wood, and renewed the attack on Rolleston. Like Harper they also climbed the long ridge from the pass and, arriving on the summit in thick mist, considered the mountain conquered. (The Goldney ridge separates the upper valleys of the Bealey and Otira rivers.) Some years later when Mannering climbed nearby Phipps Peak he could see that his Rolleston climb had ended on the low peak. The real summit, a tougher proposition altogether, lay further back, invisible from the road.

Rolleston from the south. *This recent winter aerial photograph shows Mount Rolleston's forbidding southern aspect, looking up Crow Icefall to the neve and high peak summit (2271m). The icefall was first climbed in 1934 during an ascent of the peak by Cedric Turner and Ernie Rich.* The Press

Winter climbing. *Mount Rolleston can be a demanding ascent in winter. This climber is punching his way in soft snow up the south face of the mountain above Crow Icefall.* Malcolm Conway

Mount Rolleston is an attractive mountain, "a splendid pile", as Sid Odell described it, standing well above its neighbours in the middle of the National Park. It is 2271m high, fourth in rank but with its superiors all 16km away on the western boundary. The high peak climbs steeply from the Crow Glacier neve, the expanse of smooth snow field at the head of the icefall. Sometimes a degree of skilled ice work is required to gain the summit rocks. Popular routes to the top include the Rome ridge, the upper Goldney ridge, and the Otira face. On the mountain's south side there is an entertaining climb up the Crow river and icefall, and a variety of routes from the upper Waimakariri itself. Combinations of any two of these provide interesting traverses, the most common being from the Bealey to the Waimakariri.

Apart from tourists riding up to see the White glaciers, and ascents of a few peaks near Arthur's Pass, there was no further interest in the region until the turn of the century except for the activities of botanist Dr Leonard Cockayne and his family and friends. Fascinated by the beauty and botanical wealth of the country near Arthur's Pass, and with Waimakariri country generally, he was first to suggest a hut at the White-Waimakariri confluence where Carrington Hut stands today.

About this time the valleys of the Otira and Bealey began to host surveyors and engineers preparing the way for railway development, in particular the big tunnel through the Alps, and some of the more adventurous sought recreation among nearby hills and valleys. Two of them, H. Thompson, a tunnel engineer, and J. Gilligan followed up the Otira River to its headwaters and completed the first ascent of Mount Rolleston's high peak. This climb was made in 1912, and nothing more is known about it, but in that same year a man named Murray (perhaps J. Murray, the Bealey roadman) is reported to have repeated the ascent.

The year 1912 also saw the first mountaineering in the upper reaches of the Waimakariri. Whenever he rode a coach across Arthur's Pass, Arthur Harper was impressed, like thousands of people since, with the view up the river. He nursed the idea long before Gerard Carrington that it would make an ideal mountain playground for the people of Christchurch. With his cousin Eric Harper and George Dennistoun he went up the river and pitched a tent at Camp Corner.

This is a magnificent location, sheltered and well-watered, with grassy flats and groves of mountain beech, and the scenery is superb. To the north, further up the Waimakariri, stands Carrington Peak, framed by the river and bush-covered hills, while to the west the Shaler Range, highest in the park, towers over the White valley. A short distance up White River, round a corner, its main reach is revealed, leading past the three loftiest peaks, Mounts Davie (2294m), Wakeman (2286m) and Murchison (2400m). Here lie the glaciers which were such an attraction last century. This valley passes enormous rock bluffs on the left above which stands Mount Harper, and at its head is White Col, leading over into a Wilberforce River tributary called the Burnet Stream.

Rock and ice. *The highest Waimakariri mountains are not on the main divide but on the Shaler Range in Canterbury. At left are Mounts Murchison and Wakeman and at right Mount Davie. The glaciers from left to right are the White, Marmaduke Dixon, Cahill and Kilmarnock. Panorama from Mount Harper was taken in 1934 by Gordon Buchanan. The first winter ascent of Murchison was made by Sydney Brookes and the author the following year. "We hauled ourselves on to the ice-clad summit in time to see the sun set in the Tasman Sea, and had to descend the glacier and walk back to Carrington in pitch darkness, arriving there all-in at 2 a.m."*

The Harper cousins and Dennistoun made the first ascent of Mount Davie, but overtures in the direction of Mount Murchison, the highest peak in the region, were frustrated by bad weather. The first ascent of Murchison had to wait until 1913, when C.K. Ward and A.E. Talbot, members of a Greymouth group which had become interested, were successful, and climbed Mount Harper as well.

In November, 1917, Mount Rolleston was climbed again, this time by W.D. Frazer, H. Johnston and L. Neubauer, all of Otira. Louie Neubauer was so impressed with the mountain he arranged to have his ashes (and his wife's) carried to the summit and scattered there. It was Bill Frazer who took Betty Petre up

W.D. Frazer, *one of the electric-locomotive drivers on the tunnel run, was probably Otira's best-known citizen. He was also a man for the numbers game, making 41 ascents of Mount Rolleston over the years, and driving trains through the tunnel more than 60,000 times. He compensated for the hours spent underground with an enthusiastic enjoyment of the world outside, becoming a keen explorer, mountaineer, and photographer, and was much in demand for illustrated talks on the region. He died in 1983 at age 96, still writing his memoirs.* Roy Sinclair.

Rolleston in April, 1927, the first woman to reach the high peak summit. Their route was via the Bealey River, which Frazer had pioneered, and which is now the most popular of all.

Policeman Will Calwell was another Otira citizen who almost made Mount Rolleston his own with innumerable ascents, often with Frazer. His exploits had to be carried out unobtrusively because of his superior officers in Greymouth—his off-duty hours were not meant to be that far off. Additional ascents of the high peak were made in the early 1920s by Edgar Williams, Bill Heinz and others. In the mid-1920s Heinz led the first east-west crossing of the Three Pass trip (Harman, Whitehorn and Browning) to Hokitika. At Arthur's Pass Guy Butler was active in the later 1920s, on Rolleston and other peaks.

There is no ready explanation for the explosion of interest in tramping, mountaineering, and skiing which began in the 1920s.

The next two decades saw all three accepted throughout New Zealand as recognised pastimes, and the popularity of skiing, in particular, now seems boundless. The beginnings of this revolution lay in the Waimakariri valley in the late 1920s and early 1930s, when young Canterbury climbers, bursting with energy and enterprise, swarmed into the valleys and climbed every peak until all the so-called "virgins" were conquered. In one of the parties venturing into the upper Waimakariri was a youthful J.C. Beaglehole, later to gain fame as the editor of Captain Cook's journals, who was moved to write:

> *I see afar in darkness whitely stand*
> *The unscaled peaks, the passes we have trod.*
> *These are the ancient dwellers of the land,*
> *Snowed, silent and remote, each like a god.*

The zeal of Gerard Carrington in 1925 and the investigation of the upper Waimakariri by the Canterbury Progress League party he took into the region during Easter of that year led indirectly

The last climb. *At 91 Edgar Williams, veteran climber and patron of the Canterbury Mountaineering Club, determined to celebrate his birthday with one last ascent of Mount Torlesse, accompanied by his friend, Austen Deans the artist. But age prevailed and the attempt had to be abandoned. Here Edgar rests (with Austen at right) after meeting with two other club seniors, Jim Tocker and Ambrose Banfield, passing on their way to the summit. Three months later the old veteran was dead.*

to the formation of the Christchurch Tramping Club and the building of Carrington Hut. Returning on the train, members resolved to meet again to further their new-found companionship of the hills and to compare photographs. This meeting took the form of a supper at the Rendezvous. The participants enjoyed each other's company so much, and their recent acquaintance with the great outdoors, that they voted to climb Mount Herbert the following weekend, and on the return journey across Lyttelton Harbour in the launch they formed the Christchurch Tramping Club, with Charles McCully as president and Gerard ("Charlie") Carrington as secretary-treasurer. Membership grew to 30 in the first year.

So far the enterprise was restricted to a degree — to people with cash to spare. The Waimakariri jaunt cost each participant 5 pounds, which was rather more than a week's pay for most, and beyond the means of impecunious students or trade apprentices. There was also a distinct Christ's College flavour to the affair which may have helped things along on the one hand but on the other persuaded many young fellows they were on the outside looking in. Of course any differences, real or imagined, were resolved in the years ahead, one of the enduring virtues of the climbing game being that it tends to ignore artificial barriers. When danger threatened young Canterbury mountaineers, be it on the peaks or in the rivers, they found the rope that bound them together, often truly a life line, worked better than any number of old school ties.

Apart from trips to the foothills the new club had two primary objectives: (1) to build the hut at Camp Corner, for which the Tourist Department made 60 pounds available, and (2) to complete the exploration and mapping of the Waimakariri country begun by Hilgendorf and Carrington. The hut was destined to be much more than a shelter in the mountains. Its erection, subsequent to Carrington's untimely death, became an act of faith, and its completion two or three years later a memorial to his name. It also became the spiritual home of Canterbury mountaineers, and the pivot around which climbing was established as a popular recreation for virile young men.

The new breed of amateurs who first learned their skills on Waimakariri mountains soon spread into more distant valleys of the Rakaia, Rangitata, Godley and Tasman, where success on higher, more difficult peaks was linked with that of similar young men from other centres. Many of these joined the Canterbury club because of its prestige among mountaineers, and walked up the Waimakariri to see where it all began. Tales of their adventures were often told round the fire in smoky old Carrington Hut, inspiring young listeners to visions of derring-do (provided of course they could see them through the "fug").

But all that was still in the future. Easter, 1926, saw Carrington back in the upper Waimakariri with a club party, but efforts to clear up topographical mysteries were only partly successful because of heavy fogs. Disappointed, he and his friend Christopher ("Felix") Fenwick climbed Mount Armstrong but still the mist dogged their steps.

Club president McCully and Carrington bought materials for the proposed hut and in May, 1926, "Charlie" and a party of young men from College House, with two packhorses from Truscott's Stables in Christchurch, began moving them up the river. None actually reached the hut site, but were stored at different locations on the way; it was mostly corrugated iron as the original intention was to use timber from the site for framing. Unfortunately the next vacation saw Carrington drowned in the gorge, and with him went the map showing the location of the various caches.

His death was an almost fatal blow for the young club. Members were fortunate in having a strong core of older men standing encouragingly behind them: Professors Arnold Wall and Robert Speight, and Messrs A. Dudley Dobson, P.R. Climie, A.P. Harper, H.G. Ell, W.K. McAlpine and W.A. Kennedy. Freddie Kay took Carrington's place as secretary, with Stuart Meares as treasurer. Over the years Meares gave the club

Christopher ("Felix") Fenwick, *a notable figure from earliest Canterbury Mountaineering Club days, fords the Waimakariri with companions en route to Carrington Hut. He was patron of the club in 1986, and the photograph (taken about 1928) was from the camera of his successor in that office,* Nui Robins.

The Three Passes. *One of the most popular transalpine trips crosses Harman, Whitehorn and Browning passes from the Waimakariri to Hokitika. This 1926 party pioneered the route. From left, Charles Hilgendorf, Bill Heinz, John and Gerald Nanson, John Burns* (and the photographer, Donald Carr).

tremendous help and, it was said, wore out two motorcars transporting members on club trips.

With lantern lectures (mostly by Will Kennedy), social functions and donations, the hut fund was slowly augmented until in the May holidays of 1928 Fenwick was able to lead a strong party (and another two packhorses) in a drive which saw most of the materials recovered and transported to the hut site. The horses strongly objected to carrying the long sheets of iron. Gerald Nanson, who was there, wrote:

One of the animals took fright at something and bolted. The sight of a loaded packhorse at speed across the tussock flats of the Waimakariri was unforgettable, and when the inevitable happened we were not surprised: the long load on one side dipped and, catching in a matagouri bush, "cartwheeled", tearing itself, the saddle, and the other side load free from the horse and scattering it over a wide area.

Further packing trips were required in 1928. Fenwick estimated he tramped 800km of Waimakariri riverbed in 1928-29 and still the hut was not built. In August, 1928, members were levied five shillings a head to get the job financed, but what happened then is something of a mystery. The scenario featured a man named Cox, licensee of the Bealey Hotel, and starred one Stanley Graham, a noted hunter*. It is said a verbal contract was entered into with Cox to build the hut (or get it built) for 30 pounds. Graham, whom Cox hired to do the work, hitched the hotel horses to an old coach and carted and dragged materials to the site, then proceeded to build the hut almost single-handed. The weather served him poorly, blowing away the roof framing before it was properly fixed. Cox treated him (and the club) even worse by going bankrupt, so that Graham was not paid and the club lost its hard-won cash. In the words of Ray Newton, a later club president, "Graham was rewarded by not being paid by Cox but compensated by the club with the gift of a watch ... no wonder he was made a life member!"

Christmas, 1928, saw construction advanced enough to justify an "official opening", although there was still no proper chimney and only one bunk (the one Graham built for himself). About this time Fenwick guided two Christchurch ladies to the

First Carrington Hut. *"Three Pass" trampers adjust their packs before leaving the old Carrington Hut, bound for Hokitika. This hut endured for 14 years until the river destroyed the site.* Canterbury Mountaineer

*But not the famous Stanley Graham of Kowhitirangi.

spot, one of whom was Miss Muir, matron of Christchurch Hospital. While they pottered around the valleys he carried buckets of sand to the site for projected concrete work. Later he packed in a bag of cement (51kg), and in early 1929 he and Graham built the fireplace, incorporating in it one of the axles of the old coach. At Easter that year a large party came up the river, completed the bunks, and tried to make a satisfactory chimney. Among these were Nui Robins and Fred Hulston, who took a hand in building nearly every hut erected by the club in the next 30 years or more.

Name changes were suggested and universally approved—from S.A. Wiren that the former Mount Armstrong be called Carrington Peak, and from Dr Hilgendorf that the modest little shelter be known as Carrington Memorial Hut. Immediately known simply as Carrington, it had much to be modest about, but even its many deficiencies endeared it to those prepared to endure them with youthful good humour. Sometimes the chimney discharged more smoke inside than out, no matter how often it was redesigned and rebuilt. Bunks were uncomfortable, the interior dim, and in a gale it creaked and groaned. In a loft up near the roof lay an old wind-up gramophone which at times could be persuaded to issue an excruciatingly off-key rendering of some forgotten masterpiece, and there also was a selection of tinned foodstuffs which had lost their labels ("Felix" Fenwick once heated a tin of soup from which he got a meal of hot raspberry jam!).

In the winter Carrington was colder inside than a snow cave, but it was a "home away from home" in the mountains, set in glorious surroundings, close enough for even a weekend visit, and beloved of all who tramped the Waimakariri. It had one special virtue—for the final few miles of the walk in, when energies were flagging and packs growing heavy, it stood out plainly in the distance, promising exquisite delights of unburdened sloth and, of course, a hot cuppa.

Carrington Hut today. *This modern, roomy "chalet" occupies a beech forest setting in the White River valley near its junction with the Waimakariri.*

Unfortunately the start of the 1940s saw the Waimakariri change course. The hut had been built on ground apparently untouched for centuries, with the river flowing on the far side of the wide valley floor. But club members arriving one day found the main stream only a few yards from the hut, which had to be dismantled hurriedly and carried to higher ground. Although the war was by then in progress, enough willing workers were assembled to carry in additional materials for a new shelter out of harm's way, in the bush. This one lasted 33 years, until in 1975 it was replaced with a massive Lockwood chalet with six or seven rooms. The impressive size and appearance of the new building has made no difference to the name, still formally Carrington Memorial Hut.

Easter, 1930, according to John Pascoe, marked the point at which Christchurch trampers finally graduated from hill walking and occasional foothill climbs to full-scale mountaineering and

Home in the hills. *In the hostile mountain world the simple back-country hut serves a vital need. While the elements might rage outside, a blazing fire on the hearth heats the billy for tea and dries wet socks and clothes.*

John Sampson.

exploration. Canterbury provided most of the climbers in the Mannering-Dixon era. Now a new wave of youthful amateurs was poised to attack peaks and passes, the wealth of their energy and optimism being matched only by the poverty of their resources. This did not stop them learning how to get about in the mountains — how to cross rivers, find their way through gorges, locate deer trails, and make temporary homes in the wilds; nor how to climb ridges and rock faces, master the arts of snow and ice climbing, dodge avalanches, read the weather, and survive in high places. Remarkably, for all the risks involved, only one or two lives were lost.

The uninitiated are often puzzled by people who go mountain-climbing, but these young men experienced sights and sensations which began for many a lasting love affair with the back country. A spirit of camaraderie quickly grew as they discovered a richness no other sport offered them. A weekend attempt on a peak at "The Pass" or up the Waimakariri was so filled with incident, high endeavour, fun, companionship, shared living and achievement, all crammed into perhaps 50 hours of intense activity, that for them other recreations paled by comparison.

A Friday evening at Christchurch railway station was a rarity without the appearance of at least some clinker-booted, pack-laden young men with ice axes in hand. They were there to catch a mixed goods and passenger train affectionately known as "The Perishable" (presumably because it carried goods not able to survive alternative NZR timetables). By an arrangement which might be impossible in today's impersonal world, the train stopped for their convenience at Bealey corner. The price of their tickets could not have gone far towards the cost of getting the monster started again on the upgrade.

This was in itself memorable. Which young adventurer, unloaded into the night beside the rails at Bealey, bound for Carrington Hut, could ever forget the occasion? — especially the enormous steam locomotive, perhaps a "Kb", skidding and grabbing at the rails as it strove to get moving again. Its thunder reverberated among the black hills, and when the stoker shovelled coal into the firebox the glare lit up plumes of smoke and steam billowing high into the frosty air. The long line of trucks squealed and groaned in protest as all were dragged slowly round the ascending curve towards Arthur's Pass, gaining speed until the red lights on the guard's van disappeared up the valley. As packs were shouldered, some final spur or curve drew a last curtain of silence, and only then, though close at hand in the dark, could the murmur of the river be heard.

The "done" thing then was to stumble and splash up the Waimakariri, fording the river as it was met, for 14 or 15 kilometres until Carrington Hut appeared out of the gloom. A

short rest and a meal, and the young climbers would be away again en route to some peak or other. Dawn, in itself usually a colourful affair in the mountains, might find them still in the shadow of the valley, or gaining altitude over rock and snow towards the heights, greeting the first pink light of the new day. This always seemed fresher than it was back in the city. Far below the last mists would be dissolving and the river shining like a silver ribbon in its valley. Up there a new world was already half conquered. This was a different game from rugby or soccer or hockey, with different opponents — rock pinnacles, narrow ridges, snowfields, crevasses, schrunds, icefalls — all edged with the spice of danger and testing the skill of the young mountaineer. The reward? Among other things a sense of conquest and accomplishment, and a summit hour of delicious idleness, with the world spread out below like a map in live relief.

As 1929 approached 1930, these things attracted hundreds of young Canterbury men to the sport of climbing and "pass-hopping". Among the first were Ivan Tucker and Dick Clark, who spent Labour weekend in the chilly recesses of Carrington Hut, venturing out on the Sunday to climb Mount Armstrong at the head of the Waimakariri. Christmas saw a good contingent of young men in the valley. Roger Chester, Evan and Jim Wilson, Bert Mabin and Arthur Reynolds made the second ascent of Carrington Peak, Edgar Williams, Clark and McInnes bagged the first ascent of Mount Greenlaw, and at Arthur's Pass various parties climbed Mount Rolleston. The "invasion" was beginning. It reached full flood at Easter, 1930.

Autumn in the mountains was often blessed with superbly fine weather, with still air and abundant sunshine. The writer remembers sitting on top of Mount Franklin one Easter Saturday under a clear blue sky, watching one of the old wax matches, held vertically, burn down to his fingers without a flicker. Easter of 1930 was like that.

Competition was keen for a virgin peak named Gizeh, a 2164m outlier on the Black Range above Anticrow River, at the

Silver ribbon. *From high on Camp Spur between Carrington Hut and Mount Harper the new-born Waimakariri winds a sunlit path down its bush-fringed valley. Streams joining from the right bank are Harper, Greenlaw and Anticrow, and from the left Crow and (barely visible) Bealey. Klondyke Bridge is where the river hugs the right bank in the distance, beyond Turkey Flat.*

Merle Sweney.

High peaks. *Mounts Gizeh (2164m) and Greenlaw (2292m) dominate the view from Mount Bealey of the Waimakariri valley at its junction with the Crow River (lower right) and Anticrow River leading to the Gizeh cirque.*
John Sampson.

south-west corner of the National Park. Clark, John Pascoe, and Geoff Flower planned a route up the Anticrow River, while Chester, Evan Wilson, and Sid Milne chose Greenlaw Creek. The parties agreed not to start their campaigns until 6 a.m. on April 19. The Clark party won hands down. Anticrow upper reaches are smooth travelling and the peak lies central to the cirque. Greenlaw Creek, on the other hand, is a rough-and-tumble affair, full of waterfalls and rock bluffs, which led Chester's party on to a low peak subsequently named Mount Damfool.

It was a time for young climbers to find their feet. Sometimes they surprised themselves with the extent of their own endurance. The standard was set on Easter Monday when "Boney" Chester, already acknowledged as the club's "tough guy", led Wilson and Milne into the top reaches of the Waimakariri, over Mount Rolleston, down to Arthur's Pass, and back to Carrington via the Bealey and Waimakariri valleys. This marathon effort established a measure of physical endurance by which other club members could judge their own capacity. The distance involved was 40km and the altitude gain and loss about 1677m.*

This traverse of Rolleston was a happy-go-lucky episode from the start. The party was not sure of its target even on reaching the upper Waimakariri basins, from where the heights seemed no distance away—the effects of foreshortening are always deceptive. So they left their packs, rope and spare clothing to make a dash for Rolleston. The day was hot and still; even their trousers seemed superfluous. Henrik Ibsen once said that nobody should go forth to battle for freedom and truth in his best trousers. Chester and company did better than that — they took them off and fought the mountain in their underpants.

The high peak was reached at 11.30 a.m. From there, Milne descended to the Crow neve and walked across the snow to the low peak to wait for Chester and Wilson, who were "religiously insisting on traversing the middle peak and every stray bit of rock on the ridge."

With all three peaks climbed and the day still young, the question arose what to do next. The answer was at hand — a traverse to Arthur's Pass. Apart from the long walk needed to get back to Carrington there was one other difficulty — the matter of no trousers and the unavoidable township. As Chester later recalled, "It was about 3.30 when we arrived at the Pass,

*Comparative figures for Mount Cook (as a matter of interest) are 8km and under 1500m from the Plateau Hut. The comparison is for basic physical effort. Technically of course the two mountains do not compare, but difficulties are heavily influenced by conditions, so that Mount Cook at its best could be easier than one of the more arduous routes on Rolleston at its worst.

and it seemed to our harassed faculties that the road was lined with women all parading that 'Well-I-Never' look".

But they survived their embarrassment and trudged on down to Klondyke Corner and up the Waimakariri to Carrington, avoiding on the way the crossfire of hunters shooting deer in the valley. Chester retrieved the gear from the upper Waimakariri next day.

"Gran" Clark and John Pascoe climbed three peaks that Easter — Gizeh, Carrington, and Davie (with Geoff Flower on the first two), and R.E. McInnes and H.C. Wickett climbed Carrington and Armstrong. Chester added to his bag by climbing Harper and Speight (a first ascent) with McInnes and Wickett. It was typical of Chester that he should propose adding Murchison to the day's programme. His companions held on until just below the final peak, where Wickett fell into a small schrund. While they recovered, "Boney" climbed alone up the near-vertical rock to the summit, the highest point in the National Park. Back at the hut after this tremendous day he recorded that "we pitched into a sort of stew, made by Johnnie, which stretched us out for the night".

Meanwhile another 20 club members who preferred lower levels of activity were exploring valleys and crossing passes. Sid Odell's party went up the Hawdon and crossed Walker Pass, treading in Edward Dobson's footsteps of 65 years before. Two others led by Jim Wilson and Ivan Tucker walked the "Three Pass Trip" to Hokitika, where they gathered at the Red Lion Hotel — "the rest is very vague". Stuart Meares spent his time at Camp Corner enjoying outings with friends and no doubt keeping watch lest any of his impetuous young adventurers should need help.

John Pascoe was one of the most colourful of the new breed of climbers. He was also one of the most articulate — his newspaper articles and books ably chronicled the exploits of the new wave of amateurs. These demonstrated a commonalty of rope and ice axe which discarded the collar-and-tie upper-crust image of some earlier alpinists (along with lingering remnants of college blazers, riding breeches, and muscle-binding puttees) for the informality

Easter camp. *This tent camp was typical of Easter at Carrington Hut when annual instruction courses were held for young mountaineers. The figure is that of Jim Fowlie, a "pommie" ship's photographer who came ashore and fell in love with the Waimakariri.*
Edgar Williams.

Ice climbing. *Young mountaineers try their hand at climbing on Waimakariri ice.*
Left: *Tom Newth hammers his way up a cliff in the Crow icefall, in one of the first demonstrations of piton use in this country.* **Right:** *Hundreds of young men were educated in mountain skills at Canterbury Mountaineering Club Easter instruction courses based on Carrington Hut.*
Stan Conway and The Canterbury Mountaineer.

of old clothes. This was a new breed of Kiwi do-it-yourselfers keen to make their mark in the mountains. None was more to the fore in this movement than Pascoe, whose tattered garments, red spotted 'kerchief, unshaven face, and foul-smelling curved pipe would have made his old Christ's College headmaster shudder in disbelief. His climbing companions were equally incredulous — but in their case at how his slightly-built frame coped with the enormous packs he carried into the mountains.

It has been said that if the mountaineering tyro's enthusiasm survives with good humour the trials of bad weather on his first trip, he is hooked for life. John Pascoe's first major trip was at Christmas, 1929, when he accompanied Christopher Fenwick and Brian Wyn-Irwin into the Mingha valley. It rained nearly all the time and their camp below Goat Pass turned into a swamp. Before leaving town Fenwick had to listen to a lengthy caution from Mrs Pascoe about his responsibilities as guardian of her son in the wilds — he was to be treated with care, he was to be kept dry, he was to change his socks every night, and so on. Fenwick had to leave his companions in the rain and go down valley to meet Claude Evans, the fourth member of the party, who was coming off the train. At the same time he sent a telegram (with the engine-driver) to John's mother. It read: "John very well, changes socks nightly". But when it reached Christchurch the world "well" was somehow replaced with the word "ill". Fortunately John's twin brother Paul took delivery of the telegram, made some inquiries, and managed to get the message right before Mrs Pascoe saw it.

The Mingha party was battered by incessant storms, one of which produced 15cm of rain in five hours. Eventually they had to retreat down the flooded river as best they could. As back-country baptisms went it couldn't have been much wetter — the vicar in the skies emptied the whole font over young Johnny. But he came up smiling and undaunted, if stuttering somewhat, and went on to become the best-known, most travelled, and most widely-read author-explorer-mountaineer in the country (at least until Edmund Hillary climbed Mount Everest).

This trip was part of a determination by Fenwick and Wyn-Irwin to continue the Waimakariri exploratory work begun by Carrington. Because of the weather they didn't discover much, and remained keenly aware that the Mingha was only a beginning — for to the east the vast Poulter-Esk country sprawled over what was largely a blank on the map. With Freddy Kay they were the first club members into the Poulter in 1927, to explore as far as Lake Minchin, 29km up the valley.*

In the new decade numerous young men journeyed into the Poulter to unravel its mysteries. In 1931 C.R. Hervey, C. Holdsworth, L.R. Hewitt and G.P. McElwee went up the Andrews Stream and crossed into the Poulter. Also in 1931

*It was Gerard Carrington's intention to explore the Poulter in 1926 with Fenwick and Wyn-Irwin, but the expedition got no further than the Christchurch railway yards when they were refused permission to travel on the night goods train. Rebuffed, they fried their sausages behind an advertising hoarding in Moorhouse Avenue and went home again.

Johnny and the Blizzard

Throughout his life John Dobree Pascoe (1908-1972) nursed an undimmed love for the mountains wherever and however he found them. Many of his early expeditions were dogged by the almost unceasing north-west weather which characterised the summers of early 1930s, but storms seemed only to increase his fervour.

One September night in 1936 when our bunch got off the "Perishable" goods train at Arthur's Pass and stumbled through pouring rain to the new Canterbury Mountaineering Club lodge* in the village, we found John and Doug Apperley preparing for a climb on Mount Williams, the prominent peak down valley rising above the Mingha and Edwards river junction. It mattered not that the weather couldn't be worse or that the hour was 3 a.m. Hold it, we told him, while we have some breakfast and we'll come with you.

John Pascoe *was a keen harrier and a law clerk in the family business when he caught the mountaineering "bug". He became its most effective public relations man and through his many books, articles and photographs shared with the general public his triumphs and disappointments in the Southern Alps. He was later illustrations editor for N.Z. War Histories, secretary Historic Places Trust, and Government archivist.*
Dorothy Pascoe

Johnny led us down valley a distance, across the rising Mingha and into the bush. It was raining just as hard there; the only difference was the drops were larger. In an hour or so we emerged on to snow-covered open country where the wind howled at our backs, snow flew thick and fast, and visibility was down to a few feet.

We must have looked like Polar explorers caught in an Antarctic blizzard, climbing on and up through knee-deep snow, huddled in our storm clothing, snow-goggled, bent against the blast, ice forming on our balaclavas as we doggedly followed the man in front.

After about an hour of this we struggled up a last rise and Johnny shouted "Summit!" We turned without a word and immediately began the descent. But now we were worse off, facing into a gale charged with pellets of ice which stung and bruised our faces as we charged downhill, staggering about like drunk men and falling over in the snow until at last we reached the shelter of the bush. A quick count showed all present, although more than one member thought some fingers missing. The rain in our faces as we forded the Mingha seemed almost warm by comparison.

The experience taught us something about blizzards, but little about how to survive them. During the worst part of the descent a doubt grew concerning our fate had we been on a higher mountain with no friendly bush within reach. Should we have persisted on our course and risked exhaustion and hypothermia, or should we have sought shelter on the heights (and if so, where and how)?

A few years later Bruce Banfield and the author dug experimental snow caves on Mounts Rolleston and Gizeh which proved to be warm, roomy, comfortable, convenient and completely insulated from the outside world. On the first occasion we were surprised to find a blizzard whistling past the entrance, similar to that on Mount Williams, of which there had been no hint in the perfect shelter of the cave.

Since then, snow caves have been used extensively for living quarters on high peaks, but more importantly they have saved the lives of many climbers trapped high by bad weather. The essential requirement is that they must be kept to a reasonable size so that the body heat of occupants maintains temperatures above freezing level, something that can't always be done in a larger crevasse or bergschrund.

*Destroyed by fire in late 1986.

Club stalwarts. *This Canterbury Mountaineering Club committee photograph taken in 1932 includes several members whose exploits in the hills inspired many to follow in their footsteps. Seated: Stuart Meares, Sir Arthur Dudley Dobson, Professor Robert Speight, Cuth Thornton. Standing: Evan Wilson, Jack Mitchell, Allan Willis, Ivan Tucker, Tom Beckett, Dick Caldwell, John Pascoe.* Canterbury Mountaineer.

C.J.S. Ellis and party surveyed much of the country and solved many topographical puzzles. In that same year Tom Beckett and Jack Crawshaw headed into Thompson Stream, through the Hervey Gorge, over Foy Pass, and down the Taramakau River, by much the same route George Dobson and Matt Russell took in 1865. Beckett, a very active member of the C.M.C., became an authority on the Poulter, and later the Rangitata after he had founded the Erewhon (Ashburton) branch of the club. Still others followed until eventually all the mysteries of this major region were laid bare and an important page in Waimakariri exploration was completed.

Nearer Arthur's Pass, attention was being focussed on the Mingha-Edwards-Hawdon country and its relation to the Westland valleys of the Deception and Otehake. Here lay the only low-altitude divide saddle overlooked by George Dobson in his 1865 search for the road pass. Taruahuna Pass is at the head of the Edwards valley and was unknown before 1930. The Edwards is a twin valley to the Mingha and joins it through a short, narrow gorge just before the Bealey junction. The volume of water led explorers to suspect that its extent was considerable, and one winter's day in 1930 Evan Wilson (one of the three who made the trouserless traverse of Rolleston at Easter) climbed Mount Williams, which overlooks both the Mingha and Edwards valleys. The hidden secret of the Edwards was revealed.

Armed with Wilson's photographs, Dick Clark, Felix Fenwick, Brian Wyn-Irwin and Sid Odell pushed their way through the gorge into the Edwards a few weeks later. With compass, pedometer and abney level they determined to chart the valley properly for addition to the map. They plugged a trail through the snow drifts and gazed astonished at a peak later named Falling Mountain because a good part of it had collapsed onto the pass and into the upper Otehake in the 1929 earthquake.

Next month Evan Wilson went into the Edwards alone, determined to climb one of the peaks on the eastern side of the valley. It was September and the whole place was deep in snow. Progress was slow because the best way was up the river itself, but on leaving the water his trousers froze solid like drainpipes, forcing him to shuffle back into the stream to thaw them. The cold became intense and the long, lonely, snowy valley began to look like a trap. He splashed off down the river and just made it through the gorge before darkness fell.

With Andrew Anderson, Wilson returned to the Edwards later in 1930 and climbed two mountains on the eastern side. In memory of Robert Falcon Scott and his Antarctic expedition of 20 years earlier the range was named the Polar Range, and the peaks Wilson and Bowers. A prominent peak further north, climbed a fortnight later by Doug Brough and J.B. Gill, became Mount Scott. About the same time Odell and Gill climbed The Dome, overlooking the Waimakariri. Falling Mountain was climbed by Fenwick and "Mac" Vincent, whose story under big, black headlines in his paper, *The Sun,* speculated that Taruahuna Pass might have been better for a road than Arthur's Pass — an unlikely prospect.

These ascents and explorations, including one by Odell's party into the Hawdon, almost completed what was required for a reliable map of Arthur's Pass National Park. This was produced by Lands and Survey in 1931. In canvas-backed form at five shillings a copy it became an essential item for every young tramper and climber in the years that followed.

Among these was Pascoe, returning to the Mingha in early 1931, this time with Brian Barrer and Betsy Blunden. With better organisation and more experience than on the 1929 trip they made the first ascent of Mount Oates, so prominent up the Mingha when viewed from the main highway in the lower Bealey. This completed the ascents of peaks overlooking the Edwards valley named in memory of the Antarctic expedition.

By 1934 there was only one virgin peak left in Arthur's Pass National Park — the low peak of Mount Greenlaw, a mountain in its own right. This fell in December, and its falling marked the end of the "Waimakariri Invasion". But not of course the end of mountaineering in the park.

New generations of young trampers and climbers will always find plenty to attract them to these parts. Certainly the glaciers have shrunk, and there are more huts for shelter and tracks through the gorges; otherwise the sights they see and the mountains they climb are no different from when George Dobson looked on them, and just as fresh to their eyes.

"Invasion" climbers invariably took easiest routes to summits. Some who came later with unsatisfied pioneering urges sought more difficult ways up familiar peaks. John Stanton and Margaret Clark, for example, climbed Rolleston in winter straight up the Bealey face (the one seen from the main highway lookout). The 100 metre vertical band at the start took six hours to climb, plus another six to the low peak summit. Others climbed on the south face from the Crow River and still others on the north face above Otira River.

With all such climbs risks increase with difficulty, and occasionally tragedy looms. The worst disaster in the park's history occurred on the Otira face of Mount Rolleston in June, 1966, when four young men died there in bad weather, and the Canterbury Mountaineering Club lost one of its most respected, experienced and likable members. John Harrison answered the call when rescue teams were alerted but the story of that week is a sad one.

At about 4.30 p.m. on the Sunday, as darkness approached, two men descending from Rolleston saw four young climbers

Taipoiti trap. *The little Taipoiti Stream running down from Harman's Pass is contained by rock precipices. In 1932 three men unconnected with the Mountaineering Club missed their way in a storm and occasioned the club's first search and rescue operation. One man died of exposure and another fell over the cliffs in to the river. He is seen here woefully underclad for storm conditions while Constable Robb, Andrew Anderson and Fred Cochrane consider the task of removal. The tragedy, widely publicised at the time, served to warn young climbers of mountain risks. Anderson went on to establish one of the longest and most prolific climbing careers in New Zealand mountaineering.* From Jack Cochrane.

Northern aspect. *The Otira face of Mount Rolleston shows the obvious route up snow and scree slopes at left and along to the summit, but nowadays any one of several direct routes up the face is favoured. Otira River rises in the valley below.* John Pascoe.
Right: John Harrison *climbed extensively in New Zealand and overseas. He married a daughter of David and Mary McLeod, of Grasmere.*

about two-thirds up the face. Conditions then were perfect. Their progress must have been delayed or they may have suffered some misadventure. For whatever reason they failed to return that evening, nor during the following morning. An alarm was raised and a search begun but by Monday afternoon a storm was closing in, and it was to get worse as time passed.

Searchers grew in number until the exercise became one of the largest in the history of New Zealand mountaineering. In blizzard conditions parties tramped up the Waimakariri to rendezvous with others who came over from Rolleston valley. One group climbed Mount Philistine to scan bluffs across the valley through binoculars but all they saw was driving rain and snow. Still others set up camps high on the Crow neve close to the summit and on Otira slide below the low peak adjacent to the face. High-level rescue teams from Wellington and Invercargill arrived to supplement those from Christchurch. Repeatedly men thought they could hear voices in the wind, as they edged out on to rock bluffs from the slide and down a ridge from the summit but in atrocious conditions little could be seen or done. By Thursday there was almost no hope that the young men on the face could still be alive.

Yet that was not all. About nine o'clock on Thursday evening an avalanche swept down from the low peak and overwhelmed the search camp established on a rocky knob near the neck of Otira slide. Two men survived in a tent not so directly affected, but John Harrison died when the other tent was swept away.

Friday dawned bright and clear, yet there was a gloom over everyone as black as the storm they had just lived through. A helicopter came up the valley and, flying in close, searched the soaring cliffs, but there was no trace except a rope dangling from a rock bluff into a snow chute. For those below scanning the icy face for signs of life, perhaps reviving in the sun's warmth, it seemed heartless that yesterday's murderous weather could so cynically assume today's golden smile. Some might say the four young men gambled and lost, but with John Harrison there was a difference. He came only to give what he could, and the mountain took all he was.

Mountaineering today has reached such heights of technical ability, aided by sophisticated gear undreamed of in earlier years, that new generations of climbers must look to other regions for the satisfaction which comes from hard-won conquest. Nevertheless the peaks and passes of Arthur's Pass National Park serve as a valuable training ground and still hold some of the lure which whetted the enthusiasm of young Canterbury men in the 1930s and 1940s. The challenges remain.

Some may even get fulfilment from emulating the feats of their forebears, such as the 1935 traverse by Jack Hayes and Ernie Rich of all three peaks of Rolleston, Armstrong and Carrington in one day. Or (if they are looking for something of greater duration) that of John Pascoe and Stan Conway, who over a period of 20 years climbed every named peak in Arthur's Pass National Park.

"Tuck" and the Violin

Of all the hoteliers who pulled a beer along the West Coast Road, Fred Cochrane of the Bealey was possibly the most controversial. There seemed to be no middle ground with Fred—if he wasn't for you he was against you. Travellers were fair game for whatever he could extract from them, the more the better, but for mountaineers and musterers he had a soft heart and was never slow to lend a hand or turn out for a rescue party. "The Bealey", of course, was a magnet which lightened many a tramper's steps over the last few miles of the long walk downriver. Fred would lean on his bar listening to a recital of our adventures and "shout" when the spirit moved him. More than once he turned on a free feed (he was a superb chef), or had son Albie drive us to Cass to catch the train. Most of us agreed with Ivan Tucker that Fred was "a bloody good scout".

Ivan Tucker was attracted to the upper Waimakariri at an early age. He specialised in transalpine journeys across the passes, including a memorable trip over Whitcombe Pass and down the gorge of the Whitcombe River in 1931, when the party relived all the difficulties and privations Whitcombe and Louper must have endured during the first crossing in 1865.

Ivan (or "Tuck" as he was universally known), a foundation member of the Canterbury Mountaineering Club and one of its outstanding "characters", could tell many a tale of his association with Fred and his hotel, including the time he and a companion tried to force a way up the Waimakariri in snow, and the companion collapsed and died on the way. Fred turned out immediately to bring in the body.

Then there was the night "Tuck" came downriver to discover the drinks at the Bealey were "on the house". Inquiring why, he learned it was Isobel Cochrane's 21st birthday and the lounge was already cleared for a party. Fred demanded of all at the bar which musical instrument they could play. When it came to "Tuck's" turn he said, "OK, put me down for the violin," never imagining he might have to perform. "Good," said Fred, "I'll just nip up to the loft."

He was back in a minute with a dusty old violin case, inside which was a perfectly good instrument. That rather took the wind out of Ivan's sails, and when a dance started he made some excuse, whereupon Fred said, "Well then, grab the wife and give her a dance." "Tuck", who was wearing his big clinkered boots, recalled his embarrassment:

I hadn't taken two steps before I stood on her toes. I told Fred I couldn't dance, so he said, "Go and look after the bar then, and I'll dance with her." About an hour later he closed the bar for a spell and handed me the damned violin again. By this time I was fit for anything so I had a go at it. The result couldn't have been too good because after a while Fred came up with a pained expression on his face and took the thing away and said, "Why don't you bugger off home or somewhere?"!

CHAPTER SEVENTEEN

River Recreation

Because about 350,000 people live within easy reach, more varied forms of recreation are found more often on the Waimakariri and its tributaries than possibly any other river in the country. It holds first place nationally for jetboating and salmon angling, and in Canterbury for trout angling, estuarine fishing and whitebaiting. Parts of the river are used for a multiplicity of other pursuits: for yachting, power boating, water skiing, rowing, canoeing and swimming. Many frequent its lower banks for picnics, walking, trailbiking and game shooting, while others turn to the hinterland for different reasons: for scenery appreciation, nature study, hunting, tramping, skiing and mountaineering. Most of these activities date back to the last century; indeed shooters were aiming their guns at bird life on the lower reaches before the First Four Ships dropped anchor at Lyttelton.

Fishing

Travellers going north by plane are almost into what was once Waimakariri riverbed before they are airborne, and if they look seaward as they rise, and the season is right, they will see hundreds of small black dots close-packed along the river near the mouth. This is evidence of the annual ritual of rodmen assembled to catch what they can of the 8000-odd quinnat salmon which in late summer and early autumn must run this hook-and-line gauntlet en route to their spawning grounds in the upper Waimakariri. It is thought that for every fish the anglers hook, another two manage to get safely past.

From various sources it has been estimated that the lower river and its tributaries receive about 60,000 fishing "visits" a year — 13,500 for whitebait and the remainder for salmon and trout. Another 10,000 are made to the high country tributaries and lakes, especially Lake Pearson.

There were no salmon or trout to greet the first immigrant anglers — only kahawai and mullet, inanga and eels. Those were the days when inanga (whitebait) were so plentiful that a couple of buckets could be filled in as many minutes. In his little book *Old Kaiapoi* Charles Brocklebank tells of catching so much of what has since become a somewhat rare delicacy that he often boiled the surplus and fed it to the fowls.

The introduction of English brown trout in 1867 gave fishermen hope for the kind of sport they had known in their homeland. The Waimakariri was a far cry from a willow-fringed stream in England, but good fishing was soon established in both the main river and its many tributaries and lakes. Would-be anglers carried trout fry by the thousands into the back country and released them into upland streams and lakes, with prayers

for their survival. Foremost among these was John Enys of Castle Hill, one of the piscatorial enthusiasts responsible for most of that work done in his part of the world, while successive batches released in the lower tributaries have long since made them favourite haunts of Christchurch anglers.

From about 1883 onward rainbow trout were introduced and soon showed a preference for the upcountry lakes. Mackinaw were also released in these lakes, but although they have survived for 80 years in Lake Pearson, they are still not worth catching.

As early as 1859 there were advocates for the introduction of salmon. In that year John Edward FitzGerald, writing from England, suggested the establishment of a salmon industry in the province. He was greatly influenced by the Duke of Richmond, who had made 12,000 pounds in a year from his salmon fishery, and "Fitz" thought the Canterbury Provincial Government ought to go into the business with the Australian market in mind. He had the right idea but was a little ahead of his time.

In fact, more than 40 years were to pass before salmon were successfully introduced into Canterbury rivers. The first attempt was in 1867 when 80,000 ova were secured from the McLeod River in North America, of which 20,000 were liberated in the Waimakariri. This was a failure, as were many others in subsequent years. Finally in 1901 the Government imported salmon ova and successfully introduced them to a hatchery at Hakataramea, a tributary of the Waitaki River. Releases were made in various East Coast rivers and the fish were soon established as sea-run stock in the Waimakariri.

It is unlikely that the Waimakariri will ever match the Rakaia for salmon fishing because it lacks comparable high-quality spawning reaches. All of these are above the Gorge Bridge, the most favoured being in Winding Creek and the upper Poulter. Nevertheless, as one of New Zealand's four major salmon rivers, the Waimakariri is more heavily fished for this species than its neighbours, the Rakaia, Rangitata and Waitaki, simply because it is most convenient for most anglers. The Rakaia offers much better odds: an average run of salmon there has been estimated at 16,000 to 24,000, and with the growth of hatchery releases this could rise to 100,000. By comparison the annual run in the Waimakariri, as mentioned, is probably about 8000.

Rowing

Boat races on the river were first held as part of the annual Kaiapoi sports meeting in 1858, when two- and four-oared ship's boats were raced on the North Branch. These continued on Queen's Birthdays until about 1865, when they had to be

At Kairaki. *A favourite fishing spot is near the Waimakariri mouth on the river's north bank, especially when the salmon are running.* Catchment Board

The champions. *This prize-winning Kaiapoi "four" stroked by J. Winterbourn dominated Canterbury rowing for nearly 20 years.*
Kaiapoi Museum

separated from the athletics because they were taking all the crowd. Enthusiasts gathered in Oram's Pier Hotel on October 31, 1866, to form the Kaiapoi Boating Club, which commissioned the building of two inrigged, clinker-built, four-oared boats, the *Cam* and *Isis*. Their most important use a year or two later was as ferry boats when the town's only bridge went away with the 1868 flood.

Possession of such a good course as that provided by the North Branch encouraged the early development of rowing in Kaiapoi. A newspaper of the day praised it in these glowing terms:

A finer stream of water than the Waimakariri for aquatic contests certainly could not be found in the province. An excellent view of the first and last quarter of a mile is obtained from the bridge, and the whole race up to six miles may be witnessed by riding along the bank.

The *Cam* and *Isis* were more like whale boats than racing craft, and were quickly overtaken when another club was formed and bought a racing gig from Christchurch which they named *Ariel*. With this they challenged Christchurch champion *Black Eagle* to a 10km race on the Waimakariri. They won easily by nearly a minute, and rowing in Kaiapoi was away to a flying start, two new clubs being formed soon after. One racing its locally-built boat light-heartedly named after a popular song of the day, *The Cure*, was to enjoy a life extending down the years to the present day, and a distinguished record in provincial and national rowing championships.

The first properly-organised regatta was held on a January day in 1868, marred by intermittent showers. *Lurline*, a Christchurch boat, won the big race of the day, and with it the 15-pound prize. Detailed reports of each race filled a column in the newspapers, notes for which were jotted down mile by mile by a reporter as he was "riding along the bank" — no small accomplishment in itself. Incidentally, Charles Street then extended down to Kairaki, but as the years passed the river swallowed up most of it.

Great interest was centred on the last race, for Kaiapoi boats only, over 10 kilometres. For this event feelings ran high and bets were freely exchanged. It was nearly 6 p.m. before the event got started and rain was coming on in earnest. Three boats were entered, *The Cure, Ariel* and *Undine,* but at the last moment the stroke oarsman of the *Undine* withdrew because, he said, of the weather. This occasioned "some heavy sarcasm and much unpleasantness".

The remaining boats carried on, *The Cure* leading all the way and winning by a good four minutes. One oarsman, who had rowed 24km that day at racing speed, collapsed in a faint and had to be carried ashore. As the rain poured down, fresh arguments developed on the riverbank between rival crews and their supporters, the point at issue being the untested but loudly proclaimed superiority of the *Undine*. Amid a chorus of mock cheering, a further challenge was issued and accepted, to be decided on the Monday evening.

But when the appointed time came, all contentions were swept aside by the greatest flood in the history of North Canterbury. This calamity, declared to be the worst ever to visit the province, submerged most of Kaiapoi, wrecked the town bridge, and put an end (for a while, at least) to the argument about which boat was Pride of the Waimakariri. The year, as mentioned, was 1868.

The Cure Boating Club quickly assumed a pre-eminent place in Canterbury rowing, winning the senior four-oar event every year from 1880 to 1886 inclusive at the Lyttelton regatta, and for five years at the Christchurch regatta. The crew during many of these heydays was G. Wright, R. Day, J. Perrin and J. Winterbourn, the last-named stroking the senior four for nearly 20 years. In one of the last big races at Lyttelton, from Governor's Bay to the finishing line inside the moles, his crew won 125 pounds in prizes, not much less than many a workingman earned in a year.

Old-timers reckoned the biggest crowd ever seen in Kaiapoi turned out for the Interprovincial Fours Regatta in 1874. Hundreds lined the banks, and Wright's old Swing Bridge, patched up after the 1868 flood, groaned under the weight of

The town turned out *in force for regattas on the Kaiapoi River in the 1920s, using Otto Peez's iron bridge as a grandstand. The sign at left asks, "How is this regatta financed?" and invites donations.* Kaiapoi Museum

spectators. Before its home crowd, Cure didn't do too well, fouling on the way and coming in third. Hokitika took the 100 pound first prize, crossing the line to loud barracking from a large contingent of Maori onlookers chanting "Ho-ki-ti-ka! Ho-ki-ti-ka!" The regatta was even reported in the Sydney *Bulletin,* which used the Maoris' chant for its heading to the article.

The Cure Boating Club operates today from premises close to the town bridge and its crews still feature prominently in Canterbury rowing circles. The club's greatest asset, however, lies at the wharf across the river — the historic motor vessel *Tuhoe,* which regularly makes excursion trips on the river.

Yachting and Power Boating

The Waimakariri's oldest sailing club was loosely centred in the 1870s on a group of Kaiapoi enthusiasts — Frank and Harry Parnham, Charlie Dudley, Harry Day, Bill Hills, Charlie Belcher, Harold Evans, George Blackwell, Charlie Fairweather and others — who competed in boats with names like *Hero, Fairy* and *Foam.* The Parnham brothers' first craft was a centreboard punt, and races were held between the Kaiapoi bridge and Lock's Point in the days when the North and South branches of the river joined near the present freezing works. One regatta day a Lyttelton boat arrived to show the "locals" how to sail. The Parnhams led it downriver in their *White Arrow,* pulled up their centreboard, planed across a shallow sandbar, and left the rest of the field stranded and out of the race.

The next club on the river had nothing to do initially with sailing. Formed in December, 1927, the Waimakariri Power Boat Club, with Ormsby Willcocks as its chief promoter, was concerned exclusively with the new craze for motorboats. Three races were held in 1928, with 10 boats competing, the championship going to a keen young club member named J.C. Mercer, later to gain more lasting fame as an aviator. Other well-known names among early members were those of F.D. Kestevan and W.T. Tretheway. Prizes were usually half the entry fees and a case or two of petrol. In 1929 some younger members had to be disciplined for racing noisy boats up and down the river after dark with no lights, but membership and status grew with the years.

Among the 90 members in 1930 a new element emerged. Against the names of nearly 20 the word "yacht" was listed, and while powerboats remained in the ascendancy, the club's 1932 Easter regatta at Kairaki included races for boats driven by sails as well as motors. In 1934, bowing to the winds of change, the club's name was altered to "Waimakariri Sailing and Power Boat Club", and from there on the "yachties" gradually took over. Among long-service members were David Crozier (commodore for 15 years), Harry Blanchard, Bob Grant and others. The club continues to prosper, operating from its Crozier Memorial Pavilion at Kairaki on the north bank of the river.

In 1947 some Christchurch families with baches at Stewart's Gully on the south bank of the lower Waimakariri discovered the pleasures of boating on the river. They started with simple "flatties": but soon graduated to yachts and in 1949 formed the Stewart's Gully Sailing Club. Among the enthusiasts who saw the club established and developed over the years were Chris Holland, Bill Scott, Ray Falkingham, Don Davies, Doug McIntosh, Keith Henderson and Mrs Falkingham sen. as lady convener. The club, based at its clubhouse on the riverbank close to the settlement, holds regular racing fixtures through the season, including a challenge series with the Waimakariri Club across the river, and for many years held three-day annual regattas featuring rowing, yachting and powerboat races.

Then and now. *Bill Hamilton at the controls of his first jetboat,* Whio 1, *during a trial run on the Waimakariri River in the early 1950s.* Whio 1 *marked the start of a revolution in boating which was to sweep across the whole world.* Guy Mannering. Below, *one of* Whio's *many Hamilton jetboat successors, driven by Mike Phillips, is seen scattering spray and shingle in the 1987 jetsprint contest on a twisting artificial course beside the river near Christchurch.*

Jetboating

About 10 years after Bill (Sir William) Hamilton drove his first jetboat on the Waimakariri, a handful of enthusiasts for this radical development in river travel got together and formed a club. In a year's time membership had grown to 58; now 25 years old, the New Zealand Jet Boat Association, with branches throughout the country, has a membership of 3000.

Original officers of the club were M.J.O. ("Duke") Dixon, president; Jon Hamilton, vice-president; George Davison, secretary-treasurer; and committee members Richard Johnson, Don Malcolm, Guy Mannering, John Mannering, John Montgomery and Allan Watson. Sir William filled the office of patron for many years, succeeded after his death by his son Jon.

As membership grew, jetboats on the Waimakariri became a common sight. The trip through the gorge and as far upriver as the flow would allow gave boaters the thrills no other craft could provide, especially in the rapids and shallows. Summer holidays with car, trailer and jetboat took members into remote Southern Alps valleys and up rivers like the Rakaia, Rangitata, Godley, Hopkins, Ahuriri, Matukituki, Arawata, Waiatoto and Haast—indeed into any river that could be reached on wheels. From one end of the country to the other the jetboat became the key to a whole new concept of adventurous holidaymaking.

The average Kiwi's competitive instincts soon invaded the jetboat world. Most familiar to the general public is of course the world championship marathon which at intervals is held on New Zealand rivers, and there are district races to provide members with local competition. In 1982 Canterbury held the first jetsprint contest, which now draws thousands of spectators each year to a tight artificial course on the Waimakariri above the bridges. The spectacular aquabatics of these high-speed racers are in striking contrast to Bill Hamilton's basic old *Whio I* and a demonstration of his faith in the jetboat and its amazing manoeuvrability.

In 1987 the association, founded in Canterbury, celebrates its 25th anniversary with events at which it is expected the first six presidents will be present. They are Duke Dixon, Richard Johnson, John Montgomery, Guy Mannering, Bob McLean and Trevor Fairbairn.

Hunting

Until 40 or 50 years ago hunters in the upper Waimakariri were never short of game. Red deer were so numerous they had to be shot out by government cullers to protect stock feed supplies and preserve the forests, and men were sent in to track down wild cattle which had grown to large numbers in the upper Poulter-Esk country. Today all game is scarce, but permits are still issued for hunting in Arthur's Pass National Park and Craigieburn Forest Park.

The first red deer intended for Waimakariri country were shipped from London on s.s. *Papanui* on October 2, 1908. There were 12 animals, three stags and nine hinds, each contained in a separate crate, fed during the voyage on English meadow hay, crushed maize and rock salt. The ship ran into a bad storm and three` hinds died, presumably for that reason although there was a suspicion that the crates were too small. The eight remaining animals were taken to Broken River by rail, but during that journey another hind died. The survivors endured still another 50km in wagons to Mount White and were liberated in the Poulter in late 1908.

In the following year a further eight animals (two stags and six hinds) were shipped in larger crates. All survived the journey and were released on November 24, 1909, to join their cousins already thriving somewhere up the Poulter. This was good country for deer. There was abundant food, especially for winter browsing; no guns were allowed in the early years; and there

The deer arrive. *Two wagons carrying crated deer arrived on the Poulter flats in 1908 after a long journey from England. One of the hinds surveys the strange new country while another samples local foodstuff.*

From Ray Marshall

176

were no predators. The Poulter herd spread to the Esk by 1916, to the Poulter headwaters by 1919, and the Waimakariri headwaters by 1923, and in that year met and mingled with those released in the Rakaia, by when the catchment areas of both rivers were thoroughly populated.

Although in the early 1930s future cabinet ministers Bob Semple, Dan Sullivan and Paddy Webb spent weekends at Fred Cochrane's Bealey Hotel to go rabbit shooting (the carcases were distributed to Christchurch families in need), Brer Rabbit has never flourished in the upper Waimakariri as in the wide plains riverbed. Rabbits were said to have been liberated in the South Island as early as 1844, and in time reached plague proportions. There was actually a Canterbury Rabbit Club in 1877 which met on McLean's Island for a day's sport.

There are of course remnants of other breeds, chamois, pigs, opossums and a very occasional thar, but today's shooter is most likely to be encountered on the Waimakariri aiming at game birds, mallard ducks on the lower reaches, Canada geese and paradise ducks in the back country. Back in 1864 the Christchurch Municipal Council, hoping to rid the Avon of watercress, imported 13 pairs of black swans but most, not happy with city life, went elsewhere, some to the Waimakariri near Kaiapoi.

Birth of skiing. *Some of the first skiers in New Zealand practising on the road at Arthur's Pass in 1929.*

Skiing

Winter used to be a lonely time in the Waimakariri basin, when the Craigieburns were blanketed in snow, sheep were safely down on lower country, and only the cries of keas were heard aloft. Now a crisp winter day, especially at the weekend, sees hundreds of brightly-clad young people (and some not so young) zooming down the slopes enjoying the full one of New Zealand's fastest-growing outdoor sports—and with it the exhilaration of the heights, vast panoramas of back-country scenery, and unlimited supplies of fresh air.

There are three club fields on the Craigieburn Range (Canterbury Winter Sports Club at Mount Cheeseman, North Canterbury Ski Club at Broken River, and Craigieburn Valley Ski Club) and one commercial field (Porter Heights at the head of Porter River), while two clubs (Christchurch Ski Club and Canterbury University Ski Club) operate at Temple Basin on the main divide above Arthur's Pass. Good snow usually comes to them all in winter, with a season of two, three and sometimes four months.

Temple Basin. Arthur's Pass was one of the cradles of skiing in New Zealand. Introduction there is credited to Guy Butler, who developed such an enthusiasm for the region that he bought the old public works dining rooms left over from tunnel construction and converted them into a hostel or lodge to provide the village with a place for visitors to stay. Then in 1927 he bought eight pairs of Norwegian hickory skis (all the available stock in Christchurch and Dunedin) to give his guests a novel

At Temple Basin. *A copy of Rosamund Harper's much-admired 1935 photograph of the scene from Temple Basin skifield above Arthur's Pass, with skiers practising their new skills below the Christchurch Ski Club's first hut. Across the valley (in which runs State Highway 73) the Bealey River upper reaches climb steeply to Mount Rolleston's summit.*

Canterbury Museum

pastime. From skiing along the road outside the lodge, guests progressed to skiing over the pass and even down to Otira.

But soon they were seeking greater thrills at higher altitudes. George Lockwood, Ted Ferrier and Dr Robin Page climbed round the Phipps, Temple and B'limit peaks on an investigative traverse and returned with a glowing report of the slopes beneath these near-2000m high mountains, all facing south and providing good runs of up to 450m. In the following year a young Swiss-German ski instructor, Oscar Coberger, turned up at the pass and astonished everyone with his skill on the "sticks". He opened a winter sports shop in the village and offered tuition to learners. Soon there were enough skiers to form the Christchurch Ski Club and by the winter of 1929 Arthur's Pass was well on the way to becoming a snow sports centre. The Railways Department ran cheap excursions every Sunday during the season which sometimes brought up to 1200 visitors at the height of their popularity.

By 1930 the club's membership had risen to 76 and in 1933 the first hut was built in Temple Basin at an altitude of about 1400m, with accommodation for 16. A University Ski Club developed which used the same facilities and in 1952 bought the original hut and its various additions when the Christchurch Club built its new and more commodious premises. New they might have been, but they were flattened that same year by a storm and had to be rebuilt in more robust fashion.

Temple Basin had the first ski tow in New Zealand, built in 1948 by Dr Page and his helpers. It was a short but effective affair powered by a Ford 10 petrol engine. Other landmarks in the club's history were: 1954-55, jeep track made; 1960, goods lift completed (vertical lift 446m); 1961, downhill tow installed; 1963, hut extensions completed; 1966, Page shelter opened; 1968, Cassidy tow installed. Membership in 1977 reached a peak

The old original. *The scene on opening day in 1933 of the Christchurch Ski Club's "new" hut in Temple Basin. From left: S.T. Barnett (secretary Park Board), Professor Arnold Wall, F.W. Freeman, Gwen Digby, Mrs Coates, Miss Freeburn, Roy Twyneham, George Lockwood, W. Stewart (chairman Park Board), D.G. Sullivan, M.P. (Mayor of Christchurch), Betty Brown, Ted Ferrier, Dr Otto Frankel, Guy Butler.*

at 700, including many from the West Coast. The club's four tows have a combined vertical lift of 550m and there is accommodation on the site for about 48 people.

Mount Cheeseman. Although skiing in the Waimakariri started at Arthur's Pass, the first club to be formed was in 1929 at Mount Cheeseman on the Craigieburn Range near Castle Hill, a little before the Christchurch Ski Club at Temple Basin. The idea of a Canterbury Winter Sports Club began with Allan Giles, who had been to school in Switzerland and had returned with an enthusiasm for skiing. With his sister Marion, Bill Day, Nui Robins, and some other Mountaineering Club members, he called a meeting and the club was formed with Arthur Dudley Dobson as president and Nui Robins as vice-president.

Activities were listed as skiing, ice skating, and tobogganing, and with the agreement of Rob Blackley, manager at Castle Hill station, the basins between Mounts Cheeseman and Cockayne were selected for the ski field, with a toboggan slide down through the bush, and an ice rink nearby. In that first year the club formed a 5.6km walking track from Broken River Bridge on the main highway and built what became known as Bottom Hut at an altitude of 1000m. Materials for this were dragged to the site with a horse and sledge, the finished hut providing bunks for 20 people. The toboggan run had a fall of 180m and the skating pond 1000 square metres of ice.

Winters in those days seemed longer and colder, with snow heavier and lower down in the valleys, and there was never any problem about a good thickness of ice on the pond. The 60 or 70 members enjoyed good skiing above the 1200m level. For variety there were boisterous and thrilling runs down the toboggan run, or on the pond one could attempt to master the delicate art of ice skating.

Arthur's Pass skiers could reach their destination by train, but Cheeseman's members had to brave the uncertainties of the narrow, twisting road over Porter's Pass and unbridged creeks on the way to Broken River, in motorcars which could not always be relied on to perform efficiently. As most people had to work Saturday mornings, departure time was usually about 2 p.m., with a rendezvous at Springfield Hotel. From there the cars, travelling in convoy, made for Broken River, where radiators and engine blocks had to be drained to prevent damage from frost. By then on a winter's day it would be dark, making the walk in to the hut a stumbling affair.

Most skiing then was on the lower slopes; with skins the skiers would climb perhaps 150m and enjoy a brief downhill run. Access to the snow was by a track up through bush from the top of the toboggan run to the "ski plane". Later in the season the more adventurous would climb another 300m where in due course a small hut called "Robin's Nest" was built in 1936 at the 1600m mark. For this everything had to be carried in from the road. Next year another effort saw the hut doubled in size to house 10.

There was a big increase in membership after the war. In 1947 a Middle Hut was built (with two rooms and a galley) at the 1200m level, and members turned mechanical and contrived one of the first ski tows in New Zealand, a small, portable affair which gave a vertical lift of about 30m. Another big improvement about that time came when the club got its hands on a bulldozer and in a few days converted the foot track to the Bottom Hut into a useable road.

A new Top Lodge was built in 1950 to accommodate 36, extended later to 66. The Bottom Hut was burned down in 1981 and replaced with a new 36-bunk Forest Lodge. The original hut cost 200 pounds — its replacement $170,000, but of course it is much larger and more palatial, fully carpeted and double-glazed for maximum comfort.

As early as 1947 the club organised junior ski schools, mainly for secondary school pupils, usually in the care of Nui and Joyce Robins. At these a whole new generation of skiers learned the sport and became valued members of the club.

Top Lodge and the tow were improved and extended. To bring facilities up-to-date a double T-bar tow was built in 1978 and later a Poma lift to take skiers to the top of the range, giving a total vertical rise of 400m. Another addition was a telephone system covering the field and all huts. Today Cheeseman has 1000 members and a waiting list.

Craigieburn Valley. The Craigieburn Valley Ski Club, operating the most northerly field on the range, had its genesis in the enthusiasm of a few members of the Canterbury Mountaineering Club looking for a winter activity to keep them fit for summer climbing, and which would also generate a better club spirit (climbers tend to be more compatible with mountains than mobs). In July of 1947 Geoff Harrow, John Sampson, Ed Cotter, and Ed's sister Judith traversed the spur above the

Toboggans and old-time skis *clutter the verandah of the Canterbury Winter Sports Club's old "bottom hut" on the track to the club's skifield on Mounts Cheeseman and Cockayne. In the 1950s a gale blew away not only the verandah but also the toilet (and according to one member the hole too). The club's forest lodge occupies the site today.* Nui Robins

A hut for the heights. *The Craigieburn Valley Ski Club's newsletter once carried this imaginative sketch of a hut transportation team in action.*

On Craigieburn snow. *Skiers enjoy a thrilling run on new snow at one of the Craigieburn Range's four skifields.*

present road to view and photograph the headwaters of the Craigie Burn. Their report led to the club committee deciding to establish a skiing facility in the area. The Forest Service gave permission to cut an access track and Harry Walker surveyed the route with his abney level. Over many weekends C.M.C. members turned out with grubbers, picks and shovels to make the 8km track.

Meanwhile Fred Hulston was prefabricating a hut in Christchurch. In January, 1948, this was carried in to the site by a large packing party, where Stan Muirson, Tom Newth, Alan Morgan and anyone else who could swing a hammer completed its erection by March. That Easter also saw the first of a number of private huts, and with them the advent of women on the exclusively male C.M.C. scene. (This led to the ski division becoming an autonomous body, and eventually to the club abandoning its long-standing membership restriction — a decision still opposed by many a mountaineering machismo.)

Craigieburn had access and accommodation; now it needed a rope tow. John Sampson and his willing and expert helpers attended to this in 1949 by building the "Jonsam Allbits Ski Tow", which worked so well that with a later extension to the top basin it served the club for 12 years.

In 1953 the Mountaineering Club decided the time had come for the parting of the ways, and next year the ski section became the Craigieburn Valley Ski Club. The spur of independence led to the new club deciding on a massive improvement programme which included the construction of a T-bar ski lift. Much work was put into this project which, had it been successful, would have put the club 20 years ahead of its contemporaries. Heavy prefabricated parts were carried in over the eight km of foot track and up to various construction sites on the field. While it was working, the T-bar gave much satisfaction but there were problems, and (the dedication of willing volunteers having its limits) in time they overwhelmed it. The club had to fall back on rope tows, much improved with plastic ropes and diesel power.

Eventually members tired of the long walk in from the highway and a vehicle access road was built by a contractor. The official opening in April, 1961, was performed to the skirl of bagpipes, appropriate to the valley's name, while a cavalcade of decorated vehicles made its way up the new "highway". The then Minister of Transport, Mr McAlpine, performed the opening ceremony. "This has been my home country since I was a child," he said, cutting the ribbon with a pair of hedge clippers.* The days of humping in four and eight-gallon packs of fuel for the tow motors were over.

Today the club has on-site accommodation for 80 people, and membership is about 350. Much off-season use of the facilities is made by school educational parties, especially in association with the nearby Craigieburn Forest Park headquarters. Affectionately known as "The Big One", Craigieburn skifields are serviced by three rope tows which give 600m of vertical lift taking skiers up more than 1.6km to the top of the range.

* The McAlpine family has been associated with Craigieburn station since 1917.

Broken River. The North Canterbury Ski Club, with fields at the head of Broken River, had its beginnings in the Rangiora Youth Recreational Club, an organisation in that town set up soon after World War II ended. In 1948 some members organised a winter sports section for ice-skating, skiing and tramping, with a base at Lake Lyndon, and from there members visited the new Mountaineering Club ski field at the head of Craigie Burn. Shown the likely basins next door in Broken River they determined to develop them for skiing. A track was opened up the valley of Cave Stream and a hut built at the bushline. In May, 1951, members began with picks and shovels to make this into a road, with some assistance from a crawler scoop-loader fitted with a 'dozer blade, and slowly the way to the heights was carved out of the forested hills. In February, 1952, direct connection with the Youth Recreational Club was severed and a North Canterbury Ski Club formed around a nucleus of nine enthusiasts.

As the road was pushed through the forest the better trees were taken to Rangiora and milled and the timber used for hut building. In July, 1952, members skied in the basin for the first time. By June, 1955, the road was completed to the main car park at 1050m and by 1962 there was access for utility vehicles right up to the ski field.

The first rope tow was built in 1953, powered by an old Rugby car engine mounted on a sled which was dragged and winched up the slopes to its final position. A worm reduction drive from an old tractor provided the gearing.

The next hut, Broken River Lodge, was built with timber salvaged from Balmoral State Forest after a fire and milled by voluntary labour at Rangiora. For its 21st anniversary the club

A hard road. *These photographs of young Rangiora people at Broken River may not be in the professional class but they do show something of the typical outpouring of energy, enthusiasm and sheer hard work which went into the making of the Waimakariri's four club skifields. Young enthusiasts turned forest tracks into roads, man-handled timber, iron, tow ropes and heavy machinery up to snow level, built ski tows to 1800 metres, and lodges, and after years of effort and expense finally experienced the joys of skiing on their own snow.* Pictures from Leith Newell

Left: *The Craigieburn bike (bearing the author's wife, daughter and grandson) photographed in 1984.* **Right:** *These packhorses transporting hut-building materials up the Waimakariri seem to be saying they can do better than the old Buick — and carry heavier loads, too.* From Nui Robins

Machinery in the Mountains

In the Great Depression reasonably roadworthy used cars could be bought for the equivalent of a week's wages. A handful of Mountaineering Club members including Nui Robins, Ivan Tucker, Jack Hayes and a character called "Tuppenny" Smith bought a Model T Ford in 1938 for five pounds and tried to drive it to Carrington Hut. They didn't get far.

Next Easter they renewed their efforts with a Dodge light truck and made it to the Big Bend, about eight kilometres up the riverbed. Their hilarious journey ended there because the engine's magneto failed. When they returned later with the magneto repaired, the truck and the piece of riverbed it had occupied were both gone, presumably in a flood.

For 1940 a sturdy Buick roadster was chosen. This one did well, making it nearly to the hut before expiring with a broken sump.

Again it was left in the riverbed, an incongruous monument to youthful persistence and high spirits, and again when the would-be alpine motorists returned the car had disappeared — a mystery never solved.

Legend has it that somebody once carried a bicycle to the top of Rolleston's low peak (2211m), where its only possible use might be to cycle across the snowfield leading to the high peak (after a good frost, of course). And the 1850m height of the Craigieburn Range inspired some keen cyclist to take his machine up there, presumably to enjoy a spin "among the peaks that through the cloudlands burst".

But most machinery in Waimakariri mountains is of the hardworking variety, used to haul skiers up the snowfield of their choice.

built Palmer Lodge in memory of one of its keenest and most useful members, Keith Palmer, who died at 40 years of age. By then there were 200 active senior members, 150 associate members, and 50 juniors, two five-ton trucks, a crawler loader dozer, a crawler front-end loader, a road grader, two tractors, a rope tow and an efficient generating plant — all of which were certainly a vindication of the faith and works of early members.

The club now has accommodation for 64 in three lodges, and four rope tows giving a vertical lift of over 600m. A recent addition has been a goods lift over 300m long with a vertical rise of 200m, driven by electricity.

Porter Heights. This field occupies the southernmost Craigieburn basin. It is operated by a company formed in 1967, when the original directors were P.H. Willis, R.S.A. Chaffey, A.D. Coberger and D.R. Preston. Chaffey and Coberger were former New Zealand ski champions. Access is by a good 6.5km road from S.H. 73, and the field is served by 2000m of T-bars with a vertical lift of 730m plus a rope tow and learners' tow.

Some concern was expressed in initial stages of development that the field could be susceptible to avalanche danger, and this was justified almost immediately. Only three weeks after opening, an avalanche swept down on the night of June 29, 1968, and overwhelmed a hut in which three men were asleep. Two were injured and all the existing buildings destroyed. But Porter Heights survived this setback to become one of the most popular and best-equipped of Canterbury fields. There is parking for 500 cars, a 40-bed lodge, a campervan park, cafeteria, ski school, and ample ski-hire service. It is the closest skifield to Christchurch (100km).

The "Coast-to-Coast"

The Waimakariri River and its Mingha tributary play important roles in the annual Coast-to-Coast triathlon, described as one of the toughest multi-discipline events in the world.

Competitors sprint 800m up the beach at Kumara on the West Coast, cycle 60km to Deception River in the Otira valley, stumble and run 26km up the rough Deception, over Goat Pass (1076m) and down the Mingha to Klondyke Corner in the Waimakariri, cycle 15km to Mount White Bridge, paddle kayaks 67km down the Waimakariri (including 24km through the gorge) to the high bridge on the edge of the plains, and finally cycle 70km to the Christchurch suburb of Sumner on the east coast.

The event, devised by Robin Judkins, features competitors taking either one day or two for the journey, and two-man teams sharing stages over two days. There were 69 competitors when it was first held in 1983, and 140 the next year. Since 1986 the field has been limited to 350, many of whom come from overseas.

Boxing

The so-called "manly art" was not a Waimakariri occupation in the accepted sense, but it is worth recording that the first professional boxing match in New Zealand was fought on the river's south bank, and raised such a storm that it was talked of for years afterwards. "Prize-fighting", as it was called, was strictly illegal and viewed then much as cockfighting would be today.

The date was July 8, 1862, and the bout, watched by about 600 keen spectators, was between two men named Henry Jones and George Barton. The venue was downstream a short distance from Felton's Ferry, near where the motorway bridges cross the river today. Four posts were driven into a level patch of ground and a rope strung to make the ring.

The police soon learned of this "brutal exhibition" and William Henry Revell, sub-inspector of police at Kaiapoi, arrived with two mounted constables, resolved to stop the bout before it started. They were outnumbered and although Revell cut the ropes and the constables waved loaded pistols at the crowd, the audience, many of them mounted, determined they were not to be deprived of the anticipated spectacle. Shouts of "Ride them down!" rang out from the more militant, along with suggestions that the men in uniform be taken away and tied to a nearby cabbage tree.

The fight went ahead. Stripped to the waist, Jones and Barton fought a bloody battle for more than an hour until the former was declared winner.

The sequel was heard in the Magistrate's Court at Christchurch a week later when both men were charged with assault, and in addition the more serious charge of "making an affray to the terror and disturbance of Her Majesty's subjects then present". Robert Anderson and Charles Horgan (the backers), Stephen Lawrence (sponge-holder) and George McKercher (referee) were accused of aiding and abetting. All were committed to the Supreme Court for trial by jury.

The prosecution announced that not only would these men stand trial, but also a number of others present at the fight who had interfered with the police in the course of their duty. This caused not a little disquiet among some of the more distinguished citizens of Christchurch, since the audience had included a Magistrate, several Justices of the Peace and, it was said, the Crown Prosecutor and other prominent legal men.

The defence, conducted by Mr Wynn Williams, held there was no evidence of terror being caused to any of Her Majesty's subjects. The only possible victim of an assault, he said, was Barton, and he wasn't complaining.

From the dock Jones said he had thought the prize-fight a harmless act, because the Magistrate who later sat in judgement on him had encouraged and backed them to fight, and Barton maintained that while the bout was in progress Mr Revell was sitting alongside with another gentleman drinking from a bottle and seeming to enjoy the sport equally with other spectators.

Nevertheless the jury found them guilty of assault but not of causing an affray, and each was sentenced to a month in Lyttelton gaol. Most of the others were fined 10 pounds (about a month's pay for a working man), but James Barker, who was named as ringleader of those who would "ride down" the mounted policemen, was sentenced to 14 days in gaol. He had the good sense to apologise to the court for his indiscretion, and so had his sentence reduced to seven days.

A Valuable Recreational Asset

There would be few Christchurch residents a hundred years ago who did not wish the "flaring, scaring Waimakariri" further from their doors, yet today there are benefits from its proximity which thousands enjoy. As the river was brought under control and its kingsize bed restricted, vast areas of what used to be its course became available for other purposes. Some of this land was planted in trees and some of the better country leased to pastoral farmers. Enough remained to provide Christchurch with a valuable reserve, in size considerably larger, for example, than the borough of Kaiapoi.

This is known as McLean's Island. A portion of it actually consists of the island itself, which was once in the middle of the riverbed and largely under water during major floods. Protected from the river since 1967 by stopbanks, this area now hosts a number of clubs and associations, including two golf courses, a kennel centre, custom and vintage car clubs, a place called Steam Scene where old railway engines run, the grounds of the local branch of the New Zealand Horse Society, a caravan club, and two rifle ranges, all enjoying the freedom of wide-open spaces within a few minutes of the city. Here too is Orana Park, famous for its exotic animals. Also in the vicinity, not to be overlooked, is the home of the Sun Club, where members enjoy privacy for total tanning, and Peacock Springs, a wild-life preserve based on old shingle pits transformed into ornamental ponds.

Visitors to McLean's Island are sometimes astonished to be told they are standing where the Waimakariri once flowed. Old waterways are hard to find today although they show clearly in aerial photographs. One familiar to thousands is that which runs through the Groynes, the popular picnic spot on John's Road some distance east of McLean's Island. Here the Waimakariri once thundered past in noisy argument with boulder and concrete breakwaters built to protect the Belfast-Chaneys country and the Main North Road. A spring-fed stream flows quietly there now to provide a lake-like watering place for pleasure boats and canoes, and for summer swimmers to share with resident waterfowl.

Mention of swimming may remind older trampers on the Farm Track section of Waimakariri Walkway (between the Groynes and Belfast's Darroch Street) that a stand of bluegums along the way marks the location of what was once the Waimakariri's most-favoured swimming hole.

Adventures and Misadventures

The twin curses of early Canterbury were judged to be rivers and booze. Drowning was known as the Canterbury death, while at a time when the population of Christchurch was only 7000 there were 56 public houses in the city. Few people were skilled at swimming, and in their travels across the plains, on meeting with unbridged rivers they too often plunged in and were swept away to a watery grave. If they survived this hazard John Barleycorn could be waiting for them on the other side in the form of a grog shop.

One Archibald McDonald reversed this order in 1875 when he demonstrated the perils of drinking at the Waimakariri instead of the pub. An alcoholic, he "went on the wagon" in April, but was reported to be somewhat despondent thereafter. In August he was found prostrate in the riverbed, face down in shallow water, drowned. His hat was on the bank with a stone placed on it, as if he had gone to drink and was unable to rise again.

But not everyone who drowned in the Waimakariri was trying to drink it. William Norfolk rode up to the bank and urged his steed forward, but it "propped" him into a deep pool where the current was running fast. Failing to keep a grip on the reins he was carried away — but of course not to Rangiora where his wife and five young children were waiting for him.

Hanging on to reins was one thing but grasping at a lifeline and having it come away in the hands was another. When Donald Coutts returned from the city with his wife one evening in 1872 he found the river too deep for his trap and rising fast, so he signalled for the punt. But in the middle of the river the wire cable snapped and away went punt and ferry-man.

As the clumsy craft disappeared round the bend it seemed all was lost, but soon it was to pass under White's Bridge, where salvation was at hand. A vigilant traveller had seen what was happening and threw the ferryman a rope. He caught it expertly but the other end was accidentally let go so the punt was once more adrift and threatening soon to carry its fearful occupant, rope and all, out to sea. Fortunately he managed to steer his craft ashore before finding himself in the breakers. The Coutts' access problems were solved soon after with the erection of the "Cutting Bridge", a landmark for many years until the river was straightened and it was no longer needed.

In the 1874 flood two men named Ward and Reid were carried away in their boat from Courtenay and somehow managed a highly-adventurous ride, out of control and at the mercy of the flood, until it swept them over the bar and out to sea, 42 kilometres from where they started. They managed to get back to the beach, there to be met by George Day, the Kaiapoi harbour-master, who had seen the boat sail past and hastened to do what he could. He hadn't expected to see them again — at least not alive. Reports do not say whether the men sailed under or over White's Bridge, which at one stage of that flood was completely submerged.

Bibliography

ACHESON, J.M., *Behind the Snowy Mountains* (unpublished thesis).

ACLAND, L.G.D., *The Early Canterbury Runs* (Whitcombe & Tombs 1952).

ADAMS, Grace, *Jack's Hut* (Reed 1968).

ANDERSONS Limited Christchurch, 1850-1925, a history (1925).

APPENDICES to the journals of the House of Representatives.

BARKER, Mary (Lady), *Station Life In New Zealand* (Macmillan 1870).

BATHGATE, D.A., *Doctor in the Sticks* (Collins 1972).

BROCKLEBANK, Charles, *Old Kaiapoi* (N.C. Gazette 1941).

BURDON, R.M., *King Dick* (Whitcombe & Tombs 1955) and *The Life and Times of Sir Julius Vogel* (Caxton Press1948).

CANTERBURY PROGRESS LEAGUE, *East and West, the story of the Midland Railway* (1923).

CANTERBURY PROVINCIAL PAPERS, including papers laid on the table, reports by Edward Dobson, George Dobson, Arthur Dobson, W.T. Doyne and various others, in the archives of the Canterbury Museum.

CHILDS, H.A., *The Story of Kaiapoi* (articles in the North Canterbury Gazette, 1933).

CUMBERLAND, K.B. and FOX, J.W., *New Zealand: a Regional View* (Whitcombe & Tombs 1958).

DENNIS, Andrew, *Arthur's Pass National Park, The First 50 Years* (A.P.N.P. Board 1979).

DOBSON, Sir Arthur Dudley, *Reminiscences* (Whitcombe & Tombs 1930).

DOBSON, Edward Henry, a Letter made available by Sister Angela Hill.

FURKETT, F.W., *Early New Zealand Engineers* (Reed 1953).

GILLESPIE, Oliver, *Oxford: the First 100 Years* (Oxford Historical Committee 1954).

GODLEY, Charlotte, *Letters From Early New Zealand 1850-53* (Whitcombe & Tombs 1951).

HARPER, Henry W. (Archdeacon), *Letters from New Zealand* (Hugh Rees Ltd. 1914).

HAWKINS, D.N., *Beyond the Waimakariri* (Whitcombe & Tombs 1957) and *Rangiora* (Rangiora Borough Council 1983).

JOURNAL of the Voyage of the *Acheron*, Hocken Library.

LOUGHNAN, R.A., *The Remarkable Life Story of Sir Joseph Ward* (New Century Press 1929).

MACDONALD, G.R., *The Macdonald Dictionary of Canterbury Biographies* (Canterbury Museum).

McINTYRE, W. David (editor), *The Journals of Henry Sewell* (Whitcoulls 1980).

McLEAN, John, *Piercing the Alps* (unpublished thesis).

McLENNAN, Vera, *Coaching Days and Accommodating Ways* (Hilton Press 1972).

McLEOD, David, *Many a Glorious Morning* (Whitcombe & Tombs 1970), *Alone in a Mountain World* (Reed 1972) and *Kingdom in the Hills* (Whitcombe & Tombs 1974).

MAY, Philip Ross, *Miners and Militants* (editor) (Whitcombe & Tombs 1975) and *The West Coast Gold Rushes* (Pegasus Press 1962).

NEW ZEALAND RAILWAY OBSERVER, various issues.

NEWTON, N.E.B., *History of the Otira Tunnel* (unpublished thesis).

NEWTON, Peter, *High Country Journey* (Reed 1952) and *The Boss's Story* (Reed 1966).

NORTH CANTERBURY CATCHMENT BOARD, *Waimakariri River Improvement Scheme, 1982 Review* and *Waimakariri River and Catchment Resource Survey, 1986.*

ODELL, R.S., BURROWS, C.J. and others, *Handbooks of Arthur's Pass National Park.*

POPPLE, G.L., *Malvern County, a Centennial History* (Malvern County Council 1953).

PERCIVAL, E.C. and BURROWS, C.J., *Cass* (University of Canterbury.)

PRICE, Joseph, *Memoirs* (Canterbury Museum).

RICHARDS, E.C., *Castle Hill* (1951).

ROSANOWSKI, G.J., *The Midland Railway* (unpublished thesis).

SINCLAIR, Keith, *William Pember Reeves* (Clarendon Press 1965).

TORLESSE, Charles Obins, *Diaries* (Canterbury Museum).

WARD, Patricia B., *The First Century: Kaiapoi Borough Council* (1968).

WILSON, Mingha, *In the Land of the Tui* (Sampson Low, Marston, 1894).

Much information has also been gleaned from *The Canterbury Mountaineer,* and files held by the Christchurch Press Company, Canterbury Public Library and Canterbury Museum of *The Press, The Lyttelton Times, The Weekly Press, The Canterbury Times,* and *Punch in Canterbury.*

Note. Readers particularly interested in the plains country north of the Waimakariri are recommended to read Don Hawkins' books listed above, which cover that area in rich detail.

Index

185

COPYRIGHT

CANTERBURY &
MOTOR ROA

LITHOGRAPHED AND PUBLISH
COULLS SOMERVILLE W
209 MANCHESTER STREET, CHRI
and at
DUNEDIN, WELLINGTON and AU

SCALE: Six Miles to One

TASMAN SEA

CANTERBURY BIGHT

REFERENCES

A   Accommodation or Boarding House
Br.   Bridge
G   Garage
H   Hotel
     Main Routes

COLOUR ROUTE SIGNS

SILVER and GOLD — Rakaia to Methven.

YELLOW and BROWN — Riccarton, Kirwee, Darfield, Homebush, Glentunnel, Rakaia Gorge, Mt. Somers, Mayfield, Rangitata Bridge.

BLACK and SILVER — Darfield to Springfield.

SILVER and BLUE — Geraldine, Fairlie, Tekapo, Pukaki, Omarama, Lindis Pass.

GREEN and SILVER — Sockburn to Prebbleton, Lincoln College, Springston, Doyleston, Leeston, Southbridge, Rakaia Huts.

CREAM and BLACK — Bluff to Picton.

KHAKI and SILVER — Waipara to Hanmer.

TABLE OF DISTANCES

From Christchurch	Miles	From Christchurch	Miles	From Christchurch	Miles	From Hokitika	Miles	From Hokitika	Miles	From Greymouth
AKAROA	52	KAIAPOI	12	REEFTON	201	ARAHURA	4	OKURU PORT (Bridle Track from Waiho)	200	AHAURA
AMBERLEY	30	KAIKOURA, Coastal Route	120	SOUTHBRIDGE	32	BRUCE BAY (Bridle Track from Waiho)	125	OTIRA	58	BARRYTOWN
ASHBURTON	53	KAIKOURA, Inland Route	120	SPRINGFIELD	41	FERGUSON'S	30			BLACKBALL
ASHBURTON, via Ellesmere Bridge	60	LAKE COLERIDGE	76	SUMNER	8	GOLDSBOROUGH	102	OVERLOOK HILL, via Rimu	8	BRUNNER
ASHLEY GORGE	46	LAKE PUKAKI	175	TIMARU, via Ashburton	117	GREYMOUTH	34	PUKEKURA	35	DOBSON
BEALEY, via Rail Christchurch to Cass	82	LAKE TEKAPO	145	TIMARU, via Rakaia Gorge	128	HAAST (Bridle Track from Waiho)	191	PUNAKAIKI (Blowhole)	60	DUNGANVILLE
BLENHEIM, Coastal Route	215	LINCOLN	12	WAIAU TOWNSHIP	76	HARI HARI	53	ROSS	40	KOKIRI
BLENHEIM, Inland Route	225	LITTLE RIVER	35	WAIHO GORGE (Franz Josef Glacier)	246	HOKITIKA GORGE	20	BUATAPU (one mile from Lake Mahinapua)	222	KUMARA
CHEVIOT	78	LYTTELTON, via Zig Zag	12	WAIKARI	45	JACKSON'S BAY (Bridle Track from Waiho)		STAFFORD	3	MARSDEN
CULVERDEN	62	METHVEN, via Rakaia Gorge	67	WAIMAKARIRI GORGE BRIDGE	41	KAKAPOTAHI (Little Waitaha)	32			MITCHELL'S (Lake Brunner)
DUNEDIN	246	METHVEN, via Ashburton	62	WAIMATE	146	KANIERI	3	TERAMAKAU	25	MOANA
DUNSANDEL	25	MURCHISON, via Reefton and Maruia	277	WAIPARA	37	KARANGARUA (Copland Track)	120	TOTARA FLAT	57	MOONLIGHT
DUNSANDEL, via Ellesmere Bridge	30	NELSON	290	WEHEKA (Fox Glacier)	263	KOITERANGI	11	UPPER KOKATAHI (Kokatahi Gorge—Five mile walk)		NGAHERE
ELLESMERE BRIDGE		NEW BRIGHTON	7	WESTPORT	251	KOKATAHI	11			OTIRA
FAIRLIE, via Cattle Valley	119	OAMARU	171			KUMARA	18	WAIHO GORGE (Franz Josef Glacier)		PAROA
GERALDINE	88	OXFORD	40	#### Suitable Picnic Grounds		KUMARA JUNCTION	15	WAITANGI	73	PUNAKAIKI
GLENTUNNEL	38	PICTON		ASHLEY GORGE	46	LAKE BRUNNER (Mitchell's, via Kumara)		WEHEKA (Fox Glacier)	107	REEFTON
GREYMOUTH	153	PEEL FOREST	83	KAIRAKI BEACH	15	LAKE IANTHE	49			RUNANGA
HANMER	92	PORTER'S PASS		LEITHFIELD BEACH	26	LAKE KANIERI	12			RURU
HERMITAGE, Mt. Cook, via Cattle Valley	211	RAKAIA	35	WAIKUKU BEACH	20	LAKE MAHINAPUA				STILLWATER
HOKITIKA	156	RAKAIA, via Ellesmere Bridge		SELWYN HUTS	24	LAKE MAPOURIKA				TERAMAKAU SETTLEMENT
HONORATA	38	RAKAIA GORGE	56	KENNEDY'S BUSH (Good Tea Rooms)		MATAINUI	71			TOTARA FLAT
INVERCARGILL	285	RANGIORA	14	MT. PLEASANT (Good Tea Rooms)		MOUNT HERCULES	58			
		RANGITATA	44	RAKAIA HUTS						
		RANGITATA BRIDGE	79							